The Gerald F. Fitzgerald Collection of

Polar Books, Maps, and Art

D1516743

The Gerald F. Fitzgerald Collection of

Polar Books, Maps, and Art

at The Newberry Library

A Catalogue

Compiled by David C. White *and* Patrick Morris

Edited by Robert W. Karrow, Jr.

Chicago

The Newberry Library

2000

Typesetting by Impressions Book and Journal Services, Madison, Wisconsin
Printing by Edwards Brothers, Ann Arbor, Michigan

Printed in the United States of America

Cover and Dust Jacket
"Melville Island from Banks Land" by Samuel G. Cresswell [no. **165**]

Library of Congress Cataloging-in-Publication Data

Gerald F. Fitzgerald Collection (Newberry Library)
   The Gerald F. Fitzgerald Collection of polar books, maps, and art at
the Newberry Library : a catalogue / compiled by David C. White and
Patrick Morris ; edited by Robert W. Karrow, Jr.
        p.   cm.
     Includes bibliographical references and index.
     ISBN 0-911028-68-4 — ISBN 0-911028-70-6 (pbk.)
     1. Gerald F. Fitzgerald Collection (Newberry Library)—Catalogs.
2. Polar regions—Bibliography—Catalogs.   3. Polar
regions—Maps—Bibliography—Catalogs.   4. Polar regions—In
art—Bibliography—Catalogs.   I. White, David C. (David Charles), 1962–
II. Morris, Patrick A. (Patrick Anthony), 1960–   III. Karrow, Robert W.
IV. Title.
Z6005.P7 G47   2000
016.909′091—dc21   00-011085

Table of Contents

Black and White Illustrations

Color Plates

Following Page 68

Arctic

Antarctic

Foreword

No job is more pleasant for a librarian than celebrating the acquisition of an important collection, unless it is welcoming the arrival of an energetic and committed trustee and generous benefactor. Both these pleasures have been mine, thanks to the collection of, and the person of, Gerald F. Fitzgerald.

Gerald is an avid and wide-ranging bookman who has also formed (and continues to build) important collections in American history and cartography. He has been a member of the Caxton Club, Chicago's bibliophilic society, since 1981, but his association with the Newberry Library goes back to the mid 1970s, when he participated in a course in the history of cartography taught by David Woodward, the first director of our Hermon Dunlap Smith Center for the History of Cartography. Gerald soon became a Library Associate, joined the President's Fellows in 1985, and was a founding member of the President's Circle in 1994, the year he became a Trustee.

When he offered to give his much-treasured collection of polar books and maps to the Newberry, we accepted eagerly. Our collections in discovery and exploration were already very strong, and here was a chance to widen that scope to include the world's last frontiers. Moreover, our Edward E. Ayer Collection is a rich source of material on the North American Eskimo peoples and on Arctic and sub-arctic Canada, and Gerald's books would supplement those holdings admirably. And finally, our world-class cartographic collections would be enriched by several hundred rare and unusual maps. That the collection came with its own catalogue is a librarian's dream, and we are thrilled to be able to offer that catalogue now to the world of scholarship.

Charles T. Cullen
President and Librarian
The Newberry Library

Introduction

Gerald F. Fitzgerald

People are often curious as to how someone living in the suburbs of Chicago would get interested in polar material. The interest developed quite by accident in the 1950s while working in Chicago's Loop. In those days there were a number of book stores carrying a variety of used hardbound books and a surprising number of what were to become rare books. Forty years later all these old, low-rent buildings with rundown bookstores have disappeared.

Being a curious and catholic reader, I was attracted by Captain George Back's *Narrative of the Arctic Land Expedition to the Mouth of the Great Fish River and along the Shores of the Arctic Ocean in the Years 1833, '34 and '35*. I purchased it for a small sum and was most astonished at reading the report of this fabulous overland expedition through Canada up to Great Slave Lake, Artillery Lake, and on up to the Great Fish River, which today is generally called Back's River. This river, which flows into the Arctic Sea, is frozen 10½ to 11 months of the year and had never before been visited by a European. Along the way Back observed, more than 160 years before the Surgeon General of the United States, that a considerable number of northern Indians had cancer of the mouth, which he presumed came from their constant chewing of tobacco. Among the many interesting events related was a duel contemplated by several of his junior officers over the affections of a beautiful young Indian woman known as Green Stockings. I recently read that a prominent family in Vancouver traced its ancestry to one of Back's officers and the beauteous Green Stockings. It was a fascinating book, and before long, I was acquiring more books on Arctic exploration, and later, Antarctic material.

The casual reader would be surprised to find out how much material has been written in a variety of languages on the polar regions. I spent considerable months identifying my collection through the *Arctic Bibliography*, Spence, and the OCLC. Ultimately, my collection of Arctic and Antarctic material became larger than any of my other collections, which include Americana, Voyages and travel, General and military history, Banking and economics, Atlases and maps, Africa and sport, and Celestial material.

Introduction

The great age of polar exploration literally died with World War I, and the later explorers had the advantage of aircraft, radios, snowmobiles, Global Positioning Systems, better equipment, etc. For many years I hoped to visit the high Arctic, and in 1991, took a marvelous trip by air, which started on Baffin Island, where Frobisher thought he had found gold (it was fool's gold), and which took me as high as the northwest coast of Ellesmere Island to the weather station Eureka at 80° north, 690 miles from the North Pole. Along the way, I visited the graves of three of Sir John Franklin's sailors at Beechey Island. Today adventurous types can go all the way to the North Pole by airplane (the Canadian government makes certain there is a second plane with you in case of a mishap) or visit Antarctica and fly over the South Pole.

Occasionally, one is asked who were the most important polar explorers. This is not an easy question to answer. One could, however, say who was the luckiest. That would be Captain Sir William Edward Parry, who took several trips from the British Isles through the Arctic channels, pushing the knowledge of the Arctic farther and farther to the west and north. For decades after, those channels were frozen, and history could not be repeated. Unluckiest may have been Captain Sir John Franklin, who got caught in the polar ice and thought it would ultimately thaw out and free his ship. It did not, and by the time his weak and starving crew tried to reach the Arctic shore, it was too late.

When it comes to leadership, I am under the impression that Sir Ernest Shackleton was the greatest of all, with Roald Amundsen close behind. Shackleton, who suffered a number of misfortunes, never lost a man, something few other polar explorers could say. He once got within 100 miles of the South Pole, but turned back because he feared for the lives of his companions. The most exciting book I've read on polar exploration is Alfred Lansing's *Endurance*, on Shackleton's 1914 expedition. Beset in ice, the ship *Endurance* drifted with the floes for eleven months before being crushed and sinking. The men then spent another six months making their way by sled and boat to Elephant Island, an inhospitable speck on the edge of the continent. Knowing that their only hope was to reach the whaling station on South Georgia Island, 870 miles away through treacherous seas, Shackleton and five companions set off in an open boat. Seventeen days later, after the most extraordinary heroic efforts, they reached South Georgia and crossed the unexplored island on foot. Shackleton then organized the relief effort that rescued the crew on Elephant Island, without any loss of life. It's a story every person interested in leadership should read.

Amundsen prepared better than any other explorer, and spent his entire life practicing in the harsh winters of mountainous Norway. His feats of being the first through the Northwest Passage and first to the South Pole are living proof of his intelligence, skill, and infinite patience with detail. To this day, Captain Robert Falcon Scott is a greater hero in Britain than Shackleton or Amundsen, however I heard a story once that has colored my view of Scott ever since. During a trip to London, John Maggs, managing director of Maggs Brothers, Berkeley Square, arranged for me to meet Peter Wordie, son of the famous explorer, scholar, and president of the Royal Geographical Society, Sir James Mann Wordie, who was second in command on Elephant Island. This meeting allowed me to acquire his father's fantastic Arctic and Antarctic working map collection. Peter Wordie told me that when he was a young boy, he overheard Sir Raymond Priestley telling his father a story about Scott's first expedition. It seems that Albert B. Armitage had commented to Scott that he thought they should practice with the use of skis and dogs while waiting for the Antarctic summer. Scott replied with disdain, "Gentlemen don't practice."

My opinion of these polar pioneers is summed up in a statement by Sir Edmund Hillary: "For scientific discovery, give me Scott; for speed and efficiency of travel, Amundsen, but when disaster strikes and all hope is gone, get down on your knees and pray for Shackleton."

No collection of a specialized nature can be put together without the help of a number of dealers alert to one's collection and happy to accommodate. Particular thanks is owed to the aforementioned John Maggs and his staff, Bernard Quaritch, also of London, Don Lake of Toronto, J. Pratt of West Side Books in Ann Arbor, Jean & Jerome Parmer of San Diego, Bob Finch of High Latitude in Bainbridge, Washington, Hamill & Barker of Evanston, Illinois, the late Van Allen Bradley, Patrick McGahem of Ottawa, Francis Edwards of London, Bauman of Philadelphia, Branner's of Copenhagen, William Reese of New Haven, and Gaston Renard of Australia. I'm also grateful to Mary Beth Beal and Harry L. Stern, who guided me and appraised my collection.

I am particularly indebted to David C. White and Patrick Morris for their putting in academic order the catalogue descriptions, to Betty Marsh for doing all the word processing, and to Robert W. Karrow, Jr., who edited this catalogue and encouraged me to present the collection to the Newberry.

References Cited

AB
Arctic Bibliography, prepared for and in cooperation with the Department of Defense under direction of the Arctic Institute of North America. [Washington, DC]: Department of Defense, 1953–1965.

Church
George Watson Cole, *A Catalogue of Books Relating to the Discovery and Early History of North and South America Forming a Part of the Library of E. D. Church*. New York: Dodd, Mead & Co., 1907; reprinted Mansfield, Conn.: Maurizio Martino, 1995.

Falk
Marvin W. Falk, *Alaskan Maps: A Cartobibliography of Alaska to 1900*. New York: Garland Publishing, 1983.

Haskell
Daniel C. Haskell, *The United States Exploring Expedition, 1838–42, and its Publications, 1844–1874: A Bibliography*. New York: New York Public Library, 1942.

Hill
The Hill Collection of Pacific Voyages, ed. By Ronald Louis Silveira de Braganza and Charlotte Oakes; annot. By Jonathan A. Hill. San Diego: University Library, University of California, San Diego, 1974–83.

Howes
Wright Howes, *U.S.iana (1650–1950): A Selective Bibliography in Which are Described 11,620 Uncommon and Significant Books Relating to the Continental Portion of the United States*. Rev. & enlgd. ed. New York: R. R. Bowker Co. for the Newberry Library, 1962.

References Cited

Jolly
David C. Jolly, *Maps in British Periodicals*. Brookline, Mass.: The Author, 1990–91.

Karrow
Robert W. Karrow, Jr., *Mapmakers of the Sixteenth Century and their Maps: Bio-Bibliographies of the Cartographers of Abraham Ortelius, 1570.* Chicago: Speculum Orbis Press for the Newberry Library, 1993.

Klein
Christopher M. Klein, *Maps in Eighteenth-Century British Magazines: A Checklist.* Hermon Dunlap Smith Center for the History of Cartography, Occasional Publication no. 3. Chicago: The Newberry Library, 1989.

Koeman
Cornelis Koeman, *Atlantes neerlandici: Bibliography of Terrestrial, Maritime, and Celestial Atlases and Pilot Books, Published in the Netherlands up to 1880.* Amsterdam: Theatrum Orbis Terrarum, 1967–85.

Lada-Mocarski
Valerian Lada-Mocarski, *Bibliography of books on Alaska published before 1868.* New Haven : Yale University Press, 1969.

Lande
Lawrence M. Lande, *A checklist of printed and manuscript material relating to the Canadian Indian, also relating to the Pacific North West Coast.* Lawrence Lande Foundation for Canadian Historical Research, Publications, no. 9. Montréal : McGill University, 1974.

Mickwitz and Miekkavaara
Ann-Mari Mickwitz and Leena Miekkavaara, *The A. E. Nordenskiöld Collection in the Helsinki University Library: Annotated Catalogue of Maps Made up to 1800.* Helsinki: Helsinki University Library, 1979–95.

NMM
National Maritime Museum, *Catalogue of the library.* London: H.M.S.O., 1968– .

Nordenskiöld
Adolf Erik Nordenskiöld, *Facsimile-Atlas to the Early History of Cartog-*

raphy. Stockholm, 1889; reprinted New York: Kraus Reprint, 1961; Dover, 1973.

OCLC
OCLC Online Union Catalog, the world's largest bibliographic database, is available as "FirstSearch" at many libraries and (by subscription) on the Internet at www.ref.oclc.org.

Pedley
Mary Sponberg Pedley, *Bel et utile: The Work of the Robert de Vaugondy Family of Mapmakers.* Tring, Eng.: Map Collector Pubs., 1992.

Phillips
Philip Lee Phillips, *A List of Geographical Atlases in the Library of Congress.* Washington: Government Printing Office, 1909– . Later volumes ed. By Clara E. LeGear.

Sabin
Joseph Sabin, *Bibliotheca Americana: A Dictionary of Books Relating to America, from its Discovery to the Present Time.* New York, 1868–1936.

Shirley
Rodney W. Shirley, *The Mapping of the World: Early Printed World Maps, 1472–1700.* London: Holland Press, 1983.

Smith
Dwight La Vern Smith, *The American and Canadian west : a bibliography.* Santa Barbara, Calif. : American Bibliographical Center-Clio Press, 1979.

Spence
Sydney A. Spence, *Antarctic miscellany : books, periodicals, & maps relating to the discovery and exploration of Antarctica.* [2d ed.] edited by J. J. H. & J. I. Simper. London : J. J. H. Simper, 1980.

Stevens
Henry Newton Stevens, *The world described in thirty large two-sheet maps, by Herman Moll, geographer. Being a collection exhibiting many different issues of each map.* London: H. Stevens, Son & Stiles, 1952. Photocopy of typescript.

References Cited

Streeter
The Celebrated Collection of Americana Formed by the Late Thomas Winthrop Streeter. New York: Parke-Bernet Galleries, 1966–69.

Tooley *Ant.*
R. V. Tooley, *Early Antarctica : a glance at the beginnings of cartographic representation of the South Polar regions.* Map collectors' series ; no. 2. London : Map Collectors' Circle, 1963.

Tooley *Dict.*
R. V. Tooley, *Tooley's Dictionary of mapmakers.* Tring, Eng.: Map Collector Publications, 1979. The first volume of a revised edition was published in 1999.

Tooley *FMA*
R. V. Tooley, *French mapping of the Americas: the De l'Isle, Buache, Dezauche Succession (1700–1830).* Map collectors' series, no. 33. London: Map Collectors' Circle, 1967.

TPL
Toronto Public Library, *A Bibliography of Canadiana: Being Items in the Public Library of Toronto, Canada Relating to the Early History and Development of Canada,* ed. By Frances M. Staton and Marie Tremaine. Toronto: The Library, 1934.

Wagner
Henry Raup Wagner, *The cartography of the northwest coast of America to the year 1800.* Berkeley, Calif.: University of California press, 1937.

Wickersham
James Wickersham, *A bibliography of Alaskan literature, 1724–1924 containing the titles of all histories, travels, voyages, newspapers, periodicals, public documents, etc., printed in English, Russian, German, French, Spanish, etc., relating to, descriptive of, or published in Russian America or Alaska, from 1724 to and including 1924.* Miscellaneous publications of the Alaska Agricultural College and School of Mines ; v. 1. Cordova, Alaska: Cordova Daily Times Print, 1927.

Books and Manuscripts

Abramson, Howard S.   **[1]**
Hero in Disgrace: The Life of Arctic
Explorer Frederick A. Cook [by] Howard
S. Abramson. Foreword by Warren Cook
Sr., President of the Frederick A. Cook
Society. New York: Paragon House, 1991.
> Octavo, white hardboard covers, silver titles on green
>   cloth spine, dust jacket.
> xix, 250 p., frontispiece (double-page map), [8] leaves
>   of plates (including 1 map).
> First edition.
> Reference: OCLC 22279699.

Abruzzi, Duke of the
(See Amedeo of Savoy)

Adams, Harry, Lt. (1876–)   **[2]**
Beyond the Barrier With Byrd. An
Authentic Story of the Byrd Antarctic
Exploring Expedition. By Lieutenant
Harry Adams, U.S. Navy, Ret. With an
Introduction by the Editor. Chicago and
New York: M.A. Donohue & Company,
[1932].
> Octavo, decorated blue cloth with gilt titles, dust
>   jacket.
> xvi p., 1 l., 19–253 p., frontispiece, [15] leaves of
>   plates.
> First edition.
> References: Spence 8, OCLC 1720341.

Adams, Paul (1937–)   **[3]**
Arctic Island Hunter. By Paul Adams. With
a Foreword by Sysselmann Odd Birketvedt
(Governor of Spitzbergen). London:
George Ronald, [1961].
> Octavo, original red cloth, black titles, dust jacket.
> 136 p., illustrations.
> Reference: OCLC 3418811.

Adams, Richard (1920–) and
Ronald Lockley   **[4]**
Voyage Through the Antarctic. New York:
Alfred A. Knopf [Distributed by Random
House], 1983.
> Octavo, quarter bound blue cloth on gray boards with
>   silver titles, dust jacket.
> 160 p., [8] leaves of plates, illustrations.
> First American edition.
> Reference: OCLC 8669556.

Adie, Raymond J.
(See Priestley, Raymond Edward, Sir)

Alberts, Fred G.
(See Bertrand, Kenneth J.)

Allen, Arthur S.   **[5]**
Under Sail to Greenland. Being an
Account of the Voyage of the Cutter
"Direction", Arthur S. Allen, Jr., Captain,
to Greenland in the Summer of 1929
Together with the Log, Letters and Other
Memoranda. Illustrated with Photographs
Taken on the Cruise. New York: Privately
printed [Marchbanks Press], 1931.
> Royal octavo, decorated dark blue hardboard cover,
>   gold titles on tan cloth spine.
> 91, [1] p., frontispiece (portrait), [11] leaves of plates,
>   endpaper design sketches of "Direction", fold-out
>   map.
> Edition of 900 copies.
> References: AB 287, OCLC 9376929.

Amdrup, G. C. (et al.) [6]
Report on the Danmark Expedition to the North-East Coast of Greenland 1906–1908. København: I Kommission Hos C.A. Reitzel, 1913.
> Super octavo, original paper wrappers, untrimmed.
> 474 p., photo illustrations, 23 loose folded maps and plates.
> Meddelelser om Grønland, Bd. XLI.
> Reference: OCLC 29131901.

Amedeo of Savoy, Luigi (1873–1933) [7]
Farther North Than Nansen. Being the Voyage of the Polar Star by H.R.H. The Duke of the Abruzzi. London: Howard Wilford Bell, 1901.
> Tall octavo, original decorated cream cloth, stamping and titles in black and yellow.
> 2 p. 1., 97, [1] p., frontispiece, [3] leaves of plates (1 folded).
> First edition.
> References: AB 10422, OCLC 385000.

Amedeo of Savoy, Luigi (1873–1933) [8]
On the "Polar Star" in the Arctic Sea by H.R.H. Luigi Amedeo of Savoy, Duke of the Abruzzi with the Statements of Commander U. Cagni upon the Sledge Expedition to 86°34' North, and of Dr. A. Cavalli Molinelli upon His Return to the Bay of Teplitz. Translated by William Le Queux. New York: Dodd Mead & Co.; London: Hutchinson & Co., 1903.
> Quarto, 2 volumes, original decorated blue cloth with gilt titles.
> Paged continuously. Volume 1: xvi, 346 p., xvii-xxii, frontispiece (portrait), [10] leaves of plates, illustrations, portraits, map; Volume 2: viii, 347–702 p., ix-xii; frontispiece (portrait), [6] leaves of plates (2 folded), illustrations, portraits, 4 maps (2 folded in pocket).
> First American edition.
> References: OCLC 889229, cf. AB 10423.

American Geographical Society of New York [9]
The Polar Exploring Expedition: A Special Meeting of the American Geographical & Statistical Society, Held March 22, 1860. New York: Printed for the Society, 1860.
> Octavo, stitched in original blue paper covers.
> 30 p., folded map.
> Treats of the proposed expedition by Isaac I. Hayes.
> Reference: OCLC 10856761.

American Geographical Society of New York [10]
The Polar Exploring Expedition: A Special Meeting of the American Geographical & Statistical Society, Held March 22, 1860. New York: Printed for the Society, 1860.
> Octavo, stitched in original blue paper covers.
> 40 p., folded map.
> Treats of the proposed expedition by Isaac I. Hayes.
> Pp. [31]-40: Appendix. Proceedings of Various Scientific Societies Relative to Dr. Hayes' Proposed Arctic Expedition.
> Reference: OCLC 4715985.

Amherst College [11]
American Painters of the Arctic. An Exhibit at Mead Art Gallery, Amherst College, Amherst, MA, Feb. 1-March 2: and at Coe Kerr Gallery, Inc., New York City, March 11-April 5, 1975. [Amherst, Mass.: Amherst College, 1975?].
> Royal octavo, white wrappers, slightly soiled and chipped, unpaginated.
> [52] p., illustrations.
> Includes 86 black and white reproductions of paintings by Salmon, Hamilton, Hicks, Church, Hayes, Bradford, Bierstadt, Stokes, Dellenbaugh, Fejes, Poor, et al.
> Edition of 2,500 copies.
> Reference: OCLC 15008828.

Amundsen, Roald Engelbregt Gravning (1872–1928)
The Amundsen Photographs (See Huntford, Roland)

Amundsen, Roald Engelbregt Gravning (1872–1928) [12]
My Life As an Explorer. Garden City, New York: Doubleday, Page & Company, 1927.

Octavo, original blue cloth with gilt titles, dust jacket.
4 p. 1., 282 p., frontispiece, illustrations (facsimiles), diagrams, 2 maps. Note to reviewer on loose slip of orange paper is placed facing p. 282.
First edition.
References: Spence 25, AB 398, OCLC 1262597.

Amundsen, Roald Engelbregt Gravning (1872–1928) [13]

My Polar Flight. By Captain Amundsen. With 45 Illustrations and 2 Charts. London: Hutchinson & Co., [1925].

Octavo, original blue cloth cover with gilt spine titles.
5 p., [3]-292 p., frontispiece (portrait), [26] leaves of plates, 2 maps.
Published in New York under title *Our Polar Flight* (**19** below).
References: AB 411, OCLC 8585403.

Amundsen, Roald Engelbregt Gravning (1872–1928) [14]

"The North West Passage." Being the Record of a Voyage of Exploration of the Ship "Gjöa" 1903–1907. By Roald Amundsen, with a Supplement by First Lieutenant Hansen, Vice-Commander of the Expedition. With about One Hundred and Thirty-nine Illustrations and Three Maps. New York: E.P. Dutton and Company, 1908.

Octavo, 2 volumes, original blue cloth with gilt titles.
Volume 1, xiii, 335 p., frontispiece (portrait), [22] leaves of plates, illustrations, 2 maps (1 folded); Volume 2, ix, 397 p.; frontispiece, [21] leaves of plates, illustrations, folded map.
"Published November 23rd, 1907."
Reference: OCLC 1728175.

Amundsen, Roald Engelbregt Gravning (1872–1928) [15]

The South Pole: An Account of the Norwegian Antarctic Expedition in the "Fram," 1910–1912. By Roald Amundsen. With Maps and Numerous Illustrations. In Two Volumes. Translated from the Norwegian by A.G. Chater. London: John Murray, 1912.

Octavo, 2 volumes, original decorated red cloth with gilt titles.
Volume I: xxxv, 392 p., frontispiece (portrait), [55] leaves of plates, illustrations, 2 maps (1 folded colored); Volume 2: x, 449 p., frontispiece (portrait), [43] leaves of plates (1 folded), illustrations, 10 maps and charts (1 folded). Volumes 1 and 2 have pencil marks in text, map facing p. 438 (volume 2) has small tear.
First edition.
References: Spence 16, OCLC 13627006.

Amundsen, Roald Engelbregt Gravning (1872–1928) [16]

The South Pole: An Account of the Norwegian Antarctic Expedition in the "Fram," 1910–1912. By Roald Amundsen. Translated from Norwegian by A.G. Chater. New York: Barnes & Noble, [1976].

Octavo, 2 volumes in one, original blue cloth with gilt titles, dust jacket.
xxxv, 449 p., illustrations, maps (some folded).
References: OCLC 2569432, cf. Spence 16.

Amundsen, Roald Engelbregt Gravning (1872–1928) [17]

"To the North Magnetic Pole and Through the Northwest Passage"—p.249–273 of Annual Report to Board of Regents of the Smithsonian Institution For the Year ending June 30, 1906. "Read at the Royal Geographical Society, February 11, 1907. Reprinted by permission from The Geographical Journal, London, Volume XXIX, May, 1907." Washington: Government Printing Office, 1907.

Octavo, original green cloth with gilt titles.
Collation for entire volume: li, 546 p. p. 249–273, [4] leaves of plates, folded map.
Amundsen report preceded 1908 book 'The Northwest Passage."
Reference: OCLC 41140315.

Amundsen, Roald Engelbregt Gravning (1872–1928) and Lincoln Ellsworth (1880–1951) [18]

First Crossing of the Polar Sea. By Roald Amundsen and Lincoln Ellsworth with

Additional Chapters by Other Members of the Expedition. New York: George H. Doran Company, MCMXXVII [1927].

> Octavo, blue cloth with yellow titles.
> x p., 1 l., 13–324 p., frontispiece, [11] leaves of plates, 2 maps (l folded).
> First edition.
> References: AB 409, OCLC 1519992.

Amundsen, Roald Engelbregt Gravning (1872–1928) and Lincoln Ellsworth (1880–1951) [19]

Our Polar Flight. The Amundsen-Ellsworth Polar Flight. By Roald Amundsen, Lincoln Ellsworth and Other Members of the Expedition. Illustrated from Photographs Taken on the Expedition. New York: Dodd, Mead and Company, 1925.

> Octavo, original decorated blue cloth with gilt titles.
> viii, 373 p., frontispiece (portrait), [19] leaves of plates (including 3 maps).
> Published in London under title *My Polar Flight* (**13** above).
> First American edition.
> References: AB 411, OCLC 1262603.

Anderson, William R. (1921–) [20]

Nautilus—90—North. By Commander William R. Anderson, U.S.N. with Clay Blair, Jr. Photographs by John Krawczyk, U.S.N. Cleveland and New York: The World Publishing Company, [1959].

> Octavo, original decorated turquoise cloth with silver titles, dust jacket torn.
> 251 p., illustrations.
> First edition.
> Reference: OCLC 598715.

Andrée, Salomon August (1854–1897), et al. [21]

The Andrée Diaries. Being the Diaries and Records of S.A. Andrée, Nils Strindberg & Knut Fraenkel Written during Their Balloon Expedition to the North Pole in 1897 and Discovered on White Island in 1930, Together with a Complete Record of the Expedition and Discovery. Authorized Translation from the Official Swedish Edition by Edward Adams-Ray. With 103 Illustrations and 6 Maps, Plans and Diagrams. London: John Lane, [1931].

> Octavo, original red cloth with gilt titles.
> xx, 471 p., frontispiece (portrait), [40] leaves of plates, illustrations, facsimiles, maps (3 folded).
> First English edition.
> Reference: OCLC 2990295.

Andrée, Salomon August (1854–1897), et al. [22]

Andree's Story: The Complete Record of His Polar Flight, 1897. From the Diaries and Journals of S.A. Andrée, Nils Strindberg, & K. Fraenkel Found on White Island in the Summer of 1930 and Edited by the Swedish Society for Anthropology and Geography. Translated from the Swedish by Edward Adams-Ray. New York: The Viking Press, 1930.

> 8vo., original decorated blue cloth with silver titles.
> xvi, 389 p., frontispiece, [21] leaves of plates, illustrations, diagrams, facsimiles, maps (1 folded).
> First American edition.
> References: AB 17273, OCLC 999343.

Antarctic Bibliography [23]

Antarctic Bibliography. Prepared at the Library of Congress and Sponsored by the Office of Antarctic Programs, National Science Foundation. Volume I—1965. [Washington: Government Printing Office, 1965].

> Quarto, original blue cloth cover with gilt titles.
> vi, [1], 506 p.
> George A. Doumani, Editor.
> Contains subject, author, geographic and grantee indexes.
> Reference: OCLC 1064353.

Antarctic Bibliography
(See also U.S. Naval Photographic
Interpretation Center)

Antarctic Treaty [24]
Convention on the Regulation of Antarctic
Mineral Resource Activities. Wellington,
N.Z.: Special Consultative Meeting on
Antarctic Mineral Resources, 2 June 1988.

In blue cloth drop-spine box with gilt titles on leather
label.
98 p.
With "Final Report of the Fourth Special Antarctic
Treaty Consultative Meeting on Antarctic Mineral
Resources" (6 p.).
Reference: Cf. OCLC 20645409.

Arctic Bibliography. [25]
Prepared for and in Cooperation with the
Department of Defense under Direction of
the Arctic Institute of North America.
[Washington, DC]: Department of
Defense, 1953–1965.

Thick octavo, 3 volumes, original blue cloth with gilt
titles.
Maps.
Reference: OCLC 24072047.

Arctic Experiences. [26]
Containing Captain George E. Tyson's
Wonderful Drift on the Ice-Floe, a History
of the Polaris Expedition, the Cruise of the
Tigress, and Rescue of the Polaris
Survivors. To which is added, a General
Arctic Chronology. Edited by E. Vale
Blake. New York: Harper & Brothers,
Publishers, 1874.

Octavo, original decorated green cloth with gilt titles.
486 p., plus 6 pages of advertisements, frontispiece
(portrait), [9] leaves of plates, illustrations,
portraits, 2 maps.
First edition.
References: AB 1694, OCLC 11387379.

Arctic Miscellanies. [27]
A Souvenir of the Late Polar Search. By

the Officers and Seamen of the Expedition.
London: Colburn and Co., Publishers,
1852.

Octavo, contemporary half calf, gilt spine. Spine weak.
xviii, 347 p., colored lithographic frontispiece.
Edited by James Donnett.
First edition.
Reference: OCLC 9617800.

The Arctic World. [28]
Its Plants, Animals and Natural
Phenomena. With a Historical Sketch of
Arctic Discovery, Down to the British
Polar Expedition: 1875–76. London,
Edinburgh and New York: T. Nelson and
Sons, [n.d.].

Large quarto, original decorated red cloth with gilt
titles and edges.
viii, 339 p., frontispiece (portrait), [24] leaves of plates,
illustrations, map.
Reference: Cf. OCLC 4341677.

Armitage, Albert B. (1864–1943) [29]
Cadet to Commodore, by Albert B.
Armitage. With a Foreword by the Right
Honorable Viscount Inchcape. London,
New York [etc.]: Cassell and Company,
Ltd., [1925].

8vo., original decorated blue cloth with gilt and blue
titles.
xii, 307, [1] p., frontispiece (portrait).
References: Spence 68, OCLC 2191522.

Armitage, Albert B. (1864–1943) [30]
Two Years in the Antarctic; Being a
Narrative of the British National Antarctic
Expedition, by Albert B. Armitage.
London: Edward Arnold, 1905.

Octavo, quarter morocco on green boards with gilt
titles.
xix, 315 p., frontispiece, [15] leaves of plates,
illustrations, folded map.
Prefatory note signed: Fridtjof Nansen.
References: Spence 67, OCLC 943829.

Armstrong, Alexander, Sir (1819–1899) [31]
A Personal Narrative of the Discovery of

The North-West Passage; with Numerous Incidents of Travel and Adventure during Nearly Five Years' Continuous Service in the Arctic Regions While in Search of the Expedition under Sir John Franklin. By Alex. Armstrong, M.D., R.N. Fellow of the Royal Geographical Society; Late Surgeon and Naturalist of H.M.S. 'Investigator.' London: Hurst and Blackett, 1857.

> Octavo, original decorated blue cloth with gilt titles.
> xxii, [2], 616 p., color frontispiece, folded map.
> First edition.
> References: AB 682, OCLC 2060040.

Armstrong, Terence E.   **[32]**
The Russians in the Arctic: Aspects of Soviet Exploration and Exploitation of the Far North, 1937–57. Fair Lawn, NJ: Essential Books, 1958.

> Octavo, blue cloth with gilt titles, dust jacket.
> 182 p., [8] leaves of plates, illustrations, 6 maps, maps
>   on endpapers.
> First American edition.
> Reference: OCLC 486706.

Arnold, Harry John Philip (1932–   )
                                             [33]
Photographer of the World: The Biography of Herbert Ponting. London: Hutchinson, [1969].

> Quarto, original blue cloth with gilt titles, dust jacket.
> 175 p., frontispiece (portrait), [30] leaves of plates.
> First edition.
> References: Spence 71, OCLC 177066.

Asher, Georg Michael (–1902)   [34]
Henry Hudson the Navigator. The Original Documents in which His Career is Recorded, Collected, Partly Translated, and Annotated, with an Introduction, by G.M. Asher, LL.D. The Hakluyt Society 1860. London: Printed for the Hakluyt Society, M.DCCC.LX [1860].

> Octavo, contemporary full calf, rebacked, marbled
>   edges and endpapers, gilt titles on red and black
>   labels, raised bands.

> ccxviii p., 1 l., 292 p., 2 folded maps.
> Works Issued by the Hakluyt Society, no. 27.
> Reference: OCLC 1549878.

Astrup, Eivind (1871–1895)   [35]
With Peary Near the Pole, By Eivind Astrup. With Illustrations from Photographs and Sketches by the Author. Translated from the Norwegian by H.J. Bull. London: C. Arthur Pearson Ltd., 1898.

> 8vo., original decorated burgundy cloth, gilt-stamped
>   spine.
> 362 p., frontispiece (portrait), [5] leaves of plates, black
>   and white text illustrations, folded map.
> References: AB 777, OCLC 1426353.

Auburn, F. M.   **[36]**
Antarctic Law & Politics. Bloomington: Indiana University Press, 1982.

> Octavo, blue cloth with gilt titles, dust jacket.
> xx, 361 p., 4 maps.
> Reference: OCLC 7923347.

Austin, Oliver L. (1903–   )   [37]
Antarctic Bird Studies. Oliver L. Austin, Jr., Editor. Antarctic Research Series, v. 12. [Washington]: American Geophysical Union of the National Academy of Sciences — National Research Council, 1968.

> Quarto, original blue cloth with gilt titles.
> ix, 262 p., illustrations, maps.
> Reference: OCLC 453231.

Australasian Antarctic Expedition, 1911–1914
(See Mawson, Douglas, Sir)

Back, George (1796–1878)   [38]
Arctic Artist: The Journal and Paintings of George Back, Midshipman with Franklin, 1819–1822, Edited by C. Stuart Houston; Commentary by I. S. MacLaren. Montreal;

Buffalo: McGill-Queen's University Press, 1994.

> Quarto, black cloth, dust jacket.
> xxviii, 403 p., illustrations (some colored), maps.
> Rupert's Land Record Society Series, v. 3.
> Reference: OCLC 31799471.

Back, George (1796–1878) [39]
Narrative of an Expedition in H.M.S. Terror, Undertaken with a View to Geographical Discovery on the Arctic Shores, in the Years 1836–7. By Captain Back, R.N., Commander of the Expedition. Illustrated by a Map and Plates. London: John Murray, MDCCCXXXVIII [1838].

> Octavo, original decorated blue cloth with gilt titles.
> vii, 456 p., frontispiece, [11] leaves of plates, folded map.
> First edition.
> References: AB 850, Sabin 2617, OCLC 1275534.

Back, George (1796–1878) [40]
[Narrative of an Expedition in HMS Terror (1838), plates only, bound for presentation]. 1840.

> Gilt-tooled leather spine on marbled boards, gilt titles on red leather label.
> 12 plates.
> On cover: "Sir George Back R.N. to Mary Minshull 1840."

Back, George (1796–1878) [41]
Narrative of the Arctic Land Expedition to the Mouth of the Great Fish River, and along the Shores of the Arctic Ocean, in the Years 1833, 1834 and 1835; By Captain Back, R.N., Commander of the Expedition. Illustrated by a Map and Plates. London: John Murray, MDCCCXXXVI [1836].

> Large quarto, original decorated purple cloth (spine faded) with gilt titles. Binder's title: Captain Back's Journal.
> x, 633 p., [16] leaves of plates, illustrations, map.
> References: AB 851, OCLC 4263717.

Back, George (1796–1878) [42]
Narrative of the Arctic Land Expedition to the Mouth of the Great Fish River, and along the Shores of the Arctic Ocean, in the Years 1833, 1834 and 1835. By Captain Back, R.N., Commander of the Expedition. Illustrated by a Map. Philadelphia: E.L. Carey & A. Hart, 1836.

> Octavo, original blue cloth-backed boards, paper label on spine.
> 4, viii, [1], 10–456 p., frontispiece (folded map), map on p. 72.
> References: AB 853, OCLC 12492059.

Baffin, William
(See Markham, Clements Robert, Sir)

Bain, J. Arthur [43]
Life of Fridtjof Nansen: Scientist and Explorer. Including an Account of the 1893–1896 Expedition. By J. Arthur Bain. With Numerous Illustrations and Map. London & Sheffield: Simpkin, Marshall, Hamilton, Kent & Co. Ltd., & J. Arthur Bain, 1897.

> Octavo, original decorated red cloth with gilt and black titles.
> x, 290 p., frontispiece (portrait), [11] leaves of plates, illustrations, map.
> Reference: OCLC 4100624.

Balch, Edwin Swift (1856–1927) [44]
Antarctica. Philadelphia: Press of Allen, Lane & Scott, 1902.

> Quarto, modern red buckram with gilt titles.
> 230 p., folded maps.
> First edition.
> References: Spence 83, OCLC 1699768.

Balchen, Bernt (1899–) [45]
Come North with Me. An Autobiography by Bernt Balchen. New York: E.P. Dutton & Co., 1958.

> Octavo, blue cloth with blue titles, dust jacket.
> 318 p., frontispiece (portrait), [11] leaves of plates, illustrations, 3 maps.

First edition.
Reference: OCLC 486315.

Baldwin, Evelyn Briggs (1862–1933) [46]

The Search for the North Pole or Life in the Great White World. A Complete and Connected Story of Arctic Explorations, Superbly Illustrated from Real Scenes. Replete with Anecdote, Incident, Thrilling Adventure, and Intensely Interesting Information. The Book with a Purpose Consecrated to Further Polar Investigation. By Evelyn Briggs Baldwin, A.M. Sold only by Subscription. Chicago, 1896.

> Octavo, original decorated gray cloth with black titles.
> 520 p., frontispiece (portrait), [31] leaves of plates, illustrations, maps.
> References: AB 1009, OCLC 6079695.

Bale, Shelby G.

(See Conference on United States Polar Exploration)

Ballantyne, Robert Michael (1825–1894) [47]

The Giant of the North or Pokings round the Pole. By R.M. Ballantyne. London: James Nisbet & Co., 1882.

> Octavo, original decorated red cloth with black and gilt titles.
> vi, 432 p., frontispiece, [6] leaves of plates (including added title-page, engraved), illustrations.
> Reference: OCLC 20761737.

Bank, Ted [48]

Birthplace of the Winds [by] Ted Bank II. New York: Thomas Y. Crowell Company, [1956].

> Octavo, original quarter gray cloth on blue boards, red titles, dust jacket.
> xii, [1], 274 p., [8] leaves of plates, illustrations, plan, 6 maps, maps on endpapers.
> Reference: OCLC 1264488.

Banks, Michael (1922–) [49]

Greenland. Newton Abbot: David &

Charles; Totowa, NJ: Rowman & Littlefield, 1975.

> Octavo, original blue cloth with gilt titles, dust jacket.
> 208 p., [8] leaves of plates, illustrations, 8 maps (1 double-page).
> Reference: OCLC 1418968.

Barber, Noel (1909–) [50]

The White Desert. [London]: Hodder & Stoughton, Ltd., [1958].

> Octavo, original blue cloth with gilt titles, dust jacket.
> viii, 9–205 p., frontispiece (map), [12] leaves of plates.
> References: Spence 86, OCLC 2978724.

Barker, James P. [51]

The Log of a Limejuicer: the Experiences under Sail of James P. Barker, Master Mariner, as Told to Roland Barker. New York: The MacMillan Company, 1936.

> Octavo, original decorated blue cloth with blue titles.
> xiv, 251 p., frontispiece (portrait), [11] leaves of plates.
> References: Later printing of Spence 91, OCLC 1700564.

Barr, William and Glyndwr Williams [52]

Voyages in Search of a Northwest Passage, 1741–1747. Edited by William Barr and Glyndwr Williams. London: The Hakluyt Society, 1994–95.

> Octavo, light blue cloth with gilt titles, dust jackets.
> Works issued by the Hakluyt Society, 2nd Series, vols. 177, 181.
> Contents: Volume 1. The Voyage of Christopher Middleton 1741–1742 (xii, 333 p., illustrations, maps) — Volume 2. The Voyage of William Moor and Francis Smith 1746–1747 (xv, 393 p., illustrations, maps).
> Reference: OCLC 30763887.

Barrington, Daines (1727–1800) [53]

Instances of Navigators Who Have Reached High Northern Latitudes. Read at a Meeting of the Royal Society, May 19, 1774. [London]: Sold by Benjamin White, Fleet-Street, [1774?].

> Octavo, modern wrappers.

8 p.
First printing?
References: Sabin 3630, TPL 450, OCLC 13624561.

Barrington, Daines (1727–1800) [54]

Miscellanies, by the Honourable Daines Barrington. Including Tracts on the Possibility of Reaching the North Pole. London: Printed by J. Nichols. Sold by B. White, MDCCLXXXI [1781].

>   Quarto, contemporary calf, skillfully rebacked, gilt-decorated boards and spine, gilt titles on red leather label.
>   iv, viii, 470, 471*-[478*], 471–540, 547–557, [1] p., 2 portraits, 5 genealogical tables, 2 maps.
>   John W. Robertson's copy.
>   References: AB 1092, Howes B177, OCLC 2474122.

Barrow, John, Sir (1764–1848) [55]

An Auto-Biographical Memoir of Sir John Barrow, Bart., Late of the Admiralty; Including Reflections, Observations, & Reminiscences at Home and Abroad, from Early Life to Advanced Age. London: John Murray, 1847.

>   Octavo, old three-quarter morocco with raised bands and gilt decorations on spine, marbled boards, edges & endpapers. Endpaper cut.
>   xi, 515 p., frontispiece (portrait). Review and obituary attached.
>   First edition.
>   Reference: OCLC 9868039.

Barrow, John, Sir (1764–1848) [56]

A Chronological History of Voyages into the Arctic Regions; Undertaken Chiefly for the Purpose of Discovering a North-East, North-West or Polar Passage between the Atlantic and Pacific: From the Earliest Periods of Scandinavian Navigation, to the Departure of Recent Expeditions, under the Orders of Captains Ross and Buchan. By John Barrow, F.R.S. London: John Murray, 1818.

>   Octavo, contemporary blue cloth skillfully rebacked, bound without half-title, gilt titles on red leather label.

[6], 379, 48 p., frontispiece (folded map), illustrations.
References: Lada-Mocarski 76. OCLC 13614689.

Barrow, John, Sir (1764–1848) [57]

A Chronological History of Voyages into the Arctic Regions (1818): Undertaken Chiefly for the Purpose of Discovering a North-East, North-West or Polar Passage between the Atlantic and Pacific. By John Barrow. A Reprint with a New Introduction by Christopher Lloyd. London: David & Charles Reprints, [1971].

>   Octavo, original blue cloth with gilt titles on blue label, dust jacket.
>   x, 379, 48 p., frontispiece (folded map), illustrations.
>   Reprint of the 1818 edition.
>   References: Sabin 3660, OCLC 4141426.

Barrow, John, Sir (1764–1848) [58]

Voyages of Discovery and Research within the Arctic Regions, from the year 1818 to the Present Time: Under the Command of the Several Naval Officers Employed by Sea and Land in Search of a North-west Passage from the Atlantic to the Pacific; with Two Attempts to Reach the North Pole. Abridged and Arranged from the Official Narratives, with Occasional Remarks. By Sir John Barrow, Bart., F.R.S., AN. ÆT. 82, Author of 'A Chronological History of Voyages into the Arctic Regions.' With Portrait and Maps. London: John Murray, 1846.

>   Octavo, original decorated blue cloth with gilt titles, hinges repaired. Binder's title: Arctic Voyages of Discovery.
>   xiv, 530 p., frontispiece (portrait), 2 maps (1 folded).
>   First edition.
>   References: AB 1096, OCLC 2321028.

Bartlett, Robert Abram (1875–1946) [59]

The Log of Bob Bartlett. The True Story of Forty Years of Seafaring and

Exploration. By Captain Robert A. Bartlett, Master Mariner. 27 Illustrations. New York & London: G.P. Putnam's Sons, 1929.

> Octavo, original decorated blue cloth with gilt titles.
> xii, 352 p., frontispiece (portrait), [26] leaves of plates.
> Inscribed copy by Bartlett.
> References: AB 1107, OCLC 619737.

Bartlett, Robert Abram (1875–1946) [60]

Peary's Extended Exploration of Arctic Lands Culminating in the Attainment of the North Pole. Philadelphia: American Philosophical Society, 1940.

> Detached from *Proceedings of the American Philosophical Society* 82, no. 5 (June, 1940): 935–47.
> Reference: AB 1109.

Bartlett, Robert Abram (1875–1946) [61]

Sails over Ice by Captain "Bob" Bartlett. With a Foreword by Lawrence Perry. New York & London: Charles Scribner's Sons, 1934.

> Octavo, original beige cloth with green titles, dust jacket.
> xii p., 1 1., 301 p., frontispiece (portraits), [15] leaves of plates, maps on endpapers.
> Inscribed by author, with laid-in folded card with reproduction of Bartlett's schooner, "Effie M. Morrissey", inscription signed by Bartlett on back.
> References: AB 1110, OCLC 1344764.

Bartlett, Robert Abram (1875–1946) and Ralph T. Hale [62]

The Last Voyage of the Karluk, Flagship of Vilhjalmar Stefansson's Canadian Arctic Expedition of 1913–16, as Related by Her Master, Robert A. Bartlett, and Here Set Down by Ralph T. Hale. Illustrated from Charts and Photographs. Boston: Small, Maynard and Company, Publishers, [1916].

Octavo, original decorated blue cloth with gilt titles.
6 p. l., 329 p., frontispiece, [21] leaves of plates, 4 maps. Prospectus laid in.
First edition.
References: AB 1112, OCLC 1053783.

Barton, George Hunt (1852–1933) [63]

Glacial Observations in the Umanak District, Greenland. By George H. Barton, S.B. [Cambridge: Massachusetts Institute of Technology, 1897].

> Quarto, original printed wrappers.
> p. 213–244, [13] leaves of plates, illustrations, map.
> At head of title: The Scientific Work of the Boston Party on the Sixth Peary Expedition to Greenland. Report B.
> Reprinted from *Technology Quarterly* 10, no. 2 (June 1897).
> Reference: OCLC 13628421.

Baum, Allyn [64]

Antarctica: The Worst Place in the World, by Allyn Baum. New York: Macmillan, [1966].

> Octavo, tan cloth with black titles, dust jacket.
> 151 p., illustrations, portraits, map.
> First edition, inscribed by author.
> References: Spence 98, OCLC 8989375.

Bayliss, E.P. and J.S. Cumpston [65]

Handbook and Index by E.P. Bayliss . . . and J.S. Cumpston . . . to Accompany a Map of Antarctica Produced by the Department of the Interior, 1939. Canberra: L.F. Johnston, Commonwealth Government Printer, [1939].

> Octavo, quarter morocco on orange boards, gilt titles on spine.
> 90 p. including tables, 3 maps.
> Cover mislabeled 1936.
> References: Spence 99, OCLC 12391282.

Beattie, Owen and John Geiger [66]

Frozen in Time: Unlocking the Secrets of the Franklin Expedition. New York: E. P. Dutton, [1987].

Octavo, blue cloth with silver titles, dust jacket.
xi, [1], 180 p., [12] leaves of color plates, illustrations, facsimiles, 2 maps.
First American edition.
Reference: Cf. OCLC 16684278.

Béchervaise, John [67]

The Far South, by John Béchervaise. With a Foreword by Phillip Law. Sydney: Angus & Robertson, [1961].

Octavo, original blue cloth covers with gilt titles, boards warped, dust jacket.
xvi, 103 p., [6] leaves of plates, 1 map (1 double-page), maps on endpapers.
Reference: Spence 107 (1962 edition).

Beechey, Frederick William (1796–1856) [68]

Narrative of a Voyage to the Pacific and Beering's Strait, to Co-operate with the Polar Expeditions: Performed in His Majesty's Ship Blossom, under the Command of Captain F.W. Beechey, R.N. [etc.] in the Years 1825, 26, 27, 28. Published by Authority of the Lords Commissioners of the Admiralty. In Two Parts. London: Henry Colburn and Richard Bentley, MDCCCXXXI [1831].

Quarto, 2 volumes in 1, contemporary calf, gilt and blind stamped, raised bands, gilt titles on red leather labels.
Paged continuously. Volume 1: xxi, [1], 392 p., [14] leaves of plates, 3 maps (2 folded); Volume 2: vii, [393]-742 p., [9] leaves of plates.
News clippings attached to front end papers.
First edition.
References: Spence 111, AB 1227, OCLC 21247745.

Beechey, Frederick William (1796–1856) [69]

A Voyage of Discovery towards the North Pole, Performed in His Majesty's Ships Dorothea and Trent, under the Command of Captain David Buchan, R.N. 1818; to Which is Added, a Summary of All the Early Attempts to Reach the Pacific by Way of the Pole. By Captain F.W. Beechey, R.N., F.R.S., One of the Lieutenants of the Expedition. Published by Authority of the Lords Commissioners of the Admiralty. London: Richard Bentley, 1843.

Octavo, original blind stamped blue cloth with gilt titles. Rebacked.
ix, [1] p., 1 l., 351, [1] p., frontispiece, [5] leaves of plates (2 folded), folded map.
References: AB 1230, OCLC 5350951.

Beke, Charles T.
(See Veer, Gerrit de)

Belcher, Edward, Sir (1799–1877) [70]

The Last of the Arctic Voyages; Being a Narrative of the Expedition in H.M.S. Assistance, under the Command of Captain Sir Edward Belcher, C.B. in Search of Sir John Franklin, during the Years 1852–53–54. With Notes on the Natural History, by Sir John Richardson, Professor Owen, Thomas Bell, J.W. Salter, and Lovell Reeve. In Two Volumes. Published under the Authority of the Lords Commissioners of the Admiralty. London: Lovell Reeve, 1855.

Octavo, 2 volumes, original decorated blue cloth with gilt titles. Uncut copy.
Volume 1: xx, 383 p., color frontispiece, [12] leaves of plates, illustrations, 3 folded maps; Volume 2: vii, 419 p., color frontispiece, [22] leaves of plates, illustrations, map.
References: AB 1241, Sabin 4389, OCLC 3556818.

Bellingshausen, Fabian Gottlieb von (1778?-1852) [71]

The Voyage of Captain Bellingshausen to the Antarctic Seas 1819–1821. Translated from Russian. Edited by Frank Debenham. London: The Hakluyt Society, 1945.

Octavo, 2 volumes, decorated blue cloth with gilt titles.
Volume 1: xxx, 259 p., frontispiece (portrait), [12] leaves of plates, 10 maps (2 folded); Volume 2:

viii, [261]-474 p., frontispiece (portrait), [6] leaves
of plates, 9 maps (7 folded; 1 in pocket).
First English edition.
Works Issued by the Hakluyt Society, 2nd Series, nos.
91 & 92.
References: Spence 117, OCLC 10870035.

Bellot, Joseph René (1826–1853)   [72]

Memoirs of Lieutenant Joseph René Bellot
. . . : with His Journal of a Voyage in the
Polar Seas, in Search of Sir John Franklin.
In Two Volumes. London: Hurst and
Blackett, Publishers, 1855.

Octavo, 2 volumes, original decorated brown cloth
with gilt titles, spine ends repaired, new
endpapers.
Volume 1: viii, 391 p., plus [3] p. of advertisements,
frontispiece (portrait); Volume 2: 403 p., 1
illustration.
First English edition.
References: AB 1305, OCLC 8289949.

Berens, S. L. (editor)   [73]

The "Fram" Expedition. Nansen in the
Frozen World. Preceded by a Biography of
the Great Explorer and Copious Extracts
from Nansen's "First Crossing of
Greenland," also an Account by Eivind
Astrup, of Life among People Near the
Pole, and His Journey Across Northern
Greenland with Lieutenant R.E. Peary,
U.S.N. Arranged and Edited by S.L.
Berens [etc.]. Followed by a Brief History
of the Principal Earlier Arctic Explorations,
from the Ninth Century to the Peary
Expedition, Including Those of Cabot,
Frobisher, Bering, Sir John Franklin, Kane,
Hayes, Hall, Nordenskjöld, Nares,
Schwatka, DeLong, Greely and Others. By
John E. Read [etc.]. Profusely Illustrated.
Philadelphia: A. J. Holman & Co.,
Publishers, [1897].

Octavo, original extra decorated blue cloth with gilt
titles.
2 p. l., viii, [9]-560 p., frontispiece (portrait), 112
illustrations (including portraits, maps.)
Reference: OCLC 8990369.

Bernacchi, Louis Charles (1876–1942)   [74]

Saga of the "Discovery." London &
Glasgow: Blackie & Son Limited, [1938].

Octavo, blue cloth with gilt titles.
xv, 240 p., [24] leaves of plates, 3 maps (2 folded),
map on front endpaper.
References: Spence 129, OCLC 896271.

Bernacchi, Louis Charles (1876–1942)   [75]

To the South Polar Regions: Expedition of
1898–1900. By Louis Bernacchi, F.R.G.S.
Illustrated from photographs taken by the
Author. London: Hurst & Blackett, 1901.

Octavo, turquoise cloth with gilt titles.
xvi, 348 p., frontispiece, [43] leaves of plates,
illustrations, 3 charts (2 folded).
First edition.
References: Spence 123, OCLC 1275564.

Bernacchi, Louis Charles (1876–1942)

(See also Polar Book; South Polar Times)

Bernard, Raymond W.   [76]

The Hollow Earth: The Greatest
Geographical Discovery in History Made
by Admiral Richard E. Byrd in the
Mysterious Land Beyond the Poles. The
True Origin of the Flying Saucers. By Dr.
Raymond Bernard. New York: University
Books, Inc., [1969].

Octavo, black cloth with silver titles, dust jacket.
254 p., illustrations, portraits, maps.
Reference: OCLC 46112.

Bernier, Joseph Elzear (1852–1934)   [77]

Master Mariner & Arctic Explorer: A
Narrative of 60 Years at Sea from the Logs
and Yarns of Captain J.E. Bernier. Ottawa,
Ontario: Printed by Le Droit, 1939.

Octavo, original decorated tan wrappers.
409 p., [19] leaves of plates, illustrations.
References: AB 1458, OCLC 8990607.

Bertram, George Colin Lawder   **[78]**
Arctic & Antarctic: The Technique of Polar
Travel. Cambridge [England]: W. Heffer &
Sons, Ltd., [1939].
> Octavo, original decorated blue cloth with gilt titles,
>   dust jacket.
> xii p., 1 l., 125 p., frontispiece, [12] leaves of plates,
>   illustrations, maps on endpapers.
> First edition.
> References: Spence 131, AB 1490, OCLC 8989897.

Bertrand, Kenneth J. (1910–   )   **[79]**
Americans in Antarctica, 1775–1948. New
York: American Geographical Society,
1971.
> Quarto, original gray cloth with gilt titles on black
>   labels.
> xvi, 554 p., [11] leaves of plates, 26 maps.
> First edition.
> American Geographical Society Special Publication No.
>   39.
> Reference: OCLC 1236432.

Bertrand, Kenneth J. and
   Fred G. Alberts   **[80]**
Geographic Names of Antarctica. With a
Foreword by Meredith F. Burrill and a List
of Expeditions by Kenneth J. Bertrand and
Fred G. Alberts. Washington, D.C. : Office
of Geography, Department of Interior,
1956.
> Folio, original light blue wrappers, black titles.
> v, 332 p.
> Reference: OCLC 13937197.

Best, George V. (d. 1584)   **[81]**
The Three Voyages of Martin Frobisher, in
Search of a Passage to Cathaia and India by
the North-West, A.D. 1576–8, Reprinted
from the First Edition of Hakluyt's
Voyages, with Selections from Manuscript
Documents in the British Museum and
State Paper Office. By Rear-Admiral
Richard Collinson, C.B. London: Printed
for the Hakluyt Society, M.DCCC.LXVII
[1867].
> Octavo, original cloth.
> [vii]-xxvi p., 1 l., [3]-374, [2] p., illustrations, 2 folded
>   maps. Pencil marks *passim*.
> Works Issued by the Hakluyt Society, no. 38.
> Reference: OCLC 1549740.

Best, George V. (d. 1584)   **[82]**
The Three Voyages of Martin Frobisher in
Search of a Passage to Cathay and India by
the North-West, A.D. 1576–8. From the
Original 1578 Text of George Best.
Together with Numerous Other Versions,
Additions, etc. Now Edited, with Preface,
Introduction, Notes, Appendixes and
Bibliography, by Vilhjalmur Stefansson
[etc.] With the Collaboration of Eloise
McCaskill, AM., together with numerous
maps and illustrations. In two volumes.
London: The Argonaut Press, 1938.
> Quarto, 2 volumes, original vellum backed decorated
>   red cloth. Gilt titles on spine.
> Uncut copy.
> Volume 1: cxxx, 166 p., frontispiece (portrait), 4 plates
>   (1 folded), 4 maps (2 folded); Volume 2: vi p., 1
>   l., [1–9], 10–293 p., frontispiece (folded map), 5
>   plates, 3 maps (2 folded).
> Copy 196 of 475 numbered copies.
> Reference: OCLC 1476010.

Bickel, Lennard   **[83]**
Mawson's Will: The Greatest Survival
Story Ever Written. With Foreword by Sir
Edmund Hillary. New York: Stein & Day,
1977.
> Octavo, original quarter black cloth on decorated blue
>   boards with gilt titles, dust jacket.
> 237 p., [8] leaves of plates, illustrations, maps on
>   endpapers.
> First edition, third printing.
> Reference: OCLC 2598732.

Biddle, Richard (1796–1847)   **[84]**
A Memoir of Sebastian Cabot; with a
Review of the History of Maritime
Discovery. Illustrated by Documents from
the Rolls, Now First Published.

Philadelphia: Published by Carey and Lea, 1831.

> Octavo, three-quarter wine morocco, pebble cloth boards, gilt titles on spine.
> viii, v, [2], 8–327 p.
> First edition.
> Reference: OCLC 1597507.

Binney, George, Sir (1900–   )   **[85]**
With Seaplane and Sledge in the Arctic, by George Binney, Leader Oxford University Arctic Expedition. With a Preface by Professor W.J. Sollas [etc.]. With 40 Pages of Illustrations. London: Hutchinson & Co., [1925].

> Octavo, original decorated blue cloth with gilt titles, dust jacket.
> 287 p., frontispiece (portrait), [39] leaves of plates, folded map.
> First edition.
> References: AB 1572, OCLC 8990930.

Bixby, William   **[86]**
Track of the Bear, by William Bixby. New York: David McKay Co., Inc., [1965].

> Octavo, original turquoise cloth with black titles, dust jacket.
> ix, 309 p., [4] leaves of plates, illustrations, double-page map, maps on endpapers.
> Reference: OCLC 1330706.

Bliss, Richard W.   **[87]**
Our Lost Explorers: The Narrative of the Jeannette Arctic Expedition as Related by the Survivors, and in the Records and Last Journals of Lieutenant De Long. Revised by Raymond Lee Newcomb, Naturalist of the Expedition. With Graphic Descriptions of Arctic Siberia, the Lena and its Delta, the Native and Exiled Inhabitants of the Country, etc.; and Mr. Newcomb's Narrative of a Winter Overland Journey from the Arctic Ocean to St. Petersburg. Also an Account of the Jeannette Search Expeditions, Their Discoveries, the Burning of the Rodgers, &c., &c. With an Introduction by Rev. W.L. Gage, D.D. [With] Maps, Portraits, and Numerous Engravings. Published by Subscription Only. Hartford, Conn.: American Publishing Company; San Francisco: A.L. Bancroft & Co., 1882.

> Octavo, original gray decorated cloth (spotted) with black, silver and gilt titles.
> xv, [1], [17]-479 p. frontispiece (portrait), 21 plates, illustrations, map, plans.
> First published narrative.
> Reference: OCLC 21620397.

Blunt, George William (1802–1878)   **[88]**
Memoir of the Dangers and Ice in the North Atlantic Ocean. Eleventh Edition. New York: E. & G. W. Blunt, 1863.

> Octavo, original blue wrappers, printed label.
> vi, 32 p., folded chart.
> Reference: OCLC 4937161.

Boas, Franz (1858–1942)   **[89]**
The Central Eskimo, by Dr. Franz Boas. Seattle, WA: Shorey Book Store, 1970.

> Octavo.
> 399–669 p., [10] leaves of plates, illustrations, diagrams, music, maps (1 folded).
> Limited to 100 copies.
> Facsimile reproduction of Smithsonian Institution, Bureau of Ethnology. Sixth Annual Report, 1884-85. Washington: GPO, 1888.
> References: AB 1728, OCLC 9354003.

Bockstoce, John
(See Maguire, Rochfort)

Bodilly, Ralph Burland (1884–   )   [90]
The Voyage of Captain Thomas James for the Discovery of the North-West Passage, 1631. By Commander R.B. Bodilly, R.N. London & Toronto: J.M. Dent & Sons Ltd.; New York: E.P. Dutton & Co. Inc., 1928.

Octavo, original decorated red cloth with gilt titles,
dust jacket.
1 p. l., 215, [1] p., folded map.
Reference: OCLC 1720789.

Bond, Creina
(See Johnson, Peter)

Bonington, Chris [91]
Quest for Adventure [by] Chris
Bonington. New York: Clarkson N. Potter,
Inc., 1982.

Quarto, original blue cloth with silver titles, dust jacket.
448 p., illustrations (some color), maps.
First American Edition.
Reference: OCLC 8114941.

Bonnycastle, Richard Henry Gardyne (1909–68) [92]
A Gentleman Adventurer. The Arctic
Diaries of R.H.G. Bonnycastle. Edited and
Compiled by Heather Robertson.
[Toronto, Ont.]: Lester & Orpen Dennys,
[1984].

Quarto, original black cloth with gilt titles, dust jacket.
217, [1] p., frontispiece (portrait), [1] leaf of plates,
illustrations, facsimiles, maps.
A Richard Bonnycastle Book 2.
Reference: OCLC 13121146.

Borchgrevink, Carsten Egebert (1864–1934) [93]
First on the Antarctic Continent: Being an
Account of the British Antarctic
Expedition, 1898–1900. By C.E.
Borchgrevink, F.R.G.S., Commander of
the Expedition. With Portraits, Maps, and
186 Illustrations. London: George
Newnes, Limited, 1901.

Octavo, original decorated blue cloth with gilt titles.
xv, [1], 333 p., frontispiece (portrait), [16] leaves of
plates, illustrations, 3 folded maps.
References: Spence 152, OCLC 8989463.

Borden, Courtney Louise (Letts) [94]
The Cruise of the Northern Light:

Explorations and Hunting in the Alaskan
and Siberian Arctic, by Mrs. John Borden.
In Which the Sea-Scouts Have a Great
Adventure. New York: The Macmillan
Company, 1928.

Octavo, original decorated blue cloth with gilt titles.
xi p., 2 l., 317 p., frontispiece (portrait), illustrations
(including portraits), maps on endpapers.
First edition.
References: AB 1978, OCLC 1520152.

Borden, John [95]
Log of the Auxiliary Schooner Yacht
Northern Light, Commanded by John
Borden, [etc.], Borden-Field Museum,
Alaska-Arctic Expedition, 1927. Chicago:
Privately Printed [by R.R. Donnelley],
1929.

Quarto, tan and blue cloth with yellow title on blue
label.
[345] p., mounted frontispiece and illustrations, maps
on endpapers.
Edition limited to 100 numbered copies. This is copy
No. 1.
First edition.
Reference: OCLC 9370154.

Borup, George (1884–1912) [96]
A Tenderfoot with Peary, by George
Borup; with a Preface by G.W. Melville
[etc.]. With Forty-six Illustrations from
Photographs and a Map. New York:
Frederick A. Stokes Company, [1911].

Octavo, original decorated blue cloth with gilt and
black titles.
xvi, 317 p., frontispiece (portrait), [15] leaves of plates,
illustrations.
Lacks map.
References: AB 2022, OCLC 1520218.

Bowermaster, Jon
(See Steger, Will)

Brainard, David Legge (1856–1946) [97]
The Outpost of the Lost: An Arctic

Adventure. By David L. Brainard. Edited by Bessie Rowland James. With Salutation by A.W. Greely. Indianapolis: The Bobbs-Merrill Company, [1929].

> Octavo, blue cloth with yellow titles, dust jacket.
> 317 p., maps on endpapers.
> First edition.
> References: AB 2071, OCLC 2027965.

Brainard, David Legge (1856–1946) [98]

Six Came Back: The Arctic Adventure of David L. Brainard. Edited by Bessie Rowland James. Indianapolis and New York: The Bobbs-Merrill Company, [1940].

> Octavo, original blue cloth with gilt titles, dust jacket.
> 305 p. including frontispiece (portrait), [11] leaves of plates, maps on endpapers.
> References: AB 2073, OCLC 2168015.

Brend, William Alfred [99]

The Story of Ice in the Past and Present. By W.A. Brend. With Thirty-seven Illustrations. London, New York, Toronto: Hodder and Stoughton, [1899].

> Duodecimo, original decorated blue cloth with white and gilt titles.
> vi p., 1 l., [9]-228 p., frontispiece, 37 illustrations.

Brent, Peter Ludwig [100]

Captain Scott and the Antarctic Tragedy [by] Peter Brent. New York: Saturday Review Press, [1974].

> Quarto, original burgundy cloth with gilt titles, dust jacket.
> 223 p., color frontispiece (portrait), illustrations (some color), 3 maps.
> References: Spence 175, OCLC 884834.

Bridges, Esteban Lucas (1874–   ) [101]

Uttermost Part of the Earth [by] E. Lucas Bridges. New York: E.P. Dutton and Company, Inc., [1949]. Special edition.

> Octavo, original green cloth with gilt titles on green label.

xxi, [1], 23–558 p., frontispiece (portrait), [23] leaves of plates, 4 maps (3 folded).
> References: Spence 179, OCLC 4612247.

British Museum (Natural History) [102]

Report on the Geological Collections Made during the Voyage of the "Quest" on the Shackleton-Rowett Expedition to the South Atlantic & Weddell Sea in 1921–1922. London: Printed by order of the Trustees of the British Museum, 1930.

> Octavo, gilt decorated burgundy cloth with gilt titles.
> vi p., 3 l., 161, 1 l. p. including frontispiece, charts, drawings, maps.
> Reference: OCLC 8989555.

Britton, Beverly

(See Kearns, William H.)

Brögger, W.C. and Nordahl Rolfsen [103]

Fridtiof Nansen: 1861–1893. By W.C. Brögger and Nordahl Rolfsen. Translated by William Archer. With Numerous Illustrations and Maps. London, New York and Bombay: Longmans, Green & Co., 1896.

> Octavo, decorated blue cloth with silver titles and cover vignette.
> x, 402 p., plus 24 pages of advertisements, frontispiece (portrait), [7] leaves of plates, illustrations, 3 folded maps.
> First English edition.
> Reference: AB 2225.

Brontman, Lazar Konstantinovich [104]

On Top of the World: The Soviet Expedition to the North Pole 1937–1938. By Lazar Brontman. With a Foreword by Professor Otto Y. Schmidt (Hero of the Soviet Union). New York: Covici, Friede, [1938].

> Octavo, blue cloth with blue titles on white label.

xi, [1] p., 1 l., 15–343 [i.e. 345] p., [8] leaves of plates
(1 double), 2 maps (1 double). Double map not
included in the pagination.
References: AB 2241, OCLC 2636096.

Brown, John (1797–1861)   **[105]**
The North-West Passage, and the Plans for
the Search for Sir John Franklin: A Review,
by John Brown [etc.]. London: Published
by E. Stanford, 1858.

Octavo, original decorated blue cloth with gilt titles.
xii, 463 p., frontispiece, 2 folded maps.
Reference: OCLC 9114110.

Brown, Robert Neal Rudmose
(1879–1957)   **[106]**
A Naturalist at the Poles: the Life, Work &
Voyages of Dr. W.S. Bruce, the Polar
Explorer. By R.N. Rudmose Brown [etc.].
With Five Chapters by W.G. Burn
Murdoch [etc.]. With 38 Illustrations and
3 Maps. London: Seeley, Service & Co.
Ltd., 1923.

Octavo, original black cloth with blue titles, dust jacket.
2 p.l., 11–316 p., frontispiece (portrait), [23] leaves of
plates, illustrations, 3 maps (2 folded).
References: Spence 194, AB 2334, OCLC 2421984.

Brown, Robert Neal Rudmose
(1879–1957)   **[107]**
The Polar Regions, a Physical and
Economic Geography of the Arctic and
Antarctic. By R.N. Rudmose Brown [etc.].
With 23 maps. London: Methuen & Co.
Ltd., [1927].

Octavo, gray cloth with gilt titles.
ix, [1], 245, [1] p., 23 maps (2 folded).
First edition.
References: AB 2326, Spence 196, OCLC 8991236.

Brown, Robert Neal Rudmose
(1879–1957)   **[108]**
The Voyage of the "Scotia" Being the
Record of a Voyage of Exploration in
Antarctic Seas by Three of the Staff. With

Illustrations. Edinburgh and London:
William Blackwood and Sons, MCMVI
[1906].

Octavo, original decorated black cloth with white
titles.
xxiv, 375 p., frontispiece, [58] leaves of plates, 3 maps
(2 folded).
References: Spence 193, OCLC 4614372.

Browne, William Henry   **[109]**
Ten Coloured Views Taken during the
Arctic Expedition of Her Majesty's Ships
"Enterprise" and "Investigator," under the
Command of Captain Sir James C. Ross
[etc.]. Drawn by W.H. Browne . . . Late of
H.M.S. "Enterprise." On Stone by Charles
Haghe. With a Summary of the Various
Arctic Expeditions in Search of Captain Sir
John Franklin [etc.], and his Companions
in H.M. Ships "Erebus" and "Terror."
Dedicated, by Special Permission, to the
Lords Commissioners of the Admiralty.
London: Ackermann and Co., 1850.

Folio, green half calf, gilt titles, original yellow
endpapers.
8 pages of text, 7 tinted lithographed plates with 10
views, with 2 original sepia illustrations.
References: AB 2344, OCLC 14128912.

Bruemmer, Fred   **[110]**
Arctic Animals: A Celebration of Survival
[by] Fred Bruemmer. Ashland, Wisconsin:
NorthWord, Inc., [1986].

Quarto, blue cloth with silver titles, dust jacket.
159 p., illustrations (some color).
First edition.
Reference: OCLC 15856792.

Bruemmer, Fred   **[111]**
The Arctic World [by] Fred Bruemmer,
Principal Writer and Photographer; Dr.
William E. Taylor, Jr., General Editor;
Contributors, Ernest S. Burch, Jr. [et al.].
San Francisco: Sierra Club Books, 1985.

Folio, decorated blue cloth with silver titles, dust
jacket.

256 p., illustrations (some color).
Reference: OCLC 11783971.

Bry, Theodore de (1528–1598)   [112]
[Plates illustrating Willem Barents' Novaya
Zemlya expedition, 1594–1597, from
*Icones sive expressae et artifitiosae
delineationes qvarvndam mapparvm,
locorvm maritimorvm, insvlarvm, vrbium,
& populorum: quibus & horundem vitae,
naturae, morum, habituumque descriptio
adiuncta est . . . omnia scita et diligenti
indvstria in aes incisa, et ob ocvlos posita à
Ioan. Theod. & Joan. Israele de Bry.*
Frankfurt: Matthaeus Becker, 1601].
> Folio, disbound leaves.
> xxxvi-lviii plates, illustrations, maps.
> Detached from de Bry's *Tertia pars Indiae orientalis*
> (Frankfurt: Matthaeus Beckerus, 1601), where
> they were intended to illustrate Gerrit de Veer's
> *Tertia pars, Navigationes tres discretas.* . . .
> Letterpress text above and below engravings, versos
> blank except for plate LVIII.
> Set includes 2 issues of plate LVIII: one, from the first
> edition, first issue, contains on verso de Veer's
> map of Novaya Zemlya; the second, from the
> first edition, second issue, has a blank verso.
> References: Church 208 and 209.

Bryant, Henry G. (1859–1932)   [113]
Notes on an Early American Arctic
Expedition. By Henry G. Bryant.
[London: Printed by William Clowes and
Sons, Limited, 1909].
> Octavo, original blue printed wrappers.
> Reprinted from the *Geographical Journal* for January,
> 1909.
> Inscribed by Bryant on front cover.
> Reference: OCLC 32863760.

Bull, Colin
(See Wright, Charles S.)

Bull, Henrik Johan (1844– ?   [114]
The Cruise of the "Antarctic" to the South
Polar Regions. By H.J. Bull. With
Frontispiece by W.L. Wyllie, A.R.A., and

Illustrations by W.G. Burn Murdoch.
London and New York: Edward Arnold,
1896.
> Octavo, contemporary three-quarter calf on green
> boards, raised bands with gilt title on red leather
> label. Binder's title: The Cruse [sic] of the
> Antarctic.
> 243 p., frontispiece, [11] leaves of plates.
> First edition.
> References: Spence 210, OCLC 2438484.

**Bullen, Frank Thomas (1857–1915)
[115]**
The Cruise of the Cachalot [by] Frank T.
Bullen. New York and Chicago: A.L. Burt
Co., [1927].
> Octavo, original green cloth with yellow titles.
> xvi, 318 p., frontispiece (portrait), decorated
> endpapers.
> Reference: OCLC 2229420.

Burney, James   [116]
With Captain James Cook in the Antarctic
and Pacific: The Private Journal of James
Burney, Second Lieutenant of the
Adventure on Cook's Second Voyage,
1772–1773. Edited and with an
Introduction by Beverley Hooper.
Canberra: National Library of Australia,
1975.
> Octavo, original decorated brown cloth with gilt titles
> on blue label, dust jacket.
> xi, 112 p., [4] leaves of plates, diagrams, illustrations,
> maps, decorated endpapers.
> Reference: OCLC 2564882.

**Burpee, Lawrence Johnstone
(1873–1946)   [117]**
The Search for the Western Sea: The Story
of the Exploration of North-Western
America. By Lawrence J. Burpee. New and
Revised Edition. New York: The
MacMillan Company, 1936.
> Octavo, 2 volumes, red cloth with gilt titles.
> Paged continuously. Volume 1: lxi, 304 p.; Volume 2:
> viii p., 1 l., 305–609 p., frontispiece, 62 plates
> (including maps.)

References: Howes B-1006, Smith 1299, OCLC
  2479631.

Bursey, Jack [118]

Antarctic Night: One Man's Story of
28,224 Hours at the Bottom of the World.
New York, [etc.]: Rand McNally &
Company, [1957].

Octavo, original gray decorated cloth with blue titles,
  dust jacket.
256 p., illustrations.
Presentation copy from Bursey.
First edition.
References: Spence 220, OCLC 1269824.

Butler, William E. [119]

International Straits of the World:
Northeast Arctic Passage. By William E.
Butler. Alphen aan den Rijn, The
Netherlands: Sijthoff & Noordhoff, 1978.

Octavo, original gray cloth with green titles.
xii, 199 p.
Reference: OCLC 8730840.

Butler, William Francis, Sir
(1838–1910) [120]

The Great Lone Land: A Narrative of
Travel and Adventure in the North-West of
America. London: Sampson Low, Marston,
Searle & Rivington, 1878.

Large duodecimo, original brown pebble cloth with
  gilt and black stampings.
x p., 1 l., 386 p., 1 l., plus 32 p. of advertisements,
  frontispiece (folded map), 6 plates from
  engravings.
Eighth Edition.
Reference: OCLC 22870596.

Butler, William Francis, Sir
(1838–1910) [121]

The Wild North Land: Being the Story of
a Winter Journey, with Dogs, Across
Northern North America. By Captain W.F.
Butler [etc.]. With Illustrations and Route
Map. Fourth Edition. London: Sampson
Low, Marston, Low & Searle, 1874.

Octavo, original decorated green cloth with gilt titles.
x p., 1 l., 358 p., 1 l., plus 48 p. of advertisements,
  frontispiece (portrait), [15] leaves of plates, folded
  map.
Reference: OCLC 4636618.

Byrd, Richard Evelyn (1888–1957)
[122]

Alone [by] Richard E. Byrd. Decorations
by Richard E. Harrison. New York: G.P.
Putnam's Sons, 1938.

Octavo, original blue cloth with blue titles.
ix p., 2 l., 3–296 p., illustrations. Printed in blue ink.
First edition.
References: Spence 232, OCLC 486938.

Byrd, Richard Evelyn (1888–1957)
[123]

Discovery: The Story of the Second Byrd
Antarctic Expedition. By Richard Evelyn
Byrd, Rear Admiral, U.S.N., Ret.
Introduction by Claude A. Swanson,
Secretary of the Navy. With Illustrations
and Maps. New York: G.P. Putnam's Sons,
1935.

Octavo, original blue cloth with gilt titles, dust jacket.
xxi p., 1 l., 405 p., frontispiece (portrait), plates,
  portraits, map, maps on endpapers.
First edition.
References: Spence 229, OCLC 486493.

Byrd, Richard Evelyn (1888–1957)
[124]

Into the Home of the Blizzard, by
Commander Richard E. Byrd. On the Eve
of His Departure for the Antarctic.
Commander Byrd Explains Why He
Attempts the Exploration of the Frozen
Continent by Air and Discusses Problems
He Must Solve. [New York?]: New York
Times and The St. Louis Post-Dispatch,
1928.

Octavo, original stiff printed wrappers.
18 p., illustrated.
Privately printed, edition of 1000 copies, no. 963,
  presented to William S. Munroe.

First edition.
References: Spence 225, OCLC 395840, 2554406.

Byrd, Richard Evelyn (1888–1957) [125]

Little America: Aerial Exploration in the Antarctic. The Flight to the South Pole. By Richard Evelyn Byrd, Rear Admiral, U.S.N., Ret. With 74 Illustrations and Maps. New York and London: G.P. Putnam's Sons; The Knickerbocker Press, 1930.

> Octavo, original half vellum on blue boards, gilt titles, glassine dust jacket, boxed.
> xvi, 436 p., frontispiece (portrait), [55] leaves of plates, illustrations, portraits, maps.
> Author's autograph edition. Edition of 1000 copies.
> References: Spence 227, OCLC 3939113.

Byrd, Richard Evelyn (1888–1957) [126]

Little America: Aerial Exploration in the Antarctic. The Flight to the South Pole. By Richard Evelyn Byrd, Rear Admiral, U.S.N., Ret. With 74 Illustrations and Maps. New York and London: G.P. Putnam's Sons, 1930.

> Octavo, original blue cloth with gilt titles.
> xvi, 422 p., frontispiece (portrait), plates, portraits, maps (part folded.)
> Inscribed to Telfer MacArthur by Byrd.
> First edition.
> References: Spence 226, OCLC 486566.

Byrd, Richard Evelyn (1888–1957) [127]

Our Navy Explores Antarctica. Washington, DC: National Geographic Society, 1947.

> Octavo, stiff wraps, cloth spine. Cover title: Polar Lands.
> From *National Geographic Magazine* 92, no. 4 (October 1947): 429–522; illustrations, photographs (some color), maps.
> Reference: Spence 2146.

Byrd, Richard Evelyn (1888–1957) [128]

Skyward: Man's Mastery of the Air as Shown by the Brilliant Flights of America's Leading Air Explorer. His Life, His Thrilling Adventures, His North Pole and Trans-Atlantic Flights, Together with His Plans for Conquering the Antarctic by Air. By Richard Evelyn Byrd, Commander, U.S. Navy. New York and London: Putnam's; Knickerbocker Press, 1928.

> Octavo, original blue cloth with gilt titles, dust jacket.
> xv, 359 p., frontispiece (portrait), illustrations, portraits, folded map.
> First trade edition.
> Reference: Spence 223.

Calvert, James [129]

Surface at the Pole: The Story of USS Skate [by] Commander James Calvert, U.S.N. London: The Adventurers Club, [1963].

> Octavo, red cloth with gilt titles, dust jacket.
> viii p., 1 l., 211 p., 1 l., frontispiece, [6] leaves of plates, illustrations.
> Reference: OCLC 11897337.

Cameron, Ian (1924–) [130]

Antarctica: The Last Continent [by] Ian Cameron. Boston & Toronto: Little, Brown and Company, [1974].

> Quarto, green cloth with gilt titles, dust jacket.
> 256 p., color frontispiece (map), illustrations (some color).
> First American edition.
> References: Spence 241, OCLC 1205917.

Campbell, Victor (1875–1956) [131]

The Wicked Mate: The Antarctic Diary of Victor Campbell: An account of the Northern Party on Captain Scott's Last Expedition from the Original Manuscript in the Queen Elizabeth Library, Memorial University of Newfoundland. Edited by H.G.R. King. Foreword by Lord

Shackleton. Bluntisham, Huntington: Bluntisham Books; Alburgh, Harleston, Norfolk: Erskine Press, 1988.

> Quarto, original blue cloth with gilt titles.
> 192 p., frontispiece, illustrations, portraits, maps.
> First edition.
> Reference: OCLC 19886037.

Canada. Department of Marine and Fisheries. [132]

Report on the Dominion Government Expedition to the Northern Waters and Arctic Archipelago of the D.G.S "Arctic" in 1910. Under Command of J.E. Bernier, Officer in Charge and Fishery Officer. [Ottawa? 1911?]

> Octavo, original brown cloth with gilt titles.
> 6 p. l., [5]-161 p., illustrations, tables, folded maps.
> References: AB 2718, OCLC 4811188

Caras, Roger A. [133]

Antarctica: Land of Frozen Time [by] Roger A. Caras. With Special Charts by A. Peter Ianuzzi. Philadelphia and New York: Chilton Books, [1962].

> Octavo, original blue cloth with black titles, dust jacket.
> xi, [1] p., 1 l., 209 p., color frontispiece, illustrations, folded map.
> First edition.
> References: Spence 244, OCLC 8991751.

Carlson, William Samuel (1905–) [134]

Lifelines through the Arctic, By William S. Carlson. New York: Duell, Sloan and Pearce, [1962].

> Octavo, original cloth, dust jacket.
> xiv p., 1 l., 3–271 p., illustrations.
> First edition, inscribed by author.
> Reference: OCLC 620188.

Carstensen, Andreas Christian Riis (1844–1906) [135]

Two Summers in Greenland. An Artist's Adventures among Ice and Islands, in Fjords and Mountains. By A. Riis Carstensen. Illustrated. London: Chapman and Hall, Limited, 1890.

> Octavo, original decorated blue cloth with gilt titles.
> xxxi, [1], 185 p., frontispiece, illustrations, plates, folded map.
> References: AB 2917, OCLC 2642781.

Carter, Paul Allen (1926–) [136]

Little America: Town at the End of the World [by] Paul A. Carter. New York: Columbia University Press, 1979.

> Octavo, original black cloth with white titles, dust jacket.
> xii p., 1 l., 301 p., illustrations.
> Reference: OCLC 5007540.

Caswell, John Edwards [137]

Arctic Frontiers: United States Explorations in the Far North [by] John Edwards Caswell. Norman: University of Oklahoma Press, 1956.

> Octavo, turquoise cloth with white titles, dust jacket.
> xv, [1] p., 1 l., 3–232 p., illustrations, bibliography, maps.
> First edition.
> Reference: OCLC 486702.

Chapman, Frederick Spencer (1907–1971) [138]

Northern Lights: The Official Account of the British Arctic Air-Route Expedition. By F. Spencer Chapman. With a Foreword by Admiral Richard E. Byrd. With a Map and 32 Pages of Plates. New York: Oxford University Press, 1934.

> Octavo, original red cloth with gilt titles.
> xiv p., 1 l., 263, [1] p., frontispiece, [31] leaves of plates, maps (1 folded.)
> References: AB 2983 (pagination differs), OCLC 3418657.

Chapman, Frederick Spencer (1907–1971) [139]

Watkins' Last Expedition. By F. Spencer Chapman [etc.]. With an Introduction by

Augustine Courtauld. With 48 Pages of Plates and a Map. London: Chatto and Windus, 1934.

> Octavo, original green cloth with gilt titles.
> xv, [1], 290, [1] p., frontispiece, 47 pages of plates from photographs, maps (1 folded).
> First edition.
> References: AB 2986, OCLC 4700563.

Chapman, Walker (Robert Silverberg) [140]

The Loneliest Continent: The Story of Antarctic Discovery, by Walker Chapman. Greenwich, Connecticut: New York Graphic Society Publishers, Ltd., [1964].

> Octavo, original blue cloth with silver titles, dust jacket.
> 279 p., [8] leaves of plates, illustrations, maps.
> First edition.
> Reference: OCLC 965307.

Charcot, Jean Baptiste (1867–1936) [141]

The Voyage of the 'Why Not?' in the Antarctic: The Journal of the Second French South Polar Expedition, 1908–1910. By Dr. Jean Charcot. English Version by Philip Walsh. With Numerous Illustrations from Photographs. London, New York and Toronto: Hodder and Stoughton, [1911].

> Quarto, original decorated blue cloth with gilt titles. Ex Libris.
> viii, 315 p., folded frontispiece, [42] leaves of plates, map. Half-title is detached.
> Plate at p. 112 is detached.
> References: Spence 262, OCLC 2532005.

Chavanne, Josef (1846–1902) [142]

Die Literatur über die Polar-Regionen Erde. Von Dr. Josef Chavanne, Dr. Alois Karpf, [und] Franz Ritter v. Le Monnier. Herausgegeben von der K.K. Geographischen Gesellschaft in Wien. [Vienna, 1878].

> Octavo, unlettered black leather spine.

> xiv, [2], 335, [1] p. Preface in English and German.
> Added English title page: The literature on the Polar-Regions of the Earth.
> First edition.
> Reference: OCLC 5916744.

Cheliuskin Expedition, 1933–1934. [143]

The Voyage of the Chelyuskin. By Members of the Expedition. Translated by Alec Brown. With Numerous Plates and Maps. London: Chatto & Windus, 1935.

> Octavo, original blue cloth with blue and white titles.
> xiii p., 1 l., 325 p., 1 l., frontispiece (portrait), [31] leaves of plates, 8 diagrams and maps.
> First English edition.
> The expedition was led by Prof. Otto Julievitch Schmidt.
> Contents: Pt. I. The Chelyuskin's Story. — Pt. II. The Airmen's Stories.
> References: OCLC 13631336, cf. AB 3045.

Cheliuskin Expedition, 1933–1934. [144]

The Voyage of the Chelyuskin. By Members of the Expedition. Translated by Alec Brown. With Numerous Plates and Maps. New York: Macmillan, 1935.

> Octavo, original blue cloth with white titles.
> xiii p., 1 l., 325 p., frontispiece (portrait), [31] leaves of plates, 8 diagrams and maps.
> First American edition.
> References: AB 3045, OCLC 904926.

Cherry-Garrard, Apsley George Benet (1886–1959) [145]

The Worst Journey in the World: Antarctic, 1910–1913, by Apsley Cherry-Garrard. With Panoramas, Maps, and Illustrations by the late Doctor Edward A. Wilson and Other Members of the Expedition. In Two Volumes. London: Constable and Company Limited, [1922].

> Octavo, 2 volumes, original brown linen backed boards, paper labels.
> Paged continuously. Volume 1: lxiv, 300 p.; Volume 2: viii, 301–585 p., color frontispiece, illustrations (some color, some folded), portraits, maps (some folded).

First edition.
References: Spence 277, OCLC 13626778.

Cherry-Garrard, Apsley George Benet (1886–1959)
(See also South Polar Times)

Christensen, Lars [146]
Such is the Antarctic. By Lars Christensen. Translated by E.M.G. Jayne. London: Hodder and Stoughton, MCMXXXV [1935].

> Octavo, original blue cloth covers with black titles, pictorial dust jacket.
> xiii, [1], 15–265 p., frontispiece (portrait), [44] leaves of plates, 4 folded maps.
> First edition.
> References: Spence 292, OCLC 322555.

Christie, Eric William Hunter [147]
The Antarctic Problem. An Historical and Political Study by E.W. Hunter Christie. Foreword by Sir Reginald Leeper. London: George Allen & Unwin Ltd., [1951].

> Octavo, original blue cloth with silver titles, dust jacket.
> 336 p., [12] leaves of plates, maps (1 folded).
> References: Spence 297, OCLC 2962904.

Clark, Harold Terry (1882–) [148]
Episodes of the Amundsen-Ellsworth Arctic Flights. An Address by Harold T. Clark, Secretary to The Cleveland Museum of Natural History. Given at the Amundsen Memorial Day Services, Held at the Museum December Fourteenth 1928. [Cleveland]: The Cleveland Museum of Natural History, [1928].

> Octavo, original printed wrappers.
> 23 pp. including mounted frontispiece (portrait), 1 mounted plate.
> Reference: OCLC 4764604.

Clarke, Peter McFerrin (1920–) [149]
On the Ice, by Peter Clarke. Photographs by Warren Krupsaw. [Boston]: Burdette &

Company; Distributed by Rand McNally & Company, [1966].

> Quarto, gray cloth with white titles, dust jacket.
> 104 p., illustrations (some color), portraits, map. With letter from author.
> References: Spence 302, OCLC 914042.

Coats, William [150]
The Geography of Hudson's Bay. Being the Remarks of Captain W. Coats, in Many Voyages to That Locality, between the Years 1727 and 1751. With an Appendix, Containing Extracts from the Log of Capt. Middleton on His Voyage for the Discovery of the North-West Passage, in H.M.S. "Furnace", in 1741–2. Edited by John Barrow, Esq. [etc.]. London: Printed for the Hakluyt Society, M.DCCC.LII [1852].

> Octavo, original decorated blue cloth with gilt titles.
> x, 147, [1] p.
> Works Issued by the Hakluyt Society, no. 11.
> Reference: OCLC 2473554.

Cochrane, John Dundas (1780–1825) [151]
Narrative of a Pedestrian Journey Through Russia and Siberian Tartary, from the Frontiers of China to the Frozen Sea and Kamtchatka: Performed during the years 1820, 1821, 1822, and 1823, By Captain John Dundas Cochrane, R.N. London: John Murray, 1824.

> Octavo, contemporary three-quarter calf and marbled boards, gilt titles on red leather label.
> xvi p., 1 l., 564 p., half-title, signature clipped from title page, illustrations, 2 folded maps.
> References: AB 3249, OCLC 10625437.

Collinson, Richard (1811–1883) [152]
Journal of H.M.S. Enterprise, on the Expedition in Search of Sir John Franklin's Ships by Behring Strait, 1850–55. By Captain Richard Collinson [etc.],

Commander of the Expedition. With a Memoir of His Other Services. Edited by His Brother, Major-General T.B. Collinson (Royal Engineers). London: Sampson Low, Marston, Searle & Rivington, Limited, 1889.

> Octavo, original blue cloth with gilt titles, rebacked, original spine mounted.
> xi, [1], 531, [1] p., plus 32 p. of advertisements, color frontispiece, portrait, maps (6 folded).
> References: AB 3351, OCLC 4759900.

Comité Arctique International
(See Unveiling the Arctic)

Committee for the Preservation of the Polar Ship Fram [153]
Fram. Oslo: Aas & Wahl, [196-?].

> Octavo, original printed wrappers.
> 68 p., photographs, illustrations, facsimiles, 2 maps.
> Reference: Cf. OCLC 26630543.

Conference on United States Polar Exploration (1967: Washington, DC) [154]
United States Polar Exploration. Edited by Herman R. Friis and Shelby G. Bale, Jr. Athens, Ohio: Ohio University Press, [1970].

> Octavo, original blue cloth, dust jacket.
> xvii, [1] p., 1 l., 199 p., illustrations, maps, maps on endpapers.
> Reference: OCLC 539581.

Cook, Frederick Albert (1865–1940) [155]
My Attainment of the Pole: Being the Record of the Expedition that First Reached the Boreal Center, 1907–1909. With the Final Summary of the Polar Controversy. By Dr. Frederick A. Cook. Third Printing, 60th Thousand. New York and London: Mitchell Kennerley, MCMXIII [1913].

> Octavo, original blue cloth with blue titles.
> xx, 610, [8] p., 1 l., frontispiece (portrait), illustrations, plates, portraits, facsimiles.
> Signed by the author.
> At head of title: Press Edition.
> Laid in: Postcard to be addressed to congressman requesting a "National Investigation" into the Cook/Peary dispute.
> References: AB 3389, OCLC 1344235.

Cook, Frederick Albert (1865–1940) [156]
Return from the Pole [by] Frederick A. Cook. Edited, with an Introduction, by Frederick J. Pohl. New York: Pellegrini & Cudahy, [1951].

> Octavo, original blue cloth with gilt titles, dust jacket.
> x, 335 p., frontispiece (portrait), map.
> References: AB 21287, OCLC 1951272.

Cook, Frederick Albert (1865–1940) [157]
Through the First Antarctic Night 1898–1899: A Narrative of the Voyage of the "Belgica" among Newly Discovered Lands and over an Unknown Sea about the South Pole. By Frederick A. Cook, M.D., Surgeon and Anthropologist of the Belgian Antarctic Expedition. With an Appendix Containing a Summary of the Scientific Results. Illustrated. London: William Heinemann, 1900.

> Octavo, original decorated blue cloth with gilt titles.
> Uncut copy.
> xxiv, 478 p., color frontispiece, [80] leaves of plates, illustrations (some color), portraits, maps.
> References: Spence 311, OCLC 13626585.

Cook, Frederick Albert (1865–1940)
(See also Frederick A. Cook Society)

Cook, James (1728–1779) [158]
The Journal of H.M.S. Resolution, 1772–1775, by Captain James Cook. [Guildford, Surrey, England] Genesis Publications Limited, in association with Hedley Foine Art Books, 1981.

Folio, three-quarter leather on red boards, raised
bands, gilt titles, decorations and edges, marbled
endpapers. In red cloth slipcase with paper label.
806, [1] p., mounted color frontispiece, [8] leaves of
plates (5 color), illustrations, maps. The journal is
in facsimile.
Reference: cf. Spence 314–19.

Cook, James (1728–1779)   **[159]**

A Voyage towards the South Pole, and
round the World. Performed in His
Majesty's Ships the Resolution and
Adventure. In the Years 1772, 1773, 1774,
1775. Written By James Cook,
Commander of the Resolution. In Which is
Included, Captain Furneaux's Narrative of
his Proceedings in the Adventure during
the Separation of the Ships. In Two
Volumes. Illustrated with Maps and Charts,
and a Variety of Portraits of Persons and
Views of Places, Drawn during the Voyage
by Mr. Hodges, and Engraved by the Most
Eminent Masters. London: Printed for W.
Strahan and T. Cadell in the Strand,
MDCCLXXVII [1777].

Quarto, 2 volumes, contemporary marbled boards
and endpapers, rebacked three-quarter calf,
raised bands, gilt titles on red leather labels.
Volume 1: xi, 378 p., frontispiece (portrait); Volume 2:
vi, 396 p., 63 plates (part folded, including
maps).
First edition.
References: Spence 314, OCLC 21804489.

Cook, James (1728–1779)

(See also David, Andrew)

Cooke, Alan (1933–   ) and
Clive Holland   **[160]**

The Exploration of Northern Canada, 500
to 1920: A Chronology [by] Alan Cooke
and Clive Holland. [Toronto]: The Arctic
History Press, [1978].

Quarto, red vinyl with gilt titles, (dust jacket in two
pieces).
549, 25 p., maps (1 folded in pocket).

Edition of 1100 copies.
Reference: OCLC 4011111.

Cooper, John M.   **[161]**

Analytical and Critical Bibliography of the
Tribes of Tierra del Fuego and Adjacent
Territory. Washington: Government
Printing Office, 1917.

Octavo, green cloth with gilt titles.
ix, [1] p., 233 p., folded map.
Smithsonian Institution, Bureau of American
Ethnology. Bulletin 63.
Annotated bibliography (71p.) contains many items of
Antarctic interest.

Copland, Dudley (1901–   )   **[162]**

Livingstone of the Arctic. With a Foreword
by A.Y. Jackson. Lancaster, Ontario:
Canadian Century Publishers, [1978].

Octavo, heavy paperback.
10 p. l., 183 p., black and white maps and
illustrations.
Second printing.
Reference: OCLC 4992791.

Cordingley, Patrick

(See Limb, Sue)

Corner, George Washington (1889–   )
          [163]

Doctor Kane of the Arctic Seas.
Philadelphia: Temple University Press,
[1972].

Large octavo, original cloth, dust jacket.
xiii, 306 p., frontispiece (portrait), illustrations, maps.
Reference: OCLC 578195.

Cranz, David (1723–1777)   **[164]**

The History of Greenland: Including an
Account of the Mission Carried On by the
United Brethren in That Country. From
the German of David Crantz. With a
Continuation to the Present Time;
Illustrative Notes; and an Appendix,
Containing a Sketch of the Mission of the
Brethren in Labrador. In Two Volumes.

London: Printed for Longman, Hurst, Rees, Orme, and Brown, 1820.

> Octavo, 2 volumes, contemporary three-quarter polished calf, skillfully rebacked, raised bands, gilt titles and edges.
> Volume 1: xi, [1], 359 p.; Volume 2: vi, 323 p., frontispieces, 5 plates, 2 maps (1 folded).
> References: AB 3472, OCLC 2503131.

Cresswell, Samuel Gurney [165]
A Series of Eight Sketches in Colour (Together with a Chart of the Route), by Lieut. S. Gurney Cresswell, of the Voyage of the H.M.S. Investigator (Captain M'Clure). London: Published, July 25th, 1854, by Day and Son, Lithographers to the Queen [etc.].

> Folio, contemporary three-quarter morocco with gilt titles.
> 4 p., [9] leaves of plates, map.
> At head of title: Dedicated, by Special Permission, to Her Most Gracious Majesty the Queen.
> References: AB 3477, OCLC 14388361.

Croft, Noel A. C.
(See Glen, Alexander Richard)

Crouse, Nellis Maynard (1884–   ) [166]
The Search for the North Pole, by Nellis M. Crouse, Author of "The Search for the Northwest Passage." New York: Richard R. Smith, 1947.

> Octavo, original cloth.
> xiii, [1], [15]-376 p. including bibliography, folded map.
> References: AB 3495, OCLC 1303006.

Cumpston, J. S.
(See Bayliss, E. P.)

Cunnington, William H.
(See Sargent, Epes)

Dalrymple, Alexander (1737–1808)
[167]
An Historical Collection of the Several

Voyages and Discoveries in the South Pacific Ocean. By Alexander Dalrymple, Esq. London: Printed for the Author; And Sold by J. Nourse, Bookseller in Ordinary to His Majesty; T. Payne, at the Mews-gate; and P. Elmsley, opposite Southampton-Street, Strand, MDCCLXX [1770–1771].

> Quarto, 2 volumes in 1, rebound, mottled calf with gilt borders, gilt titles on black leather label.
> Volume 1: xxx, 24 p., 21, [22–24], 204 p., 3 p. of errata; Volume 2: 124 [p. 124 misnumbered 224], 20, [60] unnumbered pages, frontispiece, 12 plates (eight folded), 4 folded maps.
> Contents: Volume I. Being Chiefly a Literal Translation from the Spanish Writers. — Volume II. Containing the Dutch Voyages [1771].
> First edition in 1770.
> References: Sabin 18338, OCLC 5258438.

Dalrymple, Alexander (1737–1808)
[168]
Memoir of a Map of the Lands around the North-Pole, by Dalrymple. 1789. Scale 1/10 of an inch to 1° of Latitude. London: Printed by George Bigg, 1789. [Montreal: I. Ehrlich, 1973].

> Quarto, original paper wrappers.
> Map 27 x 30 cm. folded in cover 28 x 22 cm.
> Accompanied by text: 20 p.
> "Reprinted in facsimile from the original in possession of I. Ehrlich, Montreal 1973 in an edition of 75 numbered and signed copies." This is no. 29.
> Reference: OCLC 5483345.

David, Andrew [169]
The Charts & Coastal Views of Captain Cook's Voyages. Chief Editor, Andrew David; Assistant Editors for the Views, Rüdiger Joppien and Bernard Smith. London: The Hakluyt Society in Association with the Australian Academy of the Humanities, 1988-

> Folio, dark blue cloth with gilt titles, dust jackets.
> Works Issued by the Hakluyt Society, Extra Series, no. 43, etc.
> Contents: Volume 1. The Voyage of the 'Endeavour' 1768–1771, with a descriptive catalogue of all

the known original surveys and coastal views and the original engravings associated with them, together with original drawings of the 'Endeavour' and her boats (lxiv, 328 p.) — Volume 2. The Voyage of the 'Resolution' and 'Adventure' 1772–1775, with a descriptive catalogue of all the known original surveys and coastal views and the original engravings associated with them (c, 332 p.).
Reference: OCLC 18693840.

Davids, Richard C. **[170]**
Lords of the Arctic. A Journey among the Polar Bears by Richard C. Davids. Photographs by Dan Guravich. New York: Macmillan Publishing Co., Inc.; London: Collier Macmillan Publishers, [1928].
Quarto, original blue cloth with silver titles, dust jacket.
xviii p., 1 l., 140 p., [32] leaves of plates, illustrations (mostly color), bibliography.
First edition.
Reference: OCLC 8533213.

Davis, Gwilym George
(See Keely, Robert N.)

Davis, John (1550?-1605) **[171]**
The Voyages and Works of John Davis, the Navigator. Edited, with an Introduction and Notes, by Albert Hastings Markham. London: Printed for the Hakluyt Society, MDCCCLXXX [1880].
Octavo, original decorated blue cloth with gilt titles.
xcx, [1], 392 p., illustrations, facsimiles, plates, maps.
Works Issued by the Hakluyt Society, no. 59.
Reference: OCLC 1608599.

Davis, John King **[172]**
With the "Aurora" in the Antarctic 1911–1914. By John King Davis [etc.]. London: Andrew Melrose, Ltd., [1919?].
Medium octavo, gilt stamping and titles on original navy blue cloth.
xxi, [1], 183 p., frontispiece (portrait), photo plates, illustrations, maps (1 folded).
Reference: Spence 354.

Deacon, George Edward R. (1906–   ) **[173]**
The Antarctic Circumpolar Ocean by George Deacon. Cambridge [England]: Cambridge University Press, 1984.
Oblong small octavo, blue hardboard covers with black and white front photograph.
viii, 180 p., 42 illustrations including photographs, plans, maps.
First Edition.
Reference: OCLC 10299351.

Debenham, Frank (1883–1965) **[174]**
Antarctica: The Story of a Continent, by Frank Debenham [etc.]. [Foreword by Sir Vivian Fuchs]. New York: The Macmillan Company, 1961.
Octavo, gray cloth covers, dust jacket.
264 p., black and white photographs, maps, maps on endpapers.
First U.S. edition.
References: OCLC 486934, cf. Spence 360.

Debenham, Frank (1883–1965) **[175]**
Discovery and Exploration: An Atlas-History of Man's Wanderings [by] Frank Debenham. Introduction by Edward Shackleton. Garden City, NY: Doubleday & Company, [1960].
Quarto, blue cloth with silver titles, dust jacket.
272 p., illustrations (part color), portraits, maps (part color).
References: Spence 361, OCLC 485965.

Debenham, Frank (1883–1965) **[176]**
In the Antarctic: Stories of Scott's Last Expedition. By Frank Debenham, O.B.E. With Illustrations by Edward Wilson and the Author. London: John Murray, [1952].
Crown octavo, blue-stamped cream colored cloth covers, dust jacket.
vii, [1], 145, [1] p., black and white illustrations, maps on endpapers.
First edition.
References: Spence 359, OCLC 347108.

Debenham, Frank (1883–1965) **[177]**
The Quiet Land: The Diaries of Frank

Debenham, Member of the British Antarctic Expedition, 1910–1913. Edited by June Debenham Back. Foreword by Sir Vivian Fuchs. Huntingdon, England: Bluntisham Books, 1992.

> Quarto, green cloth covers with gilt titles, dust jacket.
> 207 p., black and white sketches, drawings and
> photographs.
> First edition. (Contains an account of the development
> of the Scott Polar Research Institute.)
> Reference: OCLC 26547127.

De Long, George Washington (1844–1881)   [178]

The Voyage of the Jeannette: The Ship and Ice Journals of George W. De Long, Lieutenant-Commander U.S.N., and Commander of the Polar Expedition of 1879–1881. Edited by His Wife Emma De Long. With Two Steel Portraits, Maps, and Many Illustrations on Wood and Stone. In Two Volumes. Boston and New York: Houghton Mifflin and Company, 1883.

> Octavo, 2 volumes, original decorated brown cloth
> covers with gilt and black titles.
> Paged continuously. Volume 1: xii, 440 p., map in
> pocket; Volume 2: x, [441]-911 p., frontispieces
> (Volume 1: portrait), illllustrations, portraits, maps
> (part folded).
> First edition?
> Reference: OCLC 669613.

Denmark. Commission for the Direction of the Geological and Geographical Investigations in Greenland

(See Greenland)

Denton, Vernon L. (1881–1944) [179]

The Far West Coast, by V. L. Denton. With 12 Illustrations and 7 Maps. Toronto: J. M. Dent & Sons, 1924.

> Octavo, light green cloth with black titles.
> [x], 297 p., illustrations, portraits, maps.
> References: AB 3887, OCLC 4813333.

Dixon, George (1800?–)   [180]

A Voyage Round the World; but More Particularly to the North-West Coast of America: Performed in 1785, 1786, 1787 and 1788, in the King George and Queen Charlotte, Captains Portlock and Dixon. Dedicated, by Permission, to Sir Joseph Banks, Bart. By Captain George Dixon. London: Published by Geo. Goulding, 1789.

> Quarto, original boards, rubbed, spine repaired, in tan
> cloth drop-spine box.
> xxix, [1] p., 1 l., 360, 47 p., 17 engraved plates (3
> folded), with 7 handcolored natural history plates
> by P.Mazell, half titles, tables, frontispiece, 5
> folded engraved maps (including frontispiece).
> First edition.
> References: Sabin 20364, OCLC 4541667.

Dobbs, Arthur (1689–1765)   [181]

An Account of the Countries Adjoining to Hudson's Bay, in the North-West Part of America: Containing a Description of Their Lakes and Rivers, the Nature of the Soil and Climates, and Their Methods of Commerce, &c. Shewing the Benefit to be Made by Settling Colonies, and Opening a Trade in These Parts; Whereby the French Will Be Deprived in a Great Measure of Their Traffick in Furs, and the Communication between Canada and Mississippi Be Cut Off. With an Abstract of Captain Middleton's Journal, and Observations upon his Behaviour during His Voyage, and Since His Return. To Which Are Added, I. A Letter from Bartholomew de Fonte, Vice-Admiral of Peru and Mexico; Giving an Account of His Voyage from Lima in Peru, to Prevent, or Seize upon Any Ships That Should Attempt to Find a North-West Passage to the South Sea. II. An Abstract of All the Discoveries Which Have Been Publish'd of the Islands and Countries in and Adjoining to the Great Western Ocean, between

America, India, and China, &c. Pointing Out the Advantages That May Be Made, if a Short Passage Should Be Found thro' Hudson's Streight to That Ocean. III. The Hudson's Bay Company's Charter. IV. The Standard of Trade in Those Parts of America; with an Account of the Exports and Profits Made Annually by the Hudson's Bay Company. V. Vocabularies of the Languages of Several Indian Nations Adjoining to Hudson's Bay. The Whole Intended to Shew the Great Probability of a North-West Passage, So Long Desired; and Which (If Discovered) Would Be of the Highest Advantage to These Kingdoms. By Arthur Dobbs, Esq. London: Printed for J. Robinson, at the Golden Lion in Ludgate-Street, M DCC XLIV [1744].

> Small quarto, original calf, skillfully rebacked, raised bands, gilt titles on red leather label, corners repaired. Binder's title: Dobb's Hudson's Bay.
> ii, 211 p., frontispiece (engraved folded map.)
> First edition.
> References: Sabin 20404, Streeter VI 3637, OCLC 3426391.

Dobbs, Arthur (1689–1765) [182]

An Account of the Countries Adjoining to Hudson's Bay, in the North-West Part of America . . . London: J. Robinson, 1744. [Copy 2].

> Large quarto, contemporary speckled calf, raised bands, gilt titles on red leather label, small stab-hole thru lower cover not affecting text.
> ii, 211 p., frontispiece (engraved folded map.)
> First edition.
> Bookplate of Earl of Roden.
> References: Sabin 20404, Streeter VI 3637, OCLC 3426391.

Dodge, Ernest Stanley [183]

Beyond the Capes: Pacific Exploration from Captain Cook to the Challenger, 1776–1877, by Ernest S. Dodge. With Illustrations. Boston and Toronto: Little, Brown and Company, [1971].

> Octavo, original blue cloth with gilt titles, dust jacket.
> xv, [1], 1 l., 3–429 p., illustrations (part color), portraits, maps on endpapers, maps.
> First edition.
> Reference: OCLC 146989.

Dodge, Ernest Stanley [184]

The Polar Rosses: John and James Clark Ross and Their Explorations, by Ernest S. Dodge. London: Faber and Faber, [1973].

> Octavo, blue cloth, black and gilt spine titles, dust jacket.
> 260 p., black and white photographs, illustrations, drawings, maps.
> References: Spence 374, OCLC 666485.

Doorly, Gerald Stokely (1880–) [185]

The Voyages of the 'Morning' by Captain Gerald S. Doorly, R.N.R. With Illustrations and a Map. New York: E.P. Dutton & Company, 1916.

> Octavo, original decorated blue cloth with white titles.
> xx, 223, [1] p., illustrations, folded map.
> First American edition.
> Reference: OCLC 518999.

Douglas, George M. [186]

Lands Forlorn: A Story of an Expedition to Hearne's Coppermine River. By George M. Douglas. With an Introduction by James Douglas, LL.D. With 180 Photographs by the Author, and Maps. New York: G.P. Putnam's Sons, 1914.

> Medium octavo, original decorated blue cloth with gilt titles and edges.
> xv, 285 p., color frontispiece (portrait), photo illustrations, 2 folded maps.
> References: AB 4074, OCLC 4650144.

Douglas, Mary (1857–) [187]

Across Greenland's Ice-Fields: The Adventures of Nansen and Peary on the Great Ice-Cap. By M. Douglas. London, Edinburgh, and New York: Thomas Nelson and Sons, 1897.

Octavo, original decorated blue cloth with gilt and
  blue titles.
vi p., 2 l., [9]-218 p., illustrations, portraits.
Introduction by Clements R. Markham.
Reference: OCLC 13623746.

Douglas, Mary (1857–)   [188]

The White North: With Nordenskiöld, De
Long, and Nansen. By M. Douglas.
London, Edinburgh, and New York:
Thomas Nelson and Sons, 1899.

Octavo, original decorated blue cloth with gilt and
  blue titles.
237 p., frontispiece, [15] leaves of plates, maps.
Reference: OCLC 10209669.

Downes, Prentice Gilbert (1909–)
[189]

Sleeping Island: The Story of One Man's
Travels in the Great Barren Lands of the
Canadian North, by P.G. Downes.
Illustrated with Photographs. New York:
Coward-McCann, Inc., [1943].

Octavo, original green cloth with red titles.
vii, 296 p., illustrations, plates, portraits, sketch map,
  maps on endpapers.
References: AB 4094, OCLC 1668105.

Drage, Theodore Swaine (fl. 1746–1766)
[190]

An Account of a Voyage for the Discovery
of a North-West Passage by Hudson's
Streights, to the Western and Southern
Ocean of America. Performed in the Year
1746 and 1747, in the Ship California,
Capt. Francis Smith, Commander. By the
Clerk of the California. Adorned with Cuts
and Maps. London: Printed and Sold by
Mr. Jolliffe, in St. James's-street; Mr.
Corbett, in Fleet-street; and Mr. Clarke,
under the Royal Exchange,
M.DCC.XLVIII [1748].

Octavo, 2 volumes bound in 1, contemporary calf, gilt
  edges, raised bands, gilt titles on red leather
  label, rebacked.

Volume 1: vii, 237 p.; Volume 2: 326, [18] p., 4
  plates, 6 folded maps.
References: Sabin 20808, TPL 206, Streeter 3640,
  OCLC 13628620.

Drygalski, Erich von (1865–1949)
[191]

The Southern Ice-Continent: The German
South Polar Expedition aboard the Gauss,
1901–1903, by Erich von Drygalski.
Translated by M.M. Raraty. Bluntisham,
Cambridgeshire, [England]: Bluntisham
Books; Alburgh, Harleston, Norfolk:
Erskine Press, 1989.

Quarto, decorated brown cloth with gilt and black
  titles.
xxi, 373 p., illustrations, maps.
Reference: OCLC 21184238.

Du Chaillu, Paul B. (1831–1903) [192]

The Land of the Midnight Sun: Summer
and Winter Journeys through Sweden,
Norway, Lapland and Northern Finland.
By Paul B. Du Chaillu [etc.]. With Map
and 235 Illustrations. In Two Volumes.
New York: Harper & Brothers, 1881.

Octavo, 2 volumes, original decorated blue cloth with
  gilt titles.
Volume 1: xvi, 441 p., map in end pocket; Volume 2:
  xvi, 474 p., illustrations.
Reference: OCLC 6679518.

Dugmore, Arthur Radclyffe (1870–)
[193]

The Romance of the Newfoundland
Caribou: An Intimate Account of the Life
of the Reindeer of North America. By A.A.
Radclyffe Dugmore [etc.]. Illustrated with
Paintings, Drawings and Photographs from
Life by the Author. London: William
Heinemann, MCMXIII [1913].

Quarto, original blue cloth with gilt titles, remnants of
  dust jacket.
viii, 191 p., color frontispiece, illustrations, maps (1
  folded).
First edition.
Reference: OCLC 551308.

Eames, Hugh [194]
Winner Lose All: Dr. Cook and the Theft of the North Pole, by Hugh Eames. With illustrations. Boston and Toronto: Little, Brown and Company, [1973].

> Octavo, original blue cloth with gilt titles, dust jacket.
> xv, 346 p., illustrations, map.
> First edition.
> Reference: OCLC 591501.

Egede, Hans Poulsen (1686–1758)
[195]
A Description of Greenland. Shewing the Natural History, Situation, Boundaries, and Face of the Country; the Nature of the Soil; the Rise and Progress of the Old Norwegian Colonies; the Ancient and Modern Inhabitants; Their Genius and Way of Life, and Produce of the Soil; Their Plants, Beasts, Fishes, &c. With a New Map of Greenland. And Several Copper Plates Representing Different Animals, Birds and Fishes, the Greenlanders Way of Hunting and Fishing; Their Habitations, Dress, Sports and Diversions, &c. By Mr. Hans Egede, Missionary in That Country for Twenty Five Years. Translated from the Danish. London: C. Hitch in Pater-noster Row; S. Austen in Newgate-Street; and J. Jackson near St. James's Gate, MDCCXLV [1745].

> Crown octavo, gilt-stamped recent full antique-style
> calf, raised bands, gilt titles on red leather label.
> xvi, [4], 220 p., twelve plates (including folded map.)
> First English edition.
> References: AB 4362, OCLC 6111988.

Elder, William (1806–1885) [196]
Biography of Elisha Kent Kane, by William Elder. Philadelphia: Childs and Peterson; New York: Sheldon, Blakeman & Co., 1858.

> Octavo, decorated cloth.

> 416 p., added title-page, engraved, frontispiece
> (portrait), plates, facsimiles.
> Reference: Sabin 22094.

Ellis, A. R.
(See Lashly, William)

Ellis, Henry (1721–1806) [197]
A Voyage to Hudson's Bay, by the Dobbs Galley and California, in the Years 1746 and 1747, for Discovering a North West Passage, with an Accurate Survey of the Coast, and a Short Natural History of the Country. Together with a Fair View of the Facts and Arguments from Which the Future Finding of Such a Passage is Rendered Probable. By Henry Ellis, Gent., Agent for the Proprietors in the Said Expedition. To Which is Prefixed, an Historical Account of the Attempts hitherto Made for the Finding a Passage that Way to the East-Indies. Illustrated with Proper Cuts, and a New and Correct Chart of Hudson's-Bay, with the Countries Adjacent. London: Printed for H. Whitridge, at the Royal Exchange, M.DCC.XLVIII [1748].

> Octavo, three-quarter morocco and marbled boards.
> xxviii, 336 p., Signature G. has extra 4 leaves,
> frontispiece (folded map), plates (partly folded.)
> References: Sabin 22312, OCLC 6341410.

Ellsberg, Edward (1891–   ) [198]
The Drift of the Jeannette in the Arctic Sea. Philadelphia: American Philosophical Society, 1940.

> Octavo.
> Removed from *Proceedings of the American
> Philosophical Society* 82, no. 5 (June 1940):
> 889–896.
> References: AB 4564, OCLC 8730501.

Ellsberg, Edward (1891–   ) [199]
Hell on Ice: The Saga of the "Jeannette."

By Commander Edward Ellsberg. New York: Dodd, Mead and Company, 1938.

Octavo, original cloth.
x p., 1 l., 421 p., 2 illustrations (including map), map on endpapers.
References: AB 4565, OCLC 486495.

Ellsworth, Lincoln (1880–1951) [200]

Beyond Horizons, by Lincoln Ellsworth, Lieutenant Commander, United States Naval Reserve. Garden City, NY: Doubleday, Doran and Company, Inc. MCMXXXVIII [1938].

Octavo, rust cloth.
xii, 403 p., frontispiece, black and white illustrations, 2 maps.
First edition.
References: AB 4572, Spence 415.

Ellsworth, Lincoln (1880–1951) [201]

My Flight Across Antarctica. With 38 Illustrations. Special Issue: The National Geographic, Volume LXX, Number One, July 1936. Washington, DC: National Geographic Society, 1936.

Royal octavo.
Texaco Aviation Division Report: with cut-out for sealed vial of "Texaco Aviation Oil 120" as used by Ellsworth. Magazine wrapped in printed banner, in paper publisher's box with label about use of Texaco oil in flight.

Ellsworth, Lincoln (1880–1951)

(See also Amundsen, Roald)

Evans, Edward Ratcliffe Garth, Sir

(See Mountevans, Edward R. G. R. Evans, baron)

Falk, Marvin

(See Unveiling the Arctic)

Fanning, Edmund (1769–1841) [202]

Voyages round the World; with Selected Sketches of Voyages to the South Seas, North and South Pacific Oceans, China, etc. Performed under the Command and Agency of the Author. Also, Information Relating to Important Late Discoveries; between the Years 1792 and 1832, Together with the Report of the Commander of the First American Exploring Expedition, Patronised by the United States Government, in the Brigs Seraph and Annawan, to the Southern Hemisphere. By Edmund Fanning. New York: Collins and Hannay, MDCCCXXXIII [1833].

Octavo, old half morocco, marbled edges and endpapers, front joint repaired.
xii, [13]-499 p., illustrations, 5 plates (including frontispiece).
References: Spence 454, OCLC 1109837.

Feilden, Henry W. (1838–1921)

Physical Observations
(See Nares, George Strong. Results Derived from the Arctic Expedition)

Feilden, Henry W. (1838–1921) [203]

The Post-Tertiary Beds of Grinnell Land and North Greenland. By H.W. Feilden [etc.]; and Note by J. Gwyn Jeffreys. [London, 1877].

Octavo, new wrappers.
Reprinted from *Annals and Magazine of Natural History* (December 1877): 483–94.
Reference: AB 4873.

Fess, Simeon Davidson (1961–1936) [204]

The North Pole Aftermath. Speech of Hon. S.D. Fess of Ohio In the House of Representatives, Congress of the United States, Thursday, March 4, 1915. [Washington: Government Printing Office, 1915].

Octavo, stapled.
27 p.
Reference: OCLC 5330273.

Fiala, Anthony (1871–1950) [205]
Fighting the Polar Ice, by Anthony Fiala,
Commander of the Ziegler Polar
Expedition [etc.]. With an Introduction by
W.S. Champ, and Reports by William J.
Peters, Russell W. Porter and Oliver S.
Fassig. Illustrations from Photographs and
Sketches by the Author. Also Nine, from
Paintings in Colour by Russell W. Porter
and J. Knowles Hare. New York:
Doubleday, Page & Co., 1906.

> Quarto, original cloth.
> xxii, 296, [6] p., color frontispiece, plates (part color),
>   portraits, Maps (1 folded).
> References: AB 4938, OCLC 1346296.

Fiennes, Ranulph, Sir (1944–) [206]
To the Ends of the Earth: The Transglobe
Expedition — The First Pole-to-Pole
Circumnavigation of the Globe, by Sir
Ranulph Fiennes. New York: Arbor House,
[1983].

> Octavo, dust jacket.
> 547 p., photographs (color), maps, maps on
>   endpapers.
> Foreword by HRH Prince Charles.
> Reference: OCLC 9812992.

Fienup-Riordan, Ann (1948–) [207]
Eskimo Essays: Yup'ik Lives and How We
See Them [by] Ann Fienup-Riordan. New
Brunswick and London: Rutgers University
Press, 1990.

> Octavo, paperback.
> xxii p., 1 l., 269 p., black and white photos, drawings,
>   and maps.
> Autographed copy to G. F. Fitzgerald.
> Reference: OCLC 21081004.

Fienup-Riordan, Ann (1948–) [208]
The Nelson Island Eskimo: Social and
Ritual Distribution, by Ann Fienup-
Riordan. Anchorage, Alaska: Alaska Pacific
University Press, 1983.

> Octavo, paperback.
> xxxvii, 419 p., illustrations.
> First printing.
> Autographed copy to G. F. Fitzgerald.
> Reference: OCLC 9636524.

Fienup-Riordan, Ann (1948–) [209]
The Real People and the Children of
Thunder: The Yup'ik Eskimo Encounter
with Moravian Missionaries John and Edith
Kilbuck, by Ann Fienup-Riordan. Norman,
OK and London: University of Oklahoma
Press, 1991.

> Octavo, blue cloth with white titles, dust jacket.
> x, 420 p., black and white photographs, illustrations,
>   maps.
> First edition.
> Reference: OCLC 22862586.

Fifield, Richard [210]
International Research in the Antarctic
[by] Richard Fifield. Published for the
Scientific Committee on Antarctic Research
(SCAR) and the ICSU Press by Oxford
University Press, 1987. [New York]:
Oxford University Press, 1987.

> Crown quarto, original navy blue cloth with gilt titles,
>   dust jacket.
> vi, [2], 146 p., illustrations (some color), figures, tables,
>   maps.
> First edition.
> Reference: OCLC 15793658.

Filchner, Wilhelm (1877–1957) [211]
To the Sixth Continent: The Second
German South Polar Expedition. By
Wilhelm Filchner with the Collaboration of
Expedition Members Alfred K[l]ing & Eric
Przybyllok. Translated and Edited with an
Introduction by William Barr. Bluntisham,
Huntingdon: Bluntisham Books; Banham,
Norfolk: The Erskine Press, 1994.

> A4, original dark blue cloth with silver titles.
> 42, viii, 253 p., illustrations, maps.

Translation of "Zum sechsten Erdteil" (Berlin, 1922).
Includes bibliography of Filchner's published works.
Reference: OCLC 31078352.

Finnie, Richard (1906–   )   **[212]**
The Lure of the North [by Richard
Finnie]. Philadelphia: David McKay
Company, [1940].

Quarto, original blue cloth with gilt titles, dust jacket.
xix, [1], 227 p., including frontispiece, 30 plates,
portraits, facsimiles, maps on endpapers.
References: AB 4991, OCLC 1508895.

Firth, Edith G.   **[213]**
The North West Passage, 1534–1859: A
Catalogue of an Exhibition of Books and
Manuscripts in the Toronto Public Library
Compiled by Edith G. Firth. With an
Introduction by H.C. Campbell. Toronto:
Baxter Publishing Co., 1963.

Paperback.
26, [2] p., illustrations.
Reference: OCLC 7584722.

Fisher, Alexander (d. 1838)   **[214]**
Journal of a Voyage of Discovery to the
Arctic Regions, Performed Between the
4th of April and the 18th of November,
1818 in His Majesty's Ship Alexander,
Wm. Edw. Parry, Esq. Lieutenant and
Commander. By an Officer of the
Alexander. London: Printed for Richard
Phillips; by G. Sidney, [1819].

Octavo, modern boards.
viii, 104 p., 3 plates of diagrams, 1 map.
References: AB 5021, OCLC 4889244.

Fisher, Alexander (d. 1838)   **[215]**
A Journal of a Voyage to the Arctic
Regions, in His Majesty's Ships Hecla and
Griper, in the Years 1819 & 1820. By
Alexander Fisher, Surgeon R.N. London:

Longman, Hurst, Rees, Orme, and Brown,
1821.

Octavo, contemporary boards, paper label, in brown
cloth drop-spine box.
1 p. l., [vii]-xi, 320 p., illustrations, 2 maps (including
frontispiece).
Third edition. "Four editions were published in
London, 1821, without change of text,
excepting typographic corrections." — AB.
References: AB 5022, OCLC 15056003.

Fisher, Margery and James   **[216]**
Shackleton and the Antarctic, by Margery
and James Fisher. Illustrated with
Photographs, and with Drawings by W.E.
How, Who Served with the Endurance
Expedition. Boston: Houghton Mifflin
Company, 1958.

Octavo, original gray cloth with gilt titles, dust jacket.
xvi, [2], 559 p., 48 p. of black and white photo
illustrations, portraits, maps (including relief maps
on endpapers).
References: Spence 460, OCLC 486943.

Fisher, Raymond Henry (1907–   )
            [217]
Bering's Voyages, Whither and Why [by]
Raymond H. Fisher. Seattle and London:
University of Washington Press, [1977].

Octavo, cloth, dust jacket torn.
xiii, 217 p., including bibliography, maps.
Reference: OCLC 3071755.

Fleming, John A. (1877–   )   **[218]**
The Ziegler Polar Expedition, 1903–1905.
Anthony Fiala, Commander. Scientific
Results Obtained under the Direction of
William J. Peters, Representative of the
National Geographic Society in Charge of
Scientific Work. Edited by John A.
Fleming. Washington: National Geographic
Society, 1907.

Thick medium quarto, gilt stamped green cloth, dust
jacket.
vii, [1], 630 p., 19 color plates, charts, tables,
photographs, 3 folded color maps in pocket.
Reference: OCLC 8421660.

Fleming, Launcelot
(See Portrait of Antarctica)

Fletcher, Harold (1903–)   [219]
Antarctic Days with Mawson: A Personal
Account of the British, Australian and New
Zealand Antarctic Research Expedition of
1929–31, by Harold Fletcher. London:
Angus & Robertson Publishers, [1984].

Octavo, cloth, dust jacket.
313 p., illustrations, maps on endpapers.
Reference: OCLC 12064807.

Forbes, Alexander (1882–1965)   [220]
Quest for a Northern Air Route, by
Alexander Forbes. Cambridge: Harvard
University Press, 1953.

Octavo, original cloth, dust jacket.
xiv p., 2 l., 138 p., [3] p., illustrations, portraits, maps.
First edition.
Reference: OCLC 1012903.

Force, Peter (1790–1868)   [221]
Grinnell Land. Remarks on the English
Maps of Arctic Discoveries, in 1850 and
1851, Made at the Ordinary Meeting of
the National Institute, Washington, in
May, 1852, by Peter Force. [and]
Supplement to Grinnell Land. Read at the
Ordinary Meeting of the National
Institute, July, 1853, by Peter Force.
[Washington: Robert A. Waters, Printed
1852–1853].

Octavo. The two bound together in boards, original
front wrapper for second title bound in.
23 p., folded map; 52 p., folded map.
References: OCLC 3746848 and 3767803.

Forster, Johann Reinhold (1729–1798)   [222]
History of the Voyages and Discoveries
Made in the North. Translated from the
German of John Reinhold Forster, I.U.D.
and Elucidated by Several New and
Original Maps. London: Printed for G.G.J.
& J. Robinson, Pater-Noster-Row,
M.DCC.LXXXVI [1786].

Quarto, mottled calf, rebacked.
[4], xvi, 489, [17] p., 3 folded maps.
References: Howes F296, AB 5161, OCLC 2191238.

Forster, Johann Reinhold (1729–1798)   [223]
The Resolution Journal of Johann
Reinhold Forster, 1772–1775. Edited by
Michael E. Hoare. London: The Hakluyt
Society, 1982.

Octavo, 4 volumes, light blue cloth with gilt titles, dust
jackets.
Paged continuously. Volume 1: xvii, 182 p.; Volume 2:
viii, 183–370 p.; Volume 3: viii, 371–554 p.;
Volume 4: viii, 555–831 p., color frontispiece
(volume 1), illustrations, plates (2 folded),
facsimiles, maps (1 folded).
Works Issued by the Hakluyt Society, 2nd Series, nos.
152–155.
References: OCLC 9365162, cf. Spence 464.

Foster, Coram   [224]
Rear Admiral Byrd and the Polar
Expeditions. With an Account of His Life
and Achievements, by Coram Foster.
Including by Special Permission the
Message of Congratulations from the
President of the United States, and a
Special Chapter Prepared from Data Given
by the National Geographic Society,
Washington, D.C. New York: A.L. Burt
Company, [1930].

Octavo, original cloth.
ix, [1], 11–287 p., frontispiece (portrait), plates,
portraits, map.
Reference: OCLC 1136165.

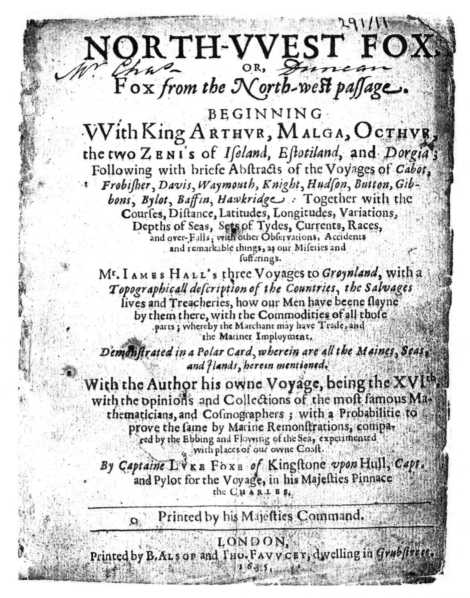

NORTH-VVEST FOX.

OR,
Fox *from the North-west passage*.

BEGINNING
VVith King ARTHVR, MALGA, OCTHVR,

the two ZENI's of *Iseland, Estotiland*, and *Dorgia*;
Following with briefe Abstracts of the Voyages of *Cabot*,
Frobisher, Davis, Waymouth, Knight, Hudson, Button, Gib-
bons, Bylot, Baffin, Hawkridge : Together with the
Courses, Distance, Latitudes, Longitudes, Variations,
Depths of Seas, Sets of Tydes, Currents, Races,
and over-Falls, with other Observations, Accidents
and remarkable things, as our Miseries and
sufferings.

Mr. IAMES HALL's three Voyages to *Groynland*, with a
Topographicall description of the Countries, the Salvages
lives and Treacheries, how our Men have beene slayne
by them there, with the Commodities of all those
parts; whereby the Marchant may have Trade, and
the Mariner Imployment.

Demonstrated in a Polar Card, wherein are all the Maines, Seas,
and Ilands, herein mentioned.

With the Author his owne Voyage, being the XVIth
with the opinions and Collections of the most famous Mathematicians, and Cosmographers; with a Probabilitie to
prove the same by Marine Remonstrations, compared by the Ebbing and Flowing of the Sea, experimented
with places of our owne Coast.

By Captaine LVKE FOXE *of* Kingstone *vpon* Hull, Capt.
and Pylot for the Voyage, in his Majesties Pinnace
the CHARLES.

Printed by his Majesties Command.

LONDON,
Printed by B. ALSOP and THO. FAWCET, dwelling in *Grubstreet*.
1635.

Captain Luke Foxe of Hull searched the northern and western reaches of Hudson Bay in 1635 looking for a Northwest Passage. Captain Thomas James had sailed in the same year and carried letters from King James to the Emperor of Japan. Fox met him in Hudson Bay and told him "You are out of the way to Japon, for this is not it." This copy was used by Miller Christy in preparing the Hakluyt Society edition of 1894.

Luke Fox, *North-VVest Fox* (1635) [**225**]

Foxe, Luke (1586–1635) [225]

North-VVest Fox, or, Fox from the North-west Passage. Beginning VVith King Arthvr, Malga, Octhvr, the Two Zeni's of Iseland, Estotiland, and Dorgia; Following with Briefe Abstracts of the Voyages of Cabot, Frobisher, Davis, Waymouth, Knight, Hudson, Button, Gibbons, Bylot, Baffin, Hawkridge: Together with the Courses, Distance, Latitudes, Longitudes, Variations, Depths of Seas, Sets of Tydes, Currents, Races, and Over-falls; with other Observations, Accidents and Remarkable Things, as Our Miseries and Sufferings. Mr. Iames Hall's Three Voyages to Groynland, with a Topographicall Description of the Countries, the Salvages Lives and Treacheries, How Our Men Have Beene Slayne by Them There, with the Commodities of All Those Parts; Whereby the Marchant may Have Trade, and the Mariner Imployment. Demonstrated in a Polar Card, Wherein Are all the Maines, Seas, and Ilands, Herein Mentioned. With the Author His Owne Voyage, Being the XVIth. with the Opinions and Collections of the Most Famous Mathematicians, and Cosmographers; with a Probabilitie to Prove the Same by Marine Remonstrations, Compared by the Ebbing and Flowing of the Sea, Experimented with Places of Our Owne Coast. By Captaine Lvke Foxe of Kingstone upon Hull, Capt. and Pylot for the Voyage, in his Majesties Pinnace the Charles. Printed by his Majesties Command. London: Printed by B. Alsop and Tho. Favvcet, dwelling in Grubstreet, 1635.

> Large duodecimo, three-quarter calf with marbled boards and endpapers, blind-stamped ornaments on spine, and gilt titles on black label. Rebacked, with portion of original spine laid down. In blue cloth drop-spine box, with gilt titles on red leather labels.
> 5 p. l., 269 p. Imperfect: lacks leaf before title-page, pages 11–14, the 2 leaves between V2–3, 2 leaves at the end, and map. Free front endpaper detached. Some portions of text supplied in pen-facsimile. Text annotated extensively throughout. This copy was used by Miller Christy in the preparation of the Hakluyt Society edition published in 1894 (**226** below).
> First edition.
> Reference: OCLC 38564781.

Foxe, Luke (1586–1635) and Thomas James (1593?-1635) [226]

The Voyages of Captain Luke Foxe of Hull, and Captain Thomas James of Bristol, in Search of a North-West Passage, in 1631–32; with Narratives of the Earlier North-West Voyages of Frobisher, Davis, Weymouth, Hall, Knight, Hudson, Button, Gibbons, Bylot, Baffin, Hawkridge, and Others. Edited, with Notes and an Introduction, by Miller Christy, F.L.S. In Two Volumes. London: Printed for the Hakluyt Society, M.DCCC.XCIV [1894].

> Octavo, 2 volumes.
> Paged continuously. Volume 1: ccxxxi, 259 p.; Volume 2: viii, [261]-681, [1], 16 p., frontispiece portraits, illustrations, 3 folded maps.
> First edition.
> Works Issued by the Hakluyt Society, nos. 88–89.
> Reference: OCLC 1487462.

Franklin, John, Sir (1786–1847) [227]

Narrative of a Journey to the Shores of the Polar Sea, in the Years 1819, 20, 21, and 22. By John Franklin, Captain R.N., F.R.S., and Commander of the Expedition. With an Appendix on Various Subjects Relating to Science and Natural History. Illustrated by Numerous Plates and Maps. Published by Authority of the Right Honourable the Earl Bathurst. London: John Murray, MDCCCXXIII [1823].

> Quarto, contemporary mottled sheep, rebacked. On spine: Franklin's Journey to the Polar Sea.

xvi, 768 p., plus 8 p. of advertisements, [34] leaves of
plates (part color), illustrations, portraits, 4 folded
maps. Plates 25–30 are numbered.
Reference: OCLC 20472340.

Franklin, John, Sir (1786–1847) [228]
Narrative of a Second Expedition to the
Shores of the Polar Sea, in the Years 1825,
1826, and 1827, by John Franklin, Captain
R.N., F.R.S., &c. and Commander of the
Expedition. Including an Account of the
Progress of a Detachment to the Eastward
by John Richardson [etc.], Surgeon and
Naturalist to the Expedition. Illustrated by
Numerous Plates and Maps. Published by
Authority of the Right Honourable the
Secretary of State for Colonial Affairs.
London: John Murray, MDCCCXXVIII
[1828].

Quarto, contemporary mottled sheep, rebacked. On
spine: Franklin's Second Journey to the Polar Sea.
xxiv, 320, [clvii], [1] p., 1 l., illustrations, 31 plates
(including frontispiece), 6 folded maps (1 color).
References: AB 5198, OCLC 4967387.

Franklin, John, Sir (1786–1847) [229]
Thirty Years in the Arctic Regions; or, The
Adventures of Sir John Franklin. New
York: H. Dayton, Publisher; Indianapolis:
Asher & Company, 1859.

Octavo, original cloth, slightly rubbed.
vi, [7]-480 p., color frontispiece.
Reference: Cf. AB 5202.

Frederick A. Cook Society [230]
[Publications]. Sullivan County Museum,
Art & Cultural Center, P.O. Box 247,
Hurleyville, NY 12747–0247.

In blue cloth drop-spine box with paper label.
Copies of Polar Priorities; Newsletters; Reprints of F. A.
Cook Articles, Accounts of Exploration, Summary
of Expeditions and Eskimo Testimony.
Reference: OCLC 33988623.

Freeden, W. von.
(See Petermann, Augustus)

Freeman, Andrew A. (1900–   ) [231]
The Case for Doctor Cook [by] Andrew A.
Freeman. New York: Coward-McCann,
Inc., [1961].

Octavo, original blue cloth.
315 p., map.
Reference: OCLC 576599.

Freuchen, Peter (1886–1957) [232]
Arctic Adventure: My Life in the Frozen
North, by Peter Freuchen. Illustrated with
Photographs and Maps. New York &
Toronto: Farrar & Rinehart, Incorporated,
[1935].

Octavo, original blue cloth.
ix, 467 p., frontispiece (portrait), illustrations, portraits,
frontispiece (portrait), maps, maps on endpapers.
References: AB 5271, OCLC 486571

Freuchen, Peter (1886–1957) [233]
Arctic Adventure: My Life in the Frozen
North. By Peter Freuchen. Illustrated with
Photographs and Maps. London and
Toronto: William Heinemann Ltd.,
[1936].

Octavo, original blue cloth.
ix, [1] p., 1 l., 3–405 p., frontispiece (portrait),
photographs (mostly portraits), maps (1 folded).
Reference: OCLC 3557648.

Freuchen, Peter (1886–1957) [234]
Eskimo, by Peter Freuchen. Translated by
A. Paul Maerker-Branden and Elsa
Branden. New York: Horace Liveright,
[1931].

Octavo, original blue cloth, dust jacket.
vii, [1], 504 p.
Frontispiece, dust jacket and introduction by Rockwell
Kent.
References: AB 5272, OCLC 10119013.

Freuchen, Peter (1886–1957) [235]
I Sailed with Rasmussen, by Peter
Freuchen. New York: Julian Messner,
1958.

Octavo, black cloth covers with turquoise cloth spine.
224 p., frontispiece (portrait), photographs, maps,
decorated endpapers.
First American edition.
Reference: OCLC 777532.

Freuchen, Peter (1886–1957) [236]

It's All Adventure [by] Peter Freuchen.
New York & Toronto: Farrar & Rinehart,
Inc., [1938].

Octavo, original red cloth.
vi, 3–508 p., frontispiece (portrait), plates, portraits,
maps on endpapers.
First edition.
Reference: OCLC 1142295.

Freuchen, Peter (1886–1957) [237]

The Law of Larion, as Translated from the
Danish by Evelyn Ramsden. London:
Evans Brothers Limited, [1954].

Octavo, red cloth, dust jacket.
v, [1], 313 p.
First English edition.
Reference: cf. OCLC 1652656.

Freuchen, Peter (1886–1957) [238]

Peter Freuchen's Adventures in the Arctic.
Edited by Dagmar Freuchen. New York:
Julian Messner Inc., [1960].

Octavo, original light blue cloth, dust jacket.
383 p., frontispiece (portrait), illustrations.
Reference: OCLC 486570.

Freuchen, Peter (1886–1957) [239]

Peter Freuchen's Book of the Eskimos.
Edited and with a Preface by Dagmar
Freuchen. [Drawings by Dagmar
Freuchen]. Cleveland and New York: The
World Publishing Company, [1961].

Octavo, original blue cloth.
441 p., maps on endpapers.
First edition.
Reference: OCLC 1033451.

Freuchen, Peter (1886–1957) [240]

Peter Freuchen's Men of the Frozen
North. Edited and with a Preface by

Dagmar Freuchen. [Drawings by Dagmar
Freuchen]. Cleveland and New York: The
World Publishing Company, [1962].

Octavo, original decorated white cloth.
315 p., 1 l., illustrations, maps on endpapers.
First edition.
Reference: OCLC 1385238.

Freuchen, Peter (1886–1957) and Finn Salomonsen [241]

The Arctic Year [by] Peter Freuchen and
Finn Salomonsen. New York: G.P.
Putnam's Sons, [1958].

Octavo, original turquoise cloth, dust jacket.
2 p. l., 438 pp. illustrations, maps, maps on
endpapers.
Reference: OCLC 1172008.

Fricker, Karl [242]

The Antarctic Regions, by Dr. Karl Fricker.
With Maps, Plates and Illustrations in the
Text. London: Swan Sonnenschein & Co.,
Limited; New York: The Macmillan
Company, 1900.

Large octavo, decorated red cloth.
xii, 292 p., frontispiece, plates, illustrations, portraits,
maps (partly folded).
Translated by A. Sonnenschein.
First English edition.
References: Spence 485, OCLC 3557994.

Friis, Herman R.

(See Conference on United States Polar
Exploration)

Fry, Howard Tyrrell [243]

Alexander Dalrymple (1737–1808) and the
Expansion of British Trade [by] Howard T.
Fry [etc.]. With a Foreword by R.A.
Skelton. [London]: Published for the
Royal Commonwealth Society by Frank
Cass & Co. Ltd., 1970.

Octavo, original blue cloth, dust jacket.
xxvii, [1], 330 p., frontispiece (portrait), genealogy
table, maps.
Imperial Studies Series, Volume 29.
Reference: OCLC 162847.

Fuchs, Vivian, Sir [244]

Antarctic Adventure: The Commonwealth Trans-Antarctic Expedition, 1955–58, by Sir Vivian Fuchs. Illustrated by Stuart Tresilian. New York: E.P. Dutton & Company, Inc., [1961].

> Octavo, blue cloth, dust jacket.
> [xvi], 189, [1] p., illustrations (some color), maps.
> First American edition.
> Reference: American edition of Spence 489.

Fuchs, Vivian, Sir [245]

Of Ice and Men: The Story of the British Antarctic Survey, 1943–73, by Sir Vivian Fuchs. Oswestry, Shropshire, England: Anthony Nelson, [1982].

> Octavo, original blue cloth, dust jacket.
> 383 p., [8] leaves of color plates, black and white illustrations, maps, maps on endpapers.
> First edition.
> Reference: OCLC 12665891.

Fuchs, Vivian, Sir and Sir Edmund Hillary [246]

The Crossing of Antarctica: The Commonwealth Trans-Antarctic Expedition, 1955–1958, by Sir Vivian Fuchs and Sir Edmund Hillary. London: Cassell, [1958].

> Octavo, original blue cloth, dust jacket.
> xv, [3], 337, [1] p., plates (part color), portraits, maps, maps on endpapers.
> First edition.
> References: Spence 490, OCLC 1978048.

Fuchs, Vivian, Sir and Sir Edmund Hillary [247]

The Crossing of Antarctica: The Commonwealth Trans-Antarctic Expedition, 1955–58, by Sir Vivian Fuchs and Sir Edmund Hillary. Illustrated. Boston and Toronto: Little, Brown and Company, [1958].

> Octavo, original blue cloth, dust jacket.
> xv, [5], 328 p., plates (part color), portraits, maps, maps on endpapers.

> First American edition.
> Reference: OCLC 14046134.

Furse, Chris [248]

Antarctic Year: Brabant Island Expedition [by] Chris Furse. Foreword by HRH Prince Charles. London [etc.]: [Croom Helm, 1986].

> Quarto, blue cloth, dust jacket.
> 235 p., [16] leaves of plates, illustrations, maps, maps on endpapers.
> First edition.
> Reference: OCLC 13332907.

Furse, Chris [249]

Elephant Island: An Antarctic Expedition. [Shrewsbury, Shropshire, England]: Anthony Nelson, [1979].

> Octavo, light blue cloth, dust jacket.
> 256 p., [4] leaves of plates, illustrations, maps.
> First edition.
> Reference: OCLC 6055230.

Gad, Finn [250]

The History of Greenland. [Volume] I: Earliest Times to 1700, by Finn Gad. Translated from the Danish by Ernst Dupont. Montreal: McGill-Queen's University Press, 1971.

> Medium octavo, original buff tone cloth cover, gold stamped spine, dust jacket.
> xiii, [1], 350 p., [16] leaves of plates, illustrations, maps.
> Reference: OCLC 163377.

Gain, Louis [251]

The Penguins of the Antarctic Regions. By L. Gain, Doctor of Science, Naturalist of the Charcot Expedition. From the Smithsonian Report for 1912, Pages 475–482 (with plates 1–9). Washington: Government Printing Office, 1913.

> Octavo, original printed wrappers.
> "Translated by permission (with additions by the author) from *La Nature* (Paris) No. 2041 July 6, 1912." — p. 475.
> Reference: Spence 495.

Gardner, Marshall B. (1854–   )   [252]
A Journey to the Earth's Interior: Or,
Have the Poles Really Been Discovered, by
Marshall B. Gardner. Revised and
Enlarged. Profusely Illustrated. Aurora,
Illinois: Published by the Author, 1920.

> Octavo.
> 456 p., 12 plates (part color), portraits, diagrams.
> References: AB 5545, OCLC 3888145.

Gatonbe, John   [253]
A Voyage into the North-West Passage.
Undertaken Anno 1612. Written by John
Gatonbe.

> Folio, modern boards.
> Detached from Awnsham Churchill, *Collection of Voyages and Travels* (London, 1732), vol. 6, pp. [241]-256, illustrations, map.
> Paper label on spine: Gatonbe. North-west Passage 1730.
> References: Sabin 13015, OCLC 17242670 [1732 edition].

Geiger, John
(See Beattie, Owen)

Geikie Correspondence   [254]
Letters (ALS and TLS) addressed to Sir
Archibald Geikie dealing with Antarctic
expeditions. Correspondents include
Robert F. Scott, Ernest Shackleton,
Douglas Mawson, Edward A. Wilson, and
Edgar Speyer.

> In full black leather drop-spine box with gold embossed border, raised bands, gilt decorations and titles on spine.
> 47 leaves.
> "Sir Archibald Geikie (1835 to 1924) was a major figure in the development of modern concepts of geology and had a strong interest in glacial geomorphology . . . The letters are a most interesting series from an important period in Antarctic history. The inception of expeditionary proposals by three of the most eminent explorers: Captain Robert Scott, Sir Ernest Shackleton, and Sir Douglas Mawson, can be traced in them. Sir Archibald is seen as a diplomatic man of science; in hindsight, the results show the efficacy of his guidance." — R.K.

> Headland, Archivist, Scott Polar Research Institute, in letter dated 11 November 1993 [included in box].

The Geographical Journal   [255]
Vol. 22, July-December 1903. London:
Royal Geographical Society, 1903.

> Octavo, half morocco and marbled boards, front joint cracked.
> With much Antarctic material, including several addresses by Sir Clements Markham.
> Reference: cf. OCLC 1570660.

German South Polar Expedition
(See Drygalski, Erich von; Filchner,
Wilhelm)

Gerritsz, Hessel (1581?-1632)   [256]
The Arctic North-East and West Passage.
Detectio freti Hudsoni, or Hessel
Gerritsz's Collection of Tracts by Himself,
Massa, and De Quir on the N.E. and W.
Passage, Siberia and Australia. Reproduced,
with the Maps, in Photolithography in
Dutch and Latin after the Editions of 1612
and 1613. Augmented with a New English
Translation by Fred. John Millard, English
Translator at Amsterdam. And an Essay on
the Origin and Design of This Collection
by S. Muller Fz. Keeper of the Records at
Utrecht. Amsterdam: Frederik Muller &
Co., 1878.

> Small quarto, original boards, title in red and black, dust jacket. Uncut copy.
> 1 p.l., xxvii, [39], [44], 47 p., illustrations, 3 maps (2 folded).
> Reference: OCLC 4925685.

Giaever, John   [257]
The White Desert: The Official Account of
the Norwegian-British-Swedish Antarctic
Expedition. By John Giaever. With
Contributions by Gordon De Q. Robin,
E.F. Roots, Valter Schytt, and Brian

BRITISH ANTARCTIC EXPEDITION, 1910.

Advisory Committee:
Major LEONARD DARWIN, R.E. (President, Royal Geographical Society).
The Right Hon. LORD STRATHCONA, G.C.M.G., &c.
Sir CLEMENTS R. MARKHAM, K.C.B., F.R.S.
The Right Hon. Sir GEORGE D. TAUBMAN GOLDIE, P.C., K.C.M.G., &c.
The Right Hon. VISCOUNT GOSCHEN.
The Right Hon. LORD HOWARD DE WALDEN.
Sir EDGAR SPEYER, Bart. (Treasurer).

Bankers:
Messrs. COCKS, BIDDULPH & CO., 43, Charing Cross, S.W.

Auditors:
Messrs. JAMES FRASER & SONS, Chartered Accountants.

36 & 38, VICTORIA STREET,
S.W.

27 . 11 . 09

Dear Sir Archibald

Thank you very much for your kind consent to join my committee. I do not anticipate any meetings and the fact that Sir Edgar Speyer acts as Treasurer is I think a guarantee that the Expedition will be run on business lines. There are I fear many persons who are not interested in Science but who like the flavour of it in connection with such an Expedition – Your name will give such persons all the satisfaction they require in that respect.

Again many thanks for permitting me to use it and for your kind wishes

Yours very truly
R Scott

Not the least of the polar explorer's tasks was raising funds. Here Scott thanks the noted geologist Sir Archibald Geikie for agreeing to join the advisory committee for his second, and last, expedition. He assures Sir Archibald that "I do not anticipate any meetings and the fact that Sir Edgar Speyer is treasurer is I think a guarantee that the expedition will be run on business lines."

Capt. R. F. Scott to Sir Archibald Geikie (A.L.S., 1909) [**254**]

Walford, and a Foreword by J.M. Wordie, President of the Royal Geographical Society. Translated from the Norwegian by E.M. Huggard. London: Chatto & Windus, 1954.

> Octavo, original blue cloth, gold-stamped.
> 304 p., 20 plates, illustrations, portraits, maps.
> First English edition.
> Reference: OCLC 3140294.

Gibbs, Wolcott (1902–1958)   [258]

Bird Life at the Pole, by Commander Christopher Robin. As told to Wolcott Gibbs. Pictures by Bruton & Bruton. New York: Morrow & Co., 1931.

> Small octavo, yellow cloth.
> 171 p., frontispiece (portrait), plates, map, decorated endpapers.
> Inscribed by author.
> Fictional, a burlesque of the First Byrd Expedition.
> Reference: OCLC 1139534.

Gilder, William Henry (1838–1900)   [259]

Among the Esquimaux with Schwatka. New York: The Century Company, 1881.

> Octavo, binding holes in margin.
> Detached from *Scribner's Monthly* (May 1881): 76–88; illustrations, map.
> Reference: OCLC 8609068.

Gilder, William Henry (1838–1900)   [260]

Ice-Pack and Tundra: An Account of the Search for the Jeannette and a Sledge Journey through Siberia. By William H. Gilder [etc.]. With Maps and Illustrations. New York: Charles Scribner's Sons, 1883.

> Octavo, original decorated green cloth, head and tail of spine slightly rubbed, joints weak.
> xi, 344 p., plus 4 p. of advertisements, frontispiece (portrait), illustrations, 3 maps (1 folded).
> First edition.
> References: AB 5744, OCLC 1984490.

Gilder, William Henry (1838–1900)   [261]

Schwatka's Search: Sledging in the Arctic in Quest of the Franklin Records. By William H. Gilder, Second in Command. With Maps and Illustrations. New York: Charles Scribner's Sons, 1881.

> Octavo, original decorated brown cloth.
> 1 l., vii-xvi, 361 p., frontispiece (portrait), illustrations, 11 plates, 2 maps.
> First edition.
> References: AB 5745, OCLC 2042163.

Gilder, William Henry (1838–1900)   [262]

The Search for Franklin. A Narrative of the American Expedition under Lieutenant Schwatka, 1878 to 1880. With Illustrations from Engravings Designed by an Artist of the Expedition. London: T. Nelson and Sons, 1882.

> Small octavo, original decorated red cloth, red and black titles with gold label.
> 127 p., [1] p. of advertisements, frontispiece (portrait), [7] leaves of plates, map.
> "Probably written by W. H. Gilder, a member of the expedition" — Brown University OCLC entry.
> Reference: OCLC 1193398.

Gilkerson, William   [263]

An Arctic Whaling Sketchbook, by William Gilkerson. Fairhaven, Massachusetts: Published by Edward J. Lefkowicz, Inc., MCMLXXXIII [1983].

> Large folio, silver-stamped gray cloth, handbound.
> 52 unnumbered pages including 9 pages of Artist's Remarks and over 135 pencil sketches.
> Colophon: *An Arctic Whaling Sketchbook* was designed by William Gilkerson to complement its parent book *American Whalers in the Western Arctic*. Edition of 120 copies [unnumbered].
> Reference: OCLC 10605819.

Gilkerson, William and John R. Bockstoce   [264]

American Whalers in the Western Arctic. The Final Epoch of the Great American

Sailing Whaling Fleet. A Portfolio of
Watercolors and Drawings by William
Gilkerson. Introduced and Related in Text
by John R. Bockstoce. Fairhaven,
Massachusetts: Edward J. Lefkowicz, Inc.,
MCMLXXXIII [1983].

> Oblong folio, half-bound in Niger Oasis over silver-
> stamped linen.
> viii, 48, [1] p., [12] leaves of plates (color), illustrations,
> maps.
> Edition of 400 copies [unnumbered]. Accompanied by
> a separate cloth portfolio containing an extra
> suite of the 12 Gilkerson plates.
> Reference: OCLC 11587334.

Giudici, Davide [265]
The Tragedy of the Italia. With the
Rescuers to the Red Tent. By Davide
Giudici, Special Correspondent of the
Corriere della Sera on board the Krassin.
New York: D. Appleton and Company,
MCMXXIX [1929].

> Octavo, original red cloth with gilt titles, dust jacket.
> xv, [1], 207, [1] p., frontispiece, 32 plates, portraits,
> map.
> References: AB 5776, OCLC 1520633.

**Glen, Alexander Richard (1912–   )
and Noel A.C. Croft** [266]
Under the Pole Star: The Oxford
University Arctic Expedition 1935–6, by
A.R. Glen. Assisted by N.A.C. Croft. With
48 Plates, 22 Maps & Diagrams. London:
Methuen Publishers, [1937].

> Quarto, original blue cloth.
> xv, [1], 365, [1] p., frontispiece, plates, illustrations,
> portraits, map (1 folded).
> References: AB 5813, OCLC 6618969.

Glenbow Museum
(See Martin, Constance)

Glines, Carroll V., (1920–   ) [267]
Polar Aviation. Edited by Lieutenant
Colonel C.V. Glines, U.S.A.F. New York:
Franklin Watts, Inc., [1964].

> Octavo, original blue cloth, dust jacket.
> xii, [3], 4–289 p., frontispiece, illustrations, portraits,
> map.
> Watts Aerospace Library; Volume 8.
> Reference: OCLC 2531973.

Godwin, George (1889–   ) [268]
Vancouver: A Life, 1757–1798. By George
Godwin [etc.]. New York: D. Appleton
and Company, MCMXXXI [1931].

> Octavo, blue cloth.
> xi, [1], 308 p., frontispiece (portrait), 9 plates (1
> folded), illustrations, portraits, 3 maps (2 folded,
> 1 in pocket).
> Reference: OCLC 1525746.

Golder, Frank Alfred (1877–1929) [269]
Bering's Voyages. An Account of the
Efforts of the Russians to Determine the
Relation of Asia and America. By F.A.
Golder. In Two Volumes. Volume I: The
Log Books and Official Reports of the First
and Second Expeditions, 1725–1730 and
1733–1742. With a Chart of the Second
Voyage by Ellsworth P. Bertholf. Volume
II: Steller's Journal of the Sea Voyage from
Kamchatka to America and Return on the
Second Expedition, 1741–42. Translated
and in Part Annotated by Leonhard
Stejneger. New York: American
Geographical Society, 1922–25, [1935
reprint].

> Large duodecimo, 2 volumes, original gray cloth, gilt
> titles and black labels on spine.
> Volume 1: x, 371 p., illustrations, tables, facsimiles,
> maps (2 folded); Volume 2 xi, [1], 290, [1] p.,
> illustrations, facsimiles, maps (2 folded.)
> American Geographical Society. Research Series; No.
> 1–2.
> References: AB 34932–3, OCLC 11830414.

Good, Dorothy
(See Kimble, George Herbert Tinley)

Goodsell, John W. (1873–1949) [270]
Letters (A.L.S.) and Documents Relating

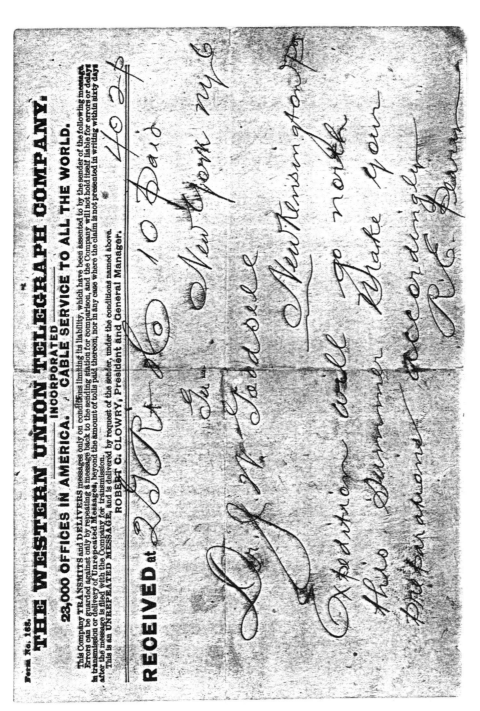

Dr. John W. Goodsell, a physician practicing near Pittsburgh, had no Arctic experience but met Peary at a social gathering and offered his services for the explorer's final assault on the pole. When the physician originally chosen could not make the trip, Peary appointed Goodsell as surgeon. He proved to be an able arctic traveler and an asset to the expedition. His memoirs were published posthumously in 1983 as *On Polar Trails* [273]

Robert Peary to John W. Goodsell (Telegram, 1908) [270]

to Dr. J. W. Goodsell, Expedition Surgeon on Peary's Final Assault on the North Pole, 1908–9. Correspondents include Goodsell, Peary, Leon Amundsen, A.W. Greely, George Borup, Elsa Barker, Jacques Suzanne, and John Wanamaker.

> 17 items in blue buckram drop-spine box. Spine label: J. W. Goodsell, Robert E. Peary. Letters and Documents.

Goodsell, John W. (1873–1949) [271]

On Polar Trails: The Peary Expedition to the North Pole, 1908–09, [by] John W. Goodsell, M.D. Revised and Edited by Donald W. Wisenhunt. Austin, Texas: Eakin Press, [1983].

> Octavo, original blue cloth, dust jacket.
> xi, [1], 202 p., frontispiece (portrait), illustrations, [2] leaves of plates, maps.
> Reference: OCLC 10346162.

Goodsir, Robert Anstruther [272]

An Arctic Voyage to Baffin's Bay and Lancaster Sound, in Search of Friends with Sir John Franklin. By Robert Anstruther Goodsir. Late President of the Royal Medical Society of Edinburgh. London: John van Voorst, M.D.CCC.L [1850].

> Octavo, original blue cloth. On spine: Goodsir's Arctic Voyage.
> [v]-viii, 152 p., plus 8 p. of advertisements, frontispiece.
> First edition.
> References: AB 5919, OCLC 7559172.

Gordon, William John [273]

Round about the North Pole, by W.J. Gordon. With Woodcuts and Other Illustrations by Edward Whymper. New York: E.P. Dutton and Company, 1907.

> Octavo, original decorated blue cloth with gilt titles.
> xii, 294 p., frontispiece (portrait), 65 plates including portraits, 6 sectional maps.
> First American edition.
> References: AB 5968, OCLC 3029302.

Gorman, James [274]

The Total Penguin [by] James Gorman.

Photographs by Frans Lanting. New York [etc.]: Prentice Hall Editions, 1990.

> Quarto, black cloth cover, gilt-stamped spine, dust jacket.
> 191, [1] p., illustrations, photographs (mostly color), map.
> First edition.
> Reference: OCLC 20690602.

Gould, Laurence M. (1896–) [275]

Cold: The Record of an Antarctic Sledge Journey, by Laurence McKinley Gould, Second in Command, Byrd Antarctic Expedition. With 47 Illustrations from Photographs by the Author, Two Maps and Two Color Reproductions of Paintings by David Paige. New York: Brewer, Warren & Putnam, 1931.

> Octavo, original blue cloth.
> ix, 275 p., color frontispiece, 32 plates (1 color), portraits, plans, facsimiles, maps (2 folded).
> References: Spence 517, OCLC 8989864.

Gould, Laurence M. (1896–) [276]

The Polar Regions in Their Relation to Human Affairs. New York: American Geographical Society, 1958.

> Octavo, paper covered boards.
> iv, 54 p., 16 plates, illustrations, map (1 folded).
> First edition.
> Bowman Memorial Lectures, Series Four.
> Reference: Spence 519.

Gould, Laurence M. (1896–) [277]

Structure of the Queen Maud Mountains, Antarctica. By Laurence M. Gould. New York: Geological Society of America, 1935.

> Octavo, green printed wrappers.
> Reprinted from *Bulletin of the Geological Society of America*, Volume 46, p. 973–984; 5 plates, illustrations, map.
> Reference: OCLC 42348975.

Great Britain. Admiralty. [278]

Additional Papers Relative to the Arctic Expedition under the Orders of Captain

Austin and Mr. William Penny. Presented
to Both Houses of Parliament by
Command of Her Majesty. Printed by
George Edward Eyre and William
Spottiswoode, Printers to the Queen's
Most Excellent Majesty. For Her Majesty's
Stationery Office, 1852.

> Folio, modern boards.
> iii, [1], 368 p., illustrations, plans, 15 lithographed
> maps (part folded).
> First edition.
> References: AB 45228, OCLC 9421627.

Great Britain. Admiralty. [279]

Arctic Expedition. Further Correspondence
and Proceedings Connected with the
Arctic Expedition. Presented to Both
Houses of Parliament by Command of Her
Majesty. London: Printed by George
Edward Eyre and William Spottiswoode,
Printers to the Queen's Most Excellent
Majesty. For Her Majesty's Stationery
Office. 1852.

> Folio, modern three-quarter calf, original blue printed
> wrappers bound in.
> On spine: Arctic Expeditions 1852 — Sir John Franklin.
> 216 p., illustrations, maps (1 folded).
> References: AB 45229, OCLC 18099558.

Great Britain. Admiralty. [280]

Arctic Expeditions. Report of the
Committee Appointed by the Lords
Commissioners of the Admiralty to Inquire
into and Report on the Recent Arctic
Expeditions in Search of Sir John Franklin,
Together with the Minutes of Evidence
Taken before the Committee, and Papers
Connected with the Subject. Presented to
Both Houses of Parliament by Command
of Her Majesty. London: Printed by
George Edward Eyre and William
Spottiswoode [etc.] For Her Majesty's
Stationery Office, 1852.

> Folio, half morocco and marbled boards.

> lix, [3], 199 p., 2 folded maps.
> References: AB 45227, OCLC 9421549.

Great Britain. Admiralty. [281]

Further Papers Relative to the Recent
Arctic Expeditions in Search of Sir John
Franklin and the Crews of H.M.S.
"Erebus" and "Terror." Presented to Both
Houses of Parliament by Command of Her
Majesty. January 1855. London: Printed by
George Edward Eyre and William
Spottiswoode, Printers to the Queen's
Most Excellent Majesty. For Her Majesty's
Stationery Office. 1855.

> Folio, later quarter calf.
> iv, 958, [2] p., illustrations, diagrams, 29 lithographic
> maps (19 folded, 8 in the text, part color), 3
> plates (2 color).
> References: AB 45245, TPL 3549, OCLC 9410198.

Great Britain. Admiralty. [282]

Further Papers Relative to the Recent
Arctic Expeditions in Search of Sir J.
Franklin, and the Crews of Her Majesty's
Ships "Erebus" and "Terror;" Including
the Reports of Dr. Kane and Messrs.
Anderson and Stewart. And
Correspondence Relative to the
Adjudication of £10,000 as a Reward for
Ascertaining the Fate of the Crews of Her
Majesty's Ships "Erebus" and "Terror." (In
Continuation of Papers Presented in
September 1854–5.) Presented to the
House of Commons. London: Printed by
Harrison and Sons, [1856].

> Folio, paper covers, stitched as issued.
> v, 95 [1] p., plan, map (right edge of map is
> damaged).
> Reference: AB 45249.

Great Britain. Admiralty. [283]

[Collection of 10 pamphlets on Arctic
expeditions].

> Folio, stitched, original paper wrappers. In brown
> cloth drop-spine box with red morocco label.

Binder's title: Sir John Franklin.
CONTENTS:
(1) Arctic Expedition, 1875–6. "Alert" and "Discovery."
Admiralty letter to Commander-in-Chief, Portsmouth,
3rd November, 1876.
    2 p., 1 l. [25 11/76 — H & S 2604].
(2) Arctic Expedition, 1875–6. Northern Sledging Party.
Commander Markham's Journal.
    32 p. [25 1/77 — H & S 3154].
(3) Arctic Expedition, 1875–6. Eastern sledging Party.
Lieutenant Rawson's Journal.
    14 p. [25 1/77 — H & S 3155].
(4) Arctic Expedition, 1875–6. Reports of Proceedings
of Captain G.S. Nares.
    38 p. [25 1/77 — H & S 3156].
(5) Arctic Expedition, 1875–6. Eastern Sledging Party.
Lieutenants Beaumont and Rawson. Orders and
Reports.
    25 p., illustration, [25 1/77 — H & S 3157].
(6) Arctic Expedition, 1875–6. Western Sledging Party.
Lieutenant Aldrich — Orders & Reports.
    7 p. [25 1/77 — H & S 3158].
(7) Arctic Expedition, 1875–6. Northern Sledging Party.
Commander Markham. Instructions and Report.
    5 p. [25 1/77 — H & S 3159].
(8) Arctic Expedition, 1875–6. Reports of Proceedings
of Captain Stephenson (when detached).
    19 p. [25 1/77 — H & S 3160].
(9) Arctic Expedition, 1875–6. Medical Report. Dr.
Colan.
    6 p. [25 1/77 — H & S 3161].
(10) Arctic Expedition. Papers and Correspondence
relating to Equipment and Fitting out of the Arctic
Expedition of 1875, including Report of the Admiralty
Arctic Committee. Presented to both Houses of
Parliament by Command of Her Majesty. London:
Printed by George Edward Eyre and William
Spottiswoode, Printers to the Queen's most excellent
Majesty. For Her Majesty's Stationery Office, 1875.
    40 p. Back cover lacking.
Reference: OCLC 33366250.

Gt. Brit. Parliament, 1745   [284]

Anno Regni Georgii II Regis . . . At the
Parliament Begun and Holden at
Westminster the First Day of December,
Anno Dom. 1741 . . . An Act for Giving a
Publick Reward to Such Person or Persons,
His Majesty's Subject or Subjects, as Shall
Discover a North West Passage through
Hudson's Streights, to the Western and
Southern Ocean of America. London:
Printed by Thomas Baskett . . . and by the
assigns of Robert Baskett, 1745.
    Folio, quarter morocco and cloth.

[2], 483–86 p.
NUC 0441559, Lada-Mocarski 25 (note).

Greely, Adolphus W. (1844–1935) [285]

The Greely Arctic Expedition as Fully
Narrated by Lieut. Greely, U.S.A. and
other Survivors. Full Account of the
Terrible Sufferings on the Ice, and Awful
Tales of Cannibalism! Commander Schley's
Report. Wonderful Discoveries by Lieut.
Greely, the American Army officer, and His
Little Band of Heroes. Philadelphia:
Published by Barclay & Company, [1885].
    Octavo, original wrappers, wrappers chipped and
        spine wanting, short tears to margins
        throughout.
    [19]-105, [1] p., illustrations.
    Reference: OCLC 6128664.

Greely, Adolphus W. (1844–1935) [286]

Handbook of Arctic Discoveries, by A.W.
Greely, Brigadier-General United States
Army [etc.]. Edited by Professor David P.
Todd. Boston: Roberts Brothers,
MDCCCXCVI [1896].
    Sextodecimo, original decorated red cloth.
    x p., 2 l., [3]-257 p., frontispiece (portrait), 11 maps (5
        folded).
    Columbian Knowledge Series No. 3.
    Reference: OCLC 26957357.

Greely, Adolphus W. (1844–1935) [287]

The Polar Regions in the Twentieth
Century. Their Discovery and Industrial
Evolution, by A.W. Greely, Major-General
U.S. Army, Retired. London, Bombay and
Sydney: George G. Harrap & Company
Ltd., [1929].
    Octavo, original red cloth.
    222, [1] p., frontispiece (portrait), plates, illustrations,
        folded map (color). Imperfect: map wanting.
    Reference: OCLC 1970520.

Greely, Adolphus W. (1844–1935) [288]

Reminiscences of Adventure and Service. A
Record of Sixty-Five Years. By Major-

General A.W. Greely, U.S.A., Retired. Illustrated. New York & London: C. Scribner's Sons, 1927.

> Octavo, original red cloth.
> xi p., 1 l., 356 p., frontispiece (portrait), illustrations, 15 plates, portraits, facsimiles.
> Reference: OCLC 1702438.

Greely, Adolphus W. (1844–1935) [289]
Report on the Proceedings of the United States Expedition to Lady Franklin Bay, Grinnell Land, by Adolphus A. Greely [etc.]. Washington: Government Printing Office, 1888.

> Quarto, 2 volumes, original brown cloth.
> Volume 1: viii, 545 p., 30 plates, illustrations, maps (part folded.) Volume 2: vi, [2], 738 p., 13 plates, illustrations, maps. With card of compliments from A.W. Greely, Chief Signal Officer.
> Reference: OCLC 2042048.

Greely, Adolphus W. (1844–1935) [290]
Three Years of Arctic Service: An Account of the Lady Franklin Bay Expedition of 1881–84, and the Attainment of the Farthest North. By Adolphus W. Greely, Lieutenant U.S. Army, Commanding the Expedition. With Nearly One Hundred Illustrations Made from Photographs Taken by the Party, and with the Official Maps and Charts. New York: Scribner's Sons, 1886.

> Octavo, 2 volumes, original pictorial cloth, joints cracked.
> Volume 1: xxv, [1], 428 p., frontispiece, 16 plates, illustrations, portraits, maps (part folded); Volume 2: xii, [1], 444 p., frontispiece, 25 plates, illustrations, portraits, maps, (part folded, 1 in pocket).
> References: AB 6118, OCLC 1248645.

Greely, Adolphus W. (1844–1935) [291]
True Tales of Arctic Heroism in the New World. By Major-General A. W. Greely, U. S. Army, Gold Medalist Royal Geographical Society and of Société de

Géographie. Illustrated. New York: Charles Scribner's Sons, 1923.

> Octavo, original red cloth with color lithograph mounted on front panel.
> xi, [3], 385 p., frontispiece, 3 plates, maps.
> References: Cf. AB 6119, OCLC 8971566.

Green, Fitzhugh (1888–1947) [292]
Dick Byrd — Air Explorer. An Intimate Story of a Great Air Explorer, Whose Spectacular Flights to the North and South Poles, across the Atlantic Ocean and Other Adventures have Thrilled Red-blooded Men and Boys the World Over. By Fitzhugh Green [etc.]. With 31 illustrations. New York and London: G.P. Putnam's Sons, 1928.

> Octavo, original black-stamped red cloth.
> viii, 267, [1] p., plus 4 p. of advertisements, frontispiece (portrait), 30 plates.

Green, Fitzhugh (1888–1947) [293]
Peary: The Man Who Refused to Fail. By Fitzhugh Green. With 20 Illustrations. New York and London: G.P. Putnam's Sons, 1926.

> Octavo, original blue cloth, dust jacket.
> viii, 404 p., frontispiece (portrait), 19 plates, portraits, maps on endpapers.
> First edition.
> Reference: AB 6126, OCLC 1534992.

Greenland [294]
Greenland. Published by the Commission for the Direction of the Geological and Geographical Investigations in Greenland. Editors: M. Vahl, G.C. Amdrup, L. Babé, and Ad. S. Jensen. Copenhagen: C.A. Reitzel, Publisher; London: Humphrey Milford, Oxford University Press, 1928–29.

> Quarto, 3 volumes, in original green printed wrappers.
> Includes black-and-white photographs, diagrams, portraits, facsimiles, maps (folded map at end of vol. 3).

Contents: Volume 1. The Discovery of Greenland,
Exploration and Nature of the Country (ii, 575 p.)
— Volume 2. The Past and Present Population of
Greenland ([ii], 415 p.) — Volume 3. The
Colonization of Greenland and its history until
1929 ([ii], 468 p.).
References: AB 6138, OCLC 933595.

Grier, Mary C. (1907–) [295]
Oceanography of the North Pacific Ocean,
Bering Sea and Bering Strait: A
Contribution Toward a Bibliography.
Compiled by Mary C. Grier, Librarian,
Oceanographic Laboratories. Seattle, WA:
Published by the University of Washington,
1941.

Octavo, printed wrappers.
v-xxii p., 1 l., 290 p.
University of Washington Publications. Library Series.
Volume 2, May, 1941.
References: AB 6193, OCLC 1825197.

Gromov, Mikhail M. (1899–) [296]
Across the North Pole to America, by M.
Gromov, Hero of the Soviet Union, Order
of Lenin, etc. Member of the Supreme
Soviety of the U.S.S.R. Moscow: Foreign
Languages Publishing House, 1939.

Duodecimo, original printed wrappers.
37, [1] p., 4 black and white photograph illustrations.
Reference: OCLC 537855.

Guttridge, Leonard F. [297]
Icebound: The Jeannette Expedition's
Quest for the North Pole. By Leonard F.
Guttridge. Annapolis, Maryland: Naval
Institute Press, 1986.

Octavo, brown cloth with gilt titles, dust jacket
repaired.
xx p., 1 l., 357 p., illustrations, maps on endpapers.
First edition.
Reference: OCLC 13395944.

Hale, Ralph T.
(See Bartlett, Robert Abram)

Hall, Charles Francis (1821–1871)
[298]
Arctic Researches and Life Among the
Esquimaux: Being the Narrative of an
Expedition in Search of Sir John Franklin,
in the Years 1860, 1861, and 1862. By
Charles Francis Hall. With Maps and One
Hundred Illustrations. New York: Harper
& Brothers, Publishers, 1865.

Octavo, original brown cloth with gilt titles.
xxviii, [29]-595 p., frontispiece (portrait), added title-
page (illustrated), 18 plates, illustrations, maps (1
folded).
First American edition.
References: AB 6485, OCLC 5357849.

Hall, Charles Francis (1821–1871)
[299]
Narrative of the North Polar Expedition.
U.S. Ship Polaris, Captain Charles Francis
Hall Commanding. Edited under the
Direction of the Honorable G.M.
Robeson, Secretary of the Navy, by Rear-
Admiral C.H. Davis, U.S.N. U.S Naval
Observatory, 1876. Washington:
Government Printing Office, 1876.

Thick quarto, original cloth.
1 p. l., 696 p. with appendix, frontispiece, illustrations,
plates, portraits, maps.
First edition.
References: AB 18382, OCLC 1011127.

Hall, Charles Francis (1821–1871)
[300]
Narrative of the Second Arctic Expedition
Made by Charles F. Hall: His Voyage to
Repulse Bay, Sledge Journeys to the Straits
of Fury and Hecla and to King William's
Land, and Residence among the Eskimos
During the Years 1864-'69. Edited under
the Orders of the Hon. Secretary of the
Navy, by Professor J.E. Nourse,
U.S.N. U.S. Naval Observatory, 1879.

Large quarto, red cloth with gilt titles.

5 p. l., L, 644 p., frontispiece (portrait), 7 plates,
  illustrations, folded facsimile, 20 maps (8 folded
  including 1 in pocket).
References: AB 6486, OCLC 23237070.

Hall, Sam [301]

The Fourth World: The Heritage of the
Arctic and Its Destruction. New York:
Alfred A. Knopf, 1987.

Octavo, brown cloth with silver titles, dust jacket.
x p., 3 l., [3]-240 p., 4 maps.
First American Edition.
Reference: cf. OCLC 20527511.

Hall, Thomas F. (1841–1933) [302]

Has the North Pole Been Discovered? An
Analytical and Synthetical Review of the
Published Narratives of the Two Arctic
Explorers, Dr. Frederick A. Cook and Civil
Engineer Robert E. Peary, U.S.N. Also a
Review of the Action of the U.S.
Government. By Thomas F. Hall.
Illustrated with Maps, Charts, Diagrams
and Tables. Boston: Richard G. Badger;
Toronto: The Copp Clark Co., Limited,
[1917].

Octavo, original red cloth.
539 p., 17 plates and maps (1 folded in pocket),
  charts (part folded), diagrams.
Author's signed presentation copy.

Halle, Louis Joseph (1910–   ) [303]

The Sea and the Ice: A Naturalist in
Antarctica, by Louis J. Halle. With an
Introduction by Les Line. Illustrated with
Photographs, Maps, and Diagrams.
Boston: Published in Cooperation with the
National Audubon Society by Houghton
Mifflin Company, 1973.

Octavo, original blue cloth with silver titles, dust jacket.
xv, 286 p., illustrations, maps, maps on endpapers.
First edition.
References: Spence 556, OCLC 609188.

Handlin, Oscar

(See Mirsky, Jeannette)

Hansen, Frederik Carl Christian (1870–1934) [304]

Outlines of the Geography and History of
Greenland for the Use of Anthropologists.
With a New Large Survey Chart of
Greenland, 5 Historical Maps, 6 Landscape
Views, 19 Portraits and a Bibliography, by
Fr. C.C. Hansen [etc.]. Reprinted from
Carl M. Fürst and Fr. C.C. Hansen: Crania
Groenlandica, Copenhagen 1915.
Copenhagen: Printed by J. Jörgensen &
Co. (Ivar Jantzen), 1915.

Folio, original printed wrappers.
40 p., [6] leaves of plates, illustrations, portraits,
  facsimiles, 6 maps (1 folded).
Reference: OCLC 10857439.

Hansen, H.

(See Mikkelsen, Ejnar)

Harber, Giles Bates (1849–1925) [305]

Letter from the Secretary of the Navy,
Transmitting Report of Lieut. G.B.
Harber, U.S.N., Concerning the Search for
the Missing Persons of the Jeannette
Expedition, and the Transportation of the
Remains of Lieutenant-Commander De
Long and Companions to the United
States. Washington: Government Printing
Office, [1884].

Octavo, original blue printed wrappers.
75 p., [4] leaves of plates, 1 folded map.
Also issued as 48th Congress, First Session, House Ex.
  Doc. No. 163.
Copies one and two.
Reference: OCLC 13623857 and 4118418.

Hardy, Alister Clavering, Sir [306]

Great Waters: A Voyage of Natural History
to Study Whales, Plankton, and the Waters
of the Southern Ocean, by Sir Alister
Hardy. New York and Evanston: Harper &
Row, Publishers, 1967.

Octavo, original blue cloth, dust jacket.

542 p., frontispiece, 38 plates (6 color), illustrations,
portraits, maps, maps on endpapers.
First American edition.
Reference: OCLC 12884416.

Harrington, Richard [307]

Northern Exposures: Canada's Backwoods
and Barrens Pictured in Monochrome and
Color, by Richard Harrington. Text and
Arrangement by Clifford Wilson. New
York: Henry Schuman, Inc.; Toronto:
Thomas Nelson & Sons Ltd., 1953.

Quarto, original blue cloth with silver titles.
119 p., color frontispiece, illustrations (part color),
map.
Reference: OCLC 1713105.

Hartwig, George Ludwig (1813–1880) [308]

The Polar World: A Popular Description of
Man and Nature in the Arctic and
Antarctic Regions of the Globe. By Dr. G.
Hartwig [etc.]. With Additional Chapters
and One Hundred and Sixty-three
Illustrations. New York: Harper &
Brothers, Publishers, 1869.

Quarto, original purple cloth, rubbed, back joint
cracked, heavily faded on spine.
xvi, [17]-486 p., plus 10 p. of advertisements,
frontispiece, illustrations.
References: AB 6733, OCLC 962166.

Haskell, Daniel Carl (1883–) [309]

The United States Exploring Expedition,
1838–1842 and Its Publications, 1844–
1874. A Bibliography by Daniel C.
Haskell. With an Introductory Note by
Harry Miller Lydenberg. New York:
Greenwood Press, Publishers, [1968].

Octavo, brown cloth.
xii, 188 p., frontispiece (portrait), illustrations, portraits.
Reprint of 1942 edition.
References: Spence 566, OCLC 10912.

Hayes, Isaac Israel (1832–1881) [310]

An Arctic Boat Journey in the Autumn of
1854, by Isaac I. Hayes, Surgeon of the
Second Grinnell Expedition. Edited, with
an Introduction and Notes, by Dr. Norton
Shaw. London: Richard Bentley, Publisher
in Ordinary to Her Majesty, 1860.

Octavo, original blue cloth with gilt titles.
xliii, 379, [1] p., folded map.
Portion torn from blank outer margin of prelim leaf xi-
xii. p. 107/108 torn in outer margin. Appendix
pages uncut.
First edition.
References: AB 6789, OCLC 22148896.

Hayes, Isaac Israel (1832–1881) [311]

The Land of Desolation: Being a Personal
Narrative of Observation and Adventure in
Greenland. By Isaac I. Hayes, M.D. [etc.].
Illustrated. New York: Harper & Brothers,
Publishers, 1872.

Octavo, original decorated green cloth with gilt titles.
357 p., frontispiece, 20 plates, illustrations, portraits.
References: AB 6792, OCLC 10856945.

Hayes, Isaac Israel (1832–1881) [312]

The Open Polar Sea: A Narrative of a
Voyage of Discovery towards the North
Pole in the Schooner "United States." By
Dr. I.I. Hayes. New York: Published by
Hurd and Houghton, 1867.

Octavo, half calf, marbled boards, endpapers and
edges.
xxiv, 454 p., frontispiece (portrait), 9 plates including
maps, illustrations, tailpieces.
First edition.
References: AB 6795, Sabin 31020, OCLC 1470066.

Hayes, Isaac Israel (1832–1881)

(See also American Geographical Society of
New York)

Hayes, James Gordon (1877–) [313]

Antarctica: A Treatise on the Southern
Continent. By J. Gordon Hayes [etc.].
London: The Richards Press Limited,
[1928].

Quarto, original blue cloth with gilt titles.
xv, 448 p., frontispiece, 15 plates of photographs,
    diagrams, maps (part folded), 4 folded maps in
    pocket).
First edition.
References: Spence 574, OCLC 3009556.

Hayes, James Gordon (1877–) [314]

The Conquest of the North Pole: Recent Arctic Exploration, by J. Gordon Hayes. New York: The Macmillan Company, 1934.

Octavo, original blue cloth with gilt titles.
317, plus [3] p. of advertisements, frontispiece, 15
    plates, portraits, 11 maps and diagrams (3
    folded.
References: AB 6800, OCLC 1801542.

Hayes, James Gordon (1877–) [315]

The Conquest of the South Pole. Antarctic Explorations, 1906–1931. By J. Gordon Hayes. London: Thornton Butterworth Limited, [1932].

Octavo, original green cloth.
9–318 p., plus [2] p. of advertisements, frontispiece,
    23 plates, portraits, 11 maps and diagrams.
References: Spence 575, OCLC 1802187.

Hayes, James Gordon (1877–) [316]

Robert Edwin Peary. A Record of his Explorations 1866–1909. London: Grant Richards & Humphrey Toulmin, [1929].

Octavo, original cloth.
xv, 299 p., 1 l., frontispiece, 7 plates, 7 maps (four
    folded in pocket) and diagrams.
References: AB 6801, OCLC 268267.

Headland, Robert K. (1944–) [317]

Chronological List of Antarctic Expeditions and Related Historical Events [by] R.K. Headland. Cambridge [England]: Cambridge University Press, [1989].

Quarto, blue cloth, dust jacket.
vii, [3], 730 p., 29 plates, 4 graphs, 27 maps.
First edition.
Reference: OCLC 18778733.

Headland, Robert K. (1944–) [318]

The Island of South Georgia [by] Robert Headland. Cambridge, [England]: Cambridge University Press, [1984].

Octavo, original blue cloth, dust jacket.
xvi, 293 p., illustrations, portraits, maps.
Reference: OCLC 10163039.

Hearne, Samuel (1745–1792) [319]

Journals of Samuel Hearne and Philip Turnor. Edited with Introduction and Notes by J. B. Tyrrell. Toronto: The Champlain Society, 1934.

Medium octavo, original crested red cloth.
xviii, 611 p., added title-page, 19 sketch maps and 7
    maps (6 folded; 2 in pocket), plans, facsimiles.
Publications of the Champlain Society; XXI.
No. 283 of 500 copies.
Reference: OCLC 4536159.

Hearne, Samuel (1745–1792) [320]

A Journey from Prince of Wales's Fort in Hudson's Bay to the Northern Ocean. Undertaken by Order of the Hudson's Bay Company, for the Discovery of Copper Mines, a North West Passage, &c. In the Years 1769, 1770, 1771 & 1772. By Samuel Hearne. London: Printed for A. Strahan and T. Cadell: And Sold by T. Cadell Jun. and W. Davies (Successors to Mr. Cadell,) in the Strand. 1795.

Quarto, later three-quarter morocco and marbled
    boards, raised bands.
xliv, 458, [2] p., frontispiece, 3 plates (part folded), 5
    maps (part folded), map facing p. 1 is detached.
References: Hill p. 141, Streeter 3642, TPL 445, OCLC
    2352041.

Hearne, Samuel (1745–1792) [321]

A Journey from Prince of Wales's Fort, in Hudson's Bay, to the Northern Ocean. Undertaken by Order of the Hudson's Bay Company, for the Discovery of Copper Mines, a North-West Passage, &c. in the Years 1769, 1770, 1771 & 1772. By

Samuel Hearne. Dublin: Printed for P. Byrne and J. Rice, 1796.

> Octavo, calf with label.
> 2 p. l., iii-L, 459, [1] p., 4 folded plates, 5 folded maps.
> Reference: OCLC 3409555.

Helm, A.S. and J.H. Miller   [322]

Antarctica by A.S. Helm and J.H. Miller. The Story of the New Zealand Party of the Trans-Antarctic Expedition. Wellington, New Zealand: R.E. Owen, Government Printer, 1964.

> Medium octavo, black cloth, gilt-stamped spine.
> 435 p., [20] leaves of plates (8 color), maps on endpapers.
> First edition.

Henderson, Daniel (1880–1955) [323]

The Hidden Coasts: A Biography of Admiral Charles Wilkes. New York, Sloane Associates, Publishers, 1953.

> Octavo, original blue linen spine on cream boards, dust jacket.
> 306 p., portrait, map on endpapers.
> Reference: OCLC 425149.

Henry, Thomas Robert (1893–   ) [324]

The White Continent—The Story of Antarctica [by] Thomas R. Henry. New York, William Sloane Associates, Publishers, [1950].

> Octavo, white spine on blue boards.
> xii, [2], 3–257 p., map.
> References: Spence 584, OCLC 20591050.

Herbert, Marie   [325]

The Snow People [by] Marie Herbert. New York: G.P. Putnam's Sons, [1973].

> Octavo, original white cloth, dust jacket.
> 4 p. l., 277, [1] p., maps on endpapers.
> First American edition.
> Reference: OCLC 782792.

Herbert, Wally   [326]

The Noose of Laurels—Robert E. Peary and the Race to the North Pole [by] Wally Herbert. New York: Atheneum, 1989.

> Octavo, black spine on white boards, dust jacket.
> 395 p., [8] leaves of plates, illustrations, maps.
> Reference: OCLC 19125417.

Heyerdahl, Thor, Søren Richter, and Hjalmar Riiser-Larsen   [327]

Great Norwegian Expeditions by Thor Heyerdahl, Søren Richter, and Hj. Riiser-Larsen. Oslo: Dreyers Forlag, [1954?].

> Quarto, original blue cloth with gilt titles, dust jacket.
> 231, [1] p., photographs (some color), maps.
> "Special edition printed for the American-Scandinavian Foundation, New York."
> Reference: OCLC 1703012.

Hillary, Edmund, Sir

(See Fuchs, Vivian, Sir)

Hoare, Michael E.

(See Forster, Johann Reinhold. Resolution Journal)

Hobbs, William H. (1864–1952) [328]

An Explorer-Scientist's Pilgrimage: The Autobiography of William Herbert Hobbs. Ann Arbor: J.W. Edwards, Inc., [1952].

> Octavo, original red cloth, dust jacket.
> 3 p. l., 222 p., frontispiece (portrait), [13] leaves of plates, portraits, maps.
> First edition. Signed copy.
> Reference: OCLC 727737.

Hobbs, William H. (1864–1952) [329]

Explorers of the Antarctic, by William Herbert Hobbs [etc.] With Fourteen Half-tone Portraits. New York: House of Field, Inc., Publishers, 1941.

> Octavo, original cream and blue linen with blue and silver labels.
> 334 p., frontispiece (portrait), [7] leaves of plates (portraits), map on endpapers.
> First edition.
> References: Spence 597, OCLC 616934.

Hobbs, William H. (1864–1952) [330]

Exploring About the North Pole of the

Winds, by William Herbert Hobbs [etc.].
Decorations by the Author. With 29
Illustrations and Maps. New York and
London: G.P. Putnam's Sons, 1930.

> Octavo, original blue cloth, dust jacket.
> viii, 376 p., frontispiece (portrait), [12] leaves of plates,
> illustrations (including maps, plan), portraits,
> maps on endpapers.
> First edition.
> References: AB 7150, OCLC 1520853.

Hobbs, William H. (1864–1952) [331]

On Some Misrepresentations of Antarctic
History. A Review of the Discoveries of
Antarctica within the American Sector as
Revealed by Maps and Documents. By
William Herbert Hobbs, University of
Michigan . . . Transactions of the American
Philosophical Society held at Philadelphia
for Promoting useful knowledge. New
Series, Volume XXXI, Part I, January
1939. [London]: William Clowes & Sons,
[1939].

> Octavo, original blue printed wrappers.
> Reprinted from *The Geographical Journal* 94 (October
> 1939): 309–330, 2 maps.
> Reference: Spence 2272.

Hobbs, William H. (1864–1952) [332]

Peary, by William Herbert Hobbs. With 27
Maps, 13 Half-tones, 10 Records and
Diagrams and 36 Drawings by the Author
after Photographs by Peary and others.
New York: The Macmillan Company,
1936.

> Octavo, original blue cloth, dust jacket.
> xv, 502 p., frontispiece (portrait), illustrations, 7 plates,
> portraits, diagrams, maps (2 folded).
> First edition. Presentation copy from author.
> References: AB 7160, Spence 596, OCLC 1375070.

Hobbs, William H. (1864–1952) [333]

The Progress of Discovery and Exploration
within the Arctic Region [by] William
Herbert Hobbs. [Syracuse, NY]:

Association of American Geographers,
c.1937.

> Quarto.
> Reprinted from *Annals of The Association of American
> Geographers* 27, no. 1 (March 1937): 1–22. 4
> maps.
> Signed by author.
> References: AB 7161, OCLC 22996468.

Holland, Clive

(See Cooke, Alan; Markham, Clements
Robert, Sir)

Hood, Robert (1797–1821) [334]

To the Arctic by Canoe 1819–1821. The
Journal and Paintings of Robert Hood,
Midshipman with Franklin. Edited by C.
Stuart Houston. Montreal and London:
McGill-Queen's University Press [for] The
Arctic Institute of North America, [1974].

> Large quarto, beige cloth with brown and gilt titles,
> dust jacket.
> xxxv, 217 p., [12] leaves of plates (part color),
> illustrations, facsimiles, 5 maps.
> Reference: OCLC 1384343.

Hooper, William H. (1827–1854) [335]

Ten Months among the Tents of the Tuski,
with Incidents of an Arctic Boat
Expedition in Search of Sir John Franklin,
as Far as the MacKenzie River, and Cape
Bathurst. By Lieut. W.H. Hooper, R.N.
With a Map and Illustrations. London:
John Murray, 1853.

> Octavo, original purple cloth, gilt titles. On spine: The
> Tents of the Tuski.
> xv, [1], 417 p., [1] p., color frontispiece, 3 plates
> (color), illustrations, map (folded.)
> First edition.
> References: AB 7395, OCLC 6806896.

Hoppin, Benjamin (1851–1923) [336]

A Diary Kept While with the Peary Arctic
Expedition of 1896, by B. Hoppin. [New
Haven, Conn.? : s.n.], 1900.

> Octavo, original gray cloth with gilt titles.

83 p., frontispiece (map), 1 plate.
References: AB 7401, OCLC 11501276.

Hosking, Eric John and Bryan Sage [337]

Antarctic Wildlife: Photographs by Eric Hosking. Text by Bryan Sage. London and Canberra: Croom Helm, [1982].

> Quarto, original black cloth with gilt titles, dust jacket.
> 160 p., photographs (mostly color).
> Reference: OCLC 8911869.

Huish, Robert (1777–1850) [338]

The Last Voyage of Capt. Sir John Ross, R.N. Knt. to the Arctic Regions; for the Discovery of a Northwest Passage; Performed in the Years 1829–30–31–32 and 33. To Which is Prefixed an Abridgement of the Former Voyages of Ross, Parry & Other Celebrated Navigators to the Northern Regions. Compiled from Authentic Information and Original Documents, Transmitted by William Light, Purser's Steward to the Expedition. Illustrated by Engravings from Drawings Taken on the Spot. By Robert Huish [etc.]. London: John Saunders, MDCCCXXXVI [1836].

> Octavo, half calf, raised bands.
> 2 p.l., ii, 716, 44 p. (wanting), frontispiece (portrait), added title page (engraved), 1 folded table, 6 plates, 1 map.
> First edition.
> References: Sabin 33626, TPL 1779, AB 7529, OCLC 2103756.

Hummel, Monte (1946–) [339]

Arctic Wildlife [by] Monte Hummel. [Secaucus, N.J.]: Chartwell Books, Inc., [1984].

> Folio, original pictorial cloth, dust jacket.
> 160 p., color illustrations.
> Reference: OCLC 13071482.

Hunt, William R. [340]

Arctic Passage: The Turbulent History of the Land and People of the Bering Sea, 1697–1975 [by] William R. Hunt. New York: Charles Scribners Sons, [1975].

> Octavo, original turquoise cloth, dust jacket.
> xv, 395 p., illustrations, map.
> First edition.
> Reference: OCLC 1530869.

Hunt, William R. [341]

To Stand at the Pole: The Dr. Cook—Admiral Peary North Pole Controversy [by] William R. Hunt. New York: Stein and Day, Publishers, 1981.

> Octavo, blue cloth spine on yellow boards, dust jacket.
> 288 p., [9] leaves of plates, illustrations, map.
> First edition.
> Reference: OCLC 7460137.

Huntford, Roland (1927–) [342]

The Amundsen Photographs. Edited and Introduced by Roland Huntford. New York: The Atlantic Monthly Press, [1987].

> Medium quarto, brown cloth with gilt titles, dust jacket.
> 199 p., frontispiece (portrait), photographs (mostly color).
> First American edition.
> Copies One and Two.
> Reference: OCLC 16276743.

Huntford, Roland (1927–) [343]

Scott & Amundsen, by Roland Huntford. New York: G.P. Putnam's Sons, [1980].

> Octavo, original black cloth with silver titles, dust jacket.
> xx, 665 p. including index and bibliography, [16] leaves of plates, 13 maps.
> First American edition.
> Reference: OCLC 6092576.

Huntford, Roland (1927–) [344]

Shackleton [by] Roland Huntford. New York: Atheneum, 1986.

> Octavo, black cloth with white spine, silver and gilt titles, dust jacket.
> xx, 774, [1] p., [12] leaves of plates, 9 maps, map on endpapers.

Hurley, Frank (1890–1962) **[345]**
Argonauts of the South, [by] Captain
Frank Hurley [etc.]. Being a Narrative of
Voyagings and Polar Seas and Adventures
in the Antarctic with Sir Douglas Mawson
and Sir Ernest Shackleton. With 75
Illustrations and Maps. New York and
London: G.P. Putnam's Sons, 1925.
> Octavo, original green cloth with gilt titles.
> xv, 290 p., frontispiece, [35] leaves of plates, 2 folded
> maps.
> References: Spence 615, OCLC 1346057.

Hurley, Frank (1890–1962)
(See Ponting, Herbert George)

Hutchison, Isobel Wylie (1889–)
[346]
On Greenland's Closed Shore: The
Fairyland of the Arctic, by Isobel Wylie
Hutchison. With a Preface by Dr. Knud
Rasmussen. With Illustrations and Map.
Edinburgh and London: William
Blackwood & Sons Ltd., 1930.
> Octavo, original green cloth with gilt titles, dust jacket.
> xviii, 395 p. frontispiece (portrait), [11] leaves of plates,
> map.
> References: AB 7599, OCLC 13630811.

Huxley, Elspeth (1907–) **[347]**
Scott of the Antarctic [by] Elspeth Huxley.
New York: Atheneum, 1978.
> Octavo, original red cloth with gilt titles.
> xiv p., 1 l., 303 p., [8] leaves of plates, 3 maps.
> Reference: OCLC 3516431.

Hyde, Alexander (1814–81) et al. [348]
The Frozen Zone and Its Explorers: A
Comprehensive Record of Voyages,
Travels, Discoveries, Adventures and
Whale-Fishing in the Arctic Regions for
One Thousand Years. With a Full and
Reliable History of the Late Expedition
under Charles Francis Hall in the Ill-fated
Polaris, Embracing the Discoveries and
Death of Its Commander; the Fearful Six
Months' Drift on the Ice; John Herran's
Diary; the Wreck of the Steamer; and the
Final Escape of Captain Buddington [sic]
and Companions in Open Boats. Also, an
Account of the Search Made for the
Castaways by the Tigress and Juniata.
Illustrated with One Hundred and
Seventy-Five Engravings and Maps.
Written, and Compiled from Authentic
Sources, by Alexander Hyde, A.M., Rev.
A.C. Baldwin, and Rev. W.L. Gage. To
Which is Added a Sketch of Dr. Kane, by
Prof. Charles W. Shields, D.D., of
Princeton College. Published by
Subscription Only. Hartford, Connecticut:
Columbian Book Company; Toledo, Ohio:
W.E. Bliss & Co.; San Francisco,
California: F. Dewing & Co., 1874.
> Thick octavo, embossed original dark green cloth with
> gilt titles.
> xvi, [1], 800 p., plus [4] p. of advertisements,
> frontispiece, 68 plates (including portraits), 5
> maps (1 folded), facsimiles. Stained.
> References: AB 7619, OCLC 3474519.

Illustrated Arctic News **[349]**
Facsimile of the Illustrated Arctic News,
Published on Board H.M.S. Resolute:
Capt. Horatio T. Austin, C.B. in Search of
the Expedition under Sir John Franklin.
Dedicated by Special Permission to the
Lords Commissioners of the Admiralty, by
Their Lordships Obedient Servants, Lieut.
Sherard Osborne [!] & Mr. Geo. F.
McDougall. London: Published by
Ackermann & Co., By appointment to Her
Majesty the Queen, H.R.H. Prince Albert,
H.R.H. The Dutchess of Kent & The
Royal Family. 15th March 1852. Contains
Five Numbers: October 31, November 30,

The staging of grand balls and theatrical productions was a time-honored way of coping with the tedium of a polar winter. Another was the production of a ship-board newspaper. The *Illustrated Arctic News* was handwritten and circulated on board Captain Horatio Austin's *Resolute* when she wintered in 1850 on her Franklin searching expedition. On the return to London, a facsimile of the paper was published to cater to the tremendous interest in Arctic affairs.

Show Bill from *Facsimile of the Ilustrated Arctic News* (1852) [**349**]

December 31, 1850; January 31 and
March 14, 1851.

> Large folio, blue decorated cloth with gilt titles.
> 57 p., color title vignette, illustrations (part colored),
>   lithographed.
> First edition.
> Reference: OCLC 7537222.

Ingstad, Helge Marcus (1899–   ) [350]
Land Under The Pole Star: A Voyage to
the Norse Settlements of Greenland and
the Saga of the People That Vanished [by]
Helge Ingstad. Translated from the
Norwegian by Naomi Walford. London:
Jonathan Cape, 1966.

> Octavo, blue cloth spine on gray boards, gilt titles,
>   dust jacket.
> ix, [1], 11–381 p., 46 plates, illustrations, facsimiles,
>   maps, maps on endpapers.
> Reference: OCLC 2933298.

**International Polar Expedition,
    1882–1883.**   [351]
Report of the International Polar
Expedition to Point Barrow, Alaska, in
Response to the Resolution of the House
of Representatives of December 11, 1884.
Washington: Government Printing Office,
1885.

> Large quarto, original red cloth with gilt titles.
> 2 p. l., 3–695 p., color frontispiece, 20 plates (2 color),
>   illustrations, plan, 2 maps (1 folded.)
> Report of Lt. P.H. Ray, Expedition Commander.
> U.S. 48th cong., 2d sess., H. Ex. Doc. 44.
> References: AB 7747, OCLC 3346550.

**International Symposium on Arctic
    Geology**   [352]
Geology of the Arctic: Proceedings of the
First International Symposium on Arctic
Geology. Held in Calgary, Alberta, January
11–13, 1960, under the Auspices of the
Alberta Society of Petroleum Geologists.
[Toronto]: University of Toronto Press,
1961.

> Octavo, 2 volumes, original blue cloth with gilt titles.
> Paged continuously. Volume 1: xv, 732 p. illustrations,
>   profiles, tables, maps; Volume 2: vi, [4], 737–
>   1196 p., illustrations, profiles, tables, maps.
> Reference: OCLC 545238.

Jack, Robert   [353]
Arctic Living: The Story of Grimsey, [by]
Robert Jack. Foreword by Vilhjalmur
Stefansson. Toronto: The Ryerson Press,
[1955].

> Octavo, original brown cloth with yellow titles, dust
>   jacket.
> x, 181 p., [2] leaves of plates.
> Inscribed by author.
> Reference: OCLC 2677746.

Jacka, Fred and Eleanor
(See Mawson, Douglas. Mawson's
Antarctic Diaries)

Jackson, Frederick G. (1860–1938)
                                    [354]
A Thousand Days in the Arctic, by
Frederick G. Jackson [etc.]. With Preface
by Admiral Sir F. Leopold McClintock
[etc.]. Illustrated from Photographs by the
Author and Drawings by R.W. Macbeth,
A.R.A., Clifford Carlton, Harry C.
Edwards, & F.W. Frohawk, from Data
Furnished by the Author. With Five
Original Maps. In Two Volumes. New
York and London: Harper & Brothers,
1899.

> Octavo, 2 volumes, original blue cloth with gilt titles.
> Volume 1: xxi, 551 p., 2 frontispiece (portraits), 39
>   plates, illustrations, portraits, 2 folded maps;
>   Volume 2: xv, 580 p., frontispiece (portrait), 23
>   plates, illustrations, portraits, 3 folded maps.
> First English edition.
> References: OCLC 11433696.

Jackson, Frederick G. (1860–1938)
                                    [355]
A Thousand Days in the Arctic, by
Frederick G. Jackson [etc.]. With Preface

by Admiral Sir F. Leopold McClintock [etc.]. Illustrated from Photographs by the Author and Drawings by R.W. Macbeth, A.R.A., Clifford Carleton, Harry C. Edwards, & F.W. Frohawk, from Data Furnished by the Author. With Five Original Maps. New York and London: Harper & Brothers, 1899.

> Thick octavo, original cloth, gilt edges.
> xxiii, 940 p., plus [4] p. of advertisements, frontispiece (portrait), 83 plates (1 folded), illustrations, portraits, 5 folded maps.
> References: AB 7943, OCLC 2845073.

James, Thomas (1593?-1635?)   **[356]**
The Strange and Dangerovs Voyage of Captaine Thomas James, in His Intended Discovery of the Northwest Passage into the South Sea. VVherein the Miseries Indvred both Going, Wintering, Returning; and the Rarities Observed, Both Philosophicall and Mathematicall, Are Related in This Iournall of It. Published by His Maiesties Command. To Which are Added, a Plat or Card for the Sayling in Those Seas. Divers Little Tables of the Author's, of the Variation of the Compasse, &c. With an Appendix Concerning Longitude, by Master Henry Gellibrand Astronomy Reader of Gresham Colledge in London. And an Advise Concerning the Philosophy of these Late Discoveryes, by W.W. London, Printed by Iohn Legatt, for Iohn Partridge. 1633.

> Small quarto, early nineteenth century mottled calf, modern folded chemise and morocco-backed slipcase. Arms blind-stamped on sides, edges speckled in green, smooth spine in six gilt-panelled compartments. On spine of slipcase: James's Voyage.
> [4], 120, [6] p., 1 l., 16 p., folded engraved map with portrait vignette.
> First edition.
> References: Sabin 35711, OCLC 15648089.

James, Thomas (1593?-1635?)   **[357]**
Captain Thomas James's Strange and

Dangerous Voyage in His Intended Discovery of the North-West Passage into the South Sea, in the Years 1631 and 1632. Wherein the Miseries Indured, both Going, Wintering, Returning, and the Rarities Observed, both Philosophical and Mathematical, Are Related at Large. Published by His Majestie's Command. To Which are Added a Plat or Card for the Sailing in Those Seas: Also Divers Little Tables of the Author's, of the Variation of the Compass, &c. With an Appendix Concerning Longitude, By Mr. Henry Gellibrand, Astronomy Reader of Gresham-College, London. And an Advice Concerning the Philosophy of these Late Discoveries, by W.W. [London]: Printed for Henry Lintot and John Osborn, at the Golden-Ball in Pater-noster Row, [1747].

> Detached from Awnsham Churchill, *Collection of Voyages and Travels* (London, 1732), p. [407]-466.
> Modern burgundy paper wrappers.

Jérémie, Nicholas (1669?-1732)   **[358]**
Twenty Years of York Factory, 1694–1714. Jérémie's Account of Hudson Strait and Bay, Translated from the French Edition of 1720, with Notes and Introduction, by R. Douglas, M.A. and J.N. Wallace, D.L.S. Ottawa: Thorburn and Abbott, 1926.

> Octavo, original stiff dark gray printed wrappers.
> 42 p., frontispiece, 2 plates, 3 maps (1 folded).
> References: AB 8107, OCLC 5151698.

Joerg, Wolfgang Louis Gottfried (1885–1952)   **[359]**
Brief History of Polar Exploration Since the Introduction of Flying by W.L.G. Joerg, American Geographical Society. To Accompany a Physical Map of the Arctic and a Bathymetric Map of the Antarctic. New York: American Geographical Society, 1930.

Quarto, in gray cloth slipcase.
iv, 50 p., 8 maps in text, 2 folded maps (unbound).
American Geographical Society. Special Publication
Number 11.
References: Spence 634, OCLC 2028383.

Joerg, Wolfgang Louis Gottfried (1885–1952) (editor) [360]

Problems of Polar Research: A Series of Papers by Thirty-one Authors. Edited by W.L.G. Joerg. New York: American Geographical Society, 1928.

Quarto, original gray cloth with gilt titles on black labels.
2 p. l., [iii]-iv p., 2 l., 3–479 p., illustrations, diagrams, maps (1 folded).
American Geographical Society. Special Publication Number 7.
References: Spence 633, OCLC 487431.

Joerg, Wolfgang Louis Gottfried (1885–1952) [361]

The Work of the Byrd Antarctic Expedition, 1928–1930. By W.L.G. Joerg, American Geographical Society. New York: American Geographical Society, 1930.

Octavo, original printed wrappers.
3 p. l, 71 p., illustrations (facsimiles), maps (2 folded).
References: Spence 636, OCLC 1800606.

Johansen, Hjalmar (1867–1913) [362]

With Nansen in the North: A Record of the Fram Expedition in 1893–96, by Hjalmar Johansen, Lieutenant in the Norwegian Army. Translated from the Norwegian by H.L. Braekstad. London, New York and Melbourne: Ward, Lock and Co. Limited, 1899.

Octavo, original blue cloth with gilt titles, joints weak.
viii, 351 p., plus 8 p. of advertisements, frontispiece (portrait), plates, illustrations, portrait, map, plates loose at p. 64, 312.
First English edition.
References: AB 8185, OCLC 2777037.

John, Brian (1940–) [363]

The World of Ice: The Natural History of the Frozen Regions [by] Brian John. London: Orbis Publishing, [1979].

Quarto, original blue cloth with gilt titles, dust jacket.
120 p., frontispiece, chiefly color photographs, color maps.
First English edition.
Reference: OCLC 16493016.

Johnson, Peter, Creina Bond, and Roy Siegfried [364]

Antarctica: No Single Country, No Single Sea. Text, Creina Bond and Roy Sigfried; Photography, Peter Johnson. New York: Mayflower Books, 1979.

Large quarto, original blue cloth with silver titles, dust jacket.
175, [1] p., frontispiece, color illustrations, color maps.
First American Edition.
Reference: OCLC 5980439.

Johnson, William N. [365]

Did Commander Peary "Achieve" the North Pole? An Analysis of Peary's Narrative, by W.N. Johnson. [Chicago: Printed by Dvorak & Weiser, 1915.]

Quarto, in original printed wrappers bound with cord.
2 p. l., 38, [1] p.
Reference: OCLC 6458065.

Joppien, Rüdiger

(See David, Andrew)

Joyce, Ernest E. Mills [366]

The South Polar Trail, by Ernest E. Mills Joyce. The Log of the Imperial Trans-Antarctic Expedition. With an Introduction by Hugh Robert Mill [etc.]. London: Duckworth, 1929.

Octavo, blue cloth covers.
220 p., frontispiece (portrait), 31 plates, 1 map.
First edition.
Reference: Spence 642.

Kane, Elisha Kent (1820–1857) [367]

Adrift in the Arctic Ice Pack. From the History of the First U.S. Grinnell Expedition in Search of Sir John Franklin. By Elisha Kent Kane, M.D. Edited by

Horace Kephart. New York: Outing
Publishing Company MCMXV [1915].

> Octavo, original decorated blue cloth.
> 7–402 p., plus 2 p. of advertisements, frontispiece
> (double map), illustrations.
> Outing Adventure Library, [no. 5]
> References: AB 8372, OCLC 8517446.

Kane, Elisha Kent (1820–1857)   [368]
Arctic Explorations: The Second Grinnell
Expedition in Search of Sir John Franklin,
1853, '54, '55. By Elisha Kent Kane,
M.D., U.S.N. Illustrated by Upwards of
Three Hundred Engravings, from Sketches
by the Author. The Steel Engravings
Executed under the Superintendence of
J.M. Butler, the Wood Engravings by Van
Ingen & Snyder. Philadelphia: Childs &
Peterson, 1856.

> Octavo, 2 volumes, original decorated purple cloth
> (faded) with gilt titles.
> Volume 1: 464 p., frontispiece (portrait), 11 plates,
> illustrations (including music), 2 maps; Volume 2:
> 467 p., frontispiece (portrait), added, engraved
> title-page, 7 plates, 1 folded diagram, 1 map.
> References: AB 8373, OCLC 2166415.

Kane, Elisha Kent (1820–1857)   [369]
Arctic Explorations: The Second Grinnell
Expedition in Search of Sir John Franklin,
1853, '54, '55. By Elisha Kent Kane,
M.D., U.S.N. Illustrated by Upwards of
Three Hundred Engravings, from Sketches
by the Author. The Steel Engravings
Executed under the Superintendence of
J.M. Butler, the Wood Engravings by Van
Ingen & Snyder. Philadelphia: Childs &
Peterson, 1856. [Copy 2]

> Octavo, 2 volumes, original decorated brown cloth
> (faded) with gilt titles.
> Volume 1: 464 p., frontispiece (portrait), 11 plates,
> illustrations (including music), 2 maps; Volume 2:
> 467 p., frontispiece (portrait), added, engraved
> title-page, 7 plates, 1 folded diagram, 1 map.
> References: AB 8373, OCLC 2166415.

Kane, Elisha Kent (1820–1857)   [370]
Arctic Explorations in Search of Sir John
Franklin. By Elisha Kent Kane, M.D.,
U.S.N. With Numerous Illustrations and a
Map. London, Edinburgh and New York:
T. Nelson and Sons, 1894.

> Octavo, original red cloth with gilt titles.
> x, [11]-443, [1] p., frontispiece (portrait), 13 plates,
> illustrations, folded map.
> Reference: OCLC 11450457.

Kane, Elisha Kent (1820–1857)   [371]
The Far North: Explorations in the Arctic
Regions, by Elisha Kent Kane, M.D.,
Commander, Second "Grinnell"
Expedition in Search of Sir John Franklin.
Edinburgh and London: Nimmo, 1874.

> Duodecimo, original decorated purple cloth, gilt
> edges.
> 228 p., plus 32 p. of advertisements, frontispiece,
> illustrations.
> 'The present volume is an epitome of 'Arctic
> Explorations,' an official account of the Second
> 'Grinnell' Expedition in search of Sir John
> Franklin." — Preface, p.6.
> Reference: OCLC 6351282.

Kane, Elisha Kent (1820–1857)   [372]
The U.S. Grinnell Expedition in Search of
Sir John Franklin. A Personal Narrative. By
Elisha Kent Kane, M.D., U.S.N. New
York: Harper & Brothers, Publishers,
1854.

> Octavo, original decorated purple cloth, new front
> endpapers.
> xi, [13]-552 p., frontispiece, [13] leaves of plates,
> illustrations, tables, maps (1 folded).
> First edition.
> References: AB 8381, OCLC 1333726.

**Kearns, William H., Jr. and
     Beverly Britton   [373]**
The Silent Continent, by William H.
Kearns, Jr. and Beverly Britton. Illustrated.
New York: Harper & Brothers Publishers,
[1955].

Octavo, turquoise cloth boards with black spine, dust jacket.
x p., 1 l., 237, [2] p., [8] leaves of plates, black and white illustrations, maps on endpapers.
First edition.
Reference: Spence 645.

Keating, Bern [374]

The Northwest Passage: From the Mathew to the Manhattan, 1497 to 1969. By Bern Keating, with Exclusive Color Photography by Dan Guravich. Chicago [etc.]: Rand McNally & Company, [1970].

Quarto, original blue cloth with gilt titles.
155, [4] p., illustrations (part color), portraits (part color), color maps.
Reference: OCLC 92933.

Keely, Robert N. (1860–   ) and Gwilym George Davis (1857–1918) [375]

In Arctic Seas: The Voyage of the "Kite" with the Peary Expedition, Together with a Transcript of the Log of the "Kite," by Robert N. Keely, Jr., [etc.]. and G.G. Davis [etc.]. Illustrated by Maps, Portraits and Photographic Views. Philadelphia: Rufus C. Hartranft, 1892.

Octavo, original blue cloth with gilt and silver titles.
vii, 524 p., frontispiece, illustrations (including facsimiles), 32 plates (1 color), portraits, 2 maps (1 folded).
First edition.
References: AB 8485, OCLC 2649911.

Kemp, Norman (1925–   ) [376]

The Conquest of the Antarctic, by Norman Kemp. New York: Philosophical Library, [1957].

Octavo, blue cloth with gilt titles, dust jacket.
3 p. l., 152 p., frontispiece, [7] leaves of plates, maps on endpapers.
References: Spence 648, OCLC 486932.

Kennedy, William (1813–1890) [377]

A Short Narrative of the Second Voyage of the Prince Albert, in Search of Sir John Franklin. By William Kennedy, Commanding the Expedition. With Illustrations, and a Map by Arrowsmith. London: W. H. Dalton, [1853].

Octavo, original decorated green cloth, gilt edges.
xiii, [1], xxv, [27]-202 p., frontispiece, 3 plates, folded map.
References: AB 8539, OCLC 10188012.

Kent, Rockwell (1882–1971) [378]

N by E [by] Rockwell Kent. New York: Literary Guild, 1930.

Octavo, original white cloth.
xi p., 281 p., 1 l., frontispiece, 14 plates, illustrations.
References: AB 8541, OCLC 486575.

Kent, Rockwell (1882–1971) [379]

Salamina, by Rockwell Kent. London: Faber & Faber Limited, [1936].

Octavo, original tan cloth.
352 p., 1 l., frontispiece, illustrations, 22 plates (1 color), portraits, folded map.
First English edition.
References: OCLC 13687376, cf. AB 8542.

Kent, Rockwell (1882–1971) [380]

Voyaging Southward from the Strait of Magellan, by Rockwell Kent. With Illustrations by the Author. New York and London: G.P. Putnam's Sons, 1924.

Large quarto, original decorated mustard yellow cloth, dust jacket.
xv, 184 p., frontispiece, 19 plates, illustrations, 4 maps, maps on endpapers.
First trade edition.
Reference: OCLC 1517425.

Kersting, Rudolf (1856–   ) [381]

The White World: Life and Adventures within the Arctic Circle Portrayed by Famous Living Explorers. Collected and Arranged for the Arctic Club by Rudolf Kersting. New York: Lewis, Scribner & Co., 1902.

Octavo, original pictorial blue cloth with gilt titles.

386 p., frontispiece, illustrations, 27 plates (plate at p.
15 detached), portraits, music.
At head of title: Issued under the auspices of the Arctic
Club.
References: AB 8556, OCLC 3006867.

Kimble, George Herbert Tinley (1908–) and Dorothy Good [382]

Geography of the Northlands. Edited by
George H.T. Kimble and Dorothy Good.
New York: The American Geographical
Society and John Wiley & Sons, Inc.;
London: Chapman & Hall, Ltd., [1955].

Octavo, original blue cloth with black labels.
x, 534 p., illustrations, maps (1 folded).
American Geographical Society. Special Publication;
Number 32.
Reference: OCLC 1179517.

King, H.G.R. [383]

The Antarctic, by H.G.R. King. London:
Blandford Press, [1969].

Octavo, blue cloth with gilt titles, dust jacket.
276 p., [12] leaves of plates (color), illustrations,
portraits, facsimiles, maps, maps on endpapers.
First edition.
Reference: Spence 654.

King, H.G.R.

(See also Campbell, Victor; Wilson,
Edward Adrian)

King, Richard (1811?-1876) [384]

Narrative of a Journey to the Shores of the
Arctic Ocean, in 1833, 1834, and 1835;
under the Command of Capt. Back, R.N.
By Richard King, M.R.C.S. &c., Surgeon
and Naturalist to the Expedition. In Two
Volumes. London: Richard Bentley,
Publishers in Ordinary to His Majesty,
1836.

Octavo, 2 volumes, rebound in three-quarter blue
morocco, raised bands, gilt titles. Minor damage
to title-pages of volumes 1 and 2: top right
corner of title-page for volume 1 is missing. Letter
rubbed off from volume 2 title-page. Binder's
title: The Arctic Ocean.

Volume 1: xv, [1], 312 p., frontispiece; Volume 2: viii,
321 p., frontispiece, 1 plate, 1 map.
Presentation Copy from author.
References: AB 8708, OCLC 1677940.

Kirwan, Laurence Patrick [385]

A History of Polar Exploration, by L.P.
Kirwan. New York: W.W. Norton &
Company, Inc., [1960].

Octavo, original blue cloth, dust jacket. Copy heavily
marked.
x, 374 p., [6] leaves of plates, illustrations, maps (1
folded), maps on endpapers.
First American edition.
References: Spence 665, OCLC 486318.

Klutschak, Heinrich [386]

Overland to Starvation Cove: With the
Inuit in Search of Franklin, 1878–1880
[by] Heinrich Klutschak. Translated and
edited by William Barr. Toronto, Buffalo
and London: University of Toronto Press,
1987.

Octavo, dust jacket.
xxxi, [3], 261 p., illustrations, portraits, 3 maps.
Reference: OCLC 17251632.

Knight, Errol Lorne

(See Stefansson, Vilhjalmur)

Koldewey, Karl (1837–1908) [387]

The German Arctic Expedition of 1869–
70, and Narrative of the Wreck of the
"Hansa" in the Ice. By Captain Koldewey,
Commander of the Expedition, Assisted by
Members of the Scientific Staff. With
Numerous Woodcuts, Two Coloured
Maps, Two Portraits on Steel, and Four
Chromo Lithographic Illustrations.
Translated and Abridged by the Rev. L.
Mercier [etc.]; and Edited by H.W. Bates
[etc.]. London: Sampson Low, Marston,
Low & Searle, 1874.

Quarto, original green cloth with black, silver and gold
decorations. Joints weak.

viii, 590 p., color frontispiece, 30 plates (3 color),
illustrations, 2 portraits, map, plan.
References: AB 9024, OCLC 5207882.

Kotzebue, Otto von (1787–1846) [388]
A Voyage of Discovery, into the South Sea
and Beering's Straits, for the Purpose of
Exploring a North-East Passage,
Undertaken in the Years 1815–1818, at the
Expense of His Highness the Chancellor of
the Empire, Count Romanzoff, in the Ship
Rurick, under the Command of the
Lieutenant in the Russian Imperial Navy,
Otto von Kotzebue. Illustrated with
Numerous Plates and Maps. In Three
Volumes. London: Printed for Longman,
Hurst, Rees, Orme, and Brown, 1821.

Octavo, 3 volumes, contemporary calf, raised bands,
rebacked, corners repaired.
Volume 1: xv, [1] 358 p., color frontispiece (portrait), 3
color plates, 2 maps (folded); Volume 2: 433, [1]
p., color frontispiece (portrait), 2 color plates, 4
maps (3 folded; Volume 3: 442 p., color
frontispiece (portrait), 1 plate, tables, 2 maps.
References: AB 9195, Howes K258, OCLC 647459.

Kpomassie, Tété-Michel [389]
An African In Greenland [by] Tété
Kpomassie. Translated by James Kirkup
from the Original French. Preface by Jean
Malaurie. San Diego, New York, London:
Harcourt Brace Jovanovich, Publishers,
[1983].

Octavo, original pink boards, blue spine with silver
titles, dust jacket.
xix p., 2 l., 3–298 p., [4] leaves of plates, map.
Reference: OCLC 8954712.

**LaChambre, Henri (1846–1904)
and Alexis Machuron [390]**
Andrée's Balloon Expedition in Search of
the North Pole, by Henri LaChambre and
Alexis Machuron (Andrée's Assistants in
the Preparation, Equipment and Departure
of the Balloon). With Over Fifty

Illustrations. New York: Frederick A.
Stokes Company, Publishers, [1898].

Octavo, original blue cloth with white titles.
306 p., frontispiece, 7 plates, illustrations, portraits.
First American edition.
References: AB 9536, OCLC 1456339.

Lamb, W. Kaye (1904–)
(See Mackenzie, Alexander, Sir. Journals
and Letters; Vancouver, George. Voyage of
George Vancouver)

Lanman, Charles [391]
Farthest North: or, The Life and
Explorations of Lieutenant James Booth
Lockwood, of the Greely Arctic
Expedition. By Charles Lanman. New
York: D. Appleton and Company, 1885.

Octavo, blue pictorial cloth with gilt titles.
333 p., frontispiece (portrait), 4 plates, folded map.
First edition.

Lansing, Alfred [392]
Endurance: Shackleton's Incredible
Voyage. New York, Toronto, and London:
McGraw-Hill Book Company, Inc.,
[1959].

Octavo, original blue cloth with silver titles, dust jacket.
vii, [1], 282, [2] p., frontispiece, [6] leaves of plates,
maps on endpapers.
First edition.
References: Spence 680, OCLC 597422.

**Lantzeff, George V. and
Richard A. Pierce [393]**
Eastward to Empire: Exploration and
Conquest on the Russian Open Frontier,
to 1750. Montreal and London: McGill-
Queens University Press, 1973.

Octavo, original white cloth with blue titles, dust
jacket.
x, 276 p., 15 maps.

Larsen, Henry A. [394]
The North-West Passage, 1940–1942 and

1944. The Famous Voyages of the Royal Canadian Mounted Police Schooner "St. Roch," Sergeant Henry Larsen, F.R.G.S., Commander. By kind permission of the Commissioner of the Royal Canadian Mounted Police. [Ottawa: Queen's Printer, 1969?].

> Original paper wrappers.
> 51 p., black and white photo illustrations, maps.
> First published by Vancouver City Archives in 1948.
> Reference: Cf. OCLC 203283.

Lashly, William [395]
Under Scott's Command: Lashly's Antarctic Diaries. Edited by A.R. Ellis, Lieutenant-Commander, R.N. With an Introduction by Sir Vivian Fuchs. New York: Taplinger Publishing Company, [1969].

> Octavo, original green cloth with gilt titles, dust jacket.
> 159, [1] p., [4] leaves of plates, diagram, map.
> First U.S. edition.
> Reference: Spence 686 (London edition), OCLC 28273.

Laub, Vilhelm
(See Mikkelsen, Eijnar. Alabama Expeditionen)

Lee, Charles (1913–) [396]
Snow, Ice and Penguins, by Charles Lee. A Cavalcade of Antarctic Adventures. New York: Dodd, Mead & Company, [1950].

> Octavo, original blue cloth with silver titles, dust jacket.
> xiv, 417 p., map on endpapers.
> References: Spence 699, OCLC 1522064.

Leslie, Alexander
(See Nordenskjöld, Adolf Erik. Arctic Voyages)

Leslie, John, Sir (1766–1832) [397]
Narrative of Discovery and Adventure in the Polar Seas and Regions: With Illustrations of Their Climate, Geology, and Natural History; and an Account of the Whale-Fishery. By Professor Leslie, Professor Jameson, and Hugh Murray, Esq., F.R.G.S. New York: Printed by J & J Harper, [1832].

> Duodecimo, original printed brown cloth covers, joints cracked.
> vi, [7]-373 p., plus 1 l. of advertisements, frontispiece (map), 6 plates, illustrations.
> Added title-page: Discovery and Adventure in the Polar Seas and Regions.
> At head of the title: Harper's Stereotype Edition.
> References: AB 9945, OCLC 12770464.

Letters Written during the Late Voyage [398]
Letters Written During the Late Voyage of Discovery in the Western Arctic Sea. By an Officer of the Expedition. London: Printed for Sir Richard Phillips and Co., 1821.

> Octavo, cloth-backed marbled boards, gilt titles.
> iv, 124 p., frontispiece (map), [3] leaves of plates.
> References: AB 9949, OCLC 13624309.

Levick, George Murray (1876–) [399]
Antarctic Penguins. A Study of Their Social Habits, by Dr. G. Murray Levick, R.N., Zoologist to the British Antarctic Expedition [1910–1913]. London: William Heinemann, [1914].

> Octavo, original green decorative cloth.
> x, 139, [2] p., frontispiece, [55] leaves of plates, tables.
> References: Spence 705, OCLC 685272.

Lewis, David (1917–) [400]
Ice Bird: The First Single-Handed Voyage to Antarctica, by David Lewis. New York: W.W. Norton & Company, Inc., [1976].

> Octavo, original blue cloth with gilt titles, dust jacket.
> 223, [1] p., [12] leaves of plates, illustrations, diagrams, maps on endpapers.
> First American edition.
> References: Spence 706 (London edition), OCLC 1818513.

Limb, Sue and Patrick Cordingley [401]
Captain Oates, Soldier and Explorer, [by]
Sue Limb and Patrick Cordingley. London:
B.T. Batsford, Ltd., [1982].

> Octavo, original blue cloth with gilt titles, dust jacket.
> 184 p., [12] leaves of plates, illustrations, maps.
> First edition.
> Reference: OCLC 9288198.

Lindsay, David Moore (1862–   ) [402]
A Voyage to the Arctic in the Whaler
Aurora, by David Moore Lindsay, F.R.G.S.
Boston: Dana Estes & Company,
Publishers, [1911].

> Octavo, original blue cloth with gilt and white titles.
> 3 p. l., v-ix, 11–223 p., frontispiece, 55 plates
>   (including portraits), illustrations.
> First edition.
> References: AB 10168, OCLC 1823198.

Liotard, André-Frank and
**   Robert Pommier   [403]**
Terre Adelie, 1949–1952 [par] André-
Frank Liotard [&] Robert Pommier.
Préface de Paul-Émile Victor. Paris:
Arthaud, [1952].

> Quarto, original wrappers.
> 47, [1] p., frontispiece (portraits), [34] leaves of plates
>   (part color).
> Inscribed by Paul-Émile Victor.
> Reference: OCLC 11082926.

Liversidge, Douglas (1913–   )   [404]
The Last Continent, [by] Douglas
Liversidge. [London]: Jarrolds, [1958].

> Octavo, original red cloth with silver titles, dust jacket.
> 248 p., [8] leaves of plates, 2 maps (1 folded).
> First edition.
> References: Spence 719, OCLC 498937.

Lloyd, Frederick Ebenezer John
**   (1859–1933)   [405]**
Two Years in the Regions of Icebergs, and
What I Saw There. By the Rev. F.E.J.
Lloyd [etc.]. Published under the
Direction of the Committee of General

Literature and Education Appointed by the
Society for Promoting Christian
Knowledge. London: Society for
Promoting Christian Knowledge; New
York: E. & J.B. Young & Co., [1886].

> Duodecimo, pictorial blue cloth.
> 127, [1] p., plus 8 p. of advertisements, frontispiece,
>   illustrations.
> Reference: OCLC 4166752.

Lockley, Ronald
(See Adams, Richard)

Loomis, Chauncey C. (1930–   )   [406]
Weird and Tragic Shores: The Story of
Charles Francis Hall, Explorer [by]
Chauncey C. Loomis. New York: Alfred A.
Knopf, 1971.

> Octavo, original ivory cloth, dust jacket.
> xiv, 367, xii p., 2 l., [8] leaves of plates (mostly
>   portraits), maps.
> First edition.
> Reference: OCLC 136234.

Lopez, Barry Holstun (1945–   )   [407]
Arctic Dreams: Imagination and Desire in a
Northern Landscape [by] Barry Lopez.
New York: Charles Scribner's Sons,
[1986].

> Octavo, dust jacket.
> xxix p., 1 l., 464 p., illustrations, maps.
> Signed by author.
> First edition.
> Reference: OCLC 12665576.

Lucas, Frederic A. (1852–1929)   [408]
Explorations in Newfoundland and
Labrador in 1887, made in Connection
with the Cruise of the U.S. Fish
Commission Schooner Grampus, by
Frederic A. Lucas. Washington:
Government Printing Office, 1891.

> Octavo, original printed wrappers.
> Pp. 709–728., with Plate CVI: frontispiece (map).
> Detached from the *Report of the United States*
>   *National Museum, 1888-'89.*
> Reference: OCLC 11020263.

Lundborg, Einar (1896–   )   [409]

The Arctic Rescue: How Nobile Was
Saved, by Einar Lundborg, Captain of the
Swedish Air Force. Translated by Alma
Luise Olson. New York: The Viking Press
MCMXXIX [1929].

> Octavo, original blue cloth with yellow titles.
> 221 p., frontispiece (portrait), [28] leaves of plates,
>   illustrations (including facsimiles).
> Maps on endpapers.
> Signed by author.
> References: AB 10459, OCLC 1577236.

Lyon, George Francis (1795–1832)   [410]

[Mounted Proofs, on India Paper, of
Engravings by Edward Finden for the
Journal of Parry's Second Expedition (**541**
below). London, 1824].

> A complete set of the twenty six plates. In blue cloth
>   drop-spine box with gilt titles on blue leather
>   label.
> Binder's title: Proof Plates Parry's Second Voyage.
> References: AB 13142, Sabin 58864, Hill p. 226,
>   Lande 1385, Smith 6965.

Lyon, George Francis (1795–1832)   [411]

A Brief Narrative of an Unsuccessful
Attempt to Reach Repulse Bay through Sir
Thomas Rowe's "Welcome," in His
Majesty's Ship Griper, in the Year
MDCCCXXIV. By Captain G.F. Lyon,
R.N. With a Chart and Engravings.
London: John Murray, MDCCCXXV
[1825].

> Octavo, contemporary straight grained calf (slightly
>   rubbed), raised bands, red label on spine, front
>   joint cracked.
> xvi, 198, [2] p., frontispiece (portrait), 5 plates, folded
>   map.
> First edition.
> Plate facing p. 55 has been bound as frontispiece;
>   map faces p.1. Binder's title: Lyon's Attempt to
>   Reach Repulse Bay.
> References: AB 10530, Sabin 42851, OCLC 13928430.

Lyon, George Francis (1795–1832)   [412]

The Private Journal of Captain G.F. Lyon
of H.M.S. Hecla, during the Recent
Voyage of Discovery under Captain Parry.
With a Map and Plates. London: John
Murray, 1824.

> Octavo, three-quarter polished green calf on green
>   boards, marbled edges, raised bands, gilt titles
>   on red leather labels.
> xi, [1], 468p., frontispiece, [6] leaves of plates, folded
>   map.
> References: AB 10531, OCLC 13965259.

Lyons, Henry George, Sir (1864–1944)   [413]

Miscellaneous Data Compiled by Colonel
H.G. Lyons, F.R.S. London: Printed and
Published by Harrison and Sons, Ltd., for
the Committee of the Captain Scott
Antarctic Fund, 1924.

> Quarto, original green printed wrappers.
> 75 p., large folded plan of the "Terra Nova" in rear
>   pocket, illustrations.
> At head of title: British (Terra Nova) Antarctic
>   Expedition, 1910–1913.
> References: Spence 730, OCLC 13629540.

McCain, Charles W.   [414]

History of the SS. "Beaver": Being a
Graphic and Vivid Sketch of This Noted
Pioneer Steamer and Her Romantic Cruise
for Over Half a Century on the Placid
Island-Dotted Waters of the North Pacific.
Also Containing a Description of the
Hudson's Bay Company from Its
Formation in 1670, Down to the Present
Time. Biography of Captain McNeill. The
Narrative of a Fraser River Prospector of
1859. Historical Momentoes of the
Beaver's Copper Remains. The Sad Ending
of the Author's Last Trip in Search of Old-
time Naval Relics. Important
Developments in Steam Since its

1. W. H. J. Browne, "The Bivouac," from his *Ten Coloured Views* (1850) [**109**]

2. Samuel G. Cresswell, "Sledging over Hummocky Ice," from his *A Series of Eight Sketches in Colour* (1854) [**165**]

MELVILLE ISLAND FROM BANKS' LAND.

3. Samuel G. Cresswell, "Melville Island from Banks Land," from his *A Series of Eight Sketches in Colour* (1854) [165]

4. Fridtjof Nansen, "Sunset off the North Coast of Asia," from his *Farthest North* (1897) [500]

FIRST COMMUNICATION with the NATIVES of PRINCE REGENTS BAY, as Drawn by JOHN SACKHEOUSE and Presented to CAPT ROSS. Augt 10.1818.

London Published Feby. 1819 by John Murray, Albemarle Street.

5. "First Communication with the Natives" by the Eskimo artist John Sacheuse, from Sir John Ross, *A Voyage of Discovery* (1819) [**606**]

6. Gerard Mercator, *Septentrionalium terrarum descriptio* (1595) [**M22**]

7. James Hamilton, "*Advance* and *Rescue* in the Arctic" (ca. 1852) [**P7**]

8. James Hamilton, "Beechey Island" (ca. 1852) [P9]

9. Edward A. Wilson, "Cape Evans in Winter," from Apsley Cherry-Garrard, *The Worst Journey in the World* (1922) [**145**]

10. "The *Floyd Bennett* Wings its Flight over Antarctica," from Francis T. Miller, *The Fight to Conquer the Ends of the Earth* (1930) [**477**]

11. Frank W. Stokes, "The Iceberg Still Shone in the Reflection of the Last Sun-Rays," from Nils Otto Nordenskiöld, *Antarctica* (1905)

[**524**]

12. Edward A. Wilson, "Paraselene, June 15th, 1911," from Robert F. Scott, *Scott's Last Expedition* (1913) [**629**]

13. George E. Marston, Portrait of Frank Wild, from Ernest H. Shackleton, *The Antarctic Book* (1909)
[**642**]

14. George E. Marston, "A Quiet Evening on the Barrier," from Ernest H. Shackleton, *The Heart of the Antarctic* (1909) [**645**]

15. Richard B. Adams, Portrait of Richard E. Byrd (1928) [**P1**]

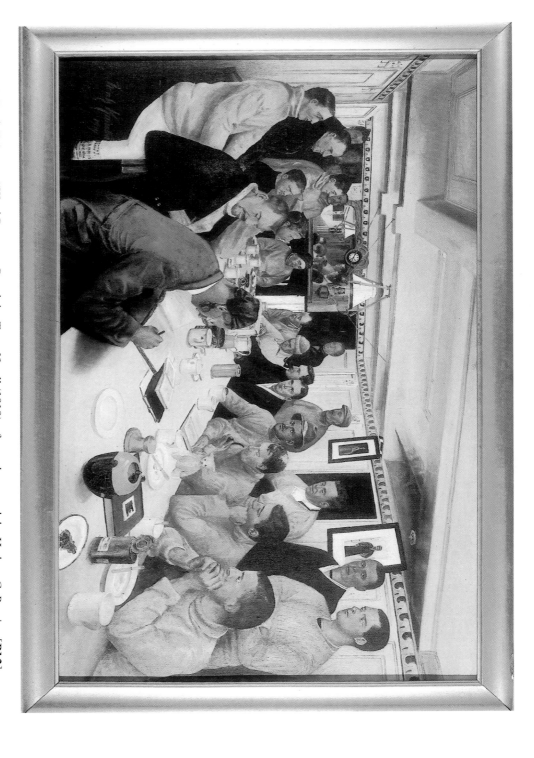

16. Frank Kniveton, "Ward Room on Board the *Terra Nova*" (1919), after a photograph by Herbert G. Ponting [**P12**]

Introduction in 1769, etc. Compiled by Charles W. McCain. Beautifully Illustrated. Vancouver, B.C.: [Evans & Hastings], 1894.

> Duodecimo, decorated red cloth with gilt titles and red edges.
> 99 p., [7] leaves of plates.
> Reference: Wickersham 4102a.

M'Clintock, Francis Leopold, Sir (1819–1907) [415]

The Voyage of the 'Fox' in the Arctic Seas. A Narrative of the Discovery of the Fate of Sir John Franklin and his Companions. By Captain M'Clintock, [etc.]. With Maps and Illustrations. London: John Murray, 1859.

> Octavo, original blue cloth with gilt titles.
> xxvii, 403 p., 3 p. of advertisements, frontispiece, [13] plates, folded facsimile, illustrations, 4 maps (3 folded, 1 folded in pocket).
> References: AB 10555, Sabine 43043, OCLC 13624551.

M'Clintock, Francis Leopold, Sir (1819–1907) [416]

The Voyage of the 'Fox' in the Arctic Seas. A Narrative of the Discovery of the Fate of Sir John Franklin and His Companions. By Captain M'Clintock, R.N., LL.D. With Maps and Illustrations. Boston: Ticknor and Fields, MDCCCLX [1860].

> Octavo, original decorated purple cloth, spine badly torn.
> xxiv, 375 p., frontispiece, 14 plates (1 folded), 4 maps (three folded).
> First American edition; "Author's Edition."
> References: AB 10556, Sabin 43043, OCLC 649567.

McClure, Robert John LeMesurier, Sir (1807–1873) [417]

The Discovery of the North-West Passage by H.M.S. "Investigator," Captain R. M'Clure, 1850, 1851, 1852, 1853, 1854. Edited by Captain Sherard Osborn [etc.], From the Logs and Journals of Capt. Robert Le M. M'Clure. Illustrated by Commander S. Gurney Cresswell, R.N. Second Edition. London: Longman, Brown, Green, Longmans, & Roberts, 1857.

> Octavo, original blue cloth.
> xix, 405 p., [4] leaves of plates, illustrations, 1 folded map (color).
> Reference: AB 10563.

M'Cormick, Robert (1800–1890) [418]

Voyages of Discovery in the Arctic and Antarctic Seas, and Round the World: Being Personal Narratives of Attempts to Reach the North and South Poles; and of an Open-boat Expedition up the Wellington Channel in Search of Sir John Franklin and Her Majesty's Ships "Erebus" and "Terror," in Her Majesty's Boat "Forlorn Hope," under the Command of the Author. To Which Are Added an Autobiography, Appendix, Portraits, Maps, and Numerous Illustrations. By Deputy Inspector-General R. M'Cormick [etc.]. In Two Volumes. London: Sampson Low, Marston, Searle and Rivington, 1884.

> Quarto, 2 volumes, later three-quarter red morocco and marbled boards.
> Volume 1: xx, 432 p., frontispiece (portrait), illustrations, 25 plates (5 folded), 2 maps; Volume 2: xii, 412 p., plus 16 p. of advertisements, frontispiece (portrait), illustrations, 33 plates, portrait, 2 maps (1 folded).
> References: AB 10582, Spence 747, OCLC 1275604.

McDonald, Archibald [419]

Peace River. A Canoe Voyage from Hudson's Bay to Pacific, by the late Sir George Simpson (Governor, Hon. Hudson's Bay Company) in 1828. Journal of the Late Chief Factor, Archibald McDonald, (Hon. Hudson's Bay Company), Who Accompanied Him. Edited, with Notes, by Malcolm McLeod,

Barrister, Etc. Ottawa: Published by J.
Durie & Son; Montreal: Dawson Bros.;
Toronto: Adam Stevenson & Co., 1872.
> Octavo, original blue cloth, gilt titles, blind stamped
> board decorations.
> xix, 119 p., map (folded).
> First edition.
> Reference: OCLC 5278637.

MacDonald, Edwin A. [420]
Polar Operations, by Edwin A.
MacDonald, Captain, U.S.N. (Retired).
Annapolis, MD: United States Naval
Institute, [1969].
> Square octavo, original white cloth with black titles,
> dust jacket.
> xiv, 239, [3] p., illustrations, maps.
> Reference: OCLC 21755.

M'Dougall, George Frederick [421]
The Eventful Voyage of H.M. Discovery
Ship "Resolute" to the Arctic regions in
Search of Sir John Franklin and the
Missing Crews of H.M. Discovery Ships
"Erebus" and "Terror," 1852, 1853, 1854.
To Which is Added, an Account of Her
Being Fallen In with by an American
Whaler after Her Abandonment in Barrow
Straits, and of Her Presentation to Queen
Victoria, by the Government of the United
States. By George F. M'Dougall, Master.
London: Longman, Brown, Green,
Longmans, & Roberts, 1857.
> Octavo, original burgundy cloth with gilt titles.
> xl, 530 p., 1 l., plus 24 p. of advertisements, color
> frontispiece, illustrations, 7 color plates, folded
> map.
> First edition.
> References: AB 10603, OCLC 1819464.

M'Dougall, George Frederick
(See also Illustrated Arctic News)

McFee, William (1881–1966) [422]
Sir Martin Frobisher, by William McFee.

London: John Lane, Bodley Head, Ltd.,
[1928].
> Octavo, original cloth.
> x p., 3 l., 288 p., frontispiece (portrait), 4 plates,
> illustrations, 4 maps (1 folded), maps on
> endpapers.
> Reference: OCLC 1330349.

McGinley, William A. (1831–1896)
[423]
Greely Relief Expedition. Reception of
Lieut. A.W. Greely, U.S.A., and His
Comrades, and of the Arctic Relief
Expedition, at Portsmouth, N.H. on
August 1 and 4, 1884. Account Prepared
at the Request of the Navy Department by
Rev. Wm. A. McGinley, of Portsmouth.
Washington: Government Printing Office,
1884.
> Octavo, original printed wrappers.
> 58 p.
> Reference: OCLC 1516000.

Machat, J. [424]
The Antarctic Question. Voyages to the
South Pole Since 1898, by J. Machat
[etc.]. From the Smithsonian Report for
1908, pages 451–480 (with Plate 1).
Washington: Government Printing Office,
1909.
> Printed wrappers.
> Title leaf plus p. 451–480, 2 maps (1 folded).
> Reference: OCLC 27414744.

Machuron, Alexis
(See LaChambre, Henri)

McInnes, William [425]
Report on a Part of the North West
Territories Drained by the Winisk and
Attawapiskat Rivers, by William McInnes.
Report on a Traverse through the
Southern Part of the North West
Territories From Lac Seul to Cat Lake in

1902, by Alfred W.G. Wilson. Ottawa: Government Printing Bureau, 1910.

> Octavo, original printed wrappers. Cover torn at spine.
> 58, 25, 7 p., frontispiece, 3 plates with large folded and colored map (no. 9A), 8 miles to inch showing explored routes on parts of the Albany, Severn and Winisk Rivers.
> References: AB 10630, OCLC 5948466.

MacInnis, Joseph B.   **[426]**
The Search for the Breadalbane [by] Joe MacInnis. New Abbot [England]: David & Charles, [1985].

> Octavo, orange cloth with gilt titles, dust jacket.
> 191 p., [11] leaves of plates, 1 map.
> Reference: OCLC 12946125, see also OCLC 23046944.

MacKenzie, Alexander, Sir (1763–1820)
                                            [427]
The Journals and Letters of Sir Alexander Mackenzie. Edited by W. Kaye Lamb. Cambridge [England]: Published for the Hakluyt Society at the University Press, 1970.

> Large octavo, blue cloth covers, dust jacket.
> viii, 551 p., frontispiece (portrait), facsimiles, 6 maps (4 folded).
> Works Issued by the Hakluyt Society, Extra Series, vol. 41.
> Reference: OCLC 136069.

MacKenzie, Alexander, Sir (1763–1820)
                                            [428]
Voyages from Montreal, on the River St. Laurence, through the Continent of North America, to the Frozen and Pacific Oceans; in the Years 1789 and 1793. With a Preliminary Account of the Rise, Progress, and Present State of the Fur Trade of that Country. Illustrated with Maps. By Alexander MacKenzie, Esq. London: Printed for T. Cadell, Jun. and W. Davies, Strand; Cobbett and Morgan, Pall-Mall; and W. Creech, at Edinburgh, by R. Noble, Old-Bailey. M.DCCC.I [1801].

> Quarto, contemporary half calf, raised bands, gilt titles.
> Binder's title: MacKenzie's Voyages.
> cxxxii, 412, [2] p., frontispiece (portrait), 3 folded maps.
> First edition.
> References: Howes M133, cf. OCLC 2844741).

McKinlay, William Laird   **[429]**
Karluk: The Great Untold Story of Arctic Exploration [by] William Laird McKinlay. Foreword by Magnus Magnusson. New York: St. Martin's Press, [1977].

> Octavo, original turquoise cloth with silver titles, dust jacket.
> xiv, 170 p., [16] leaves of plates, illustrations, 3 maps.
> "Family bookshelf edition."
> Reference: OCLC 2846587.

Mackintosh, Aeneas Lionel Acton (1879–1916)   **[430]**
Shackleton's Lieutenant. The Nimrod Diary of A.L.A. Mackintosh. British Antarctic Expedition 1907–09. Edited by Stanley Newman; Associate Editor, Richard McElrea; Research and Maps, David Harrowfield. Auckland [et al.]: Polar Publications, [1990].

> Octavo, black cloth with gilt spine titles, dust jacket.
> 144 p., frontispiece (portrait), [12] leaves of plates, maps, maps on endpapers.
> First edition.
> Reference: OCLC 26765666.

MacMillan, Donald B. (1874–   ) **[431]**
Etah and Beyond: or, Life within Twelve Degrees of the Pole, by Donald Baxter MacMillan. With Illustrations from Photographs by the Author. Boston and New York: Houghton Mifflin Company, 1927.

> Octavo, original blue cloth with gilt titles.
> xix, 287 p., frontispiece (portrait), [31] leaves of plates, map.
> First edition?
> Reference: OCLC 2482391.

MacMillan, Donald B. (1874–   ) **[432]**
Four Years in the White North, by Donald

B. MacMillan [etc.]. Illustrated from Photographs by the Author. New York and London: Harper & Brothers, Publishers, [1918].

> Octavo, original blue cloth with gilt titles.
> 10 p. l., 426 p., frontispiece, 46 plates, portraits, 3 maps (1 double).
> References: AB 10673, OCLC 887273.

MacMillan, Donald B. (1874–   )   [433]
How Peary Reached the Pole: The Personal Story of His Assistant, Donald B. MacMillan [etc.] with Illustrations Chiefly from Photographs Taken by the Author on This Expedition. Boston and New York: Houghton Mifflin Company; Cambridge [MA]: The Riverside Press, 1934.

> Octavo, original blue cloth with gilt titles.
> xii, 1 l., 306 p., frontispiece (portrait), 15 plates, facsimiles, maps on endpapers.
> References: AB 10676, OCLC 1820561.

MacMillan, Miriam   [434]
Green Seas and White Ice, by Miriam MacMillan. New York: Dodd, Mead and Company, [1948].

> Octavo, original turquoise cloth with white titles.
> xv, 287 p., [8] leaves of plates, illustrations, portraits, maps.
> References: AB 10680, OCLC 692573.

Maguire, Rochfort   [435]
The Journal of Rochfort Maguire, 1852–1854: Two Years at Point Barrow, Alaska, aboard HMS Plover in the Search for Sir John Franklin. Edited by John Bockstoce. London: The Hakluyt Society, 1988.

> Octavo, 2 volumes, dust jacket.
> Paged continuously. Volume 1: xiv, 318 p., frontispiece (portrait), illustrations, 4 maps (1 double); Volume 2: vi, 319–584 p., illustrations, map (folded).
> Works issued by the Hakluyt Society, 2nd Series, vols. 169–170.
> Reference: OCLC 19230619.

Major, Richard Henry (1818–1891)   [436]
The Voyages of the Venetian Brothers, Nicolò & Antonio Zeno, to the Northern Seas, in the XIVth Century, Comprising the Latest Known Accounts of the Lost Colony of Greenland; and of the Northmen in America before Columbus. Translated and Edited, with Notes and an Introduction, by Richard Henry Major, F.S.A., &c. London: Printed for the Hakluyt Society, M.DCCC.LXXIII 1873.

> Octavo, old three-quarter calf, marbled edges and endpapers, raised bands, black label with gilt titles.
> 3 p. l., cii p., 2 l., 64 p., plate, geneaological table, 4 folded maps (including frontispiece).
> Works issued by the Hakluyt Society, vol. 50.
> Reference: OCLC 2478959.

Malaurie, Jean   [437]
The Last Kings of Thule: With the Polar Eskimos, as They Face Their Destiny, [by] Jean Malaurie. Translated from the French by Adrienne Foulke. New York: E.P. Dutton, Inc., [1982].

> Quarto, gray boards with white cloth spine, gilt titles, dust jacket.
> xx, 489 p., [26] leaves of plates, illustrations, 11 maps.
> First American edition.
> Reference: OCLC 7283150.

Manby, George William   [438]
Journal of a Voyage to Greenland in the Year 1821. With Graphic Illustrations. By George William Manby, Esq. The Second Edition. London: Printed for G. and W.B. Whittaker, Ave-Maria Lane. MDCCCXXIII [1823].

> Octavo, modern three-quarter morocco with marbled boards and endpapers, raised bands, gilt titles and top edge.
> xi, 225, [1] p., plus [2] p. of advertisements, color frontispiece (folded map), [20] leaves of plates (5 folded), illustrations.
> Reference: AB 10844.

Mangles, James (1786–1867) **[439]**

Papers and Despatches Relating to the Arctic Searching Expeditions of 1850–51–52. Together with a Few Brief Remarks as to the Probable Course Pursued by Sir John Franklin. Illustrated by a General Map of the Polar Regions, a Chart of the Field of Search, and a Special Map of Beechey Island. Collected and Arranged by James Mangles, Commander, R.N. Second Edition, with Copious Additions. London: Francis & John Rivington, 1852.

> Octavo, original blind stamped blue cloth, paper label on spine with presentation bookplate from James Mangles to Capt. Penny. Also owned by J. Bellot, Lt., French Navy.
> 94 p., 3 maps, stained *passim*.
> References: AB 10849, OCLC 8159908.

Markham, Albert Hastings, Sir (1841–1918) **[440]**

The Great Frozen Sea. A Personal Narrative of the Voyage of the "Alert" during the Arctic Expedition of 1875–6. By Captain Albert Hastings Markham, R.N. (Late Commander of H.M.S. "Alert") [etc.]. London: Daldy, Isbister & Co., 1878.

> Thick octavo, recent half-calf binding, marbled boards, black label with gilt titles.
> xx, 440 p., frontispiece, 7 plates (2 double-page), illustrations, 2 maps (1 folded).
> First edition.
> Reference: AB 10926.

Markham, Albert Hastings, Sir (1841–1918) **[441]**

Life of Sir John Franklin and the North-west Passage. By Captain Albert Hastings Markham, R.N., A.D.C. London: George Philip & Son, 1891.

> Octavo, original cloth.
> xii, 324 p., plus 6 p. of advertisements, frontispiece (portrait), 9 plates (including facsimile), illustrations, portraits, 6 maps (2 folded).

(The World's Great Explorers and Explorations; Volume 5.)
> References: AB 10929, OCLC 3649012.

Markham, Albert Hastings, Sir (1841–1918) **[442]**

A Polar Reconnaissance: Being the Voyage of the "Isbjörn" to Novaya Zemlya in 1879, by Albert H. Markham, F.R.G.S. (Captain, Royal Navy). With Maps and Illustrations. London: C. Kegan Paul & Co., 1881.

> Octavo, original blue decorated cloth with gilt and black titles.
> xvi p., 1 l., 361 p., frontispiece (portrait), 5 plates, illustrations, 2 folded maps.
> Frontispiece is detached.
> First edition.
> References: AB 10931, OCLC 3649026.

Markham, Clements Robert, Sir (1830–1916) **[443]**

Antarctic Obsession: A Personal Narrative of the Origins of the British National Antarctic Expedition, 1901–1904, by Sir Clements Markham. Edited and Introduced by Clive Holland. Alburgh, Harleston, Norfolk [England]: Bluntisham Books: Erskine Press, 1986.

> Octavo, red cloth cover with gilt titles.
> xxv, 179 p., frontispiece (portrait), 22 plates (including maps, plans, portraits, facsimiles).
> Reference: OCLC 22890886.

Markham, Clements Robert, Sir (1830–1916) **[444]**

The Lands of Silence: A History of Arctic and Antarctic Exploration, by Sir Clements R. Markham [etc.]. Cambridge [England]: At the University Press, 1921.

> Quarto, original silver decorated blue cloth. Uncut copy.
> xii, 539 p., frontispiece (portrait), illustrations (including facsimiles), 25 plates (including portraits), maps (part folded).
> References: AB 10939, Spence 755, OCLC 3498686.

**Markham, Clements Robert, Sir
(1830–1916)** [445]
Life of Admiral Sir Leopold McClintock
[etc.], by an Old Messmate Sir Clements
Markham [etc.]. With an Introductory
Note by the Most Reverend William
Alexander [etc.]. With Portraits, Maps, and
Illustrations. London: John Murray, 1909.

> Large octavo, original blue cloth covers, armorial
> stamp.
> xx, 370 p., plus [2] p. of advertisements, frontispiece
> (portrait), 20 plates (including portraits), 7 maps
> (1 folded).
> References: AB 10940, OCLC 2322920.

**Markham, Clements Robert, Sir
(1830–1916)** [446]
A Life of John Davis, the Navigator, 1550–
1605, Discoverer of Davis Straits. By
Clements R. Markham [etc.]. New York:
Dodd, Mead & Company, Publishers,
[1889].

> Small octavo, original blue cloth with gilt titles.
> vi, [2], 301 p., plus 4 p. of advertisements, frontispiece
> (portrait), 4 plates, illustrations, facsimiles, 12
> maps (4 folded).
> (The World's Great Explorers and Explorations; Volume
> I.)
> Reference: OCLC 1509459.

**Markham, Clements Robert, Sir
(1830–1916)** [447]
The Voyages of William Baffin, 1612–
1622. Edited, with Notes and an
Introduction, by Clements R. Markham
[etc.]. London: Printed for Hakluyt Society
MDCCCLXXXI [1881].

> Octavo, later three-quarter morocco and marbled
> boards, gilt titles on spine, joints weak.
> lix, 192 p., frontispiece (portrait), 9 maps (6 folded).
> Works Issued by the Hakluyt Society, no. 63.
> Reference: OCLC 2479037.

**Markham, Clements Robert. Sir
(1830–1916)**
(See also Royal Geographical Society.
Voyage Southward)

Markham, M.E. and Florence A. [448]
The Life of Sir Albert Hastings Markham,
by M.E. and F.A. Markham. Cambridge
[England]: At the University Press, 1927.

> Octavo, original blue cloth with gilt titles.
> x, 261, [1] p., frontispiece (portrait), 4 plates, 13
> illustrations, 3 maps (1 folded).
> References: AB 10952, OCLC 2804415.

Marra, John [449]
Journal of the Resolution's Voyage in
1772, 1773, 1774, and 1775. On
Discovery to the Southern Hemisphere, by
Which the Non-Existence of an
Undiscovered Continent, between the
Equator and the 50th Degree of Southern
Latitude, is Demonstratively Proved. Also a
Journal of the Adventure's Voyage, in the
Years 1772, 1773, and 1774. With an
Account of the Separation of the Two
Ships, and the Most Remarkable Incidents
that Befel Each. Interspersed with
Historical and Geographical Descriptions
of the Islands and Countries Discovered in
the Course of Their Respective Voyages.
Illustrated with a Chart, in Which the
Tracks of Both Vessels are Accurately Laid
Down, and Other Cuts. London: Printed
for F. Newbery, at the Corner of St. Paul's
Church-Yard, 1775.

> Octavo, contemporary calf, finely rebacked, raised
> bands with red label, gilt title. On spine: Cooke's
> Voyage.
> xiii, [1], 328 p., frontispiece (folded map), 5 plates.
> First edition.
> References: Spence 758, OCLC 7351872.

Marret, Mario (1920–   ) [450]
Seven Men Among the Penguins: An
Antarctic Venture [by] Mario Marret.
Translated from the French by Edward
Fitzgerald. New York: Harcourt Brace and
Company, [1955].

> Octavo, blue cloth with silver titles.

xii, 269 p., [4] leaves of plates, illustrations, 3 maps.
First American edition.
References: Spence 762, OCLC 1522252.

Marshall, Robert (1901–1939)   [451]

Arctic Village [by] Robert Marshall. [Fairbanks]: University of Alaska Press, [1991].

Octavo, paperback reprint of 1933 edition.
xxx, 399 p., frontispiece, 39 plates, maps on
endpapers.
References: AB 10974, OCLC 22906992.

Marston, George

(See Murray, James)

Martin, Constance   [452]

James Hamilton: Arctic Watercolours (Kane). Calgary, Alberta: Glenbow Museum, 1984–85.

Quarto
52 p., illustrations.
Exhibition catalog.
Reference: OCLC 10824205

Martin, Horace T.   [453]

Castorologia; or, The History and Traditions of the Canadian Beaver. By Horace T. Martin, F.Z.S., &c. An Exhaustive Monograph, Popularly Written and Fully Illustrated. Montreal: Wm. Drysdale & Co.; London: Edward Stanford, 1892.

Octavo, original red cloth, beveled boards with gilt
edges and titles.
xvi, 238 p., frontispiece, 14 plates, illustrations,
facsimiles, 4 maps (1 double).
Reference: OCLC 512658.

Mathiassen, Therkel (1892–)   [454]

Contributions to the Geography of Baffin Land and Melville Peninsula, by Therkel Mathiassen. Copenhagen: Gyldendalske Boghandel, Nordisk Forlag, 1933.

Super octavo, original gray printed wrappers. Uncut
copy.

3 p.l., 102, [2]) p., illustrations, 3 maps (2 folded, in
pocket).
Thule Expedition, 5th, 1921–24. Report, Volume 1,
Number 3.
Compiled from diaries kept by the author and Peter
Freuchen.
Reference: AB 11068.

Mathiassen, Therkel (1892–)   [455]

Contributions to the Physiography of Southampton Island, by Therkel Mathiassen. Copenhagen: Gyldendalske Boghandel, Nordisk Forlag, 1931.

Super octavo, original gray printed wrappers.
29, [2] p., illustrations, folded map.
Thule Expedition, 5th, 1921–24. Report, Volume 1,
Number 2.
Reference: AB 11069.

Mathiassen, Therkel (1892–)   [456]

Report on the Expedition, by Therkel Mathiassen. Copenhagen: Gyldendalske Boghandel, Nordisk Forlag, 1945.

Super octavo, original gray printed wrappers, uncut.
121, [14] p., illustrations (including portraits, maps.)
Thule Expedition. 5th, 1921–24. Report, Volume 1,
Number 1.
Reference: AB 11093.

Matters, Leonard (1881–)   [457]

Through the Kara Sea. The Narrative of a Voyage in a Tramp Steamer through Arctic Waters to the Yenisie River. By Leonard Matters. With Chart and 51 Illustrations. London: Skeffington & Son, Ltd., [1932].

Octavo, brown cloth with black titles.
283, [1] p., frontispiece (portrait), [15] leaves of plates,
map.
First edition.
References: AB 11109, OCLC 4079648.

Matthiessen, Peter   [458]

Oomingmak: The Expedition to the Musk Ox Island in the Bering Sea, by Peter Matthiessen. Illustrated with Photographs. New York: Hastings House, [1967].

Octavo, red cloth with silver and black decorations,
dust jacket.

85 p., illustrations, portraits, map.
Reference: OCLC 1284965.

de Maupertuis, Pierre L. M., et al. [459]

The Figure of the Earth, Determined from Observations Made by Order of the French King, at the Polar Circle: By Messrs. DeMaupertuis, Camus, Clairaut, Le Monnier, Members of the Royal Academy of Sciences; the Abbé Outhier, Correspondent of the Academy; and Mr. Celsius, Professor of Astronomy at Upsal. Translated from the French of M. deMaupertuis. London: Printed For T. Cox, at the Royal Exchange; C. Davis, in Pater-noster-Row; J. & P. Knapton, in Ludgate-street; and A. Millar, in the Strand, MDCC.XXXVIII [1738].

Crown octavo, contemporary gilt speckled calf, spine gilt extra, leather label, raised bands.
vii, [1], 232 p., 9 folded plates, folded map, engraved vignette.
First English edition, after the original French.

Mawson, Douglas, Sir (1882–1958) [460]

Australasian Antarctic Expedition, 1911–14, under the Leadership of Sir Douglas Mawson [etc.]. Scientific Reports. Sydney: Government Printing Office, [1916–17].

Medium quarto, complete set in original wrappers. In 11 cloth slipcases with gilt titles on brown leather labels.
Series A, 5 volumes in 26 parts; Series B, 7 volumes in 10 parts; Series C, 10 volumes in 55 parts.
Reference: OCLC 11052946.

Summary of Contents:

SERIES A. Volume 1: Geographical Narrative and Cartography, by Douglas Mawson. **Volume 2:** Oceanography. Part 1: Sea-Floor Deposits from Soundings. By Frederick Chapman. With Two Plates and a Map; Part 2: Tidal Observations, by A.T. Doodson. With Three Plates and Seven Text Figures; Part 3: Soundings, by John K. Davis. With Three Plates; Part 4: Hydrological Observations, Made on Board S.Y. "Aurora," Reduced, Tabulated and Edited by Douglas Mawson; Part 5: Marine Biological Programme and other Zoological and Botanical Activities, Compiled by

Douglas Mawson. With Nine Plates and Five Maps. **Volume 3:** Geography, Physiography, Glaciology, Oceanography, and Geology. Part 1: The Metamorphic Rocks of Adelie Land, Section 1, by F.L. Stillwell. With Thirty-Five Plates and Fourteen Figures in the Text; Part 2: The Metamorphic Limestones of Commonwealth Bay, Adelie Land, by C.E. Tilley. With Two Plates; Part 3: The Dolerites of King George Land and Adelie Land, by W.R. Browne. With Two Plates; Part 4: Amphibolites and Related Rocks from The Moraines, Cape Denison, Adelie Land, by F.L. Stillwell. With Two Plates; Part 5: Magnetite Garnet Rocks from the Moraines, Cape Denison, Adelie Land, by Arthur L. Coulson. With Two Plates; Part 6: Petrological Notes on Further Rock Specimens Collected from *in situ* Occurrences, Commonwealth Bay Region, by J.O.G. Glastonbury. With Two Plates. **Volume 4:** Geology. Part 1: The Adelie Land Meteorite, by P.G.W. Bayly and F.L. Stillwell. With Two Plates; Part 2: Petrology of Rocks from Queen Mary Land, by S.R. Nockolds. With Thirty-Four Text-Figures and One Plate; Part 3: Granites of King George Land and Adelie Land, by H.S. Summers and A.B. Edwards. With an Appendix by A.W. Kleeman. With One Plate; Part 4: Acid Effusive and Hypabyssal Rocks (From the Moraines), by J.O.G. Glastonbury. With One Plate; Part 5: Basic Igneous Rocks and Metamorphic Equivalents From Commonwealth Bay, by J.O.G. Glastonbury. With Two Plates; Part 6: Certain Epidotic Rocks from The Moraines, Commonwealth Bay, by J.O.G. Glastonbury. With One Plate; Part 7: Schists and Gneisses from The Moraines, Cape Denison, Adelie Land, by A.W. Kleeman. With Five Plates; Part 8: Metamorphosed Limestones and other Calcereous Sediments from The Moraines. A Further Collection, by J.O.G. Glastonbury. With One Plate; Part 9: Some Hybrid Gneisses from The Moraines, Cape Denison, by J.O.G. Glastonbury; Part 10: A Group of Gneisses (Sillimanitic and Cordieritic) from The Moraines at Cape Denison, Antarctica. By Dr. C.E. Tilley. With One Plate; Part 11: Sedimentary Rocks, by Douglas Mawson. With Five Plates; Part 12: Record of Minerals of King George Land, Adelie Land and Queen Mary Land, by Douglas Mawson; Part 13: Catalogue of Rocks and Minerals Collected in Antarctic Lands, Prepared by Douglas Mawson. **Volume 5:** Macquarie Island: Its Geography and Geology, by Douglas Mawson. 194 Pages of text, 46 Text Figures, 2 Maps in Colour (one folded) and 37 Half-Tone Plates (3 folded).

SERIES B. Volume 1: Terrestrial Magnetism. Part 1: Field Survey and Reduction of Magnetograph Curves, by Eric Norman Webb; Part 2: Analysis and Discussion of Magnetograph Curves, by Charles Chree. With Twenty-Two Text Illustrations, Eighteen Plates, and One-Hundred-and-Twenty Tables. **Volume 2:** Terrestrial Magnetism and Related Observations. Part 1: Records of the Aurora Polaris, by Douglas Mawson. With Six Plates and Fifteen Text-Figures; Part 2: Magnetic Disturbance and its Relations to Aurora, by Charles Chree. With Fifty-Six Tables; Part 3: Magnetic Disturbance at Cape Denison, by J.M. Stagg. With Fifty-One Tables, Four Text Figures and Eight Plates; Part 4: The Transmission of Wireless Signals in Relation to Magnetic and Auroral Disturbances, by Charles Seymour Wright. With Fifty-Eight Tables and Seventeen Text Figures. **Volume 3:** Meteorology. Tabulated and Reduced Records of the Macquarie Island Station. Recorders: G.F. Ainsworth, H. Power, and A.C. Tulloch [etc.]. Reduction and Tabulation of Data by . . . B.W. Newman. With Four Plates, Two Figures in Text, and Thirteen tables. **Volume 4:** Meteorology. Tabulated and Reduced Records of the Cape Denison Station, Adelie Land, by C.T. Madigan. With Twenty Plates, Twenty-Four Figures in Text, and Sixteen Tables, and An Appendix by W.E. Bassett. **Volume 5:** Meteorology. Part 1: Records of the Queen Mary Land Station; Part 2: Meteorological Log of the S.Y. "Aurora."; Part 3: Sledge Journey Weather Records [with] Appendix: Macquarie Island Weather Notes for 1909–1910–1911. With Four Plates, Five Text Figures, and Twenty-Four Tables. **Volume 6:** Meteorology. Discussions of Observations at Adelie Land, Queen Mary Land and Macquarie Island, by Edward Kidson. With Thirty Figures in Text, and Sixty-Five Tables. **Volume 7:** Daily Weather Charts. Extending from Australia and New Zealand to the Antarctic Continent, by Edward Kidson. With Four Text Figures and Three Hundred and Sixty-Five Charts.

   SERIES C. Zoology and Botany. **Volume 1**, Part 1: Diatoms, by Albert Mann. With Six Plates; Part 2: Foraminifera, by Frederic Chapman and Walter James Parr. With Four Plates; Part 3: Parasitic Infusoria from Macquarie Island, by Professor T. Harvey Johnston. With Twenty-Six Text Figures. **Volume 2**, Part 1: Mallophaga and Siphunculata, by (The Late) Professor Launcelot Harrison. With Three Plates and Seven Text Figures; Part 2: Isopoda and Tanaidacea, by Herbert M. Hale. With Nineteen text Figures; Part 3: Ticks (Ixodoidea), by Professor T. Harvey Johnston; Part 4: Amphipoda Gammaridea, by G.E. Nicholls. With Sixty-Seven Text Figures; Part 5: Amphipoda Hyperiidea, by Dr. E.K. Barnard; Part 6: Crustacea Decapoda (in part), by Freda Bage. With One Plate; Part 7: Cirripedia, by Freda Bage. With Four Plates and One Text Figure; Part 8: Pycnogonida, by Isabella Gordon. With Eight Text Figures. **Volume 3**, Part 1: Fishes, by Edgar R. Waite. With Five Plates, Two Maps, One Chart, and Sixteen Figures in the Text; Part 2: Pterobranchia, by W.G. Ridewood. With Two Plates and Three Text Figures; Part 3: Ascidiæ Simplices, by Sir William A. Herdman. With Six Plates; Part 4: Rhabdopleura, by Professor T. Harvey Johnston. With Six Text Figures; Part 5: Ascidiæ Compositæ, by Dr. Hervé Harant and Dr. Paulette Vernières. With One Plate. **Volume 4**, Part 1: Mollusca, by C. Hedley. With Nine Plates and Three Figures in the Text; Part 2: Cephalopoda, by S. Stillman Berry. With Five Plates and Thirty Figures in the Text; Part 3: Brachiopoda, by J. Allan Thomson.

With Four Plates and One map. **Volume 5**, Part 1: Arachnida from Macquarie Island, by W.J. Rainbow. With Fourteen Figures in the Text; Part 2: Brachyura, by Mary J. Rathbun. With One Figure in the Text; Part 3: Copepoda, by G. Stewardson Brady. With Fifteen Plates; Part 4: Cladocera and Halocypridæ, by G. Stewardson Brady. With Two Plates; Part 5: Euphausiacea and Mysidacea, by W.M. Tattersall. With One Plate; Part 6: Cumaca and Phyllocarida, by W.T. Calman. With Two Plates; Part 7: Ostracoda, by Frederick Chapman. With Two Plates; Part 7: Ostracoda, by Frederick Chapman. With Two Plates; Part 8: The Insects of Macquarie Island, by R.J. Tillyard [etc.]. With Appendices by Professor C.T. Brues. With Twenty-One Text-Figures. **Volume 6**, Part 1: Calcareous Sponges, by Professor Arthur Dendy. With One Plate; Part 2: The Chætognathia, by Professor T. Harvey Johnson and B. Buckland Taylor. With Three Plates; Part 3: Polychæta, by W.B. Benham. With Six Plates and a Map; Part 4: Oligochæta of Macquarie Island, by W.B. Benham. With Five Text-Figures and a Map; Part 5: Gephyrea Inermia, by W.B. Benham. With One Plate; Part 6: Polyzoa, by L.R. Thornely. With Five Text-Figures; Part 7: Marine Free-Living Nemas, by N.A. Cobb. With Fourteen Text Figures. **Volume 7**, Part 1: Mosses, by H.A. Dixon and Rev. W. Walter Watts; Part 2: The Algæ of Commonwealth Bay, by A.H.S. Lucas. With Nine Plates; Part 3: The Vascular Flora of Macquarie Island, by T.F. Cheeseman. With Map; Part 4: Bacteriological and other Researches, by A.L. McLean. With Eleven Plates and Thirteen Text-Figures; Part 5: Ecological Notes and Illustrations of the Flora of Macquarie Island, by H. Hamilton. [with] Nineteen Plates, Two in Colours. **Volume 8**, Part 1: Echinodermata Asteriodea, by Professor René Kœhler. With Seventy-Five Plates; Part 2: Echinodermata Ophiuroidea, by Professor René Kœhler. With Fifteen Plates; Part 3: Echinodermata Echinoidea, by Professor René Kœhler. With One Hundred and Twenty-Four Plates; Part 4: Crinoidea, by Austin H. Clark. **Volume 9**, Part 1: The Bryozoa. Supplementary Report by Authur A. Livingstone. With Seven Plates and Twenty Figures in Text; Part 2: Actiniaria, by Oskar Carlgren and T.A. Stephenson. With Eighteen Figures in Text; Part 3: Alcyonaria, Madreporaria, and Antipatharia, by J. Arthur Thomson and Miss Nita Rennet. With Seven Plates; Part 4: Hydroida, by E.A. Briggs. With Two Plates and Three text Figures; Part 5: Non-Calcareous Sponges, by Maurice Burton. With One text Figure. **Volume 10**, Part 1: Trematoda, by T. Harvey Johnston. With Twenty-Eight Figures; Part 2: Acanthocephalia, by Professor T. Harvey Johnston and Effie W. Best. With Thirty-Nine Figures; Part 3: Leeches, by Professor J.P. Moore. With One Plate and One Text Figure; Part 4: Cestoda, by Professor T. Harvey Johnston. With Ninety-One Text Figures; Part 5: Parasitic Nematoda, by Professor T. Harvey Johnston. With Ten Text Figures; Part 6: Acarina, by H. Womersley. With Eleven Plates and Two Text Figures;

Part 7: Echinoderida, by Professor T. Harvey Johnston.
With Seven Text Figures.

Mawson, Douglas, Sir (1882–1958) [461]

Geographical Narrative and Cartography.
Australasian Antarctic Expedition 1911–
1914. Sydney: Government Printing
Office, 1942.

>Demy quarto, original wrapper.
>364 p., 24 half-tone plates, 30 text figures, 7 map
>   plates, maps (2 folded).
>Scientific Reports. Series A, Volume 1.
>Reference: OCLC 11685332.

Mawson, Douglas, Sir (1882–1958) [462]

The Home of the Blizzard, Being the
Story of the Australasian Antarctic
Expedition, 1911–1914; by Sir Douglas
Mawson [etc.]. Illustrated in Colour and
Black and White. Also with Maps. London:
William Heinemann, [1915].

>Large octavo, 2 volumes, original blue cloth with gilt
>   and silver titles.
>Volume 1: xxx, 349 p., frontispiece (portrait), 118
>   plates (8 color), illustrations, diagrams, facsimiles,
>   7 maps; Volume 2: xiii, 337, [2] p., frontispiece,
>   103 plates (10 color), illustrations, diagrams,
>   facsimiles, 12 maps (3 folded, in pocket).
>References: Spence 774, OCLC 3009654.

Mawson, Douglas, Sir (1882–1958) [463]

Mawson's Antarctic Diaries. Edited by
Fred Jacka & Eleanora Jacka. London:
Unwin Hyman, [1988].

>Crown quarto, black cloth with gilt titles, dust jacket.
>L, 414 p., [26] leaves of plates: illustrations (some
>   color), charts, facsimiles (some color), 1 plan,
>   portraits (some color), maps.
>Reference: OCLC 18071646.

Mawson, Douglas, Sir (1882–1958)

(See also Geikie Correspondence; Price, A.
Grenfell)

May, Walter William [464]

A Series of Fourteen Sketches Made
During the Voyage up Wellington Channel
in Search of Sir John Franklin, K.C.H., and
the Missing Crews of H.M. Discovery —
Ships Erebus and Terror; Together with a
Short Account of Each Drawing. By
Commander Walter W. May, R.N., Late
Lieutenant of H.M. Discovery — Ship
Assistance (Captain Sir Edward Belcher,
C.B.). London: Published May 1, 1855, By
Day and Son, Lithographers to the Queen,
1855.

>Folio, burgundy leather label on spine, with gilt title, in
>   tan cloth drop-spine box.
>6 p., 1 l., 14 plates on 13 sheets.
>At head of title: Dedicated, by Special Permission, to
>   The Right Hon. Sir James R.G. Graham, Bart.,
>   G.C.B., M.P.
>Reference: OCLC 16897974.

Mc *Names beginning with Mc are entered
as if spelled Mac, e.g. McCain is entered as
MacCain*

Mear, Roger and Robert Swan [465]

A Walk to the Pole: To the Heart of
Antarctica in the Footsteps of Scott, by
Roger Meer and Robert Swan. With
Research and Additional Material by
Lindsay Fulcher. New York: Crown
Publishers, Inc., [1987].

>Octavo, blue cloth with silver titles, dust jacket.
>xiii, [1], 306 p., illustrations (chiefly color photographs),
>   portraits, maps, maps on endpapers.
>First American edition.
>Reference: OCLC 16092953.

Mech, L. David [466]

The Arctic Wolf: Living with the Pack [by]
L. David Mech. Foreword by Roger Caras.
[Stillwater, MN]: Voyageur Press, [1988].

>Large quarto, brown cloth with gilt titles, dust jacket.
>128 p., color illustrations.
>Reference: OCLC 18711426.

Mecking, Ludwig (1879–)
(See Nordenskjöld, Nils Otto Gustaf)

Melville, George W. (1841–1912) [467]
In the Lena Delta: A Narrative of the
Search for Lieut.-Commander DeLong and
His Companions, Followed by an Account
of the Greely Relief Expedition and a
Proposed Method of Reaching the North
Pole, by George W. Melville [etc.]. Edited
by Melville Philips. With Maps and
Illustrations. London: Longmans, Green
and Co., 1885.

> Octavo, original gray cloth, black and gold titles.
> xiii p., 1 l., 497 p., frontispiece (portrait), illustrations,
>   15 plates, 4 folded maps.
> First London edition.
> Reference: OCLC 18786362.

Menster, William J. (1913–)   [468]
Strong Men South [by] William J.
Menster. Dubuque, Iowa: Stromen
Publishing Company, [1949].

> Octavo, original white cloth with blue titles.
> vii, 206 p., 8 plates (including portraits, map.)
> Presentation copy from the author.

Merk, Frederick
(See Simpson, George, Sir. Fur Trade and
Empire)

Middleton, Christopher (d.1770) [469]
A Vindication of the Conduct of Captain
Christopher Middleton, in a Late Voyage
on Board His Majesty's Ship Furnace, for
Discovering a North-west Passage to the
Western American Ocean. In Answer to
certain Objections and Aspersions of
Arthur Dobbs, Esq.; with an Appendix:
Containing the Captain's Instructions;
Councils Held; Reports of the Inferior
Officers; Letters between Mr. Dobbs, Capt.
Middleton, &c. Affidavits and Other

Vouchers Refer'd to in the Captain's
Answers, &c. With as Much of the Log-
Journal as Relates to the Discovery. The
Whole as Lately Deliver'd to the Lords
Commissioners of the Admiralty. To which
is Annex'd, an Account of the
Extraordinary Degrees and Surprizing
Effects of Cold in Hudson's-Bay, North
America, Read before the Royal Society. By
Christopher Middleton, Late Commander
of the Furnace, and F.R.S. London:
Printed by the Author's Appointment; and
Sold by Jacob Robinson, at the Golden-
Lion in Ludgate-Street, 1743.

> Octavo, half calf with marbled boards, red label on
>   spine with gilt titles. Binder's title: Conduct of
>   Captain Middleton.
> [2], 206 p., 1 l., 48 p.
> First edition.
> References: Sabin 48858, Streeter 3636, TPL 187,
>   OCLC 5322991.

Miertsching, Johann August   [470]
Frozen Ships: The Arctic Diary of Johann
Miertsching, 1850–1854. Translated and
with Introduction and Notes by L.H.
Neatby. New York: St. Martin's Press,
1967.

> Octavo, gray cloth with gilt titles, dust jacket with color
>   pictorial sketch by Lt. S. Gurney Cresswell.
> xviii, 254 p., [2] leaves of plates, black and white
>   photo illustrations, portraits, 2 maps (1 double-
>   page).
> References: AB 11387, OCLC 3428233.

Mikkelsen, Ejnar (1880–)   [471]
Conquering the Arctic Ice, by Ejnar
Mikkelsen. With Numerous Illustrations
and Maps. Philadelphia: George W. Jacobs
& Co., Publishers, 1909.

> Octavo, original decorated red cloth. Uncut copy.
> xviii, 470 p., frontispiece, illustrations, plates, portraits,
>   folded map.
> Reference: OCLC 9165394.

Mikkelsen, Ejnar (1880–) [472]
Lost in the Arctic: Being the Story of the
'Alabama' Expedition, 1909–1912. By
Ejnar Mikkelsen, Author of "Conquering
the Arctic Ice." With Numerous
Illustrations and a Map. London: William
Heinemann, MCMXIII [1913].

> Quarto, original decorated blue cloth cover with silver
> titles. Boards warped.
> xviii, 399, [1] p., frontispiece (portrait), 67 plates,
> folded map.
> References: AB 11428, OCLC 3038120.

**Mikkelsen, Ejnar (1880–),
Vilhelm Laub, and H. Hansen** [473]
Alabama Expeditionen til Grønlands
Nordøstkyst 1909–1912. Under Ledelse of
Ejnar Mikkelsen. København: I
Kommission Hos C.A. Reitzel, 1922.

> Super octavo, original printed green wrappers, uncut
> copy.
> 4 p.l., viii, 295 p., 52 plates (1 folded), 2 facsimiles (1
> folded), 5 maps (4 folded).
> Meddelelser om Grønland, Bind LII.
> References: AB 11417, OCLC 13632524.

Mill, Hugh Robert (1861–1950) [474]
The Life of Sir Ernest Shackleton [etc.] by
Hugh Robert Mill. Boston: Little, Brown
and Company, 1923.

> Octavo, original blue cloth with gilt titles.
> xv, 312 p., frontispiece (portrait), 19 plates, 4 maps.
> First American edition.
> References: Spence 796, OCLC 2997413.

Mill, Hugh Robert (1861–1950) [475]
The Life of Sir Ernest Shackleton [etc.] by
Hugh Robert Mill. London: William
Heinemann Ltd., MCMXXIV [1924].

> Octavo, original blue cloth with gilt titles.
> xv, 312 p., frontispiece (portrait), 19 plates, 4 maps.
> On verso of t.p.: Cheap edition, October 1924.
> References: Spence 797, OCLC 899892.

Mill, Hugh Robert (1861–1950) [476]
The Siege of the South Pole: The Story of

Antarctic Exploration by Hugh Robert
Mill [etc.]. With Maps, Diagrams, and
Other Illustrations, and Maps by J.G.
Bartholomew. London: Alston Rivers,
Limited, 1905.

> Octavo, original decorative green cloth with gilt titles.
> xvi, 455, [1] p., frontispiece, illustrations, 52 plates,
> maps (3 folded.)
> First edition.
> References: Spence 793, OCLC 2205392.

Mill, Hugh Robert (1861–1950)
(See also Royal Geographical Society.
Voyage Southward)

Miller, Francis T. (1877–1959) [477]
The Fight to Conquer the Ends of the
Earth: The World's Great Adventure: 1000
Years of Polar Exploration Including the
Heroic Achievements of Admiral Richard
Evelyn Byrd, by Francis Trevelyan Miller
[etc.] With Forewords by General A.W.
Greely [etc.], [and] Dr. Henry Fairfield
Osborn [etc.]. Illustrated: Photographs,
Historic Prints, Etc. Philadelphia, Chicago,
and Toronto: The John C. Winston
Company, [1930].

> Octavo, original blue decorated cloth with silver titles.
> 384 p., plus [1] p. of advertisements, color
> frontispiece, [40] leaves of plates including
> portraits, maps, facsimiles.
> References: Spence 803, cf. OCLC 4108929.

Miller, J. H.
(See Helm, A. S.)

Miller, James Martin (1859–1939)
[478]
"Old Glory" the First Flag at the North
Pole: Discovery of the North Pole; Dr.
Frederick A. Cook's Own Story of How
He Reached the North Pole April 21st,
1908, and the Story of Commander

Robert E. Peary's Discovery April 6th, 1909. Graphic and Thrilling Stories of the Greatest Achievement by Man Since Columbus Discovered America; Terrible Sufferings and Privations; the Awful Cold; Face to Face with Death by Starvation; American Pluck, Courage and Endurance Reach the Top of the World through Terrific Gales Over a Continent of Ice. Special Introduction by General A.W. Greely, U.S.A. [etc.]. Edited by Honorable J. Martin Miller [etc.]. Also Containing A True and Authentic Account of Other Great Polar Expeditions, Including Franklin, Greely, Abruzzi, Nares, Nordenskjöld, Nansen, Sverdrup, Shackelton [sic], etc. Illustrated with Half-Tone Reproductions of Photographs of Many Expeditions. Philadelphia, Pa.: American Book & Bible House, [1909].

> Quarto, three-quarter red calf with marbled boards and edges, gilt titles. Front joint cracked.
> 12 p. l, 428 p., frontispiece (portrait), [16] leaves of plates (including maps and portraits), illustrations, maps.
> Reference: OCLC 7840268.

Mirsky, Jeannette (1903–1987) [479]
Elisha Kent Kane and the Seafaring Frontier [by] Jeannette Mirsky. Edited by Oscar Handlin. Boston: Little, Brown and Company, [1954].

> Octavo, blue cloth with gilt titles, dust jacket.
> viii p., 1 l., 201 p., 1 map.
> First edition.
> Reference: OCLC 490383.

Mirsky, Jeannette (1903–1987) [480]
To the Arctic! The Story of Northern Exploration from Earliest Times to the Present, by Jeannette Mirsky. With an Introduction by Vilhjalmur Stefansson. New York: Alfred A. Knopf, 1948.

> Octavo, original blue cloth with gilt titles, dust jacket.

> xxi, [1], 334, xviii p., [6] leaves of plates, illustrations, 8 maps (1 folded).
> First Borzoi edition.
> Cellophane envelope containing newspaper reviews of this book is attached to prelim.
> References: AB 11527, OCLC 1527057.

Mirsky, Jeannette (1903–1987) [481]
To the North. The Story of Arctic Exploration from Earliest Times to the Present, by Jeannette Mirsky. New York: The Viking Press, 1934.

> Quarto, original blue cloth with silver titles, dust jacket.
> 3 p. l., ix-xx, 386 p., [16] leaves of plates, illustrations (including facsimiles), portraits, maps (1 folded).
> First edition.
> References: AB 11528, OCLC 1539692.

Mitchell, T. C. (editor) [482]
Captain Cook and the South Pacific. London: Published for the Trustees of the British Museum by British Museum Publications, Ltd., 1979.

> Quarto, original green cloth with gilt titles, dust jacket.
> 249 p., illustrations, portraits, facsimiles, maps.
> First edition.
> The British Museum Yearbook; v. 3.
> Reference: OCLC 5616259.

Mittelholzer, Walter (1894–   ) [483]
By Airplane towards the North Pole: an Account of an Expedition to Spitzbergen in the Summer of 1923, by Walter Mittelholzer [etc.]. With Forty-eight Illustrations and Four Maps. Translated from the German by Eden & Cedar Paul. Boston and New York: Houghton Mifflin Company, 1925.

> Octavo, original blue cloth with white titles.
> 176 p., frontispiece (folded map), [16] leaves of plates, 3 maps (1 folded).
> First American edition.
> Reference: OCLC 6596345.

Mitterling, Philip I. [484]
America in the Antarctic to 1840, by Philip I. Mitterling. Urbana: University of Illinois Press, 1959.

Octavo, original brown cloth with black titles, dust
jacket.
viii p., 1 l., 201 p., maps.
First edition.
References: Spence 806, OCLC 342256.

Montague, Richard [485]

Oceans, Poles and Airmen: The First
Flights over Wide Waters and Desolate Ice
[by] Richard Montague. New York:
Random House, [1971].

Octavo, original brown cloth with red and gold titles,
pictorial dust jacket.
x, 307, [2] p., [8] leaves of plates.
First edition.
Reference: OCLC 130428.

Moore, J. Hampton (1864–1950) [486]

Peary's Discovery of the North Pole: For
the Verdict of the National Geographic
Society Which Passed Upon the Report of
These Distinguished Americans Has Been
Accepted Without Question by the Royal
Geographical Society of London [etc.].
Speech of Hon. J. Hampton Moore of
Pennsylvania in the House of
Representatives, March 22, 1910.
Washington: [s.n.], 1910.

Octavo, original printed wrappers, stapled.
36 p.
Reference: OCLC 11566344.

Morgan, William James, *et al.*

(See Wilkes, Charles)

Morrison, Robert J. [487]

Russia's Shortcut to Fame [by] Robert J.
Morrison. Vancouver, WA: Morrison &
Family Publishing House, Inc., [1987].

Octavo, softbound.
311 p., [8] leaves of plates, maps.
Reference: OCLC 18407675.

Morton, Arthur Silver (1870–1945) [488]

Sir George Simpson: Overseas Governor of
the Hudson's Bay Company, a Pen Picture
of a Man of Action, by Arthur S. Morton
[etc.]. Toronto and Vancouver: J.M. Dent
& Sons, Limited, [1944].

Octavo, red cloth with black titles.
xii, 310 p., frontispiece (portrait), 5 plates, maps on
endpapers.
First edition.
Reference: OCLC 5351724.

Moss, Edward L. [489]

Shores of the Polar Sea. A Narrative of the
Arctic Expedition of 1875–6, by Dr.
Edward L. Moss, H.M.S. "Alert."
Illustrated by Sixteen Chromo-Lithographs
and Numerous Engravings from Drawings
Made on the Spot by the Author. London:
Marcus Ward & Co.; Belfast: Royal Ulster
Works, 1878.

Folio, original decorated blue cloth, gilt edges, black
and gilt titles, [rebacked, original backings laid
down].
83 p., 28 steel engravings, XVI color plates, map. The
plates are mounted chrome-lithographs, each
preceded by leaf with descriptive letterpress.
Reference: OCLC 7547855.

Mountevans, Edward R. G. R. Evans, baron (1880–1957) [490]

The Antarctic Challenged, by Admiral
Lord Mountevans. New York: John
deGraff, Inc., [1956].

Octavo, original blue cloth with gilt titles, torn dust
jacket.
vi p., 1 l., 247 p., [6] leaves of plates, illustrations,
maps on endpapers.
Reference: OCLC 2613327.

Mountevans, Edward R. G. R. Evans, baron (1880–1957) [491]

British Polar Explorers [by] Admiral Sir
Edward Evans. With 8 Plates in Colour
and 14 Illustrations in Black and White.
London: Collins, MCMXLVI [1946].

Octavo, dust jacket.
48 p., [4] leaves of plates, illustrations (some color).
Reference: OCLC 19821209.

Mountevans, Edward R. G. R. Evans, baron (1880–1957) [492]
South with Scott, by Admiral Sir Edward R.G.R. Evans [etc.]. London and Glasgow: Collins, [1912].
> Octavo, original cloth, spine faded, shaken.
> 8, 283, [1] p., frontispiece (portrait), folded plan, folded maps.

Mowat, Farley [493]
The Polar Passion. The Quest for the North Pole, with Selections from Arctic Journals [by] Farley Mowat. Boston and Toronto: Little, Brown and Company, [1967].
> Small folio, original gray cloth with gilt titles, dust jacket.
> 301 p., illustrations, facsimiles, portraits, maps.
> First American edition.
> Reference: OCLC 4086179.

Müller, Gerhard Friedrich (1705–1783) [494]
Voyages from Asia to America, for Completing the Discoveries of the North West Coast of America. To Which is Prefixed, a Summary of the Voyages Made by the Russians on the Frozen Sea, in Search of a North East Passage. Serving as an Explanation of a Map of the Russian Discoveries, Published by the Academy of Sciences at Petersburgh. Translated from the High Dutch of S. Müller, of the Royal Academy of Petersburgh. With the Addition of Three New Maps; 1. A Copy of Part of the Japanese Map of the World; 2. A Copy of DeLisle's and Buache's Fictitious Map; and 3. A large Map of Canada, Extending to the Pacific Ocean, Containing the New Discoveries Made by the Russians and French. By Thomas Jefferys, Geographer to his Majesty. London: Printed for T. Jefferys, the Corner of St. Martin's-Lane, Charing Cross, 1761.
> Quarto, modern calf, raised bands, blind-tooled in gold, red leather label with gilt titles. Folded map at back repaired. Summary of conservation treatment laid in, facing p. 76.
> viii, xliii, 76 p., 4 maps (2 large engraved folded, including frontispiece.)
> References: Sabin 51285, Streeter 3458, Hill, p.206, OCLC 4118500.

Mühry, A.
(See Petermann, August)

Mulgrave, Constantine John Phipps, 2d baron
(See Phipps, Constantine John, 2d baron Mulgrave)

Murdoch, William G. Burn (1862–) [495]
From Edinburgh to the Antarctic: An Artist's Notes and Sketches during the Dundee Antarctic Expedition of 1892–93. By W.G. Burn Murdoch. With a Chapter by W.S. Bruce, Naturalist of the Barque 'Balæna'. London and New York: Longmans, Green and Co., 1894.
> Octavo, original decorated green cloth with silver titles.
> ix p., 1 l., 364 p., plus 24 p. of advertisements, 7 plates, illustrations, 3 maps (1 folded.)
> First edition.
> References: Spence 825, OCLC 959729.

Murphey, Cecil B.
(See Vaughan, Norman D.)

Murphy, Charles J. V. (1904–) [496]
Struggle. The Life and Exploits of Commander Richard E. Byrd, by Charles J.V. Murphy. New York: Frederick A. Stokes Company, MCMXXVIII [1928].
> Octavo, original blue cloth with yellow titles.
> xii p., 1 l., 368 p., frontispiece (portrait), [3] leaves of plates.

First edition.
Reference: OCLC 307655.

Murray, George (1831–) [497]

The Antarctic Manual for the Use of the Expedition of 1901. Edited by George Murray [etc.], with a Preface by Sir Clements R. Markham [etc.]. Presented to the Expedition and Issued by the Royal Geographical Society. London: Royal Geographical Society, 1901.

Octavo, blue cloth with gilt titles.
xvi, 586 p., illustrations, 3 folded maps in pocket.
First edition.
References: Spence 829, OCLC 13628570.

Murray, George (1831–)

(See also Mill, Hugh Robert. Voyage Southward)

Murray, James and George Marston [498]

Antarctic Days. Sketches of the Homely Side of Polar Life by Two of Shackleton's Men. Illustrated by the Authors, James Murray and George Marston, and Introduced by Sir Ernest Shackleton. London: Andrew Melrose, 1913.

Quarto, original blue pictorial cloth covers, with gilt titles.
xxi, 199, [1] p., color frontispiece, [30] leaves of plates (3 color), illustrations.
Edition de Luxe of 280 copies; this is copy 264. Signed by Shackleton, Murray and Marston.
References: Spence 830, OCLC 961857.

Nansen, Fridtjof (1861–1930) [499]

Eskimo Life, by Fridtjof Nansen [etc.]. Translated by William Archer. With Illustrations. London: Longmans, Green and Co., 1893.

Octavo, green cloth with gilt titles, rebound.
xvi, 350 p., plus 24 p. advertisements, frontispiece (portrait), 15 plates, illustrations.
References: AB 11979, OCLC 2746971.

Nansen, Fridtjof (1861–1930) [500]

Fridtjof Nansen's "Farthest North": Being the Record of a Voyage of Exploration of the Ship 'Fram' 1893–96 and of a Fifteen Months' Sleigh Journey by Dr. Nansen and Lieut. Johansen. With an Appendix by Otto Sverdrup, Captain of the 'Fram', about One Hundred and Twenty Full Page and Numerous Text Illustrations, Sixteen Coloured Plates in Facsimile from Dr. Nansen's Own Sketches, Etched Portrait, Photogravures and Maps. Westminster [England]: Archibald Constable and Company, 1897.

Large octavo, 2 volumes, original green cloth with gilt titles.
Volume 1: xiii, [1] p., 1 l., 510 p., frontispiece (portrait), 55 plates (8 color), illustrations, 2 folded maps; Volume 2: xiii p., 1 l., 671, [1] p., frontispiece (portrait), 72 plates (8 color), illustrations, 2 folded maps.
First English edition.
References: AB 11983, OCLC 10857444.

Nansen, Fridtjof (1861–1930) [501]

"Farthest North": Being the Record of a Voyage of Exploration of the Ship 'Fram' 1893–96 and of a Fifteen Months' Sleigh Journey by Dr. Nansen & Lieut. Johansen. With an Appendix by Otto Sverdrup, Captain of the 'Fram', about One Hundred and Twenty Full Page and Numerous Text Illustrations and Coloured Plate in Facsimile from Dr. Nansen's Own Sketches, Portrait and Maps. In Two Volumes. London: George Newnes, Ltd., 1898.

Octavo, 2 volumes, original decorative green cloth with gilt and red titles.
Volume 1: xv, 480 p., frontispiece (portrait), 60 plates (1 color), illustrations, portraits, folded map; Volume 2: viii, 456 p., frontispiece (portrait), 51 plates, illustrations, portraits.
Reference: OCLC 4168603.

Nansen, Fridtjof (1861–1930) [502]

The First Crossing of Greenland, by Fridtjof Nansen. Translated from the Norwegian by Hubert Majendie Gepp [etc.]. With Maps and Numerous

Fritdjof Nansen (1861–1930) was the consummate explorer. In 1888, the same year he received his doctorate from Christiana University, he made the first crossing of Greenland on skis. In 1893 he organized the *Fram* expedition, in which the little ship was purposely frozen into the ice and carried by the pack across Asia. En route, he and a companion left the ship and skied to 86° 13′ for a new "farthest north." When Norway became independent in 1905, Nansen was the country's first ambassador to Great Britain and during and after World War I he performed important diplomatic and philanthropic missions.

Fridtjof Nansen by Johan Nordhagen, from Nansen's *Farthest North* (1897) [**500**]

Illustrations. In Two Volumes. London: Longmans, Green and Co., 1890.

> Octavo, 2 volumes, original decorated blue cloth with silver titles.
> Volume 1: xxii, 510 p., frontispiece (portrait), 6 plates, illustrations, 2 folded maps. Volume 2: x, 509 p., frontispiece (portrait), 4 plates, illustrations, 2 folded maps.
> Reference: OCLC 28367512.

Nansen, Fridtjof (1861–1930)   [503]
Hunting and Adventure in the Arctic, by Fridtjof Nansen. Fully Illustrated from Drawings by the Author. New York: Duffield and Company, 1925.

> Octavo, blue cloth with gilt titles. Ex Libris.
> 5 p. l, 3–462 p., frontispiece (portrait), 3 photographic plates, illustrations, maps.
> First American edition.
> References: AB 11991, OCLC 560944.

Nansen, Fridtjof (1861–1930)   [504]
In Northern Mists. Arctic Exploration in Early Times, by Fridtjof Nansen [etc.]. Translated by Arthur G. Chater. Illustrated. London: William Heinemann, MCMXI [1911].

> Quarto, 2 volumes, original blue cloth cover with gilt titles.
> Volume 1: xi, 383, [1] p., mounted color frontispiece, illustrations, facsimiles, maps; Volume 2: 4 p.l., 415, [1] p., mounted color frontispiece, illustrations, facsimiles, maps.
> First English edition
> References: AB 11993, OCLC 3562515.

Nansen, Fridtjof (1861–1930)   [505]
The Norwegian North Polar Expedition, 1893–1896: Scientific Results. Edited by Fridtjof Nansen. New York: Greenwood Press, Publishers, [1969].

> Large octavo, 6 volumes.
> Illustrations (part folded), maps (part folded).
> Reprint of the 1901–1906 edition.
> References: OCLC 57219, cf. AB 12004.

Nanton, Paul   [506]
Arctic Breakthrough. Franklin's

Expeditions 1819–1847. With an Introduction by Dr. Trevor Lloyd. Toronto and Vancouver: Clarke, Irwin, 1970.

> Octavo, brown cloth with gilt titles, dust jacket.
> xi, 262 p., frontispiece (portrait), [4] leaves of plates, maps, maps on endpapers.
> Author's signed copy.
> Reference: OCLC 158752.

Nares, George Strong (1831–1915)   [507]
Narrative of a Voyage to the Polar Sea during 1875–6 in H.M. Ships 'Alert' and 'Discovery,' by Capt. Sir G.S. Nares [etc.], Commander of the Expedition. With Notes on the Natural History by H.W. Feilden [etc.], Naturalist to the Expedition. In Two Volumes. London: Sampson Low, Marston, Searle, & Rivington, 1878.

> Octavo, 2 volumes, original green cloth with gilt and black titles.
> Volume 1: xl, 395 p., frontispiece, 3 plates, illustrations, folded map; Volume 2: viii, 378 p., plus 32 p. of advertisements, frontispiece, 9 plates, illustrations, folded map.
> First edition.
> References: AB 12026A, OCLC 2312144.

Nares, George Strong (1831–1915)   [508]
The Official Report of the Recent Arctic Expedition, by Captain Nares, R.N., Commander of the Expedition. London: John Murray, 1876.

> Octavo, contemporary brown buckram with gilt titles, library shelf mark on spine.
> 96 p., frontispiece (map).
> First edition.
> Reference: OCLC 9934749.

Nares, George Strong (1831–1915) and B. Ninnis   [509]
Results Derived from the Arctic Expedition, 1875–76. I. Physical Observations by Captain Sir George Nares, R.N., and Captain Feilden, &c. II. Medical

Report on the Eskimo Dog Disease, by Fleet Surgeon B. Ninnis, M.D. Presented to Both Houses of Parliament by Command of Her Majesty. London: Printed by George Edward Eyre and William Spottiswoode, Printers to the Queen's Most Excellent Majesty, for Her Majesty's Stationery Office, 1878.

Folio, original blue printed wrappers.
156 p., illustrations, 8 color plates (folded), tables (7 folded).
References: OCLC 10354084, cf. AB 45257.

National Foreign Assessment Center (U.S.) [510]

Polar Regions Atlas. Produced by the National Foreign Assessment Center, CIA. [Washington, D.C.]: The Agency, 1978.

Folio.
66 p., color illustrations, maps.
Reference: OCLC 4129532.

Neatby, Leslie H. [511]

Conquest of the Last Frontier. [Toronto: Longsmans Canada Limited, 1966].

Octavo, cream cloth with blue and brown titles, dust jacket.
xvi p., 1 l., 425, [6] p., plate, 4 maps.
First edition.
Reference: OCLC 6289334.

Neatby, Leslie H. [512]

Discovery in Russian and Siberian Waters [by] Leslie H. Neatby. Athens: Ohio University Press, 1973.

Octavo, original blue cloth with gilt titles, dust jacket.
vi p., 1 l., 226 p., [4] leaves of plates, (including 3 maps).
Reference: OCLC 736858.

Neatby, Leslie H. [513]

In Quest of the North West Passage [by] Leslie H. Neatby. Foreword by Dr. J. Tuzo Wilson. Toronto: Longmans, Green and Company, 1958.

Octavo, black cloth with silver titles, dust jacket.
[x] p., 1 l., 194, [1] p., [2] leaves of plates, 5 maps (2 folded).
Marked with highlighter and pencil.
Reference: OCLC 4715531.

Neatby, Leslie H. [514]

The Search for Franklin [by] Leslie H. Neatby. Edmonton: M.G. Hurtig Ltd., [1970].

Octavo, black cloth with gilt titles, dust jacket.
280, [1] p., [4] leaves of plates, 5 maps.
Marked with highlighter.
Reference: OCLC 20959655.

Neatby, Leslie H.

(see also Miertsching, Johann August)

Neider, Charles (1915–) [515]

Antarctica: Authentic Accounts of Life and Exploration in the World's Highest, Driest, Windiest, Coldest and Most Remote Continent. Edited with an Introduction and Notes by Charles Neider. New York: Random House, [1972].

Octavo, blue cloth with black spine, titles in blue and silver, dust jacket.
x, 464 p., maps on endpapers.
Reference: OCLC 287049.

Neider, Charles (1915–) [516]

Beyond Cape Horn: Travels in the Antarctic [by] Charles Neider. With Color Photographs by the Author. San Francisco: Siena Club Books, [1980].

Octavo, original blue cloth with silver titles, dust jacket.
xi, 387 p., [4] leaves of plates, 12 maps, maps on endpapers.
First edition.
Reference: OCLC 6195053.

Neider, Charles (1915–) [517]

Edge of the World: Ross Island, Antarctica. A Personal and Historical Narrative, by Charles Neider. Illustrated with Maps, Black-and-white Photographs, and with

Thirty-three Color Photographs by the
Author. Garden City: Doubleday, 1974.
> Octavo, original blue cloth with red and silver titles,
> dust jacket.
> xvi, 461 p., photographs (mostly color), 14 maps,
> maps on endpapers.
> First edition.
> References: Spence 843, OCLC 900676.

Newman, Stanley A.
(See Mackintosh, Aeneas Lionel Acton)

Ninnis, Belgrave
(See Nares, George Strong, Sir. Results
Derived from the Arctic Expedition)

Nobile, Umberto (1885–)   [518]
My Polar Flights. An Account of the
Voyages of the Airships 'Italia' and
'Norge', by Umberto Nobile. Translated
by Frances Fleetwood. New York: G.P.
Putnam's Sons, [1961].
> Octavo, blue cloth with silver titles, dust jacket.
> 288 p., [4] leaves of plates, 3 maps.
> First American edition.
> Reference: OCLC 1142432.

Noble, Louis Legrand (1813–1882)
**   [519]**
After Icebergs with a Painter: A Summer
Voyage to Labrador and around
Newfoundland, by Rev. Louis L. Noble.
New York: D. Appleton and Company,
M.DCCC.LXI [1861].
> Octavo, purple cloth with gilt titles.
> xiv, 1 l., 336 p., plus 8 p. of advertisements, added
> title-page (illustrated), 5 plates.
> References: AB 12352, Sabin 55580, OCLC 1738303.

Noice, Harold (1895–)   [520]
With Stefansson in the Arctic, by Harold
Noice, Commander of the Relief
Expedition to Wrangel Island 1923. With
Illustrations. New York: Dodd, Mead &
Company, [1924].

> Octavo, green cloth with gilt titles.
> 269, [1] p., frontispiece (portrait), 15 plates,
> illustrations, folded map.
> First edition.
> "Printed in Great Britain."
> References: AB 12380, OCLC 2125515.

Nordenskjöld, Adolf Erik (1832–1901)
**   [521]**
The Arctic Voyages of Adolf Erik
Nordenskjöld. London: Macmillan and
Company, 1879.
> Octavo, original decorated brown cloth.
> xiv, [1], 447, [1] p., frontispiece, illustrations, 3 folded
> maps.
> Preface signed: "Alexander Leslie, Editor."
> References: AB 9942, OCLC 781303.

Nordenskjöld, Adolf Erik (1832–1901)
**   [522]**
The Voyage of the Vega round Asia and
Europe, with a Historical Review of
Previous Journeys along the North Coast
of the Old World, by A.E. Nordenskiöld.
Translated by Alexander Leslie. With Five
Steel Portraits, Numerous Maps, and
Illustrations. In Two Volumes. London:
Macmillan and Co., 1881.
> Octavo, 2 volumes, original green cloth with gilt titles.
> Volume 1: xxv, 524 p., frontispiece (portrait), 166
>   illustrations, 2 portrait plates, 8 folded maps;
> Volume 2: xvii, [1] p., 1 l., 482 p., plus 1 p. of
>   advertisements, frontispiece (portrait), 132
>   illustrations, 1 portrait plate, 2 folded maps.
> First English edition.
> References: AB 12443, OCLC 13384958.

Nordenskjöld, Adolf Erik (1832–1901)
**   [523]**
The Voyage of the Vega round Asia and
Europe, with a Historical Review of
Previous Journeys along the North Coast
of the Old World, by A.E. Nordenskiöld.
Translated by Alexander Leslie. With Five
Steel Portraits, Numerous Maps, and
Illustrations. New York: Macmillan and
Co., 1882.

Octavo, green cloth with gilt titles.
xxvi, 756 p., frontispiece (portrait), 298 illustrations, 4
   portrait plates, 10 folded maps.
First American edition.
References: AB 12444, OCLC 223254.

Nordenskjöld, Nils Otto Gustaf (1869–1928)   [524]

Antarctica; or, Two Years amongst the Ice of the South Pole, by Dr. N. Otto G. Nordenskjöld and Dr. Joh. Gunnar Andersson. London: Hurst and Blackett, Limited; New York: The Macmillan Co., 1905.

Octavo, original green cloth with gilt titles.
xviii, [1], 608 p., frontispiece (portrait), illustrations, 129
   plates (4 color), portraits, 8 maps (3 folded).
First American edition.
References: Spence 861, OCLC 3768057.

Nordenskjöld, Nils Otto Gustaf (1869–1928) and Ludwig Mecking (1879–   )   [525]

The Geography of the Polar Regions, Consisting of a General Characterization of Polar Nature, by Otto Nordenskjöld, and a Regional Geography of the Arctic and the Antarctic, by Ludwig Mecking. New York: American Geographical Society, 1928.

Quarto, original gray cloth with gilt titles on black
   labels.
2 p. l., [iii]-vi p., 2 l., 3–359 p., illustrations (including
   maps), diagrams.
American Geographical Society Special Publication
   no. 8.
References: Spence 863, OCLC 1934249.

North Georgia Gazette   [526]

The North Georgia Gazette, and Winter Chronicle. Edited by Edward Sabine. London: John Murray, MDCCCXXI [1821]

Quarto, contemporary three-quarter calf and marbled
   original boards and edges, rebacked, gilt titles.
xii, 132 p.
First collected edition.
References: AB 12547, OCLC 15070269.

Nourse, Joseph Everett (1819–1889)   [527]

American Explorations in the Ice Zones: The Expeditions of DeHaven, Kane, Rodgers, Hayes, Hall, Schwatka, and DeLong; the Relief Voyages for the Jeannette by the U.S. Steamers Corwin, Rodgers, and Alliance; the Cruises of Captains Long and Raynor of the Merchant Service; the Greely Expedition and Rescue of the Survivors; the Discoveries of Lieutenant Lockwood, and the Naval Explorations in Alaska under Lieutenants Ray and Stoney. With a Brief Notice of the Antarctic Cruise under Lieutenant Wilkes, 1840, and of the Locations and Objects of the U.S. Signal Service Arctic Observers. Prepared Chiefly from Official Sources by Prof. J.E. Nourse, U.S.N. [etc.]. Third Edition. Boston: Published by B.B. Russell, [1884].

Octavo, original decorated green cloth with black,
   silver and gilt titles.
624 p., frontispiece, 35 plates (including portraits,
   illustrations, facsimiles, diagrams, maps (1
   double).
Reference: OCLC 7366017.

O'Brien, John S. (1899–1938)   [528]

By Dog Sled for Byrd: 1600 Miles across Antarctic Ice, by John S. O'Brien. Illustrations by Richard Rodgers and Ben Stahl. Chicago: Thomas S. Rockwell Company, 1931.

Octavo, original blue cloth with silver titles.
192 p., frontispiece (portrait), [6] leaves of plates,
   illustrations, maps on endpapers.
References: Spence 870, OCLC 374985.

Ommanney, Francis D. (1903–   )   [529]

South Latitude, by F.D. Ommanney. With 16 Illustrations. London, New York and Toronto: Longmans, Green and Co., [1938].

Octavo, original turquoise cloth with gilt titles.
x, [1], 308 p., frontispiece, [8] leaves of plates
(including portraits), maps on endpapers.
First edition.
References: Spence 873, OCLC 946757.

O'Reilly, Bernard (1783?–)   [530]

Greenland, the Adjacent Seas and the
North-West Passage to the Pacific Ocean,
Illustrated in a Voyage to Davis's Strait,
During the Summer of 1817. With Charts
and Numerous Plates, from Drawings of
the Author Taken on the Spot. By Bernard
O'Reilly, Esq. London: Printed for
Baldwin, Cradock and Joy, 1818.

Quarto, contemporary three-quarter calf, raised bands,
marbled boards, gilt titles. Binder's title: O'Reilly's
Greenland.
vi, [2], 293 p., frontispiece (map), 18 plates, 2 folded
maps.
First edition.
References: AB 12852, OCLC 4428935.

Osborn, Sherard (1822–1875)   [531]

Stray Leaves from an Arctic Journal; or,
Eighteen Months in the Polar Regions, in
Search of Sir John Franklin's Expedition, in
the Years 1850–51. By Lieut. Sherard
Osborn, Commanding H.M.S. Vessel,
"Pioneer." Dedicated to Lady Franklin.
London: Longman, Brown, Green and
Longmans, 1852.

Octavo, later three-quarter calf on gray boards, raised
bands.
vii p., 1 l., 320 p., color frontispiece, 3 color plates,
illustrations.
First edition.
References: AB 12899, OCLC 9062509.

Osborn, Sherard (1822–75)

(See also Illustrated Arctic News; McClure,
Robert John LeMesurier, Sir)

Outhier, Ræaginald   [532]

Journal d'un Voyage au Nord, en 1736. &
1737. Par M. Outhier, Prêtre du Diocèse
de Besançon, Correspondant de
l'Académie Royal des Sciences. A Paris:
Chez Pigot, Libraire, Quaites Augustins, à
l'image S. Jacques; Chez Durand, Libraire,
rue Saint Jacques, au Griffon, MDCCXLIV
[1744].

Quarto, modern mottled brown calf with gilt
decorations, gilt title on label, raised bands.
4 p. l., 238 p., [2] p. of advertisements, 11 folded
plates, illustrations, 5 folded maps and plans.
First edition.
Reference: Sabin 5793.

Owen, Russell (1889–1952)   [533]

The Antarctic Ocean [by] Russell Owen.
London: Museum Press Limited, [1948].

Octavo, turquoise cloth with gilt titles on decorated
white label, dust jacket.
225 p., frontispiece, 13 plates, 12 maps, maps on
endpapers.
First U.K. Edition.
References: Spence 885, OCLC 2747775.

Owen, Russell (1889–1952)   [534]

South of the Sun, by Russell Owen. New
York: The John Day Company, [1934].

Octavo, original blue cloth with silver titles, dust jacket.
288 p., illustration on title-page.
Signed by the author.
References: Spence 883, OCLC 987815.

Palmer, James C.   [535]

Thulia: A Tale of the Antarctic. By J.C.
Palmer, U.S.N. New-York: Published by
Samuel Colman, MDCCCXLIII [1843].

Octavo, gold-stamped pictorial black calf, gilt edges.
72 p., 3 plates, illustrations.
First edition.
References: Spence 890, Haskell 186.

Parfit, Michael   [536]

South Light: A Journey to the Last
Continent [by] Michael Parfit. New York:
Macmillan Publishing Company, [1985].

Octavo, purple cloth boards on blue spine, silver titles,
dust jacket.
ix p., 1 l., 306 p., frontispiece (map).
Reference: OCLC 12342193.

Parijanine, Maurice (1885–) [537]
The Krassin, by Maurice Parijanine.
Translated by Lawrence Brown. Illustrated.
New York: The Macaulay Company,
[1929].
> Octavo, black cloth, red titles.
> 216, [2] p., frontispiece, [7] leaves of plates, 1 map
> (double).
> First American edition.
> Reference: AB 13112.

Parmer, Jean M. [538]
Polar Books: Bibliography and Price Guide
Version 2.0. San Diego, CA: Jean M. and
Jerome F. Parmer, 1990.
> Quarto, spiral bound, plastic and paper cover.
> v, 106 leaves.
> 1,150 titles on Alaska, the Arctic and Antarctica.
> Reference: OCLC 22489680.

Parry, Ann [539]
Parry of the Arctic: The Life Story of
Admiral Sir Edward Parry, 1790–1855. By
Ann Parry. London: Chatto & Windus,
1963.
> Octavo, original blue cloth with gilt titles, dust jacket.
> 240 p., [8] leaves of plates, facsimile, 7 maps (1
> folded).
> First edition.
> Reference: OCLC 4276904.

Parry, William Edward, Sir (1790–1855)
[540]
[Voyage, 1st] Journal of a Voyage for the
Discovery of a North-west Passage from
the Atlantic to the Pacific; Performed in
the Years 1819–20, in His Majesty's Ships
Hecla and Griper, under the Orders of
William Edward Parry, R.N., F.R.S. and
Commander of the Expedition. With an
Appendix, Containing the Scientific and
Other Observations. Published by
Authority of the Lords Commissioners of
the Admiralty. London: John Murray,

Publisher to the Admiralty, and Board of
Longitude, MDCCCXXI [1821].
> Quarto, old three-quarter calf with marbled boards,
> edges and endpapers, gilt titles.
> xxix, 310, clxxix p., 4 l., [clxxxiiii]-cccx, frontispiece
> (folded map), [7] leaves of plates, 5 maps (3
> folded), an additional 6 plates in the
> Supplement.
> Bound with: A Supplement to the Appendix of Captain
> Parry's Voyage for the Discovery of a North-west
> Passage, in the Years 1819–20. Containing An
> Account of the Subjects of Natural History.
> London: John Murray, MDCCCXXIV [1824].]
> Pagination of supplement is continuous.
> References: Sabin 58860, OCLC 4223205.

Parry, William Edward, Sir (1790–1855)
[541]
[Voyage, 2d] Journal of a Second Voyage
for the Discovery of a North-west Passage
from the Atlantic to the Pacific; Performed
in the Years 1821–22–23, in His Majesty's
Ships Fury and Hecla, under the Orders of
Captain William Edward Parry, R.N.,
F.R.S., and Commander of the Expedition.
Illustrated by Numerous Plates. Published
by Authority of the Lords Commissioners
of the Admiralty. London: John Murray,
Publisher to the Admiralty, and Board of
Longitude, MDCCCXXIV [1824].
> Quarto, contemporary polished calf, very skillfully
> rebacked, marbled boards, edges and
> endpapers, gilt titles on red label, raised bands.
> Binder's date on spine is 1825.
> 5 p. l., xxx p., 1 l., 571, [1] p., frontispiece, [13] leaves
> of plates, 13 maps and views (8 folded).
> Imperfect: Plate facing p. 436 is lacking.
> References: AB 13142, OCLC 4106096.

Parry, William Edward, Sir (1790–1855)
[542]
[Voyage, 3d] Journal of a Third Voyage for
the Discovery of a North-west Passage
from the Atlantic to the Pacific; Performed
in the Years 1824–25, in His Majesty's
Ships Hecla and Fury, under the Orders of
Captain William Edward Parry, R.N.,

F.R.S., and Commander of the Expedition. Illustrated by Plates and Charts. Published by Authority of the Lords Commissioners of the Admiralty. London: John Murray, Publisher to the Admiralty, and Board of Longitude, MDCCCXXVI [1826].

> Large quarto, uncut in original boards, paper label. In quarter blue calf drop-spine box, gilt lettering, raised bands.
> xxvii, [1], 186 p., 1 l., 151, [1] p., frontispiece, 6 plates (1 folded), 4 maps (1 folded).
> First edition.
> References: AB 13144, OCLC 1193384.

Parry, William Edward, Sir (1790–1855) [543]

[Voyage, 4th] Narrative of an Attempt to Reach the North Pole, in Boats Fitted for the Purpose, and Attached to His Majesty's Ship Hecla, in the Year MDCCCXXVII, under the Command of Captain William Edward Parry, R.N., F.R.S., and Honorary Member of the Imperial Academy of Sciences at St. Petersburg. Illustrated by Plates and Charts. Published by Authority of His Royal Highness the Lord Admiral. London: John Murray, Publisher to the Admiralty, and Board of Longitude, MDCCCXXVIII [1828].

> Quarto, contemporary three-quarter calf, skillfully rebacked, marbled boards, edges and endpapers, gilt titles, raised bands. Binder's title: Parry's Voyage. 4th Voyage.
> xxii p., 1 l., 229, [1] p., frontispiece, 3 plates, 3 maps (1 folded).
> References: AB 13146, OCLC 4106051.

Partridge, Bellamy [544]

Amundsen, the Splendid Norseman. By Bellamy Partridge. New York: Frederick A. Stokes Company, MCMXXIX [1929].

> Octavo, blue cloth with gold titles.
> xvi, [4], 276 p., frontispiece (portrait), [3] leaves of plates, maps on endpapers.
> Fifth printing.
> Reference: Spence 898.

Payer, Julius (1842–1915) [545]

New Lands within the Arctic Circle. Narrative of the Discoveries of the Austrian Ship "Tegetthoff" in the Years 1872–1874. By Julius Payer, One of the Commanders of the Expedition. With Maps and Numerous Illustrations from Drawings by the Author. Translated from the German, with the Author's Approbation. In Two Volumes. London: Macmillan and Co., 1876.

> Octavo, 2 volumes, original decorated cloth, gilt titles. Binder's title: Austrian Arctic Voyage 1872–4.
> Volume 1: xxxi, [1], 335, [1] p., color frontispiece, 11 plates, illustrations, double map; Volume 2: xiv, 303, [1] p., frontispiece, 10 plates, illustrations, double map.
> First English edition.
> References: AB 13202, OCLC 5438645.

Peard, George (1783–1837) [546]

To the Pacific and Arctic with Beechey: The Journal of Lieutenant George Peard of H.M.S. "Blossom," 1825–1828. Edited by Barry M. Gough. Cambridge: Published for the Hakluyt Society at the University Press, 1973.

> Octavo, original blue cloth, dust jacket, gilt titles.
> x, 272 p., frontispiece (portrait), illustrations, 3 plates, 4 maps (2 folded).
> Works issued by the Hakluyt Society, 2nd Series, vol. 143.
> Reference: OCLC 900678.

Peary, Josephine Diebitsch [547]

My Arctic Journal: A Year among Ice-fields and Eskimos, by Josephine Diebitsch-Peary. With an Account of the Great White Journey across Greenland by Robert E. Peary, Civil Engineer, U.S. Navy. New York and Philadelphia: The Contemporary Publishing Company, 1893.

> Octavo, original green cloth with red and gilt titles.
> 240 p., frontispiece (portrait), 21 plates (4 colored), illustrations, portraits, 3 maps.
> First edition.
> References: AB 13221, OCLC 10065908.

Peary, Robert Edwin (1856–1920)

[548]

Nearest the Pole: A Narrative of the Polar Expedition of the Peary Arctic Club in the S.S. Roosevelt, 1905–1906, by R.E. Peary, U.S.N. With Ninety-five Photographs by the Author, Two Maps and a Frontispiece in Colour by Albert Operti. New York: Doubleday, Page & Company, 1907.

> Octavo, original green cloth with gilt titles.
> xx, 411 p., color frontispiece, [32] leaves of plates (including portraits), 2 folded maps.
> First edition.
> References: AB 13226, OCLC 494902.

Peary, Robert Edwin (1856–1920)

[549]

North Polar Exploration: Field Work of the Peary Arctic Club, 1898–1902. By R.E. Peary, Commander, U.S. Navy. From the Smithsonian Report for 1903, Pages 427–457. (With Plates I-IX). Washington: Government Printing Office, 1904.

> Octavo, original printed wrappers. Uncut copy.
> [4] leaves of plates, folded map.
> Reference: OCLC 14389488, cf. AB 13229.

Peary, Robert Edwin (1856–1920)

[550]

The North Pole. Its Discovery in 1909 under the Auspices of the Peary Arctic Club, by Robert E. Peary. With an Introduction by Theodore Roosevelt, and a Foreword by Gilbert H. Grosvenor, Director and Editor, National Geographic Society. With Eight Full-page Illustrations Reproducing Photographic Enlargements Colored by Hand; One Hundred Illustrations in Black-and-white, from Photographs; and with a Map in Colors by Gilbert H. Grosvenor. New York: Frederick A. Stokes Company, 1910.

> Octavo, original blue pictorial cloth with gilt titles and top-edge.

xxxii, 373 p., color frontispiece (portrait), [36] leaves of plates (7 color), illustrations, folded map.
> References: AB 13230, OCLC 17997189.

Peary, Robert Edwin (1856–1920)

[551]

The North Pole. Its Discovery in 1909 under the Auspices of the Peary Arctic Club, By Robert E. Peary. With an Introduction by Theodore Roosevelt, and a Foreword by Gilbert H. Grosvenor, Director and Editor, National Geographic Society. With Eight Full-page Illustrations Reproducing Photographic Enlargements Colored by Hand; One Hundred Illustrations in Black-and-white, from Photographs; and with a Map in Colors by Gilbert H. Grosvenor. New York: Frederick A. Stokes Company, 1910.

> Octavo, three-quarter blue morocco with gilt titles and top-edge, raised bands.
> xxxii, 373 p., color frontispiece (portrait), [36] leaves of plates (7 color), illustrations, folded map.
> First edition.
> At head of title: General Hubbard Edition.
> Edition of 500 numbered copies. This is number 276, signed by Peary.
> Reference: AB 13230.

Peary, Robert Edwin (1856–1920)

[552]

Northward over the "Great Ice." A Narrative of Life and Work along the Shores and upon the Interior Ice-Cap of Northern Greenland in the Years 1886 and 1891–1897. With a Description of the Little Tribe of Smith-Sound Eskimos, the Most Northerly Human Beings in the World, and an Account of the Discovery and Bringing Home of the "Saviksere," or Great Cape-York Meteorites, By Robert E. Peary [etc.] With Maps, Diagrams, and about Eight Hundred Illustrations. In Two Volumes. New York: Frederick A. Stokes Company, MDCCCXCVIII [1898].

Octavo, 2 volumes, original blue cloth with white
titles.
Volume 1: 3 p. l, xv-lxxx, 521 p.; Volume 2: 1 p. l., [v]-
xiv, 625 p., frontispieces (portraits), illustrations,
plates, portraits, 9 maps (1 folded).
First edition.
References: AB 13231, OCLC 486568.

Peary, Robert Edwin (1856–1920)
[553]

Secrets of Polar Travel, by Robert E. Peary.
Illustrated with Photographs. New York:
The Century Co., 1917.

Octavo, original decorated blue cloth with gilt titles.
ix p., 3 l., 3–312 p., frontispiece (portrait), [39] leaves
of plates.
First American edition?
References: AB 13238, OCLC 1850507.

Peary, Robert Edwin (1856–1920)
(See also Goodsell, John W.)

Perkins, Robert
[554]

Into the Great Solitude: An Arctic Journey
[by] Robert Perkins. New York: Henry
Holt and Company, [1991].

Octavo, brown half cloth/blue hardboard covers, gilt
titles, dust jacket.
xi, [1] p., 2 l., 219 p., frontispiece, illustrations,
facsimiles, maps.
First Edition, Second Printing
Reference: OCLC 22178865.

Perry, Richard
[555]

The Jeannette; and a Complete and
Authentic Narrative Encyclopedia of All
Voyages and Expeditions to the North
Polar Regions, Containing a Complete
Account of the Most Remarkable Examples
of Heroism, Endurance and Suffering on
Record. Embracing the Biography and
Voyages of Franklin, Kane, Hayes, Hall,
and De Long, with an Account of the
Development of Arctic Navigation through
the Voyages of the Norsemen, the Cabots,
Gilbert, Davis, Barentz, Hudson, Baffin,
Behring, MacKenzie, Cook, Scoresby,
Parry, Wrangell, Ross, Nares,
Nordenskiold, Schwatka, Smith, Young,
and Many Others; an Accurate Description
of All Important Scientific and
Geographical Discoveries Ever Made in the
Frozen North. By Capt. Richard Perry.
Elegantly Illustrated with Two Hundred
Engravings. Chicago: The Coburn & Cook
Publishing Company [etc.], 1882.

Octavo, original decorated red cloth with gilt titles,
marbled edges.
xvi, [17]-840 p., including frontispiece, illustrations.
References: AB 13318, OCLC 3768244.

Perry, Richard (1909–   )
[556]

The World of the Polar Bear [by] Richard
Perry. [Seattle]: University of Washington
Press, [1966].

Octavo, original blue cloth with silver titles, dust jacket.
[xi], 195 p., [4] leaves of plates, map.
First American edition.
Reference: OCLC 11009305.

Petermann, Augustus; W. von Freeden; and A. Mühry
[557]

Papers on the Eastern and Northern
Extensions of the Gulf Stream. From the
German of Dr. A. Petermann, Dr. W. von
Freeden, and Dr. A. Mühry. Translated in
the United States Hydrographic Office, in
Charge of Captain R.H. Wyman, U.S.N.,
by E.R. Knorr [with First-Sixth
Supplements]. Washington: Government
Printing Office 1871 [-1875].

Imperial octavo, 3 volumes, original three-quarter
pebbled calf and boards, marbled edges,
Volumes 1 and 3 have marbled endpapers.
Volume 1: viii, [1], 388 p., 2 folded maps.
[Supplements] Volume 2: 18, [27], 57 p., and 2
folded maps; Volume 3: 46, 16 p., and folded
map; 32 p. and map.
First English editions.
References: cf. AB 13347, OCLC 5111018.

Peterson, Roger Tory [558]
Penguins [by] Roger Tory Peterson.
Boston: Houghton Mifflin and Company,
1979.

> Quarto, black cloth with gilt titles, dust jacket.
> x, [5], 238 p., illustrations, photographs (chiefly color),
> map, endpaper color drawings by R.T.
> Peterson.
> First edition.
> Reference: OCLC 4804526.

de Peyster, John Watts (1821–1907)
[559]
The Dutch at the North Pole and the
Dutch in Maine. A Paper Read before the
New York Historical Society, 3rd March,
1857. By J. Watts de Peyster, a Member of
the Society. New York: Printed for the
Society, M DCCC LVII [1857].

> Octavo, in original printed wrappers.
> 80 p.

**Phipps, Constantine John, 2d baron
Mulgrave (1744–1792)** [560]
A Voyage towards the North Pole
Undertaken by His Majesty's Command
1773, by Constantine John Phipps.
London: Printed by W. Bowyer and J.
Nichols, For J. Nourse, Bookseller to His
Majesty, in the Strand, MDCCLXXIV
[1774].

> Quarto, contemporary decorated calf, rebacked, raised
> bands, gilt title on red label, marbled endpapers.
> viii, 253, [1] p., frontispiece (folded map), 14 folded
> plates, tables, (some folded), 2 folded maps.
> References: Sabin 62572, OCLC 13624360.

Pierce, Richard A.
(See Lantzeff, George V.)

Pike, Warburton Mayer (1861–1915)
[561]
The Barren Ground of Northern Canada,
by Warburton Pike. London and New
York: Macmillan and Co., 1892.

> Octavo, original green cloth with gilt titles.
> ix p., 1 l., 300 p., 55 p. of advertisements, 2 folded
> maps.
> References: AB 13527, OCLC 8989382.

Pike, Warburton Mayer (1861–1915)
[562]
Through the Sub-Arctic Forest: A Record
of a Canoe Journey from Fort Wrangel to
the Pelly Lakes and down the Yukon River
to the Behring Sea, by Warburton Pike
[etc.]. With Illustrations and Maps.
London and New York: Edward Arnold,
Publisher to the India Office, 1896.

> Octavo, original brown decorated cloth with black
> and gilt titles.
> xiv p., 1 l., 295 p., 32 p. of advertisements,
> frontispiece, 12 plates, illustrations, 2 folded
> maps.
> References: AB 13528, OCLC 2580939.

Polar Book [563]
The Polar Book. London: E. Allom & Co.,
Ltd., [1930].

> Octavo, original printed wrappers.
> 115 p., folded map.
> Foreword signed: L.C. Bernacchi, organizing director
> British Polar Exhibition, 1930.
> The volumes contain signature pages with the
> signatures of many prominent polar explorers,
> such as Sir Vivian Fuchs and others.
> References: Spence 125, OCLC 8989778.

Polar Record [564]
The Polar Record: A Journal of Arctic and
Antarctic Exploration and Research.
Cambridge [England]: At the University
Press, 1931- .

> Medium octavo to 1987, quarto beginning 1988. Blue
> cloth with gilt titles.
> Organ of the Scott Polar Research Institute.
> Vol. 1—date. Indexes, autographs, charts, photos,
> diagrams, maps.
> References: AB 13626–27–28–28A-29, OCLC
> 1762535.

Pommier, Robert
(See Liotard, André-Frank)

Poncins, Gontran de Montaigne, vicomte de, (1900–　) **[565]**

Kabloona [by] Gontran de Poncins, in Collaboration with Lewis Galentière. Illustrated by the Author. New York: Reynal & Hitchcock, Inc., [1941].

> Octavo, original quarter cloth on black boards, white titles on black label.
> xii, 339 p., [20] leaves of plates (4 color), illustrations, portraits, maps on endpapers.
> References: AB 13701, cf. OCLC 419644.

Ponting, Herbert George **[566]**

The Great White South: Being an Account of Experiences with Captain Scott's South Pole Expedition and of the Nature Life of the Antarctic, by Herbert G. Ponting [etc.], and an Introduction by Lady Scott. London: Duckworth & Co., [1921].

> Octavo, quarter blue morocco on blue boards, with gilt titles, ex libris.
> xxvi, 305, [1] p., frontispiece (portrait), [96] leaves of plates (including maps.)
> References: Spence 925, OCLC 1000701.

Ponting, Herbert George **[567]**

Scott's Last Voyage through the Antarctic Camera of Herbert Ponting. Edited by Ann Savours. Introduced by Sir Peter Scott. New York and Washington: Praeger Publishers, [1975].

> Crown quarto, blue cloth with silver titles, dust jacket.
> 160 p., photo illustrations (some color), maps.
> References: Spence 1031 (London edition), OCLC 995009.

Ponting, Herbert George and Frank Hurley (1890–1962) **[568]**

1910–1916: Antarctic Photographs, Herbert Ponting and Frank Hurley: Scott, Mawson and Shackleton Expeditions. Foreword by Sir Vivian Fuchs. Introduced by Jennie Boddington. New York: St. Martin's Press, 1980.

> Oblong octavo, black cloth with white titles, dust jacket.

> 119 p., [18] leaves of plates (photographs).
> First American edition.
> Reference: OCLC 5800481.

Porter, Eliot (1901–　) **[569]**

Antarctica [by] Eliot Porter. Foreword by Walter Sullivan. New York: E.P. Dutton, [1978].

> Square folio, original white cloth with black titles, dust jacket.
> 168 p., color photographs, 3 maps, maps on endpapers.
> First edition.
> References: Spence 932, OCLC 3844068.

Porter, Russell Williams (1871–1949) **[570]**

The Arctic Diary of Russell Williams Porter. Edited by Herman Friis. Charlottesville: University Press of Virginia, 1976.

> Square quarto, original blue cloth with gilt titles, dust jacket.
> xii, 171, [1] p., color frontispiece (portrait), illustrations (some color), portraits, 4 maps.
> First edition.
> Reference: OCLC 1992152.

Portlock, Nathaniel (1748–1817) [571]

A Voyage round the World; but More Particularly to the North-West Coast of America: Performed in 1785, 1786, 1787 and 1788 in the King George and Queen Charlotte, Captains Portlock and Dixon. Embellished with Twenty Copper-plates. Dedicated, by Permission, to His Majesty, by Captain Nathaniel Portlock. London: Printed for John Stockdale, opposite Burlington-House, Piccadilly; and George Goulding, James Street, Covent Garden, M,DCC,LXXXIX [1789].

> Quarto, three-quarter burgundy morocco, gilt titles and decorations.
> xii, 384, xl p., frontispiece (portrait), [13] leaves of plates, 6 folded maps, tables.
> References: Sabin 64389, Howes 497, OCLC 1556302.

Portrait of Antarctica [572]

Portrait of Antarctica. [Photographs by Kevin Walton, Launcelot Fleming, Paul Goodall-Copestake, et al.] Foreword by HRH the Prince of Wales. London: George Philip, 1983.

> Square octavo, blue cloth with white titles, dust jacket.
> 168 p., illustrations (some color), 2 maps.
> Reference: OCLC 10356976.

Poulsom, Neville Wright [573]

The White Ribbon: A Medallic Record of British Polar Expeditions [by] Major Neville W. Poulsom. London: B.A. Seaby Ltd., [1968].

> Large octavo, black cloth with silver titles, dust jacket.
> 216 p., frontispiece, [4] leaves of plates, tables.
> Laid in: Photocopy of typescript list of "Polar Medals, 1966–1979," compiled by D. W. H. Walton (4p.).
> First edition.
> References: Spence 933, OCLC 61828.

Poulter, Thomas Charles (1897–) [574]

With Byrd in the Antarctic in Picture and Story. Buffalo and New York: J. W. Clement, [n.d.].

> Octavo, heavy paper cover, fore edge stained, cover torn at spine.
> [48] unnumbered p., photographs, illustrations.
> Cover title: The Romance of Antarctic Adventure.
> Reference: OCLC 5773654.

Pound, Reginald [575]

Scott of the Antarctic [by] Reginald Pound. New York: Coward-McCann, Inc., [1967].

> Octavo, original blue cloth with silver titles, dust jacket.
> xii, 327 p., [12] leaves of plates, 2 maps.
> First American edition.
> References: Spence 934, OCLC 1378824.

Powell, Theodore [576]

The Long Rescue, by Theodore Powell. Garden City, New York: Doubleday & Company, Inc., 1960.

> Octavo, original gray cloth with green titles, dust jacket.
> 374 p., [8] leaves of plates, maps on endpapers.
> Reference: OCLC 1492213.

Prentiss, Henry Mellen [577]

The Great Polar Current. Polar Papers: DeLong-Nansen-Peary, by Henry Mellen Prentiss. New York: Frederick A. Stokes Company, Publishers, [1897].

> Small octavo, original green decorated cloth with gilt titles and top edge.
> 4 p. l., 153 p.
> References: AB 13932, OCLC 2640127.

Price, A. Grenfell (1892–) [578]

The Winning of Australian Antarctica: Mawson's B.A.N.Z.A.R.E. Voyages 1929–31. Based on the Mawson Papers. By A. Grenfell Price [etc.]. Being Volume I, the Geographical Report, of the B.A.N.Z. Antarctic Research Expedition, 1929–31, Reports—Series A. Published for the Mawson Institute for Antarctic Research, University of Adelaide. [Sydney]: Angus and Robertson, [1962].

> Tall octavo, original cloth, dust jacket.
> xvii, 241 p., frontispiece (portrait), [15] leaves of plates, 13 maps (3 folded, 4 double).
> References: Spence 779, OCLC 594647.

Priestley, Raymond, Sir (1886–) [579]

Antarctic Adventure: Scott's Northern Party, by Raymond E. Priestly. With a Map and 150 Illustrations. London and Leipsic: T. Fisher Unwin, [1914].

> Octavo, original decorated blue cloth with silver titles, new endpapers.
> 382 p., frontispiece (portrait), [96] leaves of plates, 3 folded maps.
> References: Spence 939, OCLC 8443263.

Priestley, Raymond, Sir (1886–) [580]

Antarctic Research: A Review of British Scientific Achievement in Antarctica. Edited by Sir Raymond Priestley, Raymond J. Adie [and] G. de Q. Robin. With

Foreword by H.R.H. The Duke of Edinburgh. London: Butterworths, 1964.

Quarto, original blue cloth with silver titles, in light blue paper slipcase.
xi, 360 p., [8] leaves of plates, illustrations, portraits, diagrams, maps (part colored), 2 folded maps in portfolio).
References: Spence 942, OCLC 486849.

Pullen, William J. S. (1813–1887) [581]
The Pullen Expedition in Search of Sir John Franklin: The Original Diaries, Log and Letters of Commander W.J.S. Pullen. Selected and Introduced by H.F. Pullen. [Toronto, Ontario]: The Arctic History Press, [1979].

Octavo, blue leatherette with gilt titles, back cover detached, in paper slipcase.
230 p., [4] leaves of plates, 4 folded maps.
Edition of 1000 copies. This is copy 509.
Reference: OCLC 5232947.

Putnam, George Palmer (1887–   )
[582]
Andreé: The Record of a Tragic Adventure, by George Palmer Putnam. New York: Brewer & Warren, Inc., 1930.

Octavo, original blue cloth with white titles.
6 p. l., 11–239, [1] p., frontispiece (portrait), [15] leaves of plates, map.
First printing.
References: AB 14004, OCLC 1521362.

Putnam, George Rockwell   [583]
The Scientific Work of the Boston Party on the Sixth Peary Expedition to Greenland. Report A. Magnetic and Pendulum Observations, by G.R. Putnam, M.S. [etc.]. [Boston: Massachusetts Institute of Technology, 1897].

Octavo, original tan printed wrappers.
Reprint from *Technology Quarterly* 10, no. 1 (March 1897): 56–132, [3] leaves of plates, illustrations, maps.
Reference: cf. AB 14010.

Pyne, Stephen J.   [584]
The Ice: A Journey to Antarctica [by]

Stephen J. Pyne. Iowa City: University of Iowa Press, [1987].

Octavo, green cloth with black titles, dust jacket.
5 p. l., 428 p., [8] leaves of plates, illustrations, maps.
Second printing.
Reference: OCLC 16081934 (London edition.)

Quartermain, L.B.   [585]
South to the Pole: The Early History of the Ross Sea Sector, Antarctica [by] L.B. Quartermain. London, Wellington and Melbourne: Oxford University Press, 1967.

Large octavo, beige cloth covers, gilt titles on blue label.
xx, [1], 481 p., frontispiece (map), [13] leaves of plates, folded map, maps on endpapers.
Reference: Spence 949.

Rae, John (1813–1893)   [586]
John Rae's Correspondence with Hudson's Bay Company on Arctic Exploration, 1844–1855. Edited by E.E. Rich. Assisted by A.M. Johnson. With an Introduction by J.M. Wordie and R.J. Cyriax. London: The Hudson's Bay Record Society, 1953.

Octavo, original blue cloth with gilt titles.
cvi, [1], 401 p., 7 l., frontispiece (portrait), 1 plate, 3 maps (2 folded).
Limited edition.
(Publications of Hudson's Bay Record Society; Volume 16.)
References: OCLC 1262294 and 7504524.

Ralling, Christopher
(See Shackleton, Ernest Henry, Sir. Shackleton)

Randall, Harry (1858–   )   [587]
The Conquest of the Northwest Passage. A Treatise by Harry Randall. Minneapolis: [Murphy-Travis], 1907.

Octavo, original blue printed wrapper.
[10] p., double frontispiece (portrait and illustration).
Reference: OCLC 10856740.

Rankin, Niall   [588]
Antarctic Isle: Wild Life in South Georgia,

by Niall Rankin [etc.]. London: Collins, 1951.

> Octavo, original blue cloth with gilt titles.
> 383 p., frontispiece, [47] leaves of plates, illustrations, 3 maps (1 double), maps on endpapers.
> First edition.
> References: Spence 958, OCLC 5585021.

Rasmussen, Knud Johan Victor (1879–1933) [589]

Across Arctic America: Narrative of the Fifth Thule Expedition, by Knud Rasmussen. With 64 Illustrations and 4 Maps. New York and London: G.P. Putnam's Sons, 1927.

> Octavo, original blue cloth with gilt titles.
> xx, 388 p., frontispiece (portrait), [65] leaves of plates, 4 maps (1 folded), maps on endpapers.
> References: AB 14199, OCLC 1887987.

Rasmussen, Knud Johan Victor (1879–1933) [590]

Greenland by the Polar Sea. The Story of the Thule Expedition from Melville Bay to Cape Morris Jesup, by Knud Rasmussen. Translated from the Danish by Asta and Rowland Kenney. With Preface by Admiral Sir Lewis Beaumont, G.C.B. With Numerous Illustrations in Black and White, Eight Colour Plates, and Maps. London: William Heinemann, 1921.

> Octavo, original decorated green cloth with silver titles, dust jacket. Uncut copy.
> xxiii, 326, [1] p., color frontispiece (portrait), [47] leaves of plates (7 color), 14 maps (1 folded).
> 1st English edition.
> References: AB 14202, OCLC 5186258.

Rawlins, Dennis [591]

Peary at the North Pole: Fact or Fiction? Washington and New York: Robert B. Luce, Inc., [1973].

> Octavo, blue cloth with silver titles, dust jacket.
> 320 p., frontispiece (portrait), illustrations, portraits, facsimiles, maps, maps on endpapers.
> Reference: OCLC 693505.

Reed, William [592]

The Phantom of the Poles, by William Reed. New York: Walter S. Rockey Company, 1906.

> Octavo, original green cloth with gilt titles.
> 283 p., frontispiece (portrait), [6] leaves of plates (including portraits), illustrations.
> References: AB 14326, Spence 963, OCLC 2503355.

Rey, Louis
(See Unveiling the Arctic)

Rich, E. E.
(See Rae, John; Simpson, George, Sir)

Richardson, John, Sir (1787–1865) [593]

Arctic Ordeal: The Journal of John Richardson, Surgeon-Naturalist with Franklin, 1820–1822. Edited by C. Stuart Houston. Illustrated by H. Albert Hochbaum. Appendices by John W. Thomson (Lichenology) and Walter O. Kupsch (Geology). Foreword by W. Gillies Ross. Kingston and Montreal: McGill-Queen's University Press, 1985.

> Quarto, blue cloth with silver titles, dust jacket.
> xxxiii, [1], 349 p., frontispiece, black and white illustrations, drawings, 8 maps.
> 1985 reprint.
> Reference: OCLC 11534924.

Richardson, John, Sir (1787–1865) [594]

Arctic Searching Expedition: A Journal of a Boat-voyage through Rupert's Land and the Arctic Sea, in Search of the Discovery Ships under Command of Sir John Franklin. With an Appendix on the Physical Geography of North America. By Sir John Richardson [etc.]. In Two Volumes. Published by Authority. London: Longman, Brown, Green, and Longmans, 1851.

Octavo, 2 volumes, later three-quarter red morocco with gilt titles and top edges, marbled boards and endpapers, raised bands.
Volume 1: viii, 413, [1] p., color frontispiece, 8 color plates, illustrations, folded map (detached); Volume 2: vii, 426 p., color frontispiece, tables.
References: AB 14489, OCLC 4106148.

Richardson, John, Sir (1787–1865) [595]

Fauna Boreali-Americana; or the Zoology of the Northern Parts of British America: containing Descriptions of the Objects of Natural History Collected on the Late Northern Land Expeditions, under Command of Captain Sir John Franklin, R.N. By John Richardson [etc.] Surgeon and Naturalist to the Expeditions. Assisted by William Swainson [etc.] and the Reverend William Kirby [etc.]. Illustrated by Numerous Plates. Published under the Authority of the Right Honourable the Secretary of State for Colonial Affairs. London: John Murray, MDCCCXXIX [1829–1831].

Tall quarto, 2 volumes in uncut state. Vol. 1, rebound quarter brown cloth with original paper label; vol. 2, original green publisher's cloth with paper label.
Contents: Part First, Containing the Quadrupeds, by John Richardson (xlvi, 300 p., 28 plates) — Part Second, The Birds. By William Swainson [etc.] and John Richardson [etc.], Surgeon and Naturalist to the Expeditions [1831] (lxvi, 523, [1] p., 50 hand-colored plates).
References: AB 14502, 17331, OCLC 13607386.

Richardson, John, Sir (1787–1865) [596]

The Polar Regions, by Sir John Richardson [etc.]. Edinburgh: Adam and Charles Black, 1861.

Octavo, modern blue half calf with marbled boards and edges, gilt titles on red label, ex libris.
ix p., 1 l., 400 p., frontispiece (folded map).
"The present work is founded on an article written for the last edition of the Encyclopaedia Britannica under the same title." — Preface.
References: AB 14501, Spence 970, OCLC 13975594.

Richardson, John, Sir (1787–1865)

(See also Swainson, William. Fauna Boreali-Americana . . . Part Second)

Richter, Søren

(See Heyerdahl, Thor)

Riesenberg, Felix (1879–1939) [597]

Cape Horn: The Story of the Cape Horn Region, Including the Straits of Magellan from the Days of the First Discoverers, through the Glorious Age of Sail, to the Present Time; Recounting the Exploits of Magellan, Drake, Schouten, Fitzroy, Darwin, Melville, and Many Others, Including the Author's Own Experiences; Wherein Many New Facts Are Brought to Light, an Important Geographical Discovery is Made, and Several Great Heroes of the Sea, Foremost of Them John Davis, Are for the First Time Given Their Due. By Felix Riesenberg [etc.]. Charts by William Briesemeister [etc.]. Illustrated with Charts and Photographs. New York: Dodd, Mead & Company, 1951.

Quarto, original blue cloth with gilt titles.
xv, 452 p., [8] leaves of plates, maps on endpapers.
References: OCLC 2065706, cf. Spence 972.

Riiser-Larsen, Hjalmar

(See Heyerdahl, Thor)

Rink, Hinrich Johannes (1819–1893) [598]

Tales and Traditions of the Eskimo, with a Sketch of Their Habits, Religion, Language and Other Peculiarities, by Dr. Henry Rink [etc.]. Edited by Dr. Robert Brown [etc.]. With Numerous Illustrations, Drawn and Engraved by Eskimo.

Edinburgh and London: Blackwood and Sons, MDCCCLXXV [1875].

> Octavo, original brown pictorial cloth with gilt titles.
> xii, 472, [1] p., folded frontispiece (portrait), [5] leaves of plates (1 folded), illustrations.
> First English edition.
> References: AB 14629, OCLC 760582.

Riordan, Ann Fienup
(See Fienup-Riordan, Ann)

Roberts, Brian
(See Wilson, Edward Adrian. Edward Wilson's Birds of the Antarctic)

Robertson, Robert B. (1913–)   [599]
Of Whales and Men, by R.B. Robertson. New York: Alfred A. Knopf, 1954.

> Octavo, original turquoise cloth with gilt titles.
> xii, 299, [3] p., [8] leaves of plates, illustration.
> First edition, second printing.
> Reference: OCLC 5640945.

Robin, G. de Q.
(See Priestley, Raymond Edward, Sir. Antarctic Research)

Robson, Joseph   [600]
An Account of Six Years Residence in Hudson's Bay, from 1733 to 1736, and 1744 to 1747. By Joseph Robson, Late Surveyor and Supervisor of the Buildings to the Hudson's-bay Company. Containing a Variety of Facts, Observations, and Discoveries, Tending to Shew, I. The vast Importance of the Countries about Hudson's-Bay to Great-Britain, on Account of the Extensive Improvements That May Be Made There in Many Beneficial Articles of Commerce, Particularly in the Furs and in the Whale and Seal Fisheries. And, II. The Interested Views of the Hudson's Bay Company; and the Absolute Necessity of Laying Open the Trade, and Making it the Object of National Encouragement, as the Only Method of Keeping It Out of the Hands of the French. To Which Is Added an Appendix; Containing, I. A Short History of the Discovery of Hudson's-bay; and of the Proceedings of the English There Since the Grant of the Hudson's-bay Charter: Together with Remarks upon the Papers and Evidence Produced by that Company before the Committee of the Honourable House of Commons, in the Year 1749. II. An Estimate of the Expence of Building the Stone Fort, Called Prince of Wales's-fort, at the Entrance of Churchill-river. III. The Soundings of Nelson-river. IV. A Survey of the Course of Nelson-river. V. A Survey of Seal and Gillam's Islands. And, VI. A Journal of the Winds and Tides at Churchill-river, for Part of the Years 1746 and 1747. The Whole Illustrated, by a Draught of Nelson and Hayes's Rivers; a Draught of Churchill-river; and Plans of York-fort, and Prince of Wales's Fort. London: Printed for J. Payne and J. Bouquet in Pater-Noster-Row; Mr. Kincaid, at Edinburgh; Mr. Barry, at Glasgow; and Mr. J. Smith, at Dublin, MDCCLII [1752].

> Octavo, later half calf, marbled boards, spine label partially chipped away.
> 1 p. l., vi, 84, 95 p., frontispiece (folded map), [1] folded leaf of plates (containing 3 plans), 1 folded map.
> First edition.
> Includes 95 pages of appendices.
> References: Lande 1418, Sabin 72259, OCLC 729384.

Rodahl, Kaare (1917–)   [601]
North: The Nature and Drama of the Polar World [by] Kaare Rodahl. New York: Harper & Brothers, Publishers, [1953].

Octavo, original quarter gray cloth on black spine,
with white titles, dust jacket.
237 p., 1 l., [8] leaves of plates, maps on endpapers.
First Edition.
Reference: OCLC 486680.

Rolfsen, Nordahl
(See Brögger, W. C.)

Ronne, Finn [602]
Antarctic Command, by Finn Ronne,
Captain, USNR. Indianapolis: The Bobbs-
Merrill Company, Inc., [1961].

Octavo, original half green cloth on dark green spine
with black titles, dust jacket.
272 p., [8] leaves of plates.
First edition.
References: Spence 988, OCLC 2352572.

Ronne, Finn [603]
Antarctic Conquest: The Story of the
Ronne Expedition 1946–1948, by Finn
Ronne, Commander, U.S.N.R. New York:
G.P. Putnam's Sons, [1949].

Octavo, beige cloth with black titles, dust jacket.
xx, 299 p., frontispiece (portrait), [15] leaves of plates,
maps, maps on endpapers.
First edition.
References: Spence 986, OCLC 1522374.

Ross, James Clark, Sir (1800–1862) [604]
A Voyage of Discovery and Research in the
Southern and Antarctic Regions, During
the Years 1839–43. By Captain Sir James
Clark Ross, R.N. [etc.]. With Plates, Maps,
and Woodcuts. In Two Volumes. London:
John Murray, 1847.

Octavo, 2 volumes, original decorative blue cloth with
gilt titles.
Volume 1: lii p., 2 l., 366 p., frontispiece, [11] leaves of
plates (1 folded), 6 maps (2 folded); Volume 2: x
p., 2 l., 447, [1] p., 16 p. of advertisements,
frontispiece, [13] leaves of plates, 2 maps (1
folded).
First edition.
References: Spence 993, OCLC 5261508.

Ross, John, Sir (1777–1856) [605]
An Explanation of Captain Sabine's
Remarks on the Late Voyage of Discovery
to Baffin's Bay. By Captain John Ross,
R.N. London: John Murray, 1819.

Octavo, lacking half-title, 19th century half calf with
marbled boards, raised bands, gilt title on red
label, gilt top edge.
1 p l., 53, [1] p.
First edition.
References: Sabin 73371, Lande S1994, OCLC
16854291.

Ross, John, Sir (1777–1856) [606]
[Voyage, 1st] A Voyage of Discovery,
Made under the Orders of the Admiralty,
in His Majesty's Ships Isabella and
Alexander for the Purpose of Exploring
Baffin's Bay, and Inquiring into the
Probability of a North-West Passage. By
John Ross, K.S. Captain Royal Navy.
London: John Murray, 1819.

Quarto, half calf and boards, raised bands, gilt titles,
front joint cracked.
2 p. l., xxxix, [1], 252 p., 1 l., cxliv p., frontispiece
(folded map), [29] leaves of plates (part color,
part folded), 2 folded maps, tables, appendices.
References: AB 14873, OCLC 4559652.

Ross, John, Sir (1777–1856) [607]
[Voyage, 2d] Narrative of a Second Voyage
in Search of a North-west Passage, and of a
Residence in the Arctic Regions during the
Years 1829, 1830, 1831, 1832, 1833. By
Sir John Ross [etc.]. Including the Reports
of Commander, now Captain, James Clark
Ross [etc.] and the Discovery of the
Northern Magnetic Pole. London: A.W.
Webster, 1835.

Large quarto, 2 volumes, decorated blue cloth with
gilt titles.
Volume 1: xxxiii, 740 p., frontispiece, [28] leaves of
plates and maps (part colored, part folded);
Volume 2 (Appendix): xii, 120, cxliv, cii, [1] p.,
frontispiece (portrait), [17] leaves of plates (part
colored.)
References: AB 14866 & 14863, Sabin 73381, OCLC
1113450.

Ross, Margaret Isabel (1897–) [608]
South of Zero. The Journal of John Hale
Meredith While with the Clark-Jamison
Antarctic Expedition of 191- to 191- [*sic*].
Edited by M.I. Ross. Illustrated by John
D. Whiting. New York and London:
Harper & Brothers Publishers, 1931.
> Octavo, original blue cloth with gilt titles.
> xiv p., 1 l., 280 p., color frontispiece (portrait),
>   illustrations, maps on endpapers.
> First edition.
> Juvenile fiction.
> References: Spence 996, OCLC 657171.

Royal Geographical Society [609]
Arctic Geography and Ethnology. A
Selection of Papers on Arctic Geography
and Ethnology. Reprinted, and Presented
to the Arctic Expedition of 1875, by the
President, Council, and Fellows of the
Royal Geographical Society. London: John
Murray, 1875.
> Octavo, original blue cloth with gilt titles.
> xii, 292 p., illustrations, 2 folded maps.
> References: AB 14929, OCLC 2358927.

Royal Geographical Society [610]
The Voyage Southward of the "Discovery."
I. London to Madeira, by Hugh Robert
Mill. II. From Madeira to the Cape, by
George Murray. III. The "Discovery" and
the Relief Ship, by Sir Clements R.
Markham. London: Royal Geographical
Society, 1902.
> Octavo pamphlet, printed blue wrappers.
> 36 p., illustrations, map.
> Reprinted from *Geographical Journal* 19, no. 4 (April
>   1902): 417–52.

Rymill, John R. (1905–) [611]
Southern Lights: The Official Account of
the British Graham Land Expedition,
1934–1937, by John Rymill. With Two
Chapters by A. Stephenson and an

Historical Introduction by Hugh Robert
Mill. London: Chatto & Windus, 1938.
> Quarto, original green cloth with gilt titles.
> xv, 295, [1] p., frontispiece, [80] leaves of plates, maps
>   (part folded).
> References: Spence 1016, OCLC 8989685.

Sage, Bryan
(See Hosking, Eric John)

Salomonsen, Finn
(See Freuchen, Peter. The Arctic Year)

**Sargent, Epes (1813–1880) and
   William H. Cunnington [612]**
The Wonders of the Arctic World: A
History of All the Researches and
Discoveries in the Frozen Regions of the
North. From the Earliest Times; with
Sketches of the Cabots, Frobisher,
Hudson, Baffin, Behring, Cook, Ross,
Franklin, Parry, Back, Rae, McClintock,
Kane, Hayes, Hall, and Others, Who in
Their Perilous Explorations Defied
Hunger, Cold, Untold Sufferings and
Death Itself to Reveal the Mysteries of This
Wonderful Portion of the Globe. By Epes
Sargent, Esq. Together with a Complete
and Reliable History of the Polaris
Expedition under the Late Captain C.F.
Hall, from Official and Trustworthy
Sources, Embracing the Important
Discoveries of This Heroic Explorer, Who
Attained a Latitude Farther North than
Ever Before Reached; His Singular and
Untimely Death on the Very Eve of His
Great Triumph; the Remarkable Rescue of
Captain Tyson and Others of the Crew
from a Floating Field of Ice, Etc., Etc.,
Etc. By William H. Cunnington, Special
Correspondent of the Philadelphia Age.
With Numerous Illustrations. Sold Only by

Subscription. Philadelphia: Philadelphia Book Company; Chicago, Cincinnati or New Orleans: J.W. Goodspeed; San Francisco: A.L. Bancroft & Co., [1873].

> Octavo, original decorated red cloth with gilt titles and edges. Binder's title: The Arctic World and its Explorers.
> 651 p., double frontispiece (portraits), illustrations (some full page), map.
> At head of title: Perils and Escapes Among Icebergs!
> References: AB 15346, OCLC 11720603.

Sarychev, Gavriila Andreevich (1763–1831)   [613]

Account of a Voyage of Discovery to the North-East of Siberia, the Frozen Ocean, and the North-East Sea. By Gawrila Sarytschew, Russian Imperial Major-General to the Expedition. Translated from the Russian, and Embellished with Engravings. Amsterdam: N. Israel; New York: DaCapo Press, 1969.

> Octavo, 2 volumes in 1, original white cloth, gilt titles on blue labels.
> Volume 1: iv, [5]-70, [2] p., [4] leaves of plates (3 folded, 1 color); Volume 2: 80 p., 1 color plate.
> Reprint of original edition: London, Richard Phillips, 1806–07.
> References: Bibliotheca Australiana no. 64, OCLC 97284.

Savours, Ann   [614]

The Voyages of the Discovery: The Illustrated History of Scott's Ship [by] Ann Savours. Foreword by HRH the Duke of Edinburgh. Preface by the Late Peter Scott. London: Virgin Books, [1992].

> Octavo, blue cloth with gilt titles, dust jacket.
> xvi, 384 p., [12] leaves of plates (4 color), maps, maps on endpapers.
> First edition.
> Reference: OCLC 27962915.

Savours, Ann

(See also Ponting, Herbert George. Scott's Last Voyage; Wilson, Edward Adrian. Diary of the Discovery Expedition)

Savoy Theatre, London   [615]

Savoy Theatre. Two Weeks Beginning Monday Matinee, November 3, 1913. Matinee Daily. The Gaumont Co., Ltd., of London by Arrangement with the British Antarctic Expedition and Mr. Herbert G. Ponting Has the Honor to Present an Animated Picture Record and Lecture Illustrative and Descriptive of the Undying Story of Captain Scott and "Animal Life in the Antarctic," recorded by Herbert G. Ponting, F.R.G.S., London, Official Artist of the Expedition. . . . Lecturer Mr. Charles B. Hanford. [London, 1913].

> Broadside, 26.5 x 15 cm.

Scherman, Katharine   [616]

Spring on an Arctic Island [by] Katharine Scherman. With Illustrations. Boston and Toronto: Little, Brown and Company, [1956].

> Octavo, original blue cloth with silver titles, dust jacket.
> xvii, 331 p., [4] leaves of plates, maps on endpapers.
> First edition.
> Reference: OCLC 933398.

Schley, Winfield Scott (1839–1909)   [617]

Report of Winfield S. Schley, Commander, U.S. Navy, Commanding Greely Relief Expedition of 1884. Washington: Government Printing Office, 1887.

> Quarto, original green cloth with gilt titles.
> 75 p., frontispiece (portrait), [31] leaves of plates, 3 maps.
> References: AB 18385, OCLC 1185141.

Schley, Winfield Scott (1839–1909)   [618]

The Rescue of Greely, by Commander W.S. Schley, U.S.N., Commanding the Expedition of 1884 and Professor J.R. Soley, U.S.N. Illustrated from the Photographs and Maps of the Relief

Expedition. New York: Charles Scribner's Sons, 1885.

> Octavo, original blue cloth with gilt titles.
> vii, [1], 277 p., frontispiece (portrait), [13] leaves of plates, 3 folded maps.
> First edition.
> References: AB 15483, OCLC 2002941.

Scholes, William Arthur   [619]

Fourteen Men: The Story of the Australian Antarctic Expedition to Heard Island, by Arthur Scholes. London: George Allen & Unwin Ltd., [1951].

> Octavo, original blue cloth with red titles, dust jacket.
> 6 p. l., 273 p., 1 l., color frontispiece, [5] leaves of plates, map, maps on endpapers.
> References: OCLC 959212, cf. Spence 1032 (Melbourne edition).

Schooling, William, Sir (1860–1936)   [620]

The Governor and Company of Adventurers of England Trading into Hudson's Bay during Two Hundred and Fifty Years, 1670–1920. London: The Hudson's Bay Company, 1920.

> Tall quarto, rebound in green buckram with original stiff white covers bound in, gilt titles.
> xvi, 129, [1] p., color frontispiece (portrait), [20] leaves of plates (1 folded, 3 color), 2 maps (1 folded).
> First edition.
> Reference: OCLC 2491305.

Schulthess, Emil   [621]

Antarctica. A Photographic Survey by Emil Schulthess. [English Translation by Peter Gorge]. New York: Simon and Schuster, 1960.

> Oblong quarto, full color cover photos.
> Black and white and color photos with full descriptions, diagrams, maps.
> References: Spence 1041, OCLC 1522432.

Schwatka, Frederick (1849–1892) [622]

The Long Arctic Search: The Narrative of Lieutenant Frederick Schwatka, U.S.A.,

1878–1880, Seeking the Records of the Lost Franklin Expedition. Edited by Edouard A. Stackpole [etc.]. Mystic, Conn.: Marine Historical Association, 1965.

> Octavo, blue printed wrappers with black titles.
> 117 p., color frontispiece, illustrations, facsimiles, portraits, maps.
> Reference: OCLC 1012693.

Scoresby, William (1760–1829)   [623]

Seven Log-Books Concerning the Arctic Voyages of Captain William Scoresby, Senior, of Whitby, England. Issued in Fac-simile by the Explorers Club of New York, with Reproductions in Color of Portraits in Oils of Captain William Scoresby, Senior, and of Captain William Scoresby, Junior, D.D. Introductory Brochure Edited by Frederick S. Dellenbaugh. New York: The Explorers Club, 1916–17.

> Folio, 8 volumes in slipcase, original marbled paper boards. In blue cloth drop-spine box, gilt titles on blue label laid over larger gray label.
> Introductory volume: ix, 31 p., mounted color frontispiece (portrait), mounted color plate (portrait), illustrations, facsimiles, 4 maps (3 folded). Volumes I–VII are facsimiles.
> Volume 1 published in 1917.
> "Three Hundred Copies Printed and Plates Destroyed. This is Number 62."
> Reference: OCLC 3400376.

Scoresby, William (1789–1857)   [624]

An Account of the Arctic Regions, with a History and Description of the Northern Whale-Fishery. By W. Scoresby Jun. F.R.S.E. Illustrated by Twenty-Four Engravings. In Two Volumes. Edinburgh: Printed for Archibald Constable and Co. Edinburgh; and Hurst, Robinson and Co. Cheapside, London, 1820.

> Octavo, 2 volumes, contemporary three-quarter calf and marbled boards, raised bands, gilt title on black label, rebacked.
> Volume 1: xx, 551, Appendix 82 p., folded frontispiece, tables (part folded); Volume 2: viii,

574 p., frontispiece, [18] leaves of plates, 4 maps
(3 folded.)
References: AB 15610, OCLC 2932912.

Scoresby, William (1789–1857)   [625]

Journal of a Voyage to the Northern
Whale-Fishery; Including Researches and
Discoveries on the Eastern Coast of West
Greenland, Made in the Summer of 1822,
in the Ship Baffin of Liverpool. By William
Scoresby Junior [etc.]. Edinburgh: Printed
for Archibald Constable and Co.
Edinburgh; and Hurst, Robinson and Co.,
Cheapside, London, 1823.

Octavo, quarter tan cloth on gray boards, black titles,
uncut. Binder's title: Voyage to Greenland.
xliii, 472 p., frontispiece (folded map), [6] leaves of
plates (2 folded), folded map. Frontispiece is
detaching.
References: AB 15614, OCLC 13624707.

Scoresby-Jackson, Robert Edmund (1835–1867)   [626]

The Life of William Scoresby [etc.], by His
Nephew, R.E. Scoresby-Jackson [etc.].
London, Edinburgh, and New York: T.
Nelson and Sons, MDCCCLXI [1861].

Octavo, green cloth with gilt titles.
3 p. l., [v]-ix, [9]-406 p., frontispiece (portrait), [5]
leaves of plates (color), illustrations, diagrams,
folded map. Added title-page, engraved.
Frontispiece is detached.
First edition.
References: Sabin 78174, OCLC 4861976.

Scott, G. Firth   [627]

The Romance of Polar Exploration:
Interesting Descriptions of Arctic and
Antarctic Adventure from the Earliest Time
to the Voyage of the "Discovery" by G.
Firth Scott. With Twenty-four Illustrations.
Philadelphia: J.B. Lippincott Company;
London: Seeley & Co. Limited, 1907.

Small octavo, three-quarter red morocco with marbled
boards and endpapers, gilt titles and top edge.
351 p., frontispiece, [20] leaves of plates, 3 maps.
References: AB 15635, Spence 1042, OCLC 3572656.

Scott, James Maurice   [628]

Gino Watkins, by J.M. Scott. London:
Hodder & Stoughton, Publishers, [1935].

Octavo, blue cloth with gilt titles, dust jacket.
xviii, 317 p., color frontispiece (portrait), [28] leaves of
plates, genealogical table, 7 maps.
References: AB 15636, Spence 1044, OCLC 2750244.

Scott, Robert Falcon (1868–1912)   [629]

Scott's Last Expedition. In Two Volumes.
Volume I. Being the Journals of Captain
R.F. Scott, R.N., C.V.O. Volume II. Being
the Reports of the Journeys & the
Scientific Work Undertaken by Dr. E.A.
Wilson and the Surviving Members of the
Expedition. Arranged by Leonard Huxley,
with a Preface by Sir Clements R.
Markham [etc.]. With Photogravure
Frontispieces, 6 Original Sketches in
Photogravure by Dr. E.A. Wilson, 18
Coloured Plates (16 from Drawings by Dr.
Wilson), 260 Full-Page and Smaller
Illustrations, from Photographs taken by
Herbert C. Ponting, and Other Members
of the Expedition; Panoramas and Maps.
London: Smith, Elder & Co., 1913.

Large octavo, 2 volumes, original blue cloth with gilt
titles.
Volume 1: xxvi, 633 p., frontispiece (portrait), 122
plates (10 color, 2 folded), folded map; Volume
2: xiv p., 1 l., 534 p., frontispiece (portrait), 87
plates (8 color, 3 double), 7 folded maps.
First edition.
References: Spence 1056, OCLC 2276814.

Scott, Robert Falcon (1868–1912)   [630]

Scott's Last Expedition. In Two Volumes.
Volume I. Being the Journals of Capt. R.F.
Scott, R.N., C.V.O. Volume II. Being the
Reports of the Journeys and the Scientific
Work Undertaken by Dr. E.A. Wilson and
the Surviving Members of the Expedition.

Scott's hut at Cape Evans was built in 1911 and is still standing, preserved by the Antarctic Heritage Trust. Herbert Ponting ("Ponco"), the expedition's photographer, liked to be called a "camera artist" and his extraordinary photos provide a rich record of the Terra Nova expedition. With his hand-cranked "kinematograph" he made the first motion pictures of Antarctica.

"The Hut after the Winter," photograph by Herbert G. Ponting from *Scott's Last Expedition* (1913) [**629**]

Arranged by Leonard Huxley. With a Preface by Sir Clements Markham [etc.]. With Photogravure Frontispieces, 6 Original Sketches in Photogravure by Dr. E.A. Wilson, 18 Coloured Plates (16 from Drawings by Dr. Wilson), 260 Full-Page and Smaller Illustrations. From Photographs Taken by Herbert G. Ponting and Other Members of the Expedition, Panoramas and Maps. New York: Dodd, Mead and Company, 1913.

> Octavo, 2 volumes, original blue cloth with gilt titles.
> Volume 1: xxiv, 443 p., frontispiece (portrait), 122 plates (10 color, 2 folded), folded map (torn); Volume 2: xvi p., 1 l., 376 p., frontispiece (portrait), 87 plates (8 color, 3 double), 7 maps (5 folded).
> First American edition.
> References: Spence 1058, OCLC 1522514.

Scott, Robert Falcon (1868–1912)
[631]

"The Uttermost South." The Undying Story of Captain Scott from His Diaries. Illustrated with Photographs by Captain Robert F. Scott and H.G. Ponting, F.R.G.S. New York; London: The Ridgway Co., 1913.

> Octavo, original paper wrappers. On cover: First Publication of Captain Scott's Diary Found in His Frozen Camp.
> In *Everybody's Magazine* 29, no. 1 (July 1913): 1–17, 97–104; illustrations, portraits, maps.
> Published serially July-October, 1913; August-October issues wanting.
> Reference: cf. OCLC 14389282.

Scott, Robert Falcon (1868–1912)
[632]

The Voyage of the 'Discovery' By Captain Robert F. Scott, C.V.O., R.N. With 260 Full-Page and Smaller Illustrations by Dr. E.A. Wilson and Other Members of the Expedition, Photogravure Frontispieces, 12 Coloured Plates in Facsimile from Dr. Wilson's Sketches, Panoramas and Maps.

In Two Volumes. London: Smith, Elder, 1905.

> Large octavo, 2 volumes, original blue cloth with gilt titles, gilt decorative medallions.
> Volume 1: xix, [1], 556 p., frontispiece, 91 plates (7 color, 1 double), 3 maps (1 double, 1 folded in pocket). Volume 2: xii, 508 p., frontispiece (portrait), 91 plates (5 color, 4 double), 2 maps (1 folded in pocket).
> First English edition?
> References: Spence 1051, OCLC 911757.

Scott, Robert Falcon (1868–1912)
(See also Geikie Correspondence)

Seaver, George (1890–)
[633]
'Birdie' Bowers of the Antarctic. By George Seaver. With an Introduction by Apsley Cherry-Garrard. London: John Murray, [1944.]

> Octavo, original blue cloth with gilt titles on white label.
> xxii, 266 p., [7] leaves of plates (3 color), 2 maps (1 folded).
> Third edition.
> References: Spence 1038; cf. OCLC 1488003 and 20074588.

Seaver, George (1890–)
[634]
Edward Wilson of the Antarctic: Naturalist and Friend, by George Seaver. With Introduction by Apsley Cherry-Garrard. London: John Murray, [1933].

> Octavo, original blue cloth, gilt titles on white label.
> xxxiv, 299 p., color frontispiece (portrait), [22] leaves of plates (6 color), 3 maps (1 folded).
> First edition.
> References: Spence 1081, OCLC 13624084.

Seemann, Berthold (1825–1871) **[635]**
Narrative of the Voyage of H.M.S. Herald during the Years 1845–51, under the Command of Captain Henry Kellett, R.N., C.B.; Being a Circumnavigation of the Globe, and Three Cruizes to the Arctic Regions in Search of Sir John Franklin. By Berthold Seemann [etc.]. In Two Volumes. London: Reeve and Co., 1853.

Octavo, 2 volumes, modern three-quarter blue
morocco, gilt titles, top edges and blind-stamped
anchor decorations on spines, raised bands.
Volume 1: xvi, 322 p., color frontispiece, folded map;
Volume 2: vii, 302 p., 16 p. of advertisements,
color frontispiece.
References: AB 15680, OCLC 8004183.

Senn, Nicholas (1844–1908)   [636]

In the Heart of the Arctics, by Nicholas
Senn [etc.]. Chicago: W.B. Conkey
Company, Publishers, [1907].

Octavo, original blue pictorial cloth with gilt titles.
336 p., frontispiece (portrait), [74] leaves of plates.
References: AB 15740, OCLC 3579666.

Service, Robert William (1874–1958) [637]

Ballads of a Cheechako, by Robert W.
Service. Toronto: William Briggs, 1909.

Duodecimo, bound in full limp crimson suede, gilt
titles and edges.
138 p., frontispiece, marbled endpapers.
Reference: OCLC 21699180.

Service, Robert William (1874–1958) [638]

Collected Verse of Robert Service.
Toronto: Ryerson Press [n.d.].

Duodecimo, blue cloth with gilt titles.
xv, 811 p.
Reference: cf. OCLC 5916117.

Service, Robert William (1874–1958) [639]

Songs of a Sourdough, by Robert W.
Service. Toronto: William Briggs, 1907.

Crown octavo, original brown cloth, gilt titles with
photo illustration laid down on upper cover.
xiii, [3], 17–116 p., frontispiece (portrait), [9] leaves of
plates
Tenth edition.
Reference: OCLC 15184977.

Service, Robert William (1874–1958) [640]

The Spell of the Yukon and Other Verses,

by Robert W. Service. New York: Barse &
Hopkins, Publishers, [1907].

Duodecimo, original green cloth with gilt titles.
4 p. l., 9–126 p.
Reference: OCLC 1101781.

Shackleton, Edward (1911–) [641]

Arctic Journeys: The Story of the Oxford
University Ellesmere Land Expedition,
1934–5. By Edward Shackleton, with a
Preface by the Rt. Hon. the Lord
Tweedsmuir [etc.]. New York and
Toronto: Farrar & Rinehard, Incorporated,
[1938].

Octavo, gray cloth with blue titles, dust jacket.
2 p. l., iii-xv, 17–372 p., frontispiece, [40] leaves of
plates (1 folded), 11 tailpieces, 4 maps and
diagrams (1 folded).
References: AB 15799, OCLC 3009217.

Shackleton, Ernest Henry, Sir (1874–1922) [642]

The Antarctic Book: Winter Quarters
1907–1909. London: William Heinemann,
1909.

Quarto, original quarter vellum with gray paper
boards.
53, [2] p., [10] leaves of plates (part colored, mounted
portraits), 2 p. of signatures of the party.
Constitutes volume [3] of the special limited edition of
his "Heart of the Antarctic" (see below).
Contents: The Southern Party [4 leaves of colored
ports.] — Erebus [poem], by E. H. Shackleton. —
Bathybia, by D. Mawson.
Includes signatures of: Ernest H. Shackleton, Ray
Priestley, Frank Wild, Ernest Joyce, Bernard A.
Day, Philip L. Brocklehurst, [illegible], Eric T.
Marshall, Aeneas L. A. Mackintosh, B. Armytage,
William C. Roberts, James Murray, T. W.
Edgeworth David, Douglas Mawson.
Pp. [25–26] is a cancel leaf, containing only a cut of
Shackleton's trademark "sign of the two
penguins" in lieu of the poem "Aurora Australis,"
found in some copies.
References: Spence 1096, OCLC 3556360.

Shackleton, Ernest Henry, Sir (1874–1922) [643]

Aurora Australis: Published at Winter

Shackleton was a bibliophile and oversaw the production of the first book printed in Antarctica, the *Aurora Australis* [**643**]. The accounts of his *Nimrod* expedition were also printed in fine editions, and this etching accompanies Douglas Mawson's fantasy "Bathybia." George Marston was a very talented artist and a boon companion.

"Explosion of a Toadstool" by George E. Marston [**642**]

Ernest Shackleton served on Scott's first expedition and accompanied Scott and Edward Wilson to their "furthest south" in the summer of 1902–3. His own *Nimrod* expedition of 1907–9 got him to within 100 miles of the pole and established the route that Scott would follow in 1911–12. His *Endurance* expedition of 1914–16 came to grief when the ship was crushed in the ice, but he kept his little band together, made one of the most heroic boat trips on record to get relief, and didn't lose a man. Shackleton was an extraordinary leader who inspired respect and devotion in his men.

Portrait of E. H. Shackleton, by Beresford, London [**645**]

Quarters of British Antarctic Expedition, 1907, during the Winter Months of April, May, June, July, 1908. Illustrated with Lithographs and Etchings by George Marston. Printed at the Sign of 'The Penguins'; 77°••32' South, Longitude 166°••12' East, Antarctica.

> Quarto, quarter red leather on original packing case boards with bevelled edges restored by Middleton.
> 6 p.1, [151] p., [10] leaves of plates.
> One of 60 bound copies. Signed by "Ernest H. Shackleton, George Marston [and] Eric T. Marshall 'Lapsus Linguae' ".
> The first book printed in the Polar regions.
> References: Spence 1095, OCLC 14213274.

Shackleton, Ernest Henry, Sir (1874–1922) [644]

Aurora Australis: The British Expedition, 1907–1909. Preface by Lord Shackleton [etc.]. Introduction by John Millard. First Public Edition. Alburgh, Harleston, Norfolk: Bluntisham/Paradigm, 1986.

> Quarto, beige cloth with gilt titles, dust jacket.
> xx, [176] p., [10] leaves of plates, illustrations.
> Facsimile reprint of Spence 1095, originally published: Cape Royd, Antarctica.
> Reference: OCLC 15049695.

Shackleton, Ernest Henry, Sir (1874–1922) [645]

The Heart of the Antarctic: Being the Story of the British Antarctic Expedition, 1907–1909. By E.H. Shackleton, C.V.O. With an Introduction by Hugh Robert Mill, D.Sc., & an Account of the First Journey to the South Magnetic Pole by Professor T.W. Edgeworth David, F.R.S. London: William Heinemann, 1909.

> Quarto, 2 volumes, original vellum and vellum backed boards,
> Volume 1: xlviii, 371, [1] p., frontispiece (portrait), [111] leaves of plates (3 double, 6 color), 11 maps and diagrams; Volume 2: xv, [1], 418, [1] p., frontispiece (portrait), [102] leaves of plates (1 double, 1 folded in pocket, 6 color), illustrations, diagrams, 3 folded maps in pocket.

This special limited edition on paper watermarked "1907 BAE 1909" was accompanied by 'The Antarctic Book: Winter Quarters 1907–1909' (see above).
Edition of 300 copies. This is copy no. 290.
Reference: Spence 1096.

Shackleton, Ernest Henry, Sir (1874–1922) [646]

The Heart of the Antarctic: Being the Story of the British Antarctic Expedition, 1907–1909. By E.H. Shackleton, C.V.O. With an Introduction by Hugh Robert Mill, D.Sc. An Account of the First Journey to the South Magnetic Pole by Professor T.W. Edgeworth David, F.R.S. Philadelphia: J.B. Lippincott Company, 1909.

> Octavo, 2 volumes, original blue cloth with silver titles. Uncut copy.
> Volume 1: liii, [1], 365, [1] p., frontispiece (portrait), [73] leaves of plates (1 folded, 6 color) 10 maps and diagrams; Volume 2: xvi, 450, [1] p., frontispiece (portrait), [68] leaves of plates (1 double, 1 folded in pocket, 6 color), illustrations, 3 folded maps in pocket.
> References: Spence 1098, OCLC 3635829.

Shackleton, Ernest Henry, Sir (1874–1922) [647]

Savoy Hotel, London, June 15th 1909. Dinner to Lieut. Shackleton, M.V.O.

> Engraved menu cover, 216 x 144 mm.
> Oval photogravure vignettes of "Dinner Time, Xmas, 1908" on front cover and of "E. H. S[hackleton] February 1909" on back cover.
> Menu wanting.
> Back cover has signatures, recto and verso, of those attending dinner; many are illegible in whole or part. Those that can be identified include Philippe Millet, Leonard Darwin, Roland Bonaparte, E. H. Shackleton, Frank R. Shackleton, Kennedy Jones, Arthur Rackham, Wm. Heinemann, [Dean?] Nicholson, W. Robertson Nicoll, Clement Shorter, Ernest E. M. Joyce, Sidney Low, Kingsford Pawling, Percy W. Everett, Alfred Reid, Edmond Salvie, William T. Heald, J. Scott Keltie, [?] Marlowe, G. K. Askwith, T. H. Elliot, [?] Grey, [Chalmers?] Roberts, Chas. H. Dorman, Geo. Putnam, Jerrard Harry, Geo. E. Marston, S. S. Pawling, A.L.A.Mackintosh, E. P.

Heinemann, G. M. Chesney, Harold Hodge, Theodore A. Cook, George Lewis, B. Armytage, Philip L. Brocklehurst, Desmond O'Fallaghan.

Shackleton, Ernest Henry, Sir (1874–1922)   [648]

Shackleton, His Antarctic Writings Selected and Introduced by Christopher Ralling. London: British Broadcasting Corporation, [1983].

> Octavo, original blue cloth with silver titles, dust jacket. 263, [1] p., illustrations, photographs (some color), facsimiles, portraits, 2 maps, maps on endpapers.
> Reference: OCLC 9985481.

Shackleton, Ernest Henry, Sir (1874–1922)   [649]

Signature followed by those of ten other members of the expedition on stationery of "British Antarctic Expedition 1907. S. Y. 'Nimrod,' " with envelope.

> 1 sheet fold. to 203 x 127 mm. and envelope 117 x 145 mm.
> Includes signatures of Shackleton, Rupert A. England, Eric Marshall, Jameson B. Adams, James Murray, Philip L. Brocklehurst, John K. Davis, Aeneas L. A. Mackintosh, A. Forbes Mackay, W. A. Rupert Michell and Ernest E. Joyce.
> Both stationery and envelope have small red monogram "HL" within heart.

Shackleton, Ernest Henry, Sir (1874–1922)   [650]

South: The Story of Shackleton's Last Expedition, 1914–1917: By Sir Ernest Shackleton C.V.O.: With Eighty-Eight Illustrations and Diagrams. New York: The Macmillan Company, MCMXX [1920].

> Octavo.
> xvi, 3 l., 380 p., color frontispiece, [86] leaves of plates (1 double), maps (1 folded).
> First American edition.
> References: Spence 1109, OCLC 1456247.

Shackleton, Ernest Henry, Sir (1874–1922)

(See also Geikie Correspondence; South

Polar Times; Whitehouse, John Howard. A Visit to Nansen)

Sherman, Harold Morrow (1898–   )
(See Wilkins, George Hubert)

Shillinglaw, John J. (1830–1905) [651]

A Narrative of Arctic Discovery, from the Earliest Period to the Present Time. With the Details of the Measures Adopted by Her Majesty's Government for the Relief of the Expedition under Sir John Franklin. By John J. Shillinglaw. London: William Shoberl, Publishers, 1850.

> Small octavo, original blue cloth with gilt titles, skillfully rebacked with original spine laid down. Uncut copy.
> xx, 348 p., frontispiece (portrait), 2 folded maps in pocket on front cover.
> First edition.
> References: AB 15909, OCLC 2288343.

Siegfried, Roy
(See Johnson, Peter)

Silverberg, Robert
(See Chapman, Walker)

Simmonds, Peter Lund (1814–1897)   [652]

Sir John Franklin and the Arctic Regions: A Narrative, Showing the Progress of British Enterprise for the Discovery of the North-West Passage during the Nineteenth Century: With Detailed Notices of the Expeditions in Search of the Missing Vessels under Captain Sir John Franklin. By P.L. Simmonds [etc.]. Second Edition, Combining the Most Recent Intelligence. London: George Routledge & Co., MDCCCLI [1851].

> Small octavo, wood-engraved frontispiece, original blue cloth with gilt titles.

xvi, 286 p., [2] p. of advertisements, 2 folded maps.
Reference: OCLC 11664814.

Simmonds, Peter Lund (1814–1897) [653]

Sir John Franklin and the Arctic Regions: With Detailed Notices of the Expeditions in Search of the Missing Vessels under Sir John Franklin. By P.L. Simonds [etc.]. To Which Is Added an Account of the American Expedition, under the Patronage of Henry Grinnell, Esq., with an Introduction to the American Edition, by John C. Lord, D.D. Buffalo: George H. Derby and Co., 1852.

Octavo, original green cloth with gilt titles.
xxiii, [25]-396 p., frontispiece, [10] leaves of plates, illustrations, folded map (printed on blue paper.)
References: AB 16100, OCLC 2938365.

Simmons, George [654]

Target: Arctic. Men in the Skies at the Top of the World. Philadelphia and New York: Chilton Books, [1965].

Octavo, blue cloth with silver titles, dust jacket.
xii, 420 p., illustrations, portraits, maps.
First edition.
Reference: OCLC 486837.

Simpson, Alexander (1811–) [655]

The Life and Travels of Thomas Simpson, the Arctic Discoverer. By His Brother, Alexander Simpson [etc.]. London: Richard Bentley, Publisher in Ordinary to Her Majesty, 1845.

Octavo, original brown decorative cloth with gilt titles.
viii, 424 p., frontispiece (portrait), folded map.
References: AB 16116, OCLC 1216582.

Simpson, George, Sir (1786/7–1860) [656]

Fur Trade and Empire: George Simpson's Journal. Remarks Connected with the Fur Trade in the Course of a Voyage from York Factory to Fort George and back to York Factory 1824–1825; Together with Accompanying Documents. Edited with an Introduction by Frederick Merk. Cambridge: Harvard University Press, 1931.

Octavo, original red cloth with gilt titles.
[xxxvii], 370 p., folded map in back pocket.
Harvard Historical Studies, v. 31.
Reference: OCLC 16846762.

Simpson, George, Sir (1786/7–1860) [657]

Journal of Occurrences in the Athabasca Department by George Simpson, 1820 and 1821, and Report. Edited by E.E. Rich, [etc.]. With an Introduction by Chester Martin [etc.]. Toronto: The Champlain Society, 1938.

Medium octavo, original decorated blue cloth with gilt titles.
lix, 498, [1] p., frontispiece (portrait), 4 folded maps in pocket.
Edition of 550 copies. This is number 104.
Reference: OCLC 2502676.

Simpson, George C. (1878–) [658]

Meterology, by G. C. Simpson. Calcutta: Thacker, Spink & Company; London: Harrison and Sons, 1919–1923.

Quarto, 3 volumes, burgundy cloth with gilt titles.
At head of title: British Antarctic Expedition. 1910–1913.
Contents: Volume 1. Discussion (x, [1], 326 p., 5 folded plates, charts, graphs, maps) — Volume 2. Weather Maps and Pressure Curves (138 p., 23 folded plates) — Volume 3. Tables (xi, 835, [1]p. index, tables).
Reference: OCLC 12981433.

Simpson, George Gaylord [659]

Penguins: Past and Present, Here and There [by] George Gaylord Simpson. New Haven and London: Yale University Press, [1976].

Octavo, paperback.
xi, [1], 150 p., color frontispiece, [10] leaves of plates (3 color), 9 maps.

Third printing.
Reference: OCLC 2200175.

Simpson, Thomas (1808–1840)   [660]
Narrative of the Discoveries on the North Coast of America; Effected by the Officers of the Hudson's Bay Company during the Years 1836–39. By Thomas Simpson, Esq. London: Richard Bentley, Publisher in Ordinary to Her Majesty, 1843.

> Octavo, rebacked in three-quarter calf and marbled boards, gilt titles on black label, raised bands.
> xix, 419, [1] p., frontispiece (map), 1 folded map.
> First edition.
> References: AB 16124, OCLC 5000974.

Siple, Paul (1908–)   [661]
90 South: The Story of the American South Pole Conquest [by] Paul Siple. New York: G.P. Putnam's Sons, [1959].

> Octavo, original blue cloth with red titles.
> 384 p., [12] leaves of plates (part color), illustrations, maps, maps on endpapers.
> References: Spence 1129, OCLC 256777.

Siple, Paul A. (1908–)   [662]
A Boy Scout with Byrd, by Paul Siple. With 33 Illustrations from Photographs by the Author. New York & London: G.P. Putnam's Sons, 1931.

> Small octavo, original cloth.
> 3 p. l., iii-viii, 165 p., [4] p. of advertisements, frontispiece (portrait), [11] leaves of plates.
> References: Spence 1127, OCLC 1815561.

Smith, Bernard
(See David, Andrew)

Smith, David Murray   [663]
Arctic Expeditions from British and Foreign Shores, from the Earliest Times to the Expedition of 1875–76. By D. Murray Smith, F.R.G.S. Numerous Coloured Illustrations, Maps, and Other Engravings. Edinburgh: Thomas C. Jack, Grange Publishing Works, 1877.

> Large thick quarto, contemporary black half morocco, raised bands, gilt titles and tooling on spine, marbled edges. Binder's title: British and Foreign Arctic Expeditions.
> xiv p., 2 l., 824 p., frontispiece (portrait), 23 plates, 2 folded maps.
> First edition.
> References: AB 16282, OCLC 10241881.

Smith, William D. (1935–)   [664]
Northwest Passage, by William D. Smith. New York: American Heritage Press, [1970].

> Octavo, gray cloth with blue and white titles, dust jacket.
> 204 p., [18] leaves of plates, maps on endpapers.
> Reference: OCLC 92889.

Smolka, Harry Peter (1912–)   [665]
40,000 against the Arctic: Russia's Polar Empire, by H.P. Smolka. New York: William Morrow & Company, 1937.

> Octavo, beige cloth with blue titles.
> 308 p., frontispiece, [15] leaves of plates, facsimiles, 4 maps (2 folded.)
> First edition.
> References: AB 16350, OCLC 1259100.

Smucker, Samuel M. (1823–1863) [666]
Arctic Explorations and Discoveries during the Nineteenth Century. Being Detailed Accounts of the Several Expeditions to the North Seas, Both English and American, Conducted by Ross, Parry, Back, Franklin, M'Clure and Others. Including the First Grinnell Expedition, under Lieutenant De Haven, and the Final Effort of Dr. E.K. Kane in Search of Sir John Franklin. Edited and Completed by Samuel M. Smucker [etc.]. New York and Auburn: Miller, Orton & Co., 1857.

> Small octavo, decorative purple cloth with gilt titles.
> xiii, [24]-517 p., 4 p. of advertisements, frontispiece (portrait), illustrations, added title-page, engraved.
> First edition.
> References: AB 16351, OCLC 3677477

Snelling, William Joseph [667]

The Polar Regions of the Western Continent Explored; Embracing a Geographical Account of Iceland, Greenland, the Islands of the Frozen Sea, and the Northern Parts of the American Continent, Including a Particular Description of the Countries, the Seas, Inhabitants, and Animals of Those Parts of the World; Also a Minute Account of the Whale Fisheries, and the Dangers Attending Them; with Remarkable Adventures of Some of the Whale Fishers, Descriptions of Mount Hecla, and the Other Volcanoes of Iceland; Together with the Adventures, Discoveries, Dangers and Trials of Parry, Franklin, Lyon, and Other Navigators, in Those Regions. By W.J. Snelling [etc.]. Illustrated by a Map and Engravings. Boston: Printed for W.W. Reed, 1831.

> Octavo, contemporary tree sheep with gilt titles.
> xx, 501 p., frontispiece (map), [4] leaves of plates, added title-page, engraved.
> First edition.
> Reference: Sabin 85426.

Snow, William Parker (1817–1895) [668]

Voyage of the Prince Albert in Search of Sir John Franklin: A Narrative of Every-Day Life in the Arctic Seas. By W. Parker Snow. London: Longman, Brown, Green and Longmans, 1851.

> Octavo, original blue cloth with gilt titles.
> 3 p.l, [v]-xvi, 416 p., color frontispiece, [2] leaves of plates (color), folded map.
> References: AB 16362, OCLC 2299744.

Society for Promoting Christian Knowledge

(See Tomlinson, Charles)

Sonntag, August [669]

Professor Sonntag's Thrilling Narrative of the Grinnell Exploring Expedition to the Arctic Ocean, in the Years 1853, 1854, and 1855 in search of Sir John Franklin, under the Command of Dr. E.K. Kane, U.S.N. Containing the History of All Previous Explorations of the Arctic Ocean, from the Year 1618 Down to the Present Time; Showing How Far They Advanced Northward, What Discoveries They Made and Their Scientific Observations. The Present Whereabouts of Sir John Franklin and His Party, If They Are Still Alive. A Statement of the Only Practicable Method by Which the North Pole May Be Reached; the Reasons Why All Exploring Expeditions Have Hitherto Failed to Penetrate the Icy Barriers of the Polar Regions. Highly Important Astronomical Observations, Proving That There Is No Such Thing as Apparent Time at the North Pole; Sufferings of Dr. Kane's Exploring Party; How They Were Buried for Two Years in the Ice, Enduring a Degree of Cold Never Experienced by Any Human Being Before; Their Miraculous Escapes and Unprecedented Hardships; Their Abandonment of the Ship; and Perilous Journey of Four Hundred Miles Over the Ice. With Nearly One Hundred Splendid Engravings. By Professor August Sonntag [etc.]. Philadelphia, Penn.: Charles C. Rhodes, Inquirer Building, [1857].

> Octavo, original blind stamped black cloth with gilt titles.
> 176 p., frontispiece, [31] leaves of plates, illustrations, portraits.
> A literary imposture: "I did not write the book. It is a shameful imposition." — Letter from August Sonntag, published in the Philadelphia Evening Journal, May 19, [1857?].
> References: OCLC 7547153, cf. AB 8373.

South Polar Times [670]
The South Polar Times. London: Smith Elder & Co., 1907–1914.

> Quarto, 3 volumes, original pictorial blue cloth with gilt titles and edges. Library stamp on titles.
> Various pagings, frontispieces (2 color), illustrations (part colored), plates (part colored), folded map. Printed on one side of leaf only.
> An exact reproduction of the South Polar Times originally issued during the Antarctic expeditions of Robert F. Scott.
> Volume 1 (April-August 1902) edited by Shackleton, volume 2 (April-August 1903) by L.C. Bernacchi, volume 3 (April-October 1911) by A. Cherry-Garrard.
> Volumes 1 and 2 are no. 99 of 250, have owner's stamp on t.p. ("Dr. von Neumayer, Neustadt a. d. Haardt"), prospectus laid in volume 1; volume 3 is no. 61 of 350, has no stamp on t.p.
> References: Spence 1094, OCLC 10187942.

Sovetskaya Antarkticheskaya Ekspeditsiya (1955–   ) [671]
Atlas Antarktiki. [tom] I. [Glav. redaktor E.I. Tolstikov]. Moskva, Leningrad: Glav. Upravlenie Geodezii i Kartografii MG SSSR, 1966.

> Large folio, dust jacket.
> xxiii, 225 plates (maps).
> All map legends and explanatory text are translated in *Soviet Geography: Review & Translation* 8, nos. 5–6 (May-June 1967). See Soviet Geography, below.
> Reference: OCLC 7137521.

Soviet Geography [672]
Special Issue: Atlas of Antarctica, Vol. I, Moscow, 1966. New York: American Geographical Society, 1967.

> Octavo, original brown printed wrappers.
> Comprises *Soviet Geography: Review & Translation* 8, nos. 5–6 (May-June 1967): [ii], 261–507.
> Translation of the map legends and explanatory text of Atlas Antarktiki, vol 1 (see Sovetskaya Antarkticheskaya Ekspeditsiya, above).
> Reference: OCLC 2197891.

Sparrman, Anders (1748–1820) [673]
A Voyage to the Cape of Good Hope, towards the Antarctic Polar Circle, and round the World: but Chiefly into the Country of the Hottentots and Caffres, from the Year 1772, to 1776. By Andrew Sparrman, M.D. [etc.]. Translated from the Swedish Original. With Plates. In Two Volumes. The Second Edition, Corrected. London: Printed for G.G.J. and J. Robinson, Pater-Noster-Row, MDCCLXXXVI [1786].

> Large quarto, 2 volumes, quarter black leather on green boards.
> Volume 1: xxviii, 368 p., frontispiece, [2] leaves of plates, 1 folded map. Volume 2: viii, 356, [1] p., 2 p. of advertisements, [7] leaves of plates.
> Portion of spine missing from volume 1.
> References: Spence 1147, OCLC 5121980.

Speck, Gordon [674]
Samuel Hearne and the Northwest Passage. By Gordon Speck. Illustrated with Photographs. Caldwell, Idaho: The Caxton Printers, Ltd., 1963.

> Octavo, original cloth with black titles.
> xxii p., 1 l., 337 p., frontispiece (portrait), 37 photo illustrations, 14 maps (12 double).
> References: Ricks p. 207, OCLC 1458892.

Spence, Sydney A. [675]
Antarctic Miscellany: Books, Periodicals & Maps Relating to the Discovery and Exploration of Antarctica. Compiled by Sydney A. Spence. Edited by J.J.H. & J.I. Simper. London: [J.J.H. Simper], 1980.

> Quarto, original green cloth with gilt titles.
> xi, 220 p., illustrations.
> Second edition. Edition of 1,000 copies. This is copy number 178.
> Previous edition published in 1966 under title: Antarctica.
> Reference: OCLC 6920646.

Spence, Sydney A. [676]
Antarctica: Its Books & Papers from the Earliest to the Present Time [by] S.A. Spence. [Mitcham, England: S.A. Spence, 1966.]

they sleep in the winter, and for how
many hours a day, is a problem full
of interest. Now and again as we
walk among the Weddell's Seals
we find a Crab-eater, seldom
more than one or two, asleep
with the rest.
        When we were in the pack
ice these were our daily
food, for we saw
some every day, and
often ate them. Here they are a
rarity, and an interesting
one, as they have hitherto
been considered the peculiar
property of the pack ice.
The "Southern Cross" expedition
found one on the Great Ice
Barrier, and we saw several
as we sailed along it, but
here we have them still
farther South, and
prospect of our
from time to

                        there seems every
                        seeing them
                        time during the winter
                    and perhaps even some-
                    -thing of their family
                    arrangements in the Spring.
                        I think the
                general admiration of our
                party is divided somewhat
            between the Crab-eater and Ross'
        Seal. We have had but few opportunities
        of getting to know the latter, though
        both are very interesting. No one has
        ever met with Ross' Seal except in the
        pack ice, and possibly his coat would
        be found to vary much if seen at
                    other seasons of the year,
                    but he has only been seen
                    in summer when all have
                    had a roughish hair

Sea Leopard
chasing Emperor Penguins

E.a.W.

Edward Wilson accompanied Scott on both his expeditions and died with Scott and 'Birdy' Bowers on their return from the pole in 1912. He was the kindest of men, an extraordinary traveler in his own right, and perhaps the best artist to work in Antarctica. An indefatigable worker, he routinely spent precious rest periods making exquisite sketches of the surrounding topography. This is an illustration from *The South Polar Times*, a typed newspaper that Wilson and Shackleton produced during Scott's first expedition in 1902.

"Sea Leopard Chasing Penguins" by Edward A. Wilson [**670**]

Octavo, stiff tan printed wrappers.
viii, 82 p.
First edition. Edition of 130 copies, of which 100 were
    for sale.
Reference: OCLC 8989142.

Speyer, Edgar
(See Geikie Correspondence)

Stackpole, Edouard A.
(See Schwatka, Frederick)

Stanton, William Ragan [677]
The Great United States Exploring
Expedition of 1838–1842, by William
Stanton. Berkley: University of California
Press, [1975].

Tall octavo, original gray cloth with gilt titles on blue
    label, dust jacket.
x, 433 p., frontispiece, illustrations, maps on
    endpapers.
Reference: OCLC 1718566.

Starokadomskii, Leonid Mikhailovich (1875–1962) [678]
Charting the Russian Northern Sea Route:
The Arctic Ocean Hydrographic
Expedition, 1910–1915 [by] L.M.
Starkadomskiy. Translated and Edited by
William Barr. Montreal and London: Arctic
Institute of North America, McGill-
Queen's University Press, 1976.

Octavo, pictorial green cloth with black titles.
xxxiv, 332 p., frontispiece (portrait), [11] leaves of
    plates, illustrations.
First English Account.
Reference: OCLC 3071995.

Stefansson, Vilhjalmur (1879–1962) [679]
The Adventure of Wrangel Island, Written
by Vilhjálmur Stefánsson. With the
Collaboration of John Irvine Knight, upon
the Diary of Whose Son Errol Lorne
Knight the Narrative is Mainly Based. New
York: The Macmillan Company, 1925.

Octavo, original blue cloth with gilt titles.
xxviii p., 1 l., 424 p., frontispiece (portrait), [15] leaves
    of plates, 3 maps (1 folded), portion of front
    endpaper removed.
First edition.
References: AB 16774, OCLC 3009299.

Stefansson, Vilhjalmur (1879–1962) [680]
The Arctic Manual, by Vilhjálmur
Stefánsson. Prepared under Direction of
the Chief of the Air Corps, United States
Army. With a Special Introduction and
Index. New York: The Macmillan
Company, 1944.

Octavo, blue cloth with blue titles.
xvi, 556 p., [8] leaves of plates, illustrations, diagrams.
First trade edition.
References: AB 16785, OCLC 827436.

Stefansson, Vilhjalmur (1879–1962) [681]
Discovery. The Autobiography of
Vilhjálmur Stefánsson. New York:
McGraw-Hill Book Company, [1964].

Octavo, blue and green cloth with silver and green
    titles, dust jacket.
viii, 411 p., [10] leaves of plates, maps on endpapers.
First edition.
Reference: OCLC 8991247.

Stefansson, Vilhjalmur (1879–1962) [682]
The Friendly Arctic. The Story of Five
Years in Polar Regions. By Vilhjálmur
Stefánsson [etc.]. New York: The
Macmillan Company, 1921.

Octavo, original blue cloth with gilt titles.
xxxi, 784 p., [34] leaves of plates, 9 maps (6 folded, 2
    in pocket).
First edition, signed by author December 1921.
References: AB 16808, OCLC 255330.

Stefansson, Vilhjalmur (1879–1962) [683]
Great Adventures and Explorations from

the Earliest Times to the Present, as Told by the Explorers Themselves. Edited with an Introduction and Comments by Vilhjalmur Stefansson, with the Collaboration of Olive Rathbun Wilcox. Maps Designed by Richard Edes Harrison. New Revised Edition. New York: Dial Press, 1952.

> Octavo, reddish-brown cloth with gilt titles.
> xii, 788 p., maps, colored maps on endpapers.
> Originally published 1947.
> Reference: OCLC 332792.

Stefansson, Vilhjalmur (1879–1962)
[684]

Greenland [by] Vilhjálmur Stefánsson. Garden City, New York: Doubleday, Doran & Co., Inc., 1942.

> Octavo, original green cloth with green and silver titles on black and silver label, dust jacket.
> viii p., 1 l., 338 p., frontispiece (facsimile), [7] leaves of plates, illustrations, map, maps on endpapers.
> First edition.
> Imperfect: Plate facing p. 136 wanting.
> References: AB 16813, OCLC 408008.

Stefansson, Vilhjalmur (1879–1962)
[685]

My Life with the Eskimo, by Vilhjálmur Stefánsson. Illustrated. London and New York: The Macmillan Company, 1913.

> Octavo, original pictorial blue cloth with gilt titles, circle blind stamped on title.
> ix, 538 p., frontispiece, [59] leaves of plates, 2 folded maps.
> Presentation copy.
> References: AB 16832, OCLC 487176.

Stefansson, Vilhjalmur (1879–1962)
[686]

Northwest to Fortune: The Search of Western Man for a Commercially Practical Route to the Far East, by Vilhjálmur Stefánsson. Maps Designed by James MacDonald. New York: Duell, Sloan and Pearce, [1958].

> Octavo, original black cloth with silver titles, dust jacket.
> xix, 356 p., 10 maps.
> First edition.
> Reference: OCLC 486556.

Stefansson, Vilhjalmur (1879–1962)
[687]

The Problem of Meighen Island: Intended as the Third Chapter but Suppressed in the Publication of Unsolved Mysteries of the Arctic, by Vilhjálmur Stefánsson, of Which a Special Edition, with Introduction by Stephen Leacock and a Frontispiece by Rockwell Kent, Was Published by the Explorers Club in December, 1938. New York: Privately Printed for Mr. Joseph Robinson, 1939.

> Octavo, uncut, unbound signatures. In beige cloth box, paper label on spine.
> iii, 257–328, 2 maps.
> Signed by the author. Edition of 300 copies. This is copy number 193. The odd numbers were for the use of J. Robinson, even numbers for V. Stefánsson's use.
> References: AB 16850, OCLC 13186377.

Stefansson, Vilhjalmur (1879–1962)
[688]

Ultima Thule. Further Mysteries of the Arctic, by Vilhjálmur Stefánsson. Illustrated by Alexander Popini. New York: The Macmillan Company, 1940.

> Octavo, original blue cloth with silver titles, dust jacket.
> 4 p. l., 383 p., [5] leaves of plates, 11 maps, illustrated endpapers.
> 'This volume is No. 64 of the first one hundred copies of the first edition of Ultima Thule, autographed by the author and illustrator for members of the Explorers Club." — First prelim. leaf.
> References: AB 16871, OCLC 1494868.

Stefansson, Vilhjalmur (1879–1962)
[689]

Unsolved Mysteries of the Arctic. By Vilhjalmur Stefansson. Introduction by Stephen Leacock Telling How This Book

Came to be Written. New York: The Macmillan Company, 1939.

> Octavo, original blue-gray cloth with silver titles.
> xi, [7], 381 p., maps.
> References: AB 16873, OCLC 486687.

Steger, Will and Jon Bowermaster [690]
Crossing Antarctica [by] Will Steger and Jon Bowermaster. New York: Alfred A. Knopf, 1992.

> Octavo, gray decorative cloth with gilt titles, dust jacket.
> x, [2], 304, [2] p., [4] leaves of color plates, maps.
> First edition.
> Reference: OCLC 23732321.

Struzik, Edward (1954–)   [691]
Northwest Passage: The Quest for an Arctic Route to the East. Text by Edward Struzik. Photography by Mike Beedell. [Toronto, Ontario]: Key Porter Books [1991].

> Quarto, original blue cloth with silver titles, dust jacket.
> 152 p., photographs (chiefly color), illustrations, sketches, facsimiles, maps.
> Reference: OCLC 25876009.

Sundman, Per Olof (1922–)   [692]
The Flight of the Eagle, by Per Olof Sundman. Translated from the Swedish by Mary Sandbach. New York: Pantheon Books [1970].

> Octavo, original beige cloth with red titles, dust jacket.
> 382, [1] p., frontispiece, [4] leaves of plates, maps on endpapers.
> First American edition.
> Reference: OCLC 67574.

Sutherland, Peter Cormack   [693]
Journal of a Voyage in Baffin's Bay and Barrow Straits, in the Years 1850–1851, Performed by H.M. Ships "Lady Franklin" and "Sophia," under the Command of Mr. William Penny, in Search of the Missing Crews of H.M. Ships Erebus and Terror: With a Narrative of Sledge Excursions on the Ice of Wellington Channel; and Observations on the Natural History and Physical Features of the Countries and Frozen Seas Visited. By Peter C. Sutherland [etc.], Surgeon to the Expedition. In Two Volumes. With Maps, Plates, and Wood-Engravings. London: Longman, Brown, Green, and Longmans, 1852.

> Octavo, original brown cloth with gilt titles.
> 2 volumes. Volume 1: lii, 506 p., [34] p. of advertisements, color frontispiece, illustrations, folded map; Volume 2: vii, 363, ccxxxiii, [1] p., color frontispiece, [4] leaves of plates (2 color), illustrations, folded map.
> References: AB 17231, OCLC 4115520.

Sutton, George A.   [694]
Glacier Island: The Official Account of the British South Georgia Expedition, 1954–55. [By] George Sutton. London: Chatto & Windus, 1957.

> Octavo, original yellow cloth with black titles.
> 224 p., frontispiece (portrait), [7] leaves of plates, 4 maps (2 double).
> References: Spence 1175, OCLC 486041.

Sutton, George Miksch (1898–) [695]
High Arctic: An Expedition to the Unspoiled North, by George Miksch Sutton. Illustrated with Color Plates by the Author and with Photographs by David F. Parmlee, Stewart D. MacDonald, David R. Gray, and Philip Taylor. Toronto, Ontario: Fitzhenry & Whiteside, Limited [1971].

> Quarto, white cloth with black titles, dust jacket.
> viii p., 4 l., 3–116, [3] p., 11 color plates (6 double), illustrations.
> Reference: OCLC 13443399.

Sutton, Richard Lightburn (1878–1952)   [696]
An Arctic Safari: With Camera and Rifle in the Land of the Midnight Sun, by Richard

L. Sutton [etc.]. With More Than One Hundred Illustrations, Made from Photographs Taken by the Author and by Richard L. Sutton, Jr. [etc.], and Emmy Lou Sutton [etc.]. St. Louis: The C.V. Mosby Company, 1932.

> Octavo, blue decorated cloth (faded), with blue titles.
> 3 p.1, 11–199 p., frontispiece (portrait), illustrations, map. Copy inscribed to a former roommate on front free endpaper.
> Note: "All of the included matter previously appeared in the Kansas City Star." — Preface.
> References: AB 17247, OCLC 8990267.

Sverdrup, Otto Neumann (1854–1930) [697]

New Land: Four Years in the Arctic Regions, by Otto Sverdrup. Translated from the Norwegian by Ethel Harriet Hearn. With Illustrations and Maps. In Two Volumes. London, New York and Bombay: Longmans, Green and Co., 1904.

> Octavo, 2 volumes, original blue decorated cloth with silver titles, ex libris R.N. Rudmose-Brown.
> 2 volumes. Volume 1: xvi, 496 p., frontispiece (portrait), [31] leaves of plates, illustrations, 3 maps; Volume 2: xii, 504 p., frontispiece (portrait), [29] leaves of plates, illustrations, 5 maps (4 on 2 sheets in pocket).
> References: AB 17322, OCLC 2008281.

Swaine, Charles
(See Drage, Theodore Swaine)

Swan, Robert
(See Mear, Roger)

Talcott, Dudley Vaill (1899–) [698]
Report of the Company [by] Dudley Vaill Talcott. Illustrated with Photographs and Drawings by the Author. New York: Harrison Smith and Robert Haas, Nineteen Hundred Thirty-Six [1936].

> Quarto, original tan decorated cloth with blue titles.
> 347 (i.e. 343) p., frontispiece (portrait), [37] leaves of plates (including illustrations, photographs, 5 maps.)

> Note: Error in paging: numbers 339–342 omitted.
> References: AB 17391, OCLC 6062553.

Taylor, Thomas Griffith (1880–1963) [699]

With Scott: The Silver Lining, by Griffith Taylor [etc.]. With Nearly 200 Illustrations and Maps. London: Smith, Elder & Co., 1916.

> Octavo, original green decorated cloth with gilt and white titles.
> xiv, [1], 464 p., frontispiece (portrait), [43] leaves of plates (1 double), illustrations, maps (2 folded).
> First edition.
> References: Spence 1183, OCLC 12496191.

Thayer, David [700]
Aerial Railway for the Exploration of the Polar Zone and for Air-transit over Water and Land. By David Thayer [etc.]. Boston: Alfred Mudge & Son, Printers, 1889.

> Octavo, original brown printed wrappers, covers detached.
> 7 p., frontispiece.
> Reference: See OCLC 15304202.

Thomas, Lowell (1892–1981) [701]
Sir Hubert Wilkins: His World of Adventure. A Biography by Lowell Thomas. New York, [etc.]: McGraw-Hill Book Company, Inc. [1961].

> Octavo, original quarter blue cloth on gray boards with blue and white titles, dust jacket.
> 296, [1] p., [8] leaves of plates.
> Reference: OCLC 8989630.

Thompson, John Beswarick [702]
The More Northerly Route: A Photographic Study of the 1944 Voyage of the 'St. Roch' through the Northwest Passage. By John Beswarick Thompson. Ottawa Parks Canada, 1974.

> Square quarto, stiff brown decorated cardcover with green titles.
> 184, [1] p.
> Reference: OCLC 2967235.

Thomson, Charles Wyville, Sir (1830–1882) [703]

The Voyage of the "Challenger." The Atlantic: A Preliminary Account of the General Results of the Exploring Voyage of H.M.S. "Challenger" during the Year 1873 and the Early Part of the Year 1876. By Sir C. Wyville Thomson [etc.]. In Two Volumes. New York: Harper & Brothers, Publishers, 1878.

> Octavo, green decorated cloth with gilt titles.
> 2 volumes. Volume 1: xx, [17]-391 p., frontispiece (portrait), [14] leaves of plates (7 folded, 7 double; including maps, diagrams, charts), illustrations (many full-page); Volume 2: viii, [9]-340 p., 4 p. of advertisements; frontispiece (folded map), [28] leaves of plates (5 folded, 19 double; including maps, illustrations, diagrams, charts), illustrations.
> First American edition.
> References: See Spence 1197, OCLC 1821288.

Thomson, George Malcolm (1899–) [704]

The Search for the North West Passage [by] George Malcolm Thomson. New York: Macmillan Publishing Co., Inc., 1975.

> Octavo, original blue cloth with gilt titles, dust jacket.
> ix p., 1 l., 288 p., [8] leaves of plates, map (double).
> First American edition.
> Reference: OCLC 1366233.

Tide Water Oil Company [705]

Highlights of the Byrd Antarctic Expedition. [New York]: Tide Water Oil Company, 1930.

> Folio, printed wrapper.
> [32] p., illustrations, portraits. (pages loose)
> Reference: OCLC 2998625.

Todd, Alden L. (1918–) [706]

Abandoned: The Story of the Greely Arctic Expedition, 1881–1884. [By] A.L. Todd. Introduction by Vilhjalmur Stefansson. New York [etc.]: McGraw Hill Book Company, Inc. [1961].

> Octavo, original quarter black cloth on blue boards with blue and white titles, dust jacket.
> 323 p., 1 l., frontispiece (portrait), [6] leaves of plates, 2 maps.
> First edition.
> Reference: OCLC 8991756.

Tomlinson, Charles (1808–1897) [707]

Winter in the Arctic Regions. I. Winter in the Open Sea. II. Winter in a Secure Harbor. III. Winter in a Snow-Hut. Published under the Direction of the Committee of General Literature and Education, Appointed by the Society for Promoting Christian Knowledge. London: Printed for the Society for Promoting Christian Knowledge; Sold at the Depository [etc.] and by All Booksellers, 1846.

> Sexto-decimo, original blind-stamped green cloth with gilt titles (spine chipped and faded).
> 176 p., frontispiece (folded map), illustrations (5 full-page).
> First edition.
> Published anonymously; the 1872 edition bears Tomlinson's name.
> Inscribed on t.p.: Thomas Hope from Lady Fanning 27th April 1853.
> References: See AB 17881, OCLC 12820612.

Traill, Henry Duff (1842–1900) [708]

The Life of Sir John Franklin, R.N. by H.D. Traill [etc.]. With Maps, Portraits, and Facsimiles. London: John Murray, 1896.

> Octavo, original brown cloth with gilt titles.
> 10 p., 1 l., 454 p., 2 p. of advertisements, frontispiece (portrait), 3 plates (1 double page, 1 folded), 2 maps (1 folded).
> References: AB 17923, OCLC 6164004.

Trevor-Battye, Aubyn Bernard Rochfort [709]

Ice-Bound on Kolguev: A Chapter in the Exploration of Arctic Europe, to Which is Added a Record of the Natural History of the Island, by Aubyn Trevor-Battye [etc.].

With Numerous Illustrations by J.T. Nettleship, Charles Whymper and the Author. And Three Maps. Westminster: Archibald Constable and Company, 1895.

> Octavo, quarter green cloth on green boards with gilt titles.
> xxviii, 458 p., frontispiece, [25] leaves of plates, illustrations, 3 folded maps.
> References: AB 17973, OCLC 9129857.

Turley, Charles [710]
The Voyages of Captain Scott, Retold from "The Voyage of the 'Discovery' and "Scott's Last Expedition", by Charles Turley [etc.]. With an Introduction by Sir J.M. Barrie, Bart. With a Portrait Frontispiece in Photogravure, 4 Coloured Plates, 28 Pages of Half-tone Illustrations (Mostly from Photographs Taken by Members of the 'Terra Nova' Expedition), Facsimile and Map. London: Smith, Elder, & Co., 1914.

> Octavo, original blue decorated cloth with gilt titles.
> viii, [1], 440 p., frontispiece (portrait), [33] leaves of plates (4 color; 1 double-page), folded map.
> First edition.
> References: Spence 1215, OCLC 1843119.

Tuttle, Charles Richard [711]
Our North Land: Being a Full Account of the Canadian North-West and Hudson's Bay Route, Together with a Narrative of the Experiences of the Hudson's Bay Expedition of 1884, Including a Description of the Climate, Resources, and the Characteristics of the Native Inhabitants between the 50th Parallel and the Arctic Circle. By Charles R. Tuttle [etc.]. Illustrated with Maps and Engravings. Toronto: C. Blackett Robinson, 1885.

> Large octavo, original green decorated cloth with gilt titles.

> xvi, [17]-589 p., frontispiece (folded map), 57 illustrations (many full-page), 4 portraits, folded map.
> First edition.
> Reference: AB 18107.

U. S. Air Force (Air Training Command) [712]
Polar Guide. AFTRC Manual; 50–0-23. [Shreveport, LA]: Air Training Command [1948].

> Quarto, punched and clasp bound in stiff black wrapper with silver titles.
> Unpaginated, illustrations, diagrams, 2 large folded maps in pocket.
> Note: "Restricted."
> References: Not in AB, OCLC 8181471.

U.S. Central Intelligence Agency. National Foreign Assessment Center
(See National Foreign Assessment Center (U.S.))

U. S. Exploring Expedition, 1838–1842
(See Wilkes, Charles)

U. S. Hydrographic Office [713]
Ice Atlas of the Northern Hemisphere. Washington: Hydrographic Office, US Navy, 1946.

> Large square folio, original cloth, plastic spiral binding.
> v, 106 p., tables, 85 maps, most colored.
> First edition.
> Reference: OCLC 1521239.

U. S. Hydrographic Office [714]
Sailing Directions for Antarctica, Including the Off-lying Islands South of Latitude 60°. [Washington: Government Printing Office, 1943].

> Quarto, original white cloth with blue titles.
> 312 p., illustrations (part folded), folded map in pocket.
> At head of title: H.O. No. 138.
> Reference: Spence 424.

U.S. Hydrographic Office [715]
Sailing Directions for the East Coast of

Siberia. From Mys Otto Shmidta to Sakhalinskiy Zaliv (Sakhalin Gulf) Including Ostrov Vrangelya (Wrangel Island), Ostrov Gerald (Herald Island) Diomede Islands, Komandorskiye Ostrova (Komandorski Islands), and the Eastern, Northern, and North-western Coasts of the Okhotsk Sea. First Edition, 1947. Issued under the Authority of the Secretary of the Navy. Washington: Government Printing Office, 1947.

> Octavo, brown cloth with black titles.
> x, 482 p., illustrations, 14 maps (2 folded).
> At head of title: H.O. Pub. No. 122A.
> A stapled 2-leaf supplement to H.O. Pub. No. 122A is laid in at end.
> Stefansson's copy.
> References: AB 18372, OCLC 11098368.

U.S. Naval Photographic Interpretation Center [716]

Antarctic Bibliography. Prepared by the U.S. Naval Photographic Interpretation Center. Washington, D.C.: Government Printing Office, 1951.

> Quarto, light blue paper covers, spiral bound.
> vi, 147 p., 3 folded maps in pocket.
> At head of title: NAVAER 10–35–591.
> References: Spence 38, OCLC 3863349.

U.S. Naval Photographic Interpretation Center [717]

Antarctic Bibliography. Prepared by the U.S. Naval Photographic Interpretation Center. New York: Greenwood Press [1968].

> Quarto, blue cloth with gilt titles.
> vi, 147 p., folded map.
> Note: First Greenwood Reprint of the 1951 edition.
> References: Spence 38, OCLC 2396.

U. S. Navy. Court of Inquiry [718]

Proceedings of a Court of Inquiry Convened at the Navy Department, Washington, D.C., October 5, 1882, in Pursuance of a Joint Resolution of Congress Approved August 8, 1882, to Investigate the Circumstances of the Loss in the Arctic Seas of the Exploring Steamer "Jeannette," etc. Washington: Government Printing Office, 1883.

> Octavo, modern green cloth, gilt titles, original blue paper cover intact.
> 363 p., illustrations, maps (some folded, some colored).
> Also issued as 47th Congress, 2d session, House Executive Document 108.
> Reference: OCLC 10065980.

U.S. Revenue-Cutter Service. [719]

Cruise of the Revenue-Steamer Corwin in Alaska and the N.W. Arctic Ocean in 1881. Medical Notes by I.C. Rosse, Glaciation by J. Muir, Natural History by E. Nelson. Washington: Government Printing Office, 1883.

> Large quarto, original brown cloth with gilt titles.
> 11 plates including frontispiece.
> Reference: OCLC 16154871.

U.S. Revenue-Cutter Service. [720]

Report of the Cruise of the Revenue Marine Steamer Corwin in the Arctic Ocean in the Year 1884. By Capt. M.A. Healy, U.S.R.M, Commander. Washington: Government Printing Office, 1889.

> Quarto, original decorated brown cloth with gilt titles.
> 128 p., frontispiece, [39] leaves of plates (2 color).
> Note: also issued as 50th Congress, 1st Session. House Miscellaneous Document, Number 602.
> References: AB 18401, OCLC 13630666.

U.S. Revenue-Cutter Service [721]

Report of the Cruise of the U.S. Revenue Cutter Bear and the Overland Expedition for the Relief of the Whalers in the Arctic Ocean, from November 27, 1897, to September 13, 1898. Washington: Government Printing Office, 1899.

> Octavo, original cloth.

iv, 3–144 p., [60] leaves of plates, folded map.
Reference: AB 18402.

U. S. War Department [722]
Proceedings of the "Proteus" Court of
Inquiry on the Greely Relief Expedition of
1883. Washington: Government Printing
Office, 1884.
> Octavo, old three-quarter black morocco with gilt
> titles, marbled edges and endpapers.
> 2 p.l., 310, 265 p., [4] leaves of plates, 6 folded maps.
> References: AB 18416, OCLC 5840956.

Unveiling the Arctic [723]
Unveiling the Arctic. Louis Rey, editor;
Claudette Reed Upton and Marvin Falk,
Co-editors. Calgary: University of Calgary,
1984.
> Quarto, original paper wrappers.
> Many photo illustrations and maps.
> Papers Presented at the Conference "The History of the
> Discovery of the Arctic Regions as Seen through
> the Descriptions of Travellers and the work of
> Cartographers From Early Antiquity to the 18th
> Century", organized by Comiteé Arctique
> International and held in Rome in 1981.
> Comprises *Arctic, Journal of the Arctic Institute of
> North America* 37, no. 4 (December 1984).
> Reference: OCLC 16052815.

Upton, Claudette Reed
(See Unveiling the Arctic)

Vaeth, J. Gordon [724]
To the Ends of the Earth: The
Explorations of Roald Amundsen, by J.
Gordon Vaeth. Illustrated with
Photographs and Maps. New York: Harper
& Row, Publishers [1962].
> Octavo, original green and blue pictorial cloth covers,
> titles in green, white and red, dust jacket.
> [xii], 219 p., 1 l., illustrated double title-page,
> illustrations, 4 maps (1 double-page).
> Reference: OCLC 1369085.

Vancouver, George (1757–1798) [725]
Voyage de découvertes, a l'Océan Pacifique
du Nord, et Autour du Monde; Dans
lequel la côte Nord-Quest de l'Amérique a
été soigneusement reconnue et exactement
relevée: ordonné par le Roi d'Angleterre,
Principalement dans la vue de constater s'il
existe, à travers le continent de l'Amérique,
un passage pour les vaisseaux, de l'Océan
Pacifique du Nord à l'Océan Atlantique
septentrional; et exécuté en 1790, 1791,
1792, 1793, 1794 et 1795, Par le
Capitaine George Vancouver. Traduit de
l'Anglais. Ouvrage enrichi de Figures, avec
un grand Atlas. A Paris, de l'Imprimerier
de la République. An VIII [1799].
> Quarto, 3 volumes, contemporary mottled calf, very
> skillfully rebacked, marbled endpapers and
> edges, gilt decorations on boards and spines, gilt
> lettering on red and green labels. Binder's title:
> Voyage De Vancouver.
> Volume I: xi, [1], 491 p., [7] leaves of plates; Volume
> 2: 5 p. l., 516 p., [4] leaves of plates, 1 map;
> Volume 3: 4 p. l., 562 p., [6] leaves of plates.
> With large folio Atlas du Voyage de Vancouver.
> 4 p., [6] leaves of plates, 10 folded maps.
> References: Spence 1222, OCLC 8639733.

Vancouver, George (1757–1798) [726]
A Voyage of Discovery to the North Pacific
Ocean and around the World, 1791–1795.
With an Introduction and Appendices.
Edited by W. Kaye Lamb. London: The
Hakluyt Society, 1984.
> Octavo, 4 volumes, light blue cloth with gilt titles, dust
> jackets.
> Paged continuously. Volume 1: xx, 442 p.; Volume 2:
> ix, 443–786 p.; Volume 3: viii, 787–1230 p.;
> Volume 4: viii, 1231–1752 p. [44] pages of
> plates (some folded), illustrations, maps, portraits,
> folded map in pocket at back of volume 1.
> Works issued by the Hakluyt Society, 2nd series, vols.
> 163–166.
> Reference: OCLC 11945202.

Vaughn, Norman D. [727]
With Byrd at the Bottom of the World:
The South Pole Expedition of 1928–1930
[by] Norman D. Vaughn with Cecil B.

Murphey. 1st ed. Harrisburg, Penn.: Stackpole Books, 1990.

> Quarto.
> viii, 196 p., [16] p. of plates (photographs), maps.
> Reference: OCLC 20722908.

Veer, Gerrit de [728]

A True Description of Three Voyages by the North-East Towards Cathay and China, Undertaken by the Dutch in the Years 1594, 1595, and 1596, by Gerrit de Veer. Published at Amsterdam in the Year 1598, and in 1609 Translated into English by William Phillip. Edited by Charles T. Beke. London: For the Hakluyt Society, 1853.

> Demy octavo, original embossed blue cloth with gilt titles.
> cxlii, 291 p., [27] p. of plates, illustrations, folded maps.
> Works issued by the Hakluyt Society, vol. 13.
> Veer's account of the voyages of Willem Barents, first published in Latin as "Diarium nauticum, seu descriptio trium navigationum admirandarum."
> Reference: OCLC 3558366.

Walton, Kevin
(See Portrait of Antarctica)

Watkins, Henry George (1907–1932) [729]

The British Arctic Air Route Expedition: A Paper Read at the Special Evening Meeting of the Society on 12 December 1931, by H. G. Watkins [and] Kangerdlugsuak and Mount Forel: Two Journeys on the British Arctic Air Route Expedition: A Paper Read at the Evening Meeting of the Society on 11 April 1932, by A. Stephenson.

> Octavo, beige cloth.
> Detached from: *Geographical Journal* 79 (1932): 353–367, 466–501 ([7] leaves of plates, 3 maps [2 folded]) and *Geographical Journal* 80 (1932): 1–30, [2] leaves of plates, diagrams, 4 folded maps.
> Reference: AB 19183.

Waxell, Sven Larsson (1701–1762) [730]

The American Expedition, by Sven Waxell. With an Introduction and Note by M.A. Michael. London, Edinburgh, and Glasgow: William Hodge and Company, Limited [1952].

> Octavo, original turquoise cloth with gilt titles.
> ix, [1], 11–236 p., frontispiece (portrait), [1] folded leaf of plates, 7 folded maps, maps on endpapers.
> First edition.
> On Bering's Second Expedition, 1733–1743. Contains the only known portrait of Vitus Bering.
> References: See AB 6111 (Greely), OCLC 1526797.

Wead, Frank Wilber (1895–1947) [731]

Gales, Ice and Men. A Biography of the Steam Barkentine 'Bear', by Frank Wead. Decorations by Charles E. Pont. New York: Dodd, Mead & Company, 1937.

> Octavo, original gray cloth with blue titles, dust jacket.
> xiii, 272 p., color frontispiece, 13 plates (1 folded), illustrations, maps on endpapers.
> References: AB 19206, OCLC 1729234.

Webster, William Henry Bayley [732]

Narrative of a Voyage to the Southern Atlantic Ocean, in the Years 1828, 29, 30, Performed in H.M. Sloop Chanticleer, under the Command of the Late Captain Henry Foster, F.R.S.&C. By Order of the Lords Commissioners of the Admiralty. From the Private Journal of W.H.B. Webster, Surgeon of the Sloop. In Two Volumes. London: Richard Bentley, Publisher in Ordinary to His Majesty, 1834.

> Octavo, 2 volumes, old quarter olive leather with marbled boards and gilt titles.
> Volume 1: xi, [1], 399, [1] p., frontispiece (map), [5] leaves of plates, illustration. Volume 2: viii, 398 p., frontispiece (folded map), illustrations, tables.
> References: Spence 1245, OCLC 4716062.

Weddell, James (1787–1834) [733]

A Voyage towards the South Pole,

Performed in the Years 1822–24. Containing an Examination of the Antarctic Sea, to the Seventy-fourth Degree of Latitude: and a Visit to Tierra Del Fuego, with a Particular Account of the Inhabitants. To Which is Added, Much Useful Information on the Coasting Navigation of Cape Horn, and the Adjacent Lands. With Charts of Harbours, &c. By James Weddell, F.R.S.E. Second Edition, with Observations on the Probability of Reaching the South Pole, and an Account of a Second Voyage performed by the Beaufoy, Captain Brisbane, to the Same Seas. London: Printed for Longman, Rees, Orme, Brown, and Green, Paternoster-Row, 1827.

> Octavo, later three-quarter morocco on blue cloth boards, gilt decorations and titles.
> Binder's title: The South Pole.
> iv, 324 p., color frontispiece (portrait), [8] leaves of plates (2 folded), 8 maps (6 folded).
> References: Spence 1248; OCLC 8518655.

Weddell, James (1787–1834) **[734]**
A Voyage towards the South Pole, Performed in the Years 1822–24, Containing an Examination of the Antarctic Sea (1827). A Reprint with a New Introduction by Sir Vivian Fuchs, Director of the British Antarctic Survey. Newton Abbot David & Charles [1970].

> Octavo, original blue cloth with gilt title on blue label, dust jacket.
> x, iv, 324 p., 19 plates (6 folded), including illustrations, charts, maps.
> Facsimile reprint of 2nd edition of 1827.
> References: Spence 1250, OCLC 102578.

Weems, John Edward **[735]**
Peary: The Explorer and the Man. Based on His Personal Papers by John Edward Weems. London: Eyre & Spottiswoode [1967].

> Octavo, original gray cloth with silver titles on blue label.
> ix p., 3 l., [3]-362 p., [6] leaves of plates, maps on endpapers.
> First edition.
> Reference: OCLC 459470.

Wellman, Walter (1858–1934) **[736]**
The Aerial Age. A Thousand Miles by Airship over the Atlantic Ocean; Airship Voyages over the Polar Sea; the Past, the Present and the Future of Aerial Navigation, by Walter Wellman (Journalist, Explorer, Aeronaut). Illustrated. New York: A.R. Keller & Company, 1911.

> Octavo, original blue decorative cloth with gilt titles.
> 448 p., frontispiece (portrait), [47] leaves of plates.
> First American edition?
> Reference: OCLC 249638.

West, Wallace **[737]**
Paramount Newsreel Men with Admiral Byrd in Little America: The Story of Little America with Pictures by Paramount Newsreel Cameramen and the Story of Their Adventures. Racine, Wisconsin: Whitman Publishing Company [c. 1934].

> Small square octavo, original cloth.
> 90 p., illustrations (including portraits.)
> Reference: OCLC 33528899.

Wheildon, William Willder (1805–1892) **[738]**
The Arctic Regions. Atmospheric Theory of the Open Polar Sea and an Ameliorated Climate. Third Paper. Concord, Mass., 1814.

> Octavo, original gray printed wrappers, uncut.
> Pp. 118–140.
> At head of title: American Association for the Advancement of Science.
> "From the Proceedings of the American Association for the Advancement of Science, Portland meeting, August, 1873."
> Reference: OCLC 8990373.

Wheildon, William Willder (1805–1892)
[739]

Atmospheric Theory of the Open Polar
Sea, with Remarks on the Present State of
the Question. By William W. Wheildon.
First Paper. Boston: Elmwood
Typographia, 1872.

> Small octavo, original tan printed wrappers.
> xii p., 1 l., 20 p.
> Reference: OCLC 3218523.

Whitehouse, John Howard (1873–   )
[740]

Nansen, a Book of Homage. Edited by J.
Howard Whitehouse. London: Hodder
and Stoughton Limited [1930].

> Octavo, original blue cloth with white titles.
> 189 p., frontispiece (portrait), [5] leaves of plates, map.
> Reference: OCLC 2777076.

Whitehouse, John Howard (1873–   )
[741]

A Visit to Nansen, by J.H. Whitehouse,
and Adventure, by Sir E.H. Shackleton.
London: Oxford University Press,
Humphrey Milford, 1928.

> Octavo, original green paper boards with green cloth
> spine, paper labels.
> 23, [1] p., frontispiece (portrait), 1 plate.
> First edition.
> References: Spence 1255, OCLC 2863144.

Whitney, Harry (1873–1936)   [742]

Hunting with the Eskimos: The Unique
Record of a Sportsman's Year among the
Northernmost Tribe—the Big Game
Hunting, the Native Life and the Battle for
Existance through the Long Arctic Night.
By Harry Whitney. Illustrated with
Photographs by the Author. New York:
The Century Co., 1910.

> Octavo, original blue decorative cloth with gilt and
> blue titles.
> xiv, 453 p., frontispiece, [63] leaves of plates,
> illustrations (head and tail pieces), folded map.

First edition.
References: AB 19411, OCLC 407294.

Wild, Frank (1874–   )   [743]

Shackleton's Last Voyage. The Story of the
'Quest'. By Commander Frank Wild,
C.B.E. From the Official Journal and
Private Diary Kept by Dr. A.H. Macklin.
With a Coloured Frontispiece, Numerous
Maps and Over 100 Illustrations from
Photographs. London, New York [etc.]:
Cassell and Company, Ltd., 1923.

> Octavo, original blue decorated cloth with gilt and
> blue titles.
> xvi, 372 p., color frontispiece, [50] leaves of plates
> (including 1 chart), 12 maps in text. First edition.
> References: Spence 1259, OCLC 3534004.

Wilkes, Charles (1798–1877)   [744]

Autobiography of Rear Admiral Charles
Wilkes, U.S. Navy, 1798–1877. Editors:
William James Morgan, David B. Tyler,
Joye L. Leonhart, [and] Mary F. Loughlin.
With an Introduction by Rear Admiral
John D.H. Kane, Jr., USN (Ret.).
Washington: Naval History Division,
Department of the Navy, 1978.

> Quarto, original red cloth with gilt titles.
> xxii, 944 p., frontispiece (portrait), illustrations.
> First publication.
> Reference: OCLC 4043274.

Wilkes, Charles (1798–1877)   [745]

Narrative of the United States Exploring
Expedition during the Years 1838, 1839,
1840, 1841, 1842. By Charles Wilkes,
U.S.N., Commander of the Expedition,
Member of the American Philosophical
Society, etc. Philadelphia: Lea &
Blanchard, 1845.

> Small quarto, 5 volumes and atlas, three-quarter green
> morocco with raised bands, gilt titles, marbled
> endpapers and edges.
> Volume 1: lx, 434 p., frontispiece (portrait), [7] leaves
> of plates, 1 folded map; Volume 2: xv, 476 p.,
> frontispiece (portrait), [13] leaves of plates, 3

folded maps; Volume 3: xv, 438 p., [12] leaves
of plates; Volume 4: xvi p., 539 p., [15] leaves of
plates, 1 folded map; Volume 5: xv, 558 p., [15]
leaves of plates, 4 folded maps; Atlas: [iii], 5
folded maps (1 hand colored).
References: Spence 1262, OCLC 19800108.

Wilkins, George Hubert, Sir (1888–)
[746]

Flying the Arctic, by Captain George H.
Wilkins. New York and London: G.P.
Putnam's Sons, 1928.

Octavo, original rust cloth with gilt titles, dust jacket.
xv, 336 p., frontispiece (portrait), [15] leaves of plates.
First edition.
References: AB 19488, OCLC 1557696.

Wilkins, George Hubert, Sir (1888–)
[747]

Under the North Pole: The Wilkins-
Ellsworth Submarine Expedition, by Sir
Hubert Wilkins. [New York]: Brewer,
Warren & Putnam [1931].

Octavo, original decorated yellow cloth with black
titles.
xiv, 347 p., frontispiece (portrait), [18] leaves of plates,
facsimiles, map, maps on endpapers.
References: AB19491, OCLC 2096382.

Wilkins, George Hubert, Sir (1888–)
and Harold Morrow Sherman
(1898–)
[748]

Thoughts through Space: A Remarkable
Adventure in the Realm of Mind. By Sir
Hubert Wilkins and Harold M. Sherman.
New York: Creative Age Press, Inc., 1942.

Octavo, original decorated blue cloth with silver titles.
5 p. l., 3–421 p., [11] leaves of plates, facsimiles.
References: AB 19494, OCLC 1268975.

Williams, Glyndwr
(See Barr, William)

Williamson, James A.
[749]

The Voyages of the Cabots and the English
Discovery of North American under Henry

VII and Henry VIII, by James A.
Williamson [etc.]. Illustrated with Thirteen
Maps. London: The Argonaut Press, 1929.

Quarto, quarter Japan vellum on decorated blue
spine. Uncut copy.
xiii, 290, [1] p., frontispiece (folded map), 12 maps.

Wilson, Alfred W. G.
(See McInnes, William)

Wilson, Clifford P.
[750]

The New North in Pictures. Edited by
Clifford Wilson. Toronto, Halifax [and]
Vancouver: The Ryerson Press [1947].

Quarto, original blue cloth with gilt titles, worn dust
jacket.
223 p., chiefly photographs (some color), facsimiles,
portraits, maps.
Reference: OCLC 13625400.

Wilson, Edward Adrian (1872–1912)
[751]

Diary of the Discovery Expedition to the
Antarctic Regions, 1901–1904. Edited
from the Original Mss. in the Scott Polar
Research Institute, Cambridge by Ann
Savours. London: Blandford Press [1975].

Quarto, original blue cloth with gilt titles, dust jacket.
47 watercolors by Wilson, 416 p., 2 frontispieces
(including 1 color), [31] leaves of plates (part
color), illustrations, facsimiles, portraits, 7 maps (1
loose at end).
Reprint of 1966 edition.
Reference: Reprint of Spence 1030.

Wilson, Edward Adrian (1872–1912)
[752]

Diary of the "Terra Nova" Expedition to
the Antarctic 1910–1912. An Account of
Scott's Last Expedition Edited from the
Original Mss. in the Scott Polar Research
Institute and the British Museum by
H.G.R. King. London: Blandford Press
[1972].

Octavo, original decorated beige cloth with gilt titles,
dust jacket.

xxiii, 279 p., frontispiece (portrait), [12] leaves of color
   plates, illustrations, portraits, facsimiles, diagrams,
   10 maps.
First edition.
Reference: OCLC 573601.

Wilson, Edward Adrian (1872–1912)
[753]

Edward Wilson's Birds of the Antarctic.
Edited by Brian Roberts. From the
Original Illustrations in the Scott Polar
Research Institute, Cambridge. London:
Blandford Press [1967].

Large quarto, original decorated blue cloth with silver
   titles, dust jacket.
191 p., frontispiece (portrait), illustrations (some color),
   diagrams, maps.
Reference: OCLC 3150610.

Wolstenholme, John, Sir (1562–1639)
[754]

Exchequer receipt in Latin dated 3
December 1622, and signed by Robert
Seymer, one of the four tellers of the
exchequer, for 1000 pounds received from
Sir John Wolstenholme, Henry Garway,
Abraham Jacob, and Maurice Abbot.

Vellum slip 4.2 x 35.4 cm.
Sir John Wolstenholme was a Merchant Adventurer
   and member of the Virginia Company. Cape
   Wolstenholme was named for him by Henry
   Hudson and Wolstenholme Island and Sound by
   William Baffin. Abbot (1565–1642) was a
   governor of the East India Company, and Jacob
   was an investor in the Virginia Company.

Woodward, Frances J.
[755]

Portrait of Jane: A Life of Lady Franklin,
by Frances J. Woodward. London: Hodder
and Stoughton [1951].

Octavo, green cloth with gilt titles, faded dust jacket.
382 p., frontispiece (portrait), [6] leaves of plates, 1
   map, map on back endpaper.
Reference: OCLC 2953470.

Woollacott, Arthur P.
[756]

Mackenzie and His Voyageurs: By Canoe
to the Arctic and the Pacific, 1789–93, by
Arthur P. Woollacott. With Illustrations
and Thirty-two Photographs. London &
Toronto: J.M. Dent & Sons, Ltd., 1927.

Octavo, original decorated blue cloth with gilt titles.
x, 237 p., [16] leaves of plates, double-page map.
Reference: OCLC 2703052.

Worsley, Frank Arthur (1872–1943)
[757]

Endurance: An Epic of Polar Adventure
[by] Frank Arthur Worsley. New York:
Jonathan Cape and Harrison Smith
[1931].

Octavo, original blue cloth (faded) with white titles.
viii p., 3 l., 316 p., frontispiece, [21] leaves of plates.
First American edition.
References: Spence 1278, OCLC 1464875.

Worsley, Frank Arthur (1872–1943)
[758]

Shackleton's Boat Journey [by] F.A.
Worsley. Narrative Introduction by Sir
Edmund Hillary. New York: W.W. Norton
& Company, Inc. [1977].

Octavo, original blue quarter cloth on light blue
   boards with gilt titles, dust jacket.
220 p., [16] leaves of plates, map, maps on
   endpapers.
First edition.
Reference: OCLC 2743074.

Worsley, Frank Arthur (1872–1943)
[759]

Under Sail in the Frozen North, by
Commander F.A. Worsley [etc.]. With a
Preface by Grettir Algarsson. Fully
Illustrated. London: Stanley Paul & Co.
Ltd. [1927].

Octavo, original decorated blue cloth with gilt titles.
2 p. l., 299 p., frontispiece, [30] leaves of plates, 3
   maps (1 folded).
"Most of these photographs were taken with a Kodak
   camera" — List of Illustrations, p. 10.
First edition inscribed by "Doc" Alex. Sinclair.
References: AB 19695, OCLC 1821741.

Wrangel, Ferdinand Petrovich, baron (1796–1870) [760]

Narrative of an Expedition to the Polar Sea, in the Years 1820, 1821, 1822, & 1823. Commanded by Lieutenant, Now Admiral, Ferdinand von Wrangell, of the Russian Imperial Navy. Edited by Major Edward Sabine [etc.]. London: James Madden and Co. MDCCCXXXX [1840].

> Octavo, full calf, rebacked with original spine laid down, raised bands, gilt decorations and titles, marbled endpapers and maps.
> cxxxvii, 413 p., folded map.
> First English edition.
> References: AB 18994, OCLC 5588965.

Wrangel, Ferdinand Petrovich, baron (1796–1870) [761]

Narrative of an Expedition to the Polar Sea, in the Years 1820, 1821, 1822 and 1823. Commanded by Lieutenant, Now Admiral Ferdinand Wrangell, of the Russian Imperial Navy. New York: Harper and Brothers [1841].

> Duodecimo, original decorated brown cloth with gilt titles. Binder's title: Wrangell's Siberian and Polar Expedition.
> xvii, [2], 20–3-2 p., [8] p. of advertisements, frontispiece (folded map).
> Family library, no. 148.
> References: AB 18995, OCLC 20399930.

Wright, Charles S. (1887–1975) [762]

Silas: The Antarctic Diaries and Memoir of Charles S. Wright. Edited by Colin Bull and Pat F. Wright. Illustrated by Pat F. Wright. Columbus: Ohio State University Press, 1993.

> Octavo, blue cloth with gilt titles, in slip case embossed with Wright's silhouette.
> xxx, 1 l., 418 p., 1 l., frontispiece (portrait), illustrations, 12 maps, decorated endpapers. Added, color frontispiece.
> Signed copy, with inscribed Terra Nova presentation card.
> Reference: OCLC 25550272.

Wright, Helen Saunders (1874–) [763]

The Great White North: The Story of Polar Exploration from the Earliest Times to the Discovery of the Pole, by Helen S. Wright. New York: The Macmillan Company, 1910.

> Octavo, original decorated green cloth with gilt titles and top edge.
> xx, 489 p., [4] p. of advertisements, frontispiece (portrait), [47] leaves of plates, illustrations, 5 maps.
> References: AB 19715, OCLC 2115156.

Wright, Noel (1890–) [764]

Quest for Franklin [by] Noel Wright. London [etc.]: Heinemann [1959].

> Octavo, black cloth with blue titles.
> xii, 258 p., frontispiece (portrait), [4] leaves of plates, illustrations, facsimiles, 4 maps.
> First edition.
> Reference: OCLC 3307314.

Wright, Pat F.
(See Wright, Charles S.)

Wright, Theon [765]

The Big Nail. The Story of the Cook-Peary Feud [by] Theon Wright. New York: The John Day Company [1970].

> Octavo, original decorated white cloth with red and gilt titles, dust jacket.
> xi p., 1 l., 368 p., illustrations, portraits, 6 maps.
> Reference: OCLC 54014.

Young, Allen William, Sir (1830–1915) [766]

The Two Voyages of the 'Pandora' in 1875 and 1876. By Sir Allen Young [etc.], Commander of the Expeditions. London: Edward Stanford, 1879.

> Octavo, original decorated blue cloth with gilt titles, rebacked with original spine laid down.
> viii, 197 p., frontispiece, [8] leaves of plates, 2 folded maps.
> First edition.
> Note: Maps are in front and back pockets.
> Inscription on title page: "Mr. B. Ball from Allen Young, March 31, '79."
> References: AB 19759, OCLC 2994661.

Young, Steven B. [767]
To the Arctic: An Introduction to the Far Northern World [by] Steven B. Young, the Center for Northern Studies. New York [etc.]: John Wiley & Sons, Inc., 1989.
Wide octavo, blue cloth with white titles, dust jacket.

xiii, 354 p., black and white photographs and text illustrations.
First edition.
Reference: OCLC 18106591.

Zeno, Nicolò and Antonio
(See Major, Richard Henry)

Separate Maps

OUTLINE OF CLASSIFICATION

Separate Maps

WORLD

World—1721 [M1]

A New Map of the World from the Latest Observations, Revis'd by I. Senex. [London: John Senex, 1721?].

> 1 map : hand col. ; on sheet 53 x 58 cm.
> Probably detached from an edition of John Senex, *A New general atlas* (cf. Phillips 563).
> Eastern and western hemispheres each 27 cm. in diam.
> Insets [each 9 cm. diam.]: The Earth projected on the plane of the Equator [northern hemisphere] — The Earth projected on the plane of the Equator [southern hemisphere] — The Earth projected at the plane of the horizon of London [northern hemisphere] — The Earth projected at the plane of the horizon of London [southern hemisphere].
> Includes 2 charts showing world climate zones [each 7 cm. diam.] and vignette of an armillary sphere [7 cm.].

World—1747 [M2]

Die verfinsterte Erdkugel d[as] i[st] geographische Vorstellvng der Sonnen-od[er] Erd-Finsternis den 25ten. Iulii ao. 1748 = Le monde eclipsé ou representation geographiqve de l'eclipse de la terre ov dv soleil qui arrivera le 25 Iullet 1748. Verzeichnet von Georg Moriz Lowiz. Nürenburg: Herausgegeben in der Homaen[n]ischen Officin, 1747.

> 1 map : hand col. ; 47 x 56 cm.
> Scale ca. 1:13,000,000 at the equator.
> "Prostat in Officina Homanniana Norimb. 1747 — C.P.S.C.M.G."
> Includes 3 hemispherical maps showing eclipted areas at different times, and "Projectio orthographica telluris."
> "Sculpsit Ruprecht Adam Schneider, Fürth."
> "Illustri ac per Omnen Europam celeberrima viro Dno. Leonhardo Evlero . . ."
> Relief shown pictorially.
> Prime meridian: Ferro.
> "1tes. Blat."

World—1794 [M3]

A New Chart of the World on Wright's or Mercator's Projection: in Which Are Exhibited All the Parts Hitherto Explored or Discovered; with the Tracks of the British Circumnavigators Byron, Wallis, Carteret and Cook, &c. London: Published by Laurie and Whittle, 53 Fleet-Street, as the Act Directs, 1794 May 12.

> 1 map : hand col. ; 71 x 91 cm.
> In MS. (pencil) on verso: No. 2.
> Detached from a Laurie and Whittle atlas [cf. Phillips 716, 6012 and others].

World—1900 [M4]

The World on Mercator's Projection. London: George Philip and Son, [ca. 1900?].

> 1 map ; 20 x 30 cm.
> "Printed in Great Britain by George Philip & Son, Limited, London."
> "The London Geographical Institute. KBI."—lower right margin.
> Blank outline map: slight MS. annotation (pencil and ink).

World—1942—Projections [M5]

Six Oblique Mercator Projections: Normal Mercator and Transverse Graticule, Calculated at the Royal Geographical Society by Arthur R. Hinks, C.B.E., F.R.S. London: Waterlow & Sons, 1942.

> 7 maps, 1 graticule : col. ; on 8 sheets each 33 x 52 cm.
> Title and imprint from paper portfolio 33 x 52 cm.
> Includes 6 oblique Mercator charts based on various longitudes with "Pole 35 ½°N.," 1 traditional Mercator chart, and 1 blank transverse Mercator graticule.
> "Hinks, R.G.S., 1942"—right bottom margin of each sheet.
> Portfolio includes 3 paragraphs of text and references to *Geographical Journal* v.95 (1940) p.381 and v.97 (1941) p.353.

Separate Maps

WESTERN HEMISPHERE

Western Hemisphere—1775   [M6]

A Chart of North and South America, Including the Atlantic and Pacific Oceans, with the Nearest Coasts of Europe, Africa, and Asia. [London]: Robt. Sayer & J. Bennett, 1775 Jun.

> 1 map (incomplete) : hand col. ; 83 x 113 cm.
> "Published according to Act of Parliament. 10 June 1775, by Robt. Sayer and J. Bennett."
> Detached from Thomas Jefferys, *The American atlas* (London: Sayer and Bennett, 1775).
> Incomplete: 4 of 6 sheets present. All 6 sheets form a complete map of the Americas, made up of 3 panels (each panel formed from 2 sheets trimmed and pasted together). Lacking bottom third of map. Size of complete map, 122 x 113 cm.
> Sheets present apparently detached from 2 or 3 different copies of the atlas.
> Contents (titles of individual sheets): Chart containing part of the Icy Sea with the adjacent coast of Asia and America. — Chart comprising Greenland with the countries and islands about Baffins Bay and part of Hudson's Bay. — Chart containing the coasts of California, New Albion, and Russian discoveries to the north. . . . — North America and the West Indies, with the opposite coasts of Europe and Africa. — Chart containing the greater part of the South Sea. . . . — South America with the adjacent islands. . . .
> Lacking last 2 sheets named.
> Includes notes on history of American exploration and shows tracks of noted sea expeditions.
> References: Phillips 1166; Wagner, no. 649.

POLAR REGIONS (NORTH AND SOUTH)

Polar Regions (North and South)—1786   [M7]

Carte des deux regions polaires jusqu' au 45e degré de latitude. [Deux-Ponts, 1786].

> 2 maps ; 20 cm. in diam., within border 22 x 44 cm. (sheet size 24 x 48 cm.)
> Detached from Georges Louis Buffon, *Histoire naturelle, generale et particuliere* (Deux-Ponts: Sanson & Cie, 1785–1787), v. 13 (1786), opp. p. 290.

> At upper left: Tome XIII.
> Shows routes of Cook, Furneaux, Tasman, Halley, "Phipps," and "Pilote Olcheredin."
> For a later edition of this map, see M9 below.

Polar Regions (North and South)—1795   [M8]

The World in Three Sections Describing the Polar Regions to the Tropics: with all the Tracks of Lord Mulgrave and Captain Cook towards the North and South Poles and the Torrid Zone or Tropical Regions with the New Discoveries in the South Sea. [London: s.n., 1795].

> 3 maps ; on 1 sheet 26 x 44 cm.
> Detached from William Guthrie, *Guthrie's universal geography improved* (London: Printed for the proprietors, 1795) [OCLC 14190973].
> At upper right is visible faint offprinting (reversed) reading: Guthrie's universal geography.
> Contents: The South pole to the Tropic of Capricorn in which are traced the several attempts of Capt. Cook to discover a southern continent . . . [14 cm. dia.] — The North Pole to the Tropic of Cancer, describing the track of the Honble. Capt. Phipps, now Lord Mulgrave . . . [14 cm. dia.] — Torrid zones or tropical regions of the world, in which are laid down, the new discoveries in the Pacific Ocean or South Sea [6 x 41 cm.]

Polar Regions (North and South)—1808?   [M9]

Carte des deux regions polaires jusqu' au 45e degré de latitude. Gravé par Blanchard. [Paris, 1808?].

> 2 maps ; 20 cm. in diam., within border 22 x 44 cm. (sheet size 33 x 50 cm.)
> Detached from Georges Louis Buffon, *Histoire naturelle, generale et particuliere* (Paris, 1799–1808).
> In upper right: T. 4. P. 145
> Shows routes of Cook, Furneaux, Tasman, Halley, "Phipp," and "Pilote Otcheredin."
> For an earlier edition of this map, see M7 above.

PACIFIC OCEAN

Pacific Ocean—1840   [M10]

Track Chart of H.M.S. Fly between the 21

September 1839 and 20th March 1840.
[1840?].

> 1 map (manuscript) ; 40 x 32 cm.
> Scale ca. 1:19,000,000 at the equator.
> Title from note on verso.
> Northerly voyage from Valparaiso to Guaymas in black
>   ink and pencil; southerly in blue ink.
> The H.M.S. Fly, commanded by "Commandant Locke,"
>   aided the U.S. ship Relief outside Valparaiso (April
>   13, 1839); see Charles Wilkes, Narrative of the
>   United States exploring expedition (Philadelphia:
>   Lea & Blanchard, 1845), v. 5, p. 158.

NORTHERN HEMISPHERE

Northern Hemisphere—1584   [M11]
[Volvelle, 1584]. [Antwerp: s.n., 1584].

> 1 map ; 13 cm. in diam. on sheet 23 x 16 cm.
> Volvelle detached from Peter Apian, *Cosmographicus
>   Liber* (Antwerp, 1584), p.65–66.
> Running head: Petri Apiani et Gemmae Fris.
> Signature I at lower right.
> Latin text on verso (p.66) with running head: Secunda
>   pars cosmograph.
> References: Nordensköld, p.92, fig. 57; Shirley, p. 57;
>   Karrow, no. 7/4.

Northern Hemisphere—1714   [M12]
Hemisphere septentrional: pour voir plus
distinctement les terres arctiques, par
Guiluame Delisle de l'Academie Rle. des
Sciences. A Paris: Chez l'Auteur sur le
Quay de l'Horloge, 1714.

> 1 map : hand col. ; 44 cm. in diam.
> Detached from an atlas; MS. "2" in upper right.

Northern Hemisphere—1730   [M13]
Hemisphere septentrional pour voir plus
distinctement les terres arctiques, par
Guillaume De Lisle de l'Academie Rle. des
Sciences. A Amsterdam: chez Jean Cóvens
et Corneille Mortier libraires, [1730 or
1733].

> 1 map : hand col. ; 43 cm. in diam. on sheet 53 x 56
>   cm.
> Detached from *Atlas nouveau* (Amsterdam: Covens et
>   Mortier, 1730 or 1733) [cf. Phillips 580, 581;
>   Koeman, C&M 3–5].
> Plate mark: 466 x 520.

Northern Hemisphere—1740   [M14]
L'hemisphere septentrional pour voir plus
distinctement les terres arctiques, par
Guillaume De Lisle de l'Academie Rle. des
Sciences. Amsterdam: chez Jean Cóvens et
Corneille Mortier libraires, 1740.

> 1 map : hand col. ; 43 cm. in diam. on sheet 54 x 66
>   cm.
> Detached from *Atlas nouveau* (Amsterdam: Covens et
>   Mortier, 174-?) [cf. Phillips 595 no.2, 596 v.1 no.
>   2; Koeman, C&M 7, no. 5].
> Later state of plate first printed in 1730 (M13 above),
>   with numerous additions and the inclusion of the
>   initial article in the first title word
>   ("L'hemisphere"). Includes a letter by Swartz on
>   Russian discoveries, in parallel French and Dutch
>   texts, appearing in left and right margins, and
>   dated January 1740.
> Plate mark: 464 x 518 mm.
> In upper right corner and on verso, the number "5"
>   (pencil, contemporary [?] hand).

Northern Hemisphere—1746   [M15]
Carte du globe terrestre oú terres de
l'Hemisphere Meridl. sont supposées être
vues à travers celles de l'Hemisphere
Septentl, par Phillipe Buache per.
Geographe de S. Mte. et de l'Academie
Royale des Sciences; Gravé par G:
Delahaye. Paris: l'Auteur, 1746 Sep 3.

> 1 map : hand col. ; 23 cm. in diam.
> Scale ca. 1:11,000,000 at the Arctic pole.
> "Publié sous le Privilége de l'Acad. Rle. des
>   Sciences . . ."
> Polar projection.
> Prime meridians: Ferro, Paris.
> Descriptive text on both sides of map.
> Reference: Tooley FMA, 99.

Northern Hemisphere—1750   [M16]
Nuova carta del Polo Artico: secondo
l'ultime osservazioni. Amsterdam: Isac
Tirion, [1750].

> 1 map : hand col. ; 28 cm. in diam.
> Scale ca. 1:45,000,000.
> Relief shown pictorially.
> Prime meridian: [Ferro].
> Probably detached from Guillaume Delisle, *Atlante
>   novissimo* (Venezia, 1750) [Phillips 594].

Northern Hemisphere—1802   [M17]
Northern Hemisphere. London: W. Faden, 1802 May 1.

> 1 map : hand col. ; 57 cm. in diam.
> Scale ca. 1:34,000,000.
> Relief shown pictorially.
> Detached from an edition of Faden's *General atlas*,
>   map no. 3 (cf. Phillips 6047).

Northern Hemisphere—1818   [M18]
Northern Hemisphere. Kirkwood sculpt. [Edinburgh, 1818].

> 1 map : hand col. ; 50 cm. in diam.
> Scale ca. 1:43,000,000.
> Relief shown pictorially.
> Detached from John Thomson, *A New general atlas*
>   (Edinburgh, [1818]) [cf. Phillips 731].

Northern Hemisphere—1827   [M19]
Der Erde nördl: Halbkugel, Augsburg bei Joh. Walch. Augsburg: Joh. Walch, [1827?].

> 1 map : hand col. ; 18 cm. in diam. on sheet 22 x 26
>   cm.
> Detached from an unidentified text; "1827" in pencil
>   on verso; "3" printed in upper right corner of
>   recto.

Northern Hemisphere—1930   [M20]
Great Circle Map Showing Fairbanks, Alaska: a Geographical Center of Europe, Asia, America and the Terminus of the Pacific Yukon Highway. [Washington, D.C.]: Geological Survey, 1930.

> 1 map ; 54 x 72 cm.
> "Copyright 1930, by Ernest Walker Sawyer."
> "Engraved and printed by the U.S. Geological Survey."
> At lower right: Map no. 7.
> Accompanied by 3 p. mimeograph letter by Sawyer
>   dated Dec. 31, 1930: ". . . The primary purpose
>   of the map is to draw attention to Alaska and its
>   tremendous strategic position and value."

Northern Hemisphere—1963   [M21]
The Top of the World, Compiled and Drawn in the Cartographic Division of the National Geographic Society for the National Geographic Magazine; Lithographed by A. Hoen & Co., Baltimore, Md. Baltimore: A. Hoen & Co., 1963.

> 1 map : col. ; 71 x 68 cm.
> Scale 1:14,000,000.
> "James M. Darley, chief cartographer. Compiled by
>   R. J. Darley, R. G. Fritz, A. D. Grazzini, A. E.
>   Holdstock, R. E. McAleer and C.L. Stern. Relief by
>   J. J. Brehm."
> Includes table of airline distances.
> MS. annotation: ARCT 69–18 c.3.

ARCTIC REGIONS

Arctic Regions—1595   [M22]
Septentrionalivm Terrarum descriptio, per Gerardum Mercatorem. Cum privilegio. [Duisburg: Rumold Mercator, 1595].

> 1 map : hand col. ; 34 cm. in diam.
> Detached from Gerard Mercator, *Atlantis pars altera*.
>   . . . (Duisburg: Rumold Mercator, 1595) pl. no.
>   [6].
> References: Karrow, 56/142; Koeman, v.2, p.292,
>   map 79; NMM, v.2, p.46, pl. no. 6.
> Insets (each 6 cm. diam.): Frislant insula — Farre insule
>   — Scetland insulæ.
> Latin text on verso with following title: Polvs Arcticvs ac
>   terrarvm circvmiacentium descriptio [signature I].
> MS. "6" in upper right on verso.

Arctic Regions—1595   [M23]
Septentrionalivm Terrarum descriptio, per Gerardum Mercatorem. Cum privilegio. [Amsterdam?: Jodocus Hondius?, 1609?].

> 1 map : hand col. ; 34 cm. in diam.
> Later issue of M22 above.
> Probably detached from Gerard Mercator, *L'Atlas ou
>   méditations* . . . (Amsterdam: Jodocus Hondius,
>   1609) pl. no. [7].
> References: Koeman, Me 19 [79]; cf. Karrow, 56/142;
>   NMM, v.2 p.46, no. 140, pl 6.
> Insets (each 6 cm. diam.): Frislant insula — Farre insule
>   — Scetland insulæ.
> French text on verso with following title: Le Pole
>   Arctiqve: et la description des terres
>   septentrionales [signature K, p.41].

Arctic Regions—1600   [M24]
Polus Arcticus sive tract[us] septentrionalis.

Coloniae: ex officina typographica Jani Bussemechers, [1600].

> 1 map ; 21 cm. in diam. on sheet 27 x 34 cm.
> Detached from Matthias Quad, *Geographisch Handtbuch* (Cologne: J. Bussemacher, 1600) [Meurer, Atlantes Coloniensis, Qua 79].
> Insets (each 6 cm. diameter): Schetlant insulae. — Frislant insula. — Farre insulae.
> Latin text on verso headed "Polus Arcticus. [p.] 81."

Arctic Regions—16—?   [M25]

Pole Arctiqve, ou terre du Septentrion. [S.l.: s.n., 16—].

> 1 map : hand col. ; 14 x 19 cm.
> Scale ca. 1:44,000,000.
> Detached from unidentified text.
> Within border, lower right corner: 4.
> Relief shown pictorially.
> Prime meridian: [Ferro].

Arctic Regions—1624   [M26]

Polo settentrionale, o Boreale, et artico. [Venice: Coronelli, ca. 1690].

> 1 map : hand col. ; 36 cm. in diam. on sheet 47 x 51 cm.
> Scale ca. 1:12,000,000.
> North polar calotte from Coronelli's 3½ foot globe (ca. 1690).
> Title from spiral text (7 lines) at center of map.
> Probably detached from an edition of M. V. Coronelli's *Libro dei globi* (Venice, 1693).
> Relief shown pictorially.

Arctic Regions—1635   [M27]

[Map of Arctic Regions and Northern Hemisphere]. [Cambridge?, 1934?].

> 1 map ; 21 x 30 cm.
> Reduced facsimile.
> "The map is reproduced from [Luke Foxe,] North-West Fox, 1635. The original is in the Pepysian Library, Magdalene College. Original size 44 x 32 cm."
> MS. annotation (pencil) by J. M. Wordie, lower right: From block prepared by I. H. Cox . . . 1934.

Arctic Regions—1636   [M28]

Poli arctici et circumiacentium terrarum descriptio novissima, sumptibus Henrici Hondij. [Amsterdam: H. Hondius and J. Jansson, 1636].

> 1 map ; 43 cm. in diam.
> Detached from a Mercator-Hondius-Jansson atlas (cf. Koeman, Me 41 A [344]).
> Title on recto from cartouche in upper center.
> Small cartouche in upper right blank.
> English text on verso with following title: The Pole arctiqve, and the description of the septentrionall or Northerne Lands [signature N, p.43–44].
> Copy 1 of 2.

Arctic Regions—1636   [M29]

Poli arctici et circumiacentium terrarum descriptio novissima, sumptibus Henrici Hondij. [Amsterdam: H. Hondius and J. Jansson, 1636].

> 1 map : col. ; 43 cm. in diam.
> Detached from a Mercator-Hondius-Jansson atlas (cf. Koeman, Me 41 A [344]).
> Title on recto from cartouche in upper center.
> Small cartouche in upper right blank.
> English text on verso with following title: The Pole arctiqve, and the description of the septentrionall or Northerne Lands [signature N, p.43–44].
> Copy 2 of 2.

Arctic Regions—1636 (1638 state)   [M30]

Poli arctici et circumiacentium terrarum descriptio novissima. Sumptibus Henrici Hondij. [Amsterdam: H. Hondius and J. Jansson, 1638].

> 1 map : col. ; 43 cm. in diam.
> Detached from a Mercator-Hondius-Jansson atlas (cf. Koeman, v.2, p.397, Me 41 A [344*]).
> Title on recto from cartouche in upper center.
> Small cartouche in upper right blank.
> Latin text on verso with following title: Polus arcticus [signature C]. Whaling vignettes in margins.

Arctic Regions—1636 (1675 state)   [M31]

Poli arctici et circumiacentium terrarum descriptio novissima, per Fredericum de Wit Amstelodami. Amsteldam: Frederick de Wit, [ca. 1675].

> 1 map : col. ; 43 cm. in diam.
> Detached from a de Wit atlas (cf. Koeman, v.4, p. 518, M. Wit 1 [2]).
> Revision of map issued in various Mercator-Hondius-Jansson atlases.

Hondius imprint replaced with de Wit imprint in title
cartouche, upper center.
Small cartouche in upper right: Gedruckt 't Amsteldam
by Frederick de Wit in de Calverstraet aen den
Dam in de Witte Pascaert.
Whaling vignettes in margins.
Verso blank.
At upper right, in MS: 131.
Copy 1 of 2.

Arctic Regions—1636 (1675 state)
[M32]

Poli arctici et circumiacentium terrarum
descriptio novissima, per Fredericum de
Wit Amstelodami. Amsteldam: Frederick
de Wit, [ca. 1675].

1 map : col. ; 43 cm. in diam.
Detached from a de Wit atlas (cf. Koeman v.4, p. 518,
M. Wit 1 [2]).
Revision of map issued in various Mercator-Hondius-
Jansson atlases.
Hondius imprint replaced with de Wit imprint in title
cartouche, upper center.
Small cartouche in upper right: Gedruckt 't Amsteldam
by Frederick de Wit in de Calverstraet aen den
Dam in de Witte Pascaert.
Whaling vignettes in margins.
Verso blank.
Mounted on heavy paper.
Copy 2 of 2.

Arctic Regions—1637   [M33]

Nova et accvrata Poli Arctici et terrarum
circum iacentium descriptio. Amstelodami:
apud Ioannem Ianssonium, [1637?].

1 map : hand col. ; 40 x 52 cm.
Detached from an atlas, MS. "20" in upper right (cf.
Koeman v.2, p. 390, Me 47 [456]).
Latin text on verso with following title: Poli arctici et
regionum sub eo sitarum descriptio [no
signature, no page no., MS. "10" in upper right].
Very similar to arctic map variously issued in Blaeu
atlases, but printed from a different plate.

Arctic Regions—1638   [M34]

Regiones svb polo arctico, auctore
Guiljelmo Blaeu. [Amsterdam: s.n., ca.
1638].

1 map : hand col. ; 40 x 52 cm.
On verso, Latin text with title: Polvs arcticvs [signature
C, p. 4].

Reference: Koeman (v.1, p.135 [Bl 23 B]) lists in Latin
ed. of Blaeu atlas with title page dated 1648;
plate apparently not altered.
From collection of J. M. Wordie.
Copy 1 of 3.

Arctic Regions—1638   [M35]

Regiones svb polo arctico, auctore
Guiljelmo Blaeu. [Amsterdam: s.n., ca.
1638].

1 map : hand col. ; 40 x 52 cm.
On verso, Latin text with title: Polvs arcticvs [signature
C, p. 4].
Reference: Koeman (v.1, p.135 [Bl 23 B]) lists in Latin
ed. of Blaeu atlas with title page dated 1648;
plate apparently not altered.
Copy 2 of 3.

Arctic Regions—1638   [M36]

Regiones svb polo arctico, auctore
Guiljelmo Blaeu. [Amsterdam: Blaeu, ca.
1638].

1 map : hand col. ; 40 x 52 cm.
On verso, French text with title: Pays sovs le pole
arctiqve [signature A, p.1].
Reference: Koeman (v.1, p. 116, map 276) lists in
French ed. of Blaeu atlas with attributed date of
between 1635 and 1638.
Copy 3 of 3.

Arctic Regions—1638 (1647 state)
[M37]

Regiones svb polo arctico, auctore
Guiljelmo Blaeu. [Amsterdam: Blaeu, ca.
1647?].

1 map : hand col. ; 40 x 52 cm.
Detached from a Blaeu atlas.
On verso, Dutch text with title: Landen onder de
Noord-Pool [signature C, p. 1].
Revised state of map first issued ca. 1638; includes
dedication to Guilielmus Backer de Cornelius
(Koeman v.1, p.144, map 276*).
Copy 1 of 3.

Arctic Regions—1638 (1647 state)
[M38]

Regiones svb polo arctico, auctore
Guiljelmo Blaeu. [Amsterdam: s.n., ca.
1647?].

1 map ; 40 x 52 cm.
Detached from a Blaeu atlas.
On verso, Latin text with title: Hyperarctica, sive
  regiones svb polo boreali [signature A, p. 1].
Revised state of map first issued ca. 1638; includes
  dedication to Guilielmus Backer de Cornelius (cf.
  Koeman v.1, p.144, map 276*).
From collection of J. M. Wordie.
Copy 2 of 3.

Arctic Regions—1638 (1647 state)
[M39]

Regiones svb polo arctico, auctore
Guiljelmo Blaeu. [Amsterdam: s.n., ca.
1647?].

1 map : hand col. ; on sheet 32 x 41 cm.
Detached from a Blaeu atlas.
Incomplete copy on sheet trimmed to 32 x 41 cm.;
  verso blank.
Revised state of map first issued ca. 1638; includes
  dedication to Guilielmus Backer de Cornelius (cf.
  Koeman v.1, p.144, map 276*).
From collection of J. M. Wordie.
Copy 3 of 3.

Arctic Regions—1680 [M40]
A Map of the North-Pole and Parts
Adjoining. [Oxford: M. Pitt], 1680.

1 map : hand col. ; 45 x 58 cm.
Detached from Moses Pitt, *The English atlas* (Oxford,
  1680–1682) [Phillips 2831, v.1, no.3].
All margins ruled with 4 red lines, recto and verso.
At upper left and right on verso in manuscript: "North
  Pole."

Arctic Regions—1685 [M41]
Terres Arctiqves dites autrement
septentrionales et boreales. [S.l.: s.n.,
1685?].

1 map : hand col. ; 10 x 13 cm.
Scale ca. 1:100,000,000.
Another issue published in Pierre Duval, Le Monde ov
  la geographie vniverselle (Paris, 1670) [Phillips
  481].
Ms. "3" at top of map.

Arctic Regions—1696 [M42]
Terre Artiche, descritte dal P. M. Coronelli
M.C., Cosmografo della Sereniss.

Republica di Venetia. [Venice: Coronelli?,
1696?].

1 map ; 45 x 61 cm.
Scale ca. 1:12,000,000.
"Dedicate All' Illmo. et Eccmo. Sig. Conte Ercole Pepoli,
  Conte di Castiglione, Bragarra, Sparui, etc.
  Senatore di Bologna, Nobile Ferarese, Patritio
  Veneto."
Relief shown pictorially.
Prime meridian: Isola del Ferro.

Arctic Regions—1705 [M43]
This Draught of the North Pole is to Shew
all the Countries Near and Adjacent to It:
as also the Most Remarkable Tracks of the
Bold Discoverers of Them, and Particularly
the Attempts of Our Own Countrymen to
Find Out the N. East and N. West
Passages, by H. Moll Geographer.
[London, 1705?].

1 map : hand col. ; 42 cm. in diam. on sheet 40 x 51
  cm.
Added title at center: The North Pole.
Detached from an edition of John Harris, *Navigantium*
  atque itinerantium bibliotheca (London, between
  1705–1764), "Vol. I Page 564."
Insets: [Arctic regions, 10 cm. diam.] and "A map of
  Nova Zembla and Waygats . . ." [4 x 6 cm.].

Arctic Regions—1717 [M44]
La Premiere partie du nouveau & grand
illuminant flambeau de la mer, le
troisiéme livre. Contenant la description
des costes maritimes de Norwegue
Finmarcken, Laplandt, Russen, & l'entiere,
Mer Blanche. Comme aussi d'Islant, l'Isle
de Beeren, l'Isle de L'esperame ou
Hoopen, Spitsbergue, & l'Isle de Jean
Maye. [Amsterdam: Johannes van Keulan,
1717?].

65–82 p. ; 9 maps ; 54 x 35 cm.
Title from heading on p.65.
Detached from an edition of Johannes van Keulen, *Le*
  nouveau & grand illuminant flambeau de la mer
  . . . [Amsterdam, 1681–1736] [cf. Koeman v.4,
  p.305, 322–23, 344–45].
Signature and catchword (T2, "Ainsi") match Koeman's
  description of copy in atlas with title page date
  1717 [v.4, p.323 [Keu 54 D]].

Collation based on combination of letterpress leaves
and engraved maps.
Folio in 2s, signed R-V2, X1.
Letterpress leaves include text and woodcut profiles
detailing coasts of Finmark, Lapland, the White
Sea, Muscovy, Hitlandt and Iceland.
Engraved maps: [unnumbered]. Paskaart van 't
Noordelykste deel der Noort Zee . . . [52 x 58
cm.] — 31. Paskaart van de kust van Finmarken
. . . [51 x 59 cm.] — 32. Paskaart van 't
Noordelykste van de kust van Finmarkken
alsmede een gedeelte van Lapland . . . [52 x 58
cm. Inset: Aftbeeldinge van 't Eylandt . . .
Wardhuys (19 x 38 cm.]] — [unnumbered].
Gedaantens der Landen soo als die hun uijt der
Zee Vertoonen . . . [29 coastal profiles on sheet
54 x 63 cm.] — 33. Paskaart van de Mont van
de Witte Zee . . . [51 x 59 cm. Insets: Swetenoes
. . . (9 x 14 cm.); De Kust van Laplandt . . . (8 x
33 cm.), Lombascho . . . (6 x 14 cm.), I. Kilduyn
(10 x 19 cm.), De Rivier van Kola . . . (19 x 42
cm.]] — 34. Paskaart van de Witte Zee . . . [52 x
59 cm.] — 35. Paskaart van de Rivier de Dwina
. . . [51 x 59 cm.] — 36. Paskaart vande noord
kust van Moscovien . . . [53 x 60 cm.] — 37.
Ysland [51 x 30 cm. Insets: Spitsbergen (30 x 28
cm.); Pascaarte van Ysland, Spitsberge, en Ian
Mayen Eyland . . . (21 x 28 cm.)].
Hand colored duplicate of plate 33, "Paskaart van de
Mont van Witte Zee. . . ." filed as pl. 33, copy 2.

Arctic Regions—1728   [M45]

A Globular Draught from the North Pole
to the Latitude of 60 Degrees. [London?:
s.n., 1728?].

1 map ; 48 cm. in diam.
Detached from an atlas; plate "21".
Bookseller's [?] pencilled date on verso: 1728.

Arctic Regions—1730   [M46]

A Map of the North Pole with All the
Territories that Lye Near It, known to us
&c.: According to the Latest Discoveries,
and Most Exact Observation, by H. Moll,
Geographer. [London?: s.n., ca. 1730?].

1 map ; 20 x 27 cm.
Detached from a text; originally folded to 17 x 8 cm.

Arctic Regions—1740   [M47]

The English Pilot. The Second Part.
Describing the Sea-coasts, Capes, Head-

lands, Soundings, Sands, Shoals, Rocks and
Dangers, the Bays, Roads, Harbours,
Rivers and Ports in the Whole Northern
Navigation Shewing the Courses and
Distances from One Place to Another: The
Letting of the Tides and Currents; the
Ebbing and Flowing of the Sea. With
Many Other Things Belonging to the Art
of Navigation. . . . London: Printed for
William Mount and Thomas Page, in
Postern-Row, on Tower-Hill, MDCCXL
[1740].

[2], 29–42 p. ; 10 maps ; 47 x 32 cm.
Incomplete; includes title page (and blank verso) and
pages 29–42.
Typeset leaves include text and woodcut profiles
detailing coasts of Finmark, Lapland, the White
Sea, Greenland and Trinity Island.
Contents, 10 engraved maps: The Coast of Norway
and Lapland from North Kyn to the River Kola
[42 x 52 cm. Inset: Wardhouse Island, 11 x 15
cm.] — The Coast of Lapland from ye River of
Kola to ye Islands of Swetnoes [29 x 52 cm.
Insets: Island of Kelduyn, 13 x 17 cm. and The
River of Kola in the Great Beseck, 13 x 35 cm.] —
A Large chart of the White Sea [45 x 58 cm.
Insets: A Large draught of Swetenose, 13 x 20
cm. and Lombascho Islands at large, 9 x 8 cm.]
— A Chart of Finmarck from Sanien to North-kyn
or North Point [43 x 53 cm.] — A Chart of the
North Sea, sold by Willm. Mount and Thos. Page
on Tower Hill, London [44 x 53 cm.] — The
Northern navigation according to Mr. Wright's
projection commonly called Mercator's chart,
sold by W. Mount and T. Page on Great Tower
Hill, London [45 x 58 cm.] — A New generall
chart of the coast of ye Northern Ocean viz
Norway, Greenland, Finmark, Lapland, Moscovy,
and Nova Zembla [48 x 56 cm. Inset: The Islands
of Podesemsko, 17 x 17 cm.] — A Generall chart
of the Northern Seas. Describing the sea coast
and islands from France to Grenne=land
[imprint erased?], London [41 x 53 cm.] — A
Chart of the East Sea [44 x 54 cm.] — The Coast
of Finmarck from Dronten to Tromsound [43 x
52 cm.].
Maps described in order found; all versos blank.

Arctic Regions—1747   [M48]

A New & Accurate Map of the North
Pole, with All the Countries Hitherto

Discovered: Situated Near or Adjacent to It: As Well As Some Others More Remote, Drawn from the Latest and Best Authorities and Regulated by Astrml. Observations by Eman Bowen — [London: Emanuel Bowen?, 1747?].

> 1 map ; on sheet 41 x 54 cm.
> Scale ca. 1:21,400,000.
> Relief shown pictorially.
> Prime meridian: London.
> Includes 2 columns of text.
> Engraved plate "No. 70" at lower center.
> Probably detached from an edition of Emanuel Bowen, *A Complete system of geography* (London, 1747) [Philips 603].
> 3 lines of MS. annotation (pencil) by J. M. Wordie in right margin.
> From collection of J. M. Wordie.
> Copy 1 of 3.

Arctic Regions—1747   [M49]

A New & Accurate Map of the North Pole, with All the Countries Hitherto Discovered: Situated Near or Adjacent to It: As Well As Some Others More Remote, Drawn from the Latest and Best Authorities and Regulated by Astrml. Observations by Eman Bowen — [London: Emanuel Bowen?, 1747?].

> 1 map ; on sheet 41 x 54 cm.
> Scale ca. 1:21,400,000.
> Relief shown pictorially.
> Prime meridian: London.
> Includes 2 columns of text.
> Engraved plate "No. 110" at lower center.
> Probably detached from an edition of Emanuel Bowen, *A Complete system of geography* (London, 1747) [Phillips 603].
> Copy 2 of 3.

Arctic Regions—1747   [M50]

A New & Accurate Map of the North Pole, with All the Countries Hitherto Discovered: Situated Near or Adjacent to It: As Well As Some Others More Remote, Drawn from the Latest and Best Authorities and Regulated by Astrml.

Observations by Eman Bowen — [London: Emanuel Bowen?, 1747?].

> 1 map : hand col. ; on sheet 41 x 54 cm.
> Scale ca. 1:21,400,000.
> Relief shown pictorially.
> Prime meridian: London.
> Includes 2 columns of text.
> Engraved plate "No. 70" at lower center beneath map.
> Probably detached from an edition of Emanuel Bowen, *A Complete system of geography* (London, 1747) [Phillips 603].
> Copy 3 of 3.

Arctic Regions—1748   [M51]

A Correct Draught of the North Pole, and of All the Countries Hitherto Discovered, Intercepted between the Pole and the Parallel of 50 Degrees, Drawn from the Most Approv'd Modern Maps and Charts, and Adjusted by Astronl. Observations by Eman. Bowen. [London, 1748].

> 1 map ; 40 x 47 cm. (plate size)
> Scale ca. 1:22,500,000 at 65 N.
> "Exhibiting the most remarkable tracts of our English navigators &c. in their several attempts to find out the North East and North West passages."
> From John Harris, *Navigantium atque itinerantium bibliotheca* (London, 1748), "v. II, p. 377."
> Relief shown pictorially.
> Includes 24 lines of text on the Northwest Passage, and 14 lines of text on the sources on which the delineation of Hudson's Bay is based.

Arctic Regions—1750   [M52]

Terres Arctiques. [Paris?: s.n., ca. 1750?].

> 1 map : hand col. ; 17 x 24 cm.
> Detached from unidentified text, "Tom. 3, pag. 349."
> Originally folded to 15 x 7 cm.

Arctic Regions—1760   [M53]

A Map of the Icy Sea in Which the Several Communications with the Land Waters and Other New Discoveries Are Exhibited. J. Gibson sculp. [London: Gentleman's Magazine, 1760].

> 1 map ; 19 cm. in diam. on sheet 21 x 24 cm.
> Detached from *Gentleman's Magazine* 30 (June 1760): opp. p. 284.
> References: Klein G60.3; OCLC 10670611.

Arctic Regions—1774 [M54]

Essai d'une carte Polaire Arcticque, par le Sr. De Vaugondy Géographe ordinaire du Roi, du fue Roi de Pologne Duc de Lorraine et de Bar, de l'Academie royale de Nanci, et Censeur royale. 1774; Gravé par E. Dussy. A Paris: Chés l'Auteur Quai de l'horloge du Palais près le Pont neuf, 1774.

> 1 map : hand col. ; 48 cm. in diam.
> "Construite d'apres toutes les connoissances le plus nouvelles pour servir aux navigations et aux découvertes à faire dans la Mer Glaciale, présentée à l'Academie Royale des Sciences avec un mémoire approuvé le 24 Mars 1773 et jugé digne d'être imprimé dans le recueil des mémoires des savans étrangers."
> MS. "5" on verso, upper right.
> Reference: Pedley no. 25.
> OCLC 5316027.

Arctic Regions—1779 [M55]

Carte qui represente les differentes connoissances que l'on a eues des Terres Arctiques depuis 1650 jusqu'en 1747 ausquelles il faut comparer la carte suivante c[art]e 10, par M. de Vaugondy 1773. [Paris, 1779].

> 4 maps ; 14 x 17 cm. on sheet 42 x 50 cm.
> Scales ca. 1:25,000,000 and ca. 1:21,000,000.
> Added title: Carte de la Baye d'Hudson parcourue in 1746, par Henri Ellis pour la recherche du passage par le Nord-Ouest.
> The first three maps extend from lat. 50° to Sir Thomas Smith's Bay, and consist of versions by Sanson (1650), Delisle (1700) and Delisle (1703); the last map (by Ellis) extends from lat. 45° to lat. 60°.
> At upper right: C[art]e 9e.
> At lower right: 168.
> Detached from the atlas supplement to Diderot's *Encyclopèdie* (Paris, 1770–1779).
> References: Pedley no. 462, Phillips 1195.
> Copy 1 of 2.

Arctic Regions—1779 [M56]

Carte qui represente les differentes connoissances que l'on a eues des Terres Arctiques depuis 1650 jusqu'en 1747 ausquelles il faut comparer la carte suivante c[art]e 10, par M. de Vaugondy 1773. [Paris, 1779].

> 4 maps : partly hand col. ; 14 x 17 cm. each on sheet 40 x 47 cm.
> Scales ca. 1:25,000,000 and ca. 1:21,000,000.
> Added title: Carte de la Baye d'Hudson parcourue in 1746, par Henri Ellis pour la recherche du passage par le Nord-Ouest.
> The first three maps extend from lat. 50° to Sir Thomas Smith's Bay, and consist of versions by Sanson (1650), Delisle (1700) and Delisle (1703); the last map (by Ellis) extends from lat. 45° to lat. 60°.
> At upper right: C[art]e 9e.
> At lower right: 168.
> Detached from the atlas supplement to Diderot's *Encyclopèdie* (Paris, 1770–1779).
> References: Pedley no. 462, Phillips 1195.
> Copy 2 of 2.

Arctic Regions—1780 [M57]

North America, Plate III [the northwest sheet of a multi-sheet map of the continent]. [London, ca. 1780].

> 1 map ; 46 x 36 cm. (plate size)
> Scale ca. 1:6,250,000.
> Detached from an edition of Malachy Postelthwayt, *The Universal dictionary of trade and commerce* (London, ca. 1780).
> Relief shown pictorially.
> Prime meridian: [Ferro].
> Includes untitled inset map (23 x 23 cm.) showing "all the material discoveries . . . from Martin Frobisher in 1576, to Francis Smith in 1747" in Arctic regions including Hudson Bay, Baffin Bay, and Davis Strait.

Arctic Regions—1795 [M58]

A Map of the Countries Situate about the North Pole As Far As the 50th Degree of North Latitude. W. Barker sculp. [Philadelphia, 1795].

> 1 map ; 23 cm. in diam. on sheet 45 x 38 cm.
> Plate mark: 27 x 25 cm.
> Above map: Engraved for Carey's edition of Guthrie's Geography improved.
> Number 44 printed at upper right corner of plate and repeated in MS. at upper right corner of sheet.
> Detached from *The General atlas for Carey's edition of Guthrie's Geography improved* (Philadelphia: Matthew Carey, 1795) [Phillips 6007, no.44].

Arctic Regions—1799 [M59]

A Map of the Countries Thirty Degrees round the North Pole. Neele sculpt. Strand. London: G. G. and J. Robinson, March 1st, 1799.

> 1 map : hand col. ; 33 cm. in diam. on sheet 38 x 48 cm.
>
> Detached from C. Cruttwell, *Atlas to Cruttwell's gazetteer* (London, 1799) [Phillips 692, no. 9].
>
> Printed from a different plate than the 1800 map of the same title, published in Dublin by J. Stockdale (see M60 below).
>
> Manuscript "9" on verso.

Arctic Regions—1800 [M60]

A Map of the Countries Thirty Degrees round the North Pole. Dublin: J. Stockdale, 1800.

> 1 map : hand col. ; 33 cm. in diam. on sheet 37 x 47 cm.
>
> "Published by J. Stockdale. No. 62 Abbey St. near Carlisle Bridge, Dublin, 1800."
>
> Detached from C. Cruttwell, *Atlas to Cruttwell's gazetteer* (Dublin: J. Stockdale, 1800) [cf. Phillips 692, no. 9; OCLC 4274161.
>
> Printed from a different plate than the 1799 map of the same title, published in London by G. G. and J. Robinson (see M59 above).

Arctic Regions—1807 [M61]

Countries Surrounding the North Pole. Neele sc. Strand. London: J. Wilkes, 1807 Oct 9.

> 1 map : hand col. ; 19 cm. in diam.
>
> "London. Pubd. as the Act directs Octr. 9th 1807 by J. Wilkes."
>
> Possibly detached from the *Encyclopaedia Londinensis* (London, 1797–1829) [cf. Tooley Dict., p.665; NUC Pre-56, v.159, p.607].

Arctic Regions—1821 [M62]

Capt. Parry's Discoveries in the Polar Regions, 1819–20, Compiled and Drawn, from the Admiralty Records, by W. Lane, Hydrographer and Teacher of Navigation, Naval Academy, 79, Leadenhall Street, London. London: Robert Blachford & Co., [1821?].

> 2 maps : hand col. ; on sheet 67 x 47 cm.
>
> Title (in letterpress) surrounds circular map in middle of sheet.
>
> "Printed for, and published by, Robert Blachford & Co., chart sellers to the Admiralty and Honorable East India Company, Navigation Warehouse, 79, Leadenhall, Street, London."
>
> Contents: Plan of Lancaster Sound, penetrated by Capt. Parry, in July, 1819 [14 x 41 cm.] — Map of the North Polar regions [23 cm. diam.].
>
> On Plan of Lancaster Sound, easternmost portion is printed on a separate slip (58 x 164 mm.) and pasted over map.
>
> Letterpress text at bottom of sheet (94 lines in 2 columns, 19 x 43 cm.): Interesting particulars of the voyage.
>
> On verso in MS. (ink): Parry's discoveries.

Arctic Regions—1827 [M63]

[Canadian Arctic and Alaska, 1827].
[Bruxelles, 1827].

> 12 maps : col. ; 43 x 55 cm.
>
> Detached from P. M. G. Vandermaelen, *Atlas universal de géographie* (Bruxelles, 1827), v.4 (Phillips 749).
>
> Running title, upper left of each sheet: Amér. Sep.
>
> Contents: Iles George. No. 1. — Découvertes Boréales. No. 2 — Baie de Baffin. No. 3. — Partie de l'Amérique Russe. No. 5. — Embouchure du Fleuve Mackensie. No. 6. — Découvertes Boréales. No. 7. — Découvertes Boréales. No. 9. — Détroit de Davis. No. 10. — Partie de l'Amérique Russe. No. 13. — Presqu' Ile d'Alaska. No. 21. — Partie de l'Amérique Russe. No. 22. — Partie de l'Amérique Russe. No. 23.
>
> Lithography by H. Ode of Bruxelles.
>
> Apparently detached from different copies of the atlas, sheets 5, 13, 21–23 comprising one group and sheets 1–3, 6–7, 9–10 another.

Arctic Regions—1828 [M64]

Die Nordpolar-Laender nebst Groenland u. Spitzbergen. Weimar: Geographischen Instituts, 1828.

> 1 map : hand col. ; 25 x 43 cm. on sheet 60 x 75 cm.
>
> Scale ca. 1:200,000,000.
>
> Letterpress title above map: Geographische-statistiche und historische Charte von den Nordpolarländern und der Russischen Nordwestküste von America.
>
> Shows Russian, British, Danish possessions.
>
> Text on 3 sides.
>
> Map with title Die Nordpolarlaender . . . found in W. E. A. von Schleiben, Atlas von Amerika (Leipzig, 1830) [Phillips 1178].

Arctic Regions—1835 [M65]

[Map of the Arctic from the Pole to 59°
North, 1835]. [London]: Admiralty, 1835.

1 map ; 61 cm. in diam. on sheet 67 x 86 cm.
"Published according to Act of Parliament by Capt.
Hurd, R.N., Hydrographer to the Admiralty, 14th
Feby. 1818. Additions to 1835."
No plate no.

Arctic Regions—1850 [M66]

Chart of the Arctic Regions from the
Admiralty Surveys. London: James Wyld,
[ca. 1850?].

1 map : hand col. ; 38 cm. in diam.
Scale ca. 1:18,000,000.
"Second Edition."
Dedication: To Lady Franklin . . .
Discoveries made on eight expeditions keyed to colors.
At lower left: New Publications.

Arctic Regions—1855 [M67]

Chart of the North Polar Sea. Engraved by
J. & C. Walker. [London]: Hydrographic
Dept., 1855.

1 map ; 75 x 59 cm.
"Published at the Hydrographic Office of the Admiralty
December 24th 1855. Sold by J. D. Potter, Agent
for the Admiralty Charts 31 Poultry & King Street
Tower Hill."
At lower right: [Admiralty Chart no.] 260.
References: cf. Verner, Explorers' maps of the
Canadian Arctic 1818–1860 (Cartographica
Monograph No. 6), plate XIV (1859 state); Falk,
Alaskan maps, no. 1865–1 (1865 state).

Arctic Regions—1856 [M68]

Arctic Regions. Engraved by A. Fullarton
& Co. [London & Edinburgh?], 1856.

2 maps : col. ; on sheet 47 x 32 cm.
Title near center of sheet, between the two maps.
Possibly detached from an edition of the *Royal
illustrated atlas of modern geography* (cf. Phillips
838).
Contents: Wellington Channel, Melville Island &c. from
Admiralty chart [11 x 23 cm.] — The Arctic
regions, showing the North-West passage as
determined by Cap. R. McClure and other Arctic
voyagers, compiled by J. Hugh Johnson F.R.G.S.
[24 cm. diam.].
At upper right: III.

Arctic Regions—1867 [M69]

Expédition Française au Pôle Nord, sous le
commandement de Mr. Gustave Lambert;
régions Polaires Boréales d'après V. A.
Malte-Brun. Gravé par Erhard Schièble;
imp. Monrocq. Paris, 1867.

1 map : col. ; 24 cm. in diam.
Scale ca. 1:45,000,000.
Insets: Route de l'expédition Française, projection
etoilée du Dr. Jaeger — Régions polaires
australes — Marche supposée du pôle
magnétique — Courbes des moyennes
d'insolation au 21 Juin.
Shows French, German, and English routes.

Arctic Regions—1874 [M70]

Chart of the North Polar Sea. Engraved by
J. & C. Walker. London: Admiralty, 1874.

1 map : col. ; 78 x 60 cm..
Variously colored to show British, American, German,
Swedish, and Austrian arctic expeditions to 1874.
"Published at the Admiralty 24th December, 1855
under the superintendence of Captn.
Washington, R.N.; F.R.S. Hydrographer. Decr.,
74."
G.B. Hyd. Dept. Pl. No.: 260.
Handstamped in top margin: W. & A. K. Johnston.
Agents. Edinburgh.

Arctic Regions—1875 [M71]

North Polar Chart, Including the Atlantic
Ocean to the 50th Parallel and the Arctic
Seas from Barrow and Franklin Straits on
the West, to Novaya Zemlya and Francis
Joseph Land on the East. Engraved by
Malby & Sons. London: Admiralty, 1875
May 20.

1 map ; 65 x 91 cm.
Scale ca. 1:7,500,000.
"Published . . . under the superintendence of Captain
F. J. Evans . . ."
"Sold by J. D. Potter . . ."
"Price Two & Sixpence."
G.B. Hyd. Dept. Pl. No.: 274.

Arctic Regions—1895 [M72]

Sketch Map Showing Route of the 'Fram'
and Nansen's and Johansen's Sledge

Journey. John Bartholomew & Co. [Edinburgh]: Edinburgh Geographical Institute, 1897.

> 1 map : col. ; 22 x 40 cm.
> Issued as a folded pamphlet with panel title: Royal Geographical Society. Nansen meeting, Albert Hall, 8th February 1897.
> Shows ship and sledge routes between July 1893 and August 1895.
> In upper margin, "Royal Geographical Society" in banderole, portrait of Nansen.

Arctic Regions—1904 [M73]

North Polar Chart, Including the Arctic Seas from Gulf of Yenisei on the West to Lancaster & Smith Sounds on the East with Bering Strait and the Pacific Ocean to the 50th Parallel, 1881. Engraved by Malby & Sons. London: Admiralty, 1904.

> 1 map ; 63 x 92 cm.
> "Published at the Admiralty, 31st March 1877, under the superintendence of Captain F. J. Evans . . . Hydrographer. Sold by J. D. Potter, agent for the sale of the Admiralty charts, 145 Minories."
> "Large corrections March, 1882, June, 1882, Feb. 1885, Feb. 1899, Sepr. 1904; Small corrections X-07 XII-07 I-15 I-17 IX-17."
> MS. annotations (pencil, col. pencil, and ink) show routes of various arctic expeditions, 1879–1917.
> G.B. Hyd. Dept. Pl. No.: 278.

Arctic Regions—1920 [M74]

North Polar Chart, Including the Atlantic Ocean to the 50th Parallel and the Arctic Seas from Barrow and Franklin Straits on the West, to Novaya Zemlya and Franz Josef Land on the East. Engraved by Malby & Sons. London: Admiralty, 1920.

> 1 map ; 63 x 92 cm.
> "Published at the Admiralty, 20th May 1875, under the superintendence of Captain F. J. Evans . . . Hydrographer. Sold by J. D. Potter, agent for the sale of the Admiralty charts, 145 Minories."
> "Large corrections March 1882, Feb. 1885, Sept. 1889, May 1899, Sepr. 1904; Small corrections I-83 X-90 XI-91 II-98 IV-05 IV-07 II-16 V-17 IX-17 1919—511 1920 (I-9)—262."
> MS. annotations (pencil, col. pencil, and ink) show routes of various arctic expeditions.
> G.B. Hyd. Dept. Pl. No.: 274.

Arctic Regions—1925 [M75]

The Arctic Regions: Prepared in the Map Department of the National Geographic Society for the National Geographic Magazine. Baltimore: A. Hoen & Co., [1925].

> 1 map ; col. ; 46 x 49 cm
> "Scale 1:14,673,400 or 231.6 miles to 1 inch."
> Detached from *National Geographic Magazine* (November, 1925).
> "Copyright, 1925, by the National Geographic Society, Washington, D.C."
> Inset maps: Spitsbergen and Franz Josef Land [11 x 16 cm.] — Ellesmere Island region [15 x 14 cm.]
> Issued folded to 14 x 9 cm.

Arctic Regions—1927 [M76]

Bathymetric Map of the Arctic Basin, by Fridtjof Nansen, Revised to 1927. [New York, 1931].

> 1 map ; 19 x 30 cm. on sheet 47 x 33 cm.
> Scale 1:20,000,000.
> Soundings in meters.
> "Reproduced by special permission of the American Geographical Society of New York."
> Printed opposite map: "This chart of the polar regions has been carried on the submarine Nautilus by the Wilkins-Ellsworth Expedition. This insert is a part of copy number   of the deluxe edition of 'Under the North Pole' by Sir Hubert Wilkins [New York: Brewer, Warren & Putnam, 1931]. The actual route of the polar voyage has been entered on this chart by the Expedition's commander. Attest:"
> "Copy number" left blank; map not annotated with ship's route; no attestation.
> For description of Wilkins book, see NUC Pre-1956, v.664, p.21.

Arctic Regions—1929—Ice [M77]

Physical Map of the Arctic. [London?, 1942?].

> 1 map ; 42 cm. in diam.
> Black and white reproduction of map "Translated and revised by the American Geographical Society of New York from map in Andree's Handatlas, 8th edition, 1924."
> Probably a reproduction of a map in the collection of the Royal Geographical Society.
> "Copyright 1929. . . ."
> Show limits of pack-ice and icebergs.
> "Unexplored or unseen areas on the Arctic Basin are left white. Areas that were within the

mathematical horizon of visibility from sledge, ship, ship's masthead, or aircraft, as the case may be be, are assumed to be known. As fog has not been taken into account in the computation the map slightly exaggerates the size of the known areas."

Insets (19 x 13 cm. and smaller): Novaya Zemlya. — Jan Mayen I. — Bear Island. — Ice Fjord (Spitsbergen). — Spitsbergen (Svalbard) and Bear Island. — Smith Sound to Robeson Channel. — Franz Josef Land. — Southern Greenland. — Northernmost Greenland. — Bering Strait. — Eastern Greenland.

MS. annotations reproduced from original: 31 Oct. 1942 Arctic—Genl. Reduce AB to 16.48.

MS. annotations (in pencil) on this reproduction include additional sheet and scale calculations.

Arctic Regions—1930—Administrative and Political Divisions [M78]

Map Showing the Limits of Political Sovereignty and Claims in the Arctic. [New York: American Geographical Society, 1930].

1 map ; 26 x 33 cm.
Added title: Fig. 7—Map showing the limits of political sovereignty and claims in the Arctic.
Enlarged [?] photographic reproduction; according to an inscription on the verso (ink) the source is "W. G. L. Joerg. Brief history of Polar exploration. New York, 1930, p. 63."

Arctic Regions—1931 [M79]

Chart of the North Polar Sea. London: Admiralty, 1931.

1 map ; 78 x 64 cm.
"Published at the Admiralty 24th December 1855 under the superintendence of Capt. Washington . . . Hydrographer. Sold by J. D. Potter, agent for the Admiralty charts, 145 Minories."
"New editions, March 1882, May 1899, 24th Decr. 1931."
"Small corrections."
G.B. Hyd. Dept. Pl. No.: 260.
At upper right: 364.31.
Handstamped "Increase 50%."

Arctic Regions—1946 [M80]

North Polar Regions. New York: Geographia Map Co., Inc., [ca. 1946].

1 map : col. ; 51 x 38 cm.
"Latitudinal scale 1:16,000,000."

"Special edition printed for National Travel Club."
With key to "Explorers routes."
Issued folded to 14 x 11 cm.

Arctic Regions—1970 [M81]

The Arctic Regions, by the U.S. Naval Oceanographic Office under the Authority of the Secretary of the Navy. Washington, D.C.: The Office, 1970.

1 map : col. ; 77 x 80 cm
"6th ed., June 1948; revised 10/26/70."
U.S. Hyd. Ofc. Pl. No. 2560.
Handstamped at lower right: No. 80.
Manuscript annotation showing route of the USS Nautilus through the north pole signed "William R. Anderson, C.O. Nautilus, first transpolar voyage, 1915 EDT, 3 August 1958."
Accompanied by 6 letters (2 signed by Anderson) to or from G. F. Fitzgerald, variously dated between August 1971-February 1972.
Accompanied by 2 photostatic reproductions of another copy of the map signed by Anderson and the Nautilus crew.

Arctic Regions—1971 [M82]

Arctic Ocean, Produced in the Cartographic Division, National Geographic Society. Washington, D.C.: Judd & Detweiler, Inc., 1971.

1 map : col. ; 48 x 63 cm.
Scale 1:10,011,000.
"Supplement to National Geographic, October 1971, page 519A, vol. 140, no.4."
"Printed by Judd & Detweiller, Inc., Washington, D.C."
Includes extensive historical notes.
On verso: Arctic Ocean floor [col. bathymetric map ; 48 x 63 cm.].

NORTH AMERICA

North America—1860 [M83]

Map of North America, Exhibiting the Recent Discoveries, Geographical & Nautical, by James Wyld; J. W. del.; Stockley sc. London: James Wyld, [ca. 1860].

1 map : hand col. ; 47 x 36 cm.
Scale ca. 1:25,000,000.

Relief shown by hachures.
Probably detached from an edition of James Wyld, *A New general atlas* (London, ca. 1860) [cf. Philipps 808].

GREENLAND

Greenland—1666 [M84]
Pascaerte van Groen-Landt, Yslandt, Straet Davids en Ian Mayen eylandt, hoemen de selvige von Hitlandt en de noortcusten van Schotlandt en Yrlandt beseylen mach. [Amsterdam, 1666?].

1 map : hand col. ; 44 x 53 cm.
Possibly detached from an atlas by Pieter Goos (cf. Koeman v.4, p. 197, map 30 and p. 204, map 25).
MS. "30" on verso; verso otherwise blank.

Greenland—1745 [M85]
Nieuwe algemeene kaart van Groenland en Straet Davids, naar de alernieuwste ondekkingen in 't Licht gebracht door R. & I. Ottens te Amsterdam. Amsterdam: [Louis Renard?, 1745?].

1 map : hand col. ; 49 x 117 cm.
Title from rectangular cartouche at lower right.
Added titles: Septemtrionaliora Americæ à Groenlandia, per Freta Davidis et Hudson, ad Terram Novam, apud R. & I. Ottens. — De Noordelyckste Zee kusten van America van Groenland door de Straet Davis ende straet Hudson tot Terra Neuf.
1 map formed from 2 sheets trimmed and pasted together.
Inset: Visch Baay [Disko Bay] door Laurens Feykes [12 x 14 cm.].
Possibly detached from Louis Renard, *Atlas van Zeevaert* (Amsterdam, 1745) [cf. Mickwitz and Miekkavaara, v. 2, p. 228, pl. 32].
In MS on verso: 32.

Greenland—1800 [M86]
The Greenland Pilot, Being Three Charts for the Fisheries of Greenland and Davis's Straits, from England to the 80th Degree of North Latitude, from the Best Surveys, Corrected by Thomas Peeters and Other Masters in the Trade. London: Printed for David Steel, at the Navigation-Warehouse, no. 1, Union-Row, Minories, Little Tower-Hill, 1800 Jan 1.

3 maps ; folded to 68 x 43 cm.
Title from printed paste-on label (22 x 14 cm.) on front cover.
Imprint date from maps.
Maps all bear imprint "Published . . . by D. & E. Steel, at the Navigation Warehouse, Little Tower Hill."
Contents: [1] A Mercator's guide from England to Greenland: Davis's Straits & Hudson's Bay including all the islands, from actual surveys [63 x 164 cm. Inset: A chart of Spitsbergen, 16 x 20 cm.] — [2] A New chart of Davis's Streights from Staten Hook to the Womans Islands [56 x 95 cm.] — [3] A New chart of Davis's Streights including James Island, Waygat Island, and the Island Disko [56 x 95 cm. Inset: The Coast at the South Bay, 23 x 14 cm.].
Maps mounted back to back onto blue paper wrapper to form 4 bound folding panels.

Greenland—1889 [M87]
Greenland from the Latest Authorities; Southern Greenland, Reduced from the Survey of Captain G. Holm Showing Dr. Nansen's Route in 1888. Edinburgh & London: W. & A. K. Johnston, 1889.

2 maps : col. ; 21 x 15 cm. and 21 x 22 cm. on sheet 26 x 57 cm.
"Pubd. for the Proceedings of the Royal Geographical Society, 1889."
Issued to accompany the Proceedings 11, no. 8 (September 1889), opp. p. 524.

Greenland—1906 [M88]
Kort over Grönland, udgivet af Kommissionen for Ledelsen af de geologiske og geographiske Undersögelser i Grönland. Kjöbenhavn: Axel E. Aamodts. lith. Etabl., 1906.

1 map : col. ; 152 x 124 cm. in 4 sheets.
Scale 1:2,000,000.
Shows routes of various exploring expeditions, 1883–.
Also a second copy of sheet 2 (N. E. Greenland) in a later printing, showing information on expeditions of 1907–13.

Separate Maps

Greenland—1926 [M89]

Kort over Grönland, Syd for 75° N. Br., udgivet af Kommissionen for Ledelsen af de geologiske og geographiske Undersögelser i Grönland. Kjöbenhavn: Axel E. Aamodts. lith. Etabl., 1926.

> 1 map : col. ; 98 x 71 cm. on 2 sheets.
> Scale 1:2,000,000.
> Inset: Grönland [41 x 27 cm.].
> Shows routes of various exploring expeditions, 1883–1921.

Greenland—1930—Ice [M90]

Isforholdene. Kjøbenhavn: Axel E. Aamodt, [ca. 1930?].

> 1 map ; 45 x 49 cm.
> Outline map printed as a form intended for use in recording ice conditions; blank lines appear after headings for year, ship's name, and captain's name. Includes table of conventional symbols to use in recording data.

Greenland—1931 [M91]

Harbours and Anchorages on the West Coast of Greenland, Chiefly from the Danish Surveys, Published in 1866. Engraved by Edwd. Weller. London: Admiralty, [1931?].

> 19 maps ; 17 x 33 cm. and smaller on sheet 70 x 87 cm.
> Maps variously attributed to W. E. Parry, E. A. Inglefield, F. L. M'Clintock, J. W. Reed, Edward Belcher, and J. E. Davis.
> "Published at the Admiralty, 20th May 1875, under the superintendence of Captain F. J. Evans . . . Hydrographer. Sold by J. D. Potter, agent for the Admiralty charts, 145 Minories."
> "New editions 10th July 1925; Small corrections 1926—4-13—1927—2-1-1929—3-2 1930—7-1 1931—11-2."
> Contents: Umanak Fiord — Crown Prince or Whale Fish Islands — Kangarssuk Havn — Upernivik Hr. — Godthaab Fiord — Godthaab Havn — Frederikshaab — Arsuk Fiord — Arsuk Fiord: Torrsukatak Snaevring — Arsuk Fiord: Weber Havn — Arsuk Fiord: Christians Havn — Arsuk Fiord: Ivigtut — Nunarsuit: Bangs Havn — Arsuk Fiord: Kajartalik — Arsuk Fiord: Manitsok Havn — Igaliko Fiord and approach to Julianehaab — Godhavn or Port of Lievely — Julianehaab.
> G.B. Hyd. Dept. Pl. No.: 276.

At upper right: 130.32.
Ruled area blank in lower right (7 x 13 cm.).
Handstamped "Increase 50%."

Greenland—1931 [M92]

Grönland. Köbenhavn: Geodætisk Institut, 1931.

> 1 map : col. ; 57 x 45 cm.
> Scale 1:5,500,000.
> At lower right, beneath neat line: Efter Ad. S. Jensen.

Greenland—1946 [M93]

Grönland, 1:5,000,000. Köbenhavn: Geodætisk Institut, 1946.

> 1 map : col. ; 58 x 51 cm.
> Added title, upper left: Danmark.
> "Kortinddeling i Maalestok 1:250,000."
> Index map for the Geodætisk Institut's 1:250,000 map series; indexes Greenland sheets only.
> Coded to show sheets published and subsequently revised.
> At upper right: Plan 4.

Greenland, Eastern—1823 [M94]

East Coast of Greenland between the Parallels of 72° and 76° N., Surveyed under the Direction of Captn. Clavering by Mr. Henry Foster Admy. Midn. H.M. Sloop Griper in the Summer of 1823. [S.l.: s.n., 19—].

> 1 map ; 41 x 33 cm.
> Photostatic reproduction of manuscript map.
> Shows routes of the ship Griper; photostat annotated in red and blue ink.
> Shelfmark [?], lower right: C.90 Ak.1.
> Mounted on cloth.

Greenland, Eastern—1900 [M95]

Karta över Konung Oscars Fjord och Kejsar Frans Josefs Fjord upprättad under Svenska Grönlandsexpeditionen 1899, af P. Dusén; Astronomiska ortbestämningarna af F. Åkerblom. [Stockholm]: Photolit. Generalstabens Litografiska Anstalt, [1900?].

> 1 map : col. ; 48 x 52 cm.
> Scale 1:500,000.
> Mounted on cloth.

Greenland, Eastern—1900—Geology
[M96]

Geologisk karta över en del af Nordöstra Grönland, efter iakttagelser af den andra tyska polar expeditionen under Koldewey 1869–1870, den danska expeditionen under Ryder 1891–92 samt den svenska expeditionen på Antarctic [sic] 1889; sammanstäld ag A. G. Nathorst; C. J. O. Kjellström del. [Stockholm]: Photolitografi, Gen. Stab. Lit. Anst., [1900?].

> 1 map ; 34 x 19 cm.
> Scale 1:2,000,000.
> At upper left: Geol. Förens. Förhandl. Bd. 23. H. 4.
> At upper right: Tafl. 5.

Greenland, Eastern—1902   [M97]

Grönland med omgivelser. P. Jul. Petersen sc. Kjöbenhavn: Sökaart-Archiv, 1902.

> 1 map ; 97 x 64 cm.
> Scale 1:900,000.
> "Udgivet af det kongelige Sökaart-Archiv. Köbenhavn, 1888. Udgave 1902."
> Plate no.: 147.
> Includes MS. annotation: yellow and red points off western coast of Iceland.
> Handstamp, upper center: Kgl. Søkort-Arkiv. 9-Feb. 1934. Kjøbenhavn [oval, 2.5 x 3.5 cm.]
> Paste-on, upper center: Omsætnings-tabel [8 x 9 cm.].

Greenland, Eastern—1929   [M98]

The Coast Region of East Greenland between Scoresby Sound and Danmark Havn, from Surveys of the Cambridge Expeditions 1926 and 1929 under the Direction of J. M. Wordie and the Mapping of Other Explorers. [London]: Royal Geographical Society, 1930.

> 3 maps : col. ; on sheet 51 x 76 cm.
> Scale 1:2,000,000.
> Issued to accompany J. M. Wordie's report on the Cambridge expedition of 1929 in *Geographical Journal* 75 no. 6 (June 1930).
> Contents: [Coast of eastern Greenland, 45 x 26 cm.]
> — [Location map showing track of the ship Heimland in the Greenland Sea, 21 x 14 cm.] —

> Nordenskiöld Glacier and Petermann Peak, from a survey by R. C. Wakefield & A. Courtauld [25 x 31 cm.].
> At lower right: East Greenland. Wordie.

Greenland, Eastern—1929   [M99]

Grönlands östkyst: Indsejling til Scoresby-Sund. Opmaalt 1900. [Copenhagen?]: Styrelsen, 1929.

> 1 map ; 79 x 40 cm.
> "Ny Udgave 1929."
> Added title: Indsjling til Scoresby-Sund.
> "Partiet omkring Rosenvinges Bugt efter Scoresby-Sund Ekspeditionen 1925. Liverpool Kyst indlagt efter Söminemester Janus Sörensens Opmaaling 1928."
> "Udgivet af Styrelsen af Kolonierne i Grönland 1925."
> Includes 2 profiles, 1 x 22 cm. and 1 x 23 cm.

Greenland, Eastern—1929   [M100]

Grönlands östkyst, Kolonien i Scoresby-Sund, opmaalt 1925 af "Scoresby-Sund Ekspeditionen"; Söopmaalingen af Söminemester Janus Sörensen 1928. [Copenhagen?]: Styrelsen, 1929.

> 1 map ; 38 x 46 cm.
> "Ny Udgave 1929."
> Added title: Kolonien i Scoresby-Sund.
> "Udgivet af Styrelsen af Kolonierne i Grönland 1925."
> Inset: Amdrups Havn [15 x 25 cm.].

Greenland, Eastern—1931   [M101]

Östgrönland mellem 70° og 77° n. Br., efter de nyeste Kilder, deri indbefattet Opmaalinger udført af Lauge Kochs sidste Expeditioner. København: Geodætisk Institut, 1931.

> 1 map : col. ; 81 x 49 cm.
> Scale 1:1,000,000.

Greenland, Eastern—1932   [M102]

Eirik Raudes Land frå Sofiasund til Youngsund . . . Mælingar av Norges Svalbard- og Ishavs-undersøkelser 1929, 1931; Redaksjon K. G. Gleditsch; Astronomiske observasjonar og utrekningar

Hans S. Jelstrup . . . ; Triangulering, detaljmæling, utrekning og konstruksjon Bernard Luncke, Wilhelm Solheim. Oslo: Norges geografiske oppmåling, 1932.

> 1 map : col. ; 76 x 72 cm.
> Above title proper: Austgrønland: East Greenland.
> "Reprodusert og prenta i Norges Geografiske Opmåling 1932."

Greenland, Eastern—1933 [M103]

70 Ö.1 Scoresbysund. Köpenhavn: Geodætisk Institut, 1937.

> 1 map : col. ; 45 x 43 cm.
> Added title, upper left: Grönland 1:250,000.
> Based on 1933 survey.
> Forms part of the Geodætisk Institut's 1:250,000 map series of Denmark.
> Issued folded to 21 x 13 cm. in attached paper covers.
> Plate no.: 70 Ö.1.

Greenland, Northern—1932 [M104]

Map of North Greenland, Scale 1:300,000, Surveyed by Lauge Koch in the Years 1917–23. [Copenhagen]: Geodetic Institute of Denmark, 1932.

> 1 map : col. ; on 19 sheets each 69 x 57 cm.
> Issued with separate title page with graphic index to sheets; issued folded to 57 x 36 cm. in printed paper portfolio.
> Accompanied by bookseller's flyer briefly describing the map; flyer credits the Second Thule Expedition of 1916 led by Knud Rasmussen and the Jubilee Expedition of 1920–23 led by Lauge Koch as sources for map compilation.
> Reference: OCLC 11539736.

Greenland, Northern—1932 [M105]

[Map of north Greenland, scale 1:300,000, surveyed by Lauge Koch in the years 1917–23]. [S.l.: s.n., 1932?].

> 1 map ; 101 x 56 cm.
> Photostatic reproductions of sheets forming part of Geodætisk Institut. Map of north Greenland, scale 1:300,000 (Copenhagen, 1932).
> Sheets 13–18 trimmed, pasted together, and mounted on cloth.
> Original map compiled from sources including the Second Thule Expedition of 1916 led by Knud Rasmussen and the Jubilee Expedition of 1920–23 led by Lauge Koch.
> Reference: OCLC 11539736.

Greenland, Western—1884 [M106]

Karta över 1883 års Svenska Expedition, på Grönlands inlandsis under befäl af A. E. Nordenskiöld, af Expeditionens topograf: C. J. O. Kjellström. [Stockholm]: Gen. Stab. Lit. Anst., Stockh., [1884?].

> 1 map : col. ; 26 x 50 cm.
> Inset: Profil [of expedition's route east from Disko Bay], 6 x 38 cm.].

Greenland, Western—1931 [M107]

Arsuk Fjord, opmaalt i 1863 af Lieutenanterne Falbe og Bluhme. Stukket af E. Chr. Möller. Kjöbenhavn: Sökaart-Archiv, 1931.

> 1 map ; 58 x 86 cm.
> Added title: Grönland vestkyst.
> "Udgivet af det kongelige Sökaart-Archiv. Kjöbenhavn, 1866."
> "Rettet til 1892 . . . 1910 . . . 31 III."
> Insets: Manitsok Havn [11 x 12 cm.] — Kajartalik [9 x 10 cm.]— Fortunas Havn [9 x 45 cm.] — Webers Havn [9 x 11 cm.] — Christians Havn [11 x 9 cm.] — Torssukatak Snævring [7 x 14 cm.] — Ivigtut [6 x 17 cm.].
> Includes 4 coastal profiles, 2 x 53 cm. and smaller.
> Plate no.: 105.
> Handstamp, lower left: Kgl. Søkort-Arkiv. 9-Feb. 1934. Kjøbenhavn [oval, 2.5 x 3.5 cm.]
> Paste-on, lower left: Omsætnings-tabel [8 x 9 cm.].

Greenland, Western—1931 [M108]

Approaches to Holstenborg, Compiled from the Surveys of W. Stanton, Master, R.N. H.M.S. Phoenix, 1853–4, Navg. Lieut. George A. Broad, R.N. H.M.S. Valorous, 1875, and the Danish Chart of 1928. London: Admiralty, 1931.

> 1 map ; 49 x 65 cm.
> Added title: Greenland.
> "Published at the Admiralty, 5th May 1876, under the superintendence of Captain F. J. Evans . . . Hydrographer. Sold by J. D. Potter, agent for the Admiralty charts, 145 Minories."
> "New editions Augt. 1889. Large corrections 24th April 1931."
> "Small corrections."
> Inset: Greenland — west coast: Holstenborg Harbour [18 x 36 cm.].
> G.B. Hyd. Dept. Pl. No.: 2266.

At upper right: 120.31.
Handstamped "Increase 50%."

Greenland, Western—1932   [M109]
Grönland, sydlige del. Kjöbenhavn:
Kongelige Sökaart-Arkiv, 1932.

     1 map ; 62 x 97 cm.
     "Udgivet af det kongelige Sökaart-Arkiv Kjöbenhavn
         1889."
     "Rettet til 1890. 93. . . . 1910 . . . 32 II XII."
     Insets: Kangarsuk Havn [8 x 7 cm.] — Frederikshaab
         [15 x 12 cm.] — Arsuk Fjord [18 x 19 cm.] —
         Smallesund Havn [11 x 14 cm.] — Bangs Havn
         (Nunarsuit) [7 x 7 cm.] — Julianehaab [7 x 6
         cm.].
     Includes 3 coastal profiles, 2 x 56 cm. and smaller.
     Plate no.: 148.
     Paste-on, lower left: Omsætnings-tabel [8 x 9 cm.].
     Mounted on cloth.

Greenland, Western—1933   [M110]
Vestkysten af Grönland fra Arsuk til
Holstenborg. Kjöbenhavn: Kongelige
Sökaart-Arkiv, 1933.

     1 map ; 85 x 63 cm.
     "Udgivet af det kongelige Sökaart-Archiv. Kjöbenhavn
         1887."
     "Rettet til 1890. 93. . . . 1910 . . . 33 I."
     Insets: Hostenborg [19 x 17 cm.] — Reden ved
         Holstenborg [8 x 7 cm.] — Sukkertoppen [17 x
         20 cm.] — Havnen ved Sukkertoppen [7 x 5 cm.]
         — Indløbene til Godthaabs Fjord [24 x 21 cm.]
         — Godthaab [9 x 9 cm.] — Færingerhavnen [14
         x 15 cm.].
     Includes coastal profile (2 x 23 cm.) and "Omsætnings-
         tabel" (8 x 9 cm.).
     Last 3 named insets, the profile and the table are
         pasted onto lower half of sheet.
     Plate no.: 145.
     Mounted on cloth.
     Handstamp: Kgl. Søkort-Arkiv. 9-Feb. 1934.
         Kjøbenhavn [oval, 2.5 x 3.5 cm.].

Greenland, Western—1933   [M111]
Upernivik—Etah. Kjöbenhavn: Sökort-
Archiv, 1933.

     2 maps ; 47 x 59 cm. and 52 x 59 cm. on sheet 104 x
         66 cm.
     Scale 1:800,000.
     Added title: Grönlands vestkyst: West coast of
         Greenland.
     "Udgivet af det kongelige Sökort-Arkiv, Köbenhavn,
         April 1933."

"Reproduceret ved Geodætisk Institut."
"Rettet til (Corrected to) 19   ."
Plate no.: 315.
MS. annotation in pencil.
Handstamp, lower left: Kgl. Søkort-Arkiv. 9-Feb. 1934.
     Kjøbenhavn [oval, 2.5 x 3.5 cm.]
Mounted on cloth.

Greenland, Western—1933   [M112]
Vestkysten af Grönland fra Holstenborg til
Upernivik. P. Jul. Petersen sc. Kjöbenhavn:
Sökaart-Archiv, 1933.

     1 map ; 94 x 62 cm.
     Scale 1:750,000.
     "Udgivet af det kongelige Sökaart-Archiv. Köbenhavn,
         1888."
     "Rettet til 1895 . . . 33 I IV."
     Inset: [Western Greenland coast between 73°00' and
         74°45' N., 32 x 19 cm.]
     Plate no.: 146.
     MS. annotation in pencil.
     Handstamp, upper right: Kgl. Søkort-Arkiv. 9-Feb.
         1934. Kjøbenhavn [oval, 2.5 x 3.5 cm.]
     Paste-on, left center: Omsætnings-tabel [8 x 9 cm.].
     Mounted on cloth.

Greenland, Western—1934   [M113]
Grönland, vestlige blad. Kjöbenhavn:
Kongelige Sökaart-Arkiv, 1934.

     1 map ; 96 x 60 cm.
     Title from above neat line, upper left.
     "Udgivet af det kongelige Sökaart-Archiv 1888.
         Udgave 1902."
     "Rettet til 1891 97.1 . . . 34 I."
     Inset: Vestkysten af Grönland [14 x 12 cm.].
     Plate no.: 147.
     Paste-on, upper right: Omstætning-tabel [8 x 9 cm.]
     Handstamp, upper right: Kgl. Søkort-Arkiv. 9-Feb.
         1934. Kjøbenhavn [oval, 2.5 x 3.5 cm.]
     Mounted on cloth.

CANADA

Hudson Bay—1748   [M114]
To Arthur Dobbs, Rowland Fry, James
Douglass, Henry Douglas, John
Tomlinson, Robert Macky, William
Bowden and Samuel Smith, Esqrs., This
Chart of the Coast Where a North West

Passage was Attempted under Their Direction in the Years 1746 & 1747, Is Most Respectfully Dedicated by Their Agent & Very Humble Servt. Henry Ellis. [London: s.n.], 1748 Feb 12.

> 1 map ; 31 x 43 cm.
> Added title: This chart of the coast where a North West Passage was attempted. . . .
> "J. Mynde sc."
> Torn, mended, and mounted on cloth.
> Visible beneath cloth on verso in MS. (ink): North West Passage.
> Accompanied by p. 86–7 detached from a Henry Stevens, Son & Stiles catalog: "a most important chart in connection with the Dobbs-Middleton controversy."
> MS. annotation (pencil), lower margin: Cannot trace any other copy J M W[ordie].
> Additional MS. notes on verso distinguish between this map and another engraved by J. Mynde (A New chart of the parts where a North West Passage was sought . . . by Henry Ellis, [17 x 44 cm.]) which appears in Ellis's A Voyage to Hudson's Bay (London: H. Whitridge, 1748).

Hudson Bay—1782   [M115]

New and Accurate Chart of Hudson's Bay, in North America. Jno. Lodge sculp. London: J. Bew, 30th Novr. 1782.

> 1 map ; 17 x 22 cm.
> At upper right: Politcal Mag. Nov. 1782.
> Detached from *Political magazine* 3 (November 1782), opp. p. 686.
> References: Klein, P82.19; Jolly, POL-64.

Hudson Bay—1932   [M116]

Hudson Bay and Strait. London: Admiralty, 1932.

> 1 Map ; 73 x 98 cm.
> Added title: British North America.
> Variously attributed to W. E. Parry, G. F. Lyon, G. Back, J. G. Boulton, T. F. Smellie and to the ships "Fury," "Helca," "Griper," "Terror," and "Bayrupert."
> "Published at the Admiralty 28th June 1884, under the superintendence of Captain Sir Frederick J. Evans . . . Hydrographer. Sold by J. D. Potter, agent for the Admiralty charts, 145 Minories."
> "New editions May 1888, Aug. 1890, Jan. 1902, April 1908, 28th Decr. 1910, 1st Dec. 1924, 3rd June 1927. Large corrections 14th Augst. 1931, 23rd Sept. 1932."

> G.B. Hyd. Dept. Pl. No.: 863.
> Handstamped "Increase 50%."
> Very slight MS. annotation with orange ink.

CANADIAN ARCTIC

Canadian Arctic—1743   [M117]

This Chart of Hudson's Bay & Straits, Baffin's Bay, Strait Davis & Labrador Coast & c. Is Most Humbly Dedicated & Presented by His Majesty's Most Obedient & Faithful Subject & Servant, C. Middleton. 1743.; R. W. Seale sculp. [London, 19—].

> 1 map ; 26 x 35 cm.
> Photostatic copy of chart at the British Museum (Maps Y 0095 (2) P.24520).
> "Publish'd by C. Middleton according to Act of Parliament April 1743."
> "N.B. The principal settlements that the [Hudson's Bay] Company now has is Churchill River, York Fort, Fort Albany, Mouse River, and Slude River."
> Dedicated "To the King."

Canadian Arctic—1820   [M118]

Chart of the Discoveries and Route of His Majesty's Ships Hecla and Griper in Search of a North West Passage, under the Command of Lieutt. (now Captain) Parry, in the Years 1819 and 1820, and Drawn under His Immediate Inspection, by John Bushman Midn. R.N.; J. Walker sculpt. London: John Murray, June 1821.

> 1 map ; 23 x 96 cm.
> Detached from William Edward Parry, *Journal of a voyage for the discovery of a North-West Passage* (London, 1821).
> Continuation inset pasted on at bottom right: [Prince Regent Inlet, 11 x 11 cm. on sheet 14 x 16 cm.].

Canadian Arctic—1821   [M119]

General Chart Showing the Track of H.M. Ships Hecla and Griper, from the Orkneys to Melville Island, North Georgia. A.D. 1819, and Return in 1820. J. Walker sculpt. London: John Murray, June 1821.

1 map ; 25 x 60 cm.
Detached from William Edward Parry, *Journal of a voyage for the discovery of a North-West Passage* (London, 1821).

Canadian Arctic—1821   **[M120]**

Chart of a Part of the Western Coast of Baffins Bay. 1820. J. Walker sculpt. London: J. Murray, June 1821.

1 map ; 51 x 38 cm.
Detached from William Edward Parry, *Journal of a voyage for the discovery of a North-West Passage* (London, 1821).

Canadian Arctic—1821   **[M121]**

Plan of the Inlet Called the River Clyde: West Coast of Baffins Bay. 1820. J. Walker sculpt. London: J. Murray, June 1821.

1 map ; 23 x 32 cm.
Detached from William Edward Parry, *Journal of a voyage for the discovery of a North-West Passage* (London, 1821).
"N.B. No anchorage could be found in any part of this inlet."

Canadian Arctic—1827   **[M122]**

Discoveries of Capts. Ross, Parry & Franklin in the Arctic Regions, from the Year 1818 to 1827, J. Aspin, delt.; Hewitt, sc. Buckingham Place. [Edinburgh]: J. Thomson & Co., 1827.

1 map : hand col. ; 47 x 58 cm.
Scale at center ca. 1:7,250,000.
Insets: Part of North America [10 x 24 cm.] — Capt. Franklin's journey from Coppermine River . . . [13 x 21 cm.].
Detached from J. Thomson & Co., *A New general atlas* (Edinburgh, 1827) [Phillips 750, no. 76].
Printed "76" in upper right corner.
Includes pencilled annotations.
Tracks of Ross and Parry outlined in colors.
From collection of J. M. Wordie.
Copy 1 of 2.

Canadian Arctic—1827   **[M123]**

Discoveries of Capts. Ross, Parry & Franklin in the Arctic Regions from the Year 1818 to 1827, J. Aspin, delt.; Hewitt,

sc. Buckingham Place. [Edinburgh]: J. Thomson & Co., 1827.

1 map: hand col. ; 47 x 58 cm.
Scale at center ca. 1:7,250,000.
Insets: Part of North America [10 x 24 cm.] — Capt. Franklin's journey from Coppermine River . . . [13 x 21 cm.]
Detached from J. Thomson & Co., *A New general atlas* (Edingburgh, 1827) [Phillips 750, no. 76].
Printed "76" in upper right corner.
Tracks of Ross and Parry not colored.
Copy 2 of 2.

Canadian Arctic—1835   **[M124]**

Gulph of Boothia. Printed by Graf & Soret. [London: A. W. Webster, 1835].

1 map ; 23 x 18 cm. on sheet 24 x 31 cm
Title from prominent lettering in the Gulf.
Added title: Chart drawn by the natives.
"N.B. These marks show where the Boothians erect huts to sleep in on their journey to Acculee. Original in possession of Captain Ross."
Detached from John Ross, *Narrative of a second voyage in search of a North-West passage* (London: A. W. Webster, 1835), opp. p. 226.

Canadian Arctic—1839   **[M125]**

Cumberland Isle, from the Observations of Captain Penny of the Greenland Ship Neptune of Aberdeen, and from the Information of Enoolooapeek an Intelligent Esquimaux. 1839. [London: Parliament], 1848.

1 map ; 49 x 38 cm.
Added title: Davis Strait.
"Henry Hansard, printer."
"No. 264. Ordered by the House of Commons to be printed, 13 April, 1848."
"Published according to Act of Parliament at the Hydrographic Office of the Admiralty Feby. 12th 1840. Sold by R. B. Bate agent for the sale of the Admiralty charts 21 Poultry."
At upper right: Paper. Arctic Expedition. (No. 5.).
Detached from Great Britain. Admiralty. *Arctic Expedition . . . Copies of instructions to Captain Sir John Franklin. . .in reference to the Arctic Expedition . . .* [by Sir Robert Harry Inglis, report no. 264]. [London, 1848].

Canadian Arctic—1845   **[M126]**

Arctic America, Sheet 1: From Cape

Barrow to Cape Krusensturn, by Sir John Franklin and Messrs. Dease & Simpson, 1825 & 1837; J. & C. Walker, sculpt. London: Hydrographic Office, 1845.

> 1 map ; 45 x 61 cm.
> "London. Published according to Act of Parliament at the Hydrographic Office of the Admiralty May 10th 1845. Sold by R. B. Bate, agent for the Admiralty charts, 21 Poultry and Royal Exchange East."
> G.B. Hyd. Dept. Pl. No.: 1711.

Canadian Arctic—1849 [M127]

Arctic America, Sheet II: Containing Barrow Strait, Prince Regent Inlet, Boothia Gulf &c. with Plans of Forts. J. & C. Walker, sculpt. London: Hydrographical Office, 1849.

> 1 map ; 48 x 61 cm.
> "Sold by R. B. Bate, agent for the Admiralty charts, 21 Poultry and Royal Exchange East."
> Insets: Winter Harbor, Melville Island — Fort Bowen — Port Neill — Victoria Harbour — Batty Bay — Elizabeth Harbour — Port Leopold.
> G.B. Hyd. Dept. Pl. No.: 261.

Canadian Arctic—1849 [M128]

A Chart of Baffin Bay, with Davis & Barrow Straits, by Captn. Ross & Lieut. Parry, R.N. in 1818, 19, & 20, and the Discoveries of Capt. Parry in 1822 and 1823; Capt. Lyon in 1824, & Dr. Rae in 1847; J. & C. Walker, sculpt. London: Admiralty, 1849.

> 1 map ; 61 x 46 cm.
> "Published . . . by Capt. Hurd, R.N. Hydrographer to the Admiralty. . . ."
> "Sold by R. B. Bate, agent for the Admiralty charts, 21 Poultry."
> G.B. Hyd. Dept. Pl. No.: 262.

Canadian Arctic—1851 [M129]

Discoveries in the Arctic Sea, between Baffin Bay & Melville Island, Drawn from Official Documents by John Arrowsmith, 10 Soho Square. London: John Arrowsmith, 1851.

> 1 map : hand col. ; 44 x 63 cm.
> "Showing the coasts explored on the ice, by Capts. Ommanney & the officers of the expeditions under the command of Captain H. T. Austin R.N. C.B. and Captain W. Penny; also by the Honble. Hudson's Bay Cos. expedition under the command of Rear Admiral Sir John Ross C.B. in search of Sir John Franklin. 1850–51."
> "London, Publd. Octr. 21st 1851. . . ."

Canadian Arctic—1851 [M130]

Discoveries in the Arctic Sea up to MDCCCLI. Engraved by J. & C. Walker. London: Hydrographic Office, 1852.

> 1 map ; 62 x 94 cm.
> "London, published according to Act of Parliament at the Hydrographic Office of the Admiralty, April 8th, 1852."
> "Sold by J. D. Potter, agent for the Admiralty charts, 31 Poultry."
> G.B. Hyd. Dept. Pl. No.: 2118.

Canadian Arctic—1851 [M131]

Arctic America: Discoveries of the Searching Expeditions under the Command of Captn. H. T. Austin, R.N., C.B. & Captn. Penny. 1851. [London]: J. D. Potter, 1851.

> 1 map ; 35 x 71 cm.
> "Published by J. D. Potter, 31, Poultry 23nd [sic] Sept. 1851."
> Issued to accompany: Great Britain. Hydrographic Dept. Arctic expeditions. Report of the committee appointed by the Lords Commissioners of the Admiralty to inquire into . . . search of Sir John Franklin (London: H. M. Stationery Office, 1851).
> No plate no.
> From collection of J. M. Wordie.
> Copy 1 of 2.

Canadian Arctic—1851 [M132]

Arctic America: Discoveries of the Searching Expeditions under the Command of Captn. H. T. Austin, R.N., C.B. & Captn. Penny. 1851. [London]: J. D. Potter, 1851.

> 1 map ; 35 x 71 cm.
> Scale ca. 1:1,750,000.
> Issued to accompany: Great Britain. Hydrograhic Dept. Arctic expeditions. Report of the committee

appointed by the Lords Commissioners of the
Admiralty to inquire into . . . search of Sir John
Franklin (London: H. M. Stationery Office, 1852).

In the upper margin a contemporary hand has
inscribed quotations (from above text?),
attributed to "Captain Austin," "Captain
Ommanney," and "Captain Penny," giving their
opinions regarding the fate of the Franklin
Expedition of 1845–47.

Several manuscript annotations on map, small burn
hole at right center.

Soundings in fathoms.

Copy 2 of 2.

Canadian Arctic—1853   [M133]

Arctic Sea: Baffin Bay, Sheet 1. J. & C.
Walker, Sculpt. London: Hydrographic
Dept., 1853.

     1 map ; 62 x 48 cm.

     Scale ca. 1:4,000,000.

     "Published according to Act of Parliament at the
     Hydrographic Office of the Admiralty Decr. 14th,
     1852."

     Soundings in fathoms.

     Insets: "Disko Bay" [5 x 8 cm.], "Omenak Fiord" [6 x 7
     cm.] and "H.W.F. & C., Xlh. 8m." [i.e. North Star
     Bay, 3 x 3 cm.]

     Sectioned into 12 pieces each 22 x 13 cm. and
     mounted on cloth.

Canadian Arctic—1855   [M134]

Sketch of the Shores of Arctic America, to
Illustrate the Search for Sir John Franklin
by Captn. Collinson of H.M.S. Enterprise
1850–1-2-3-4, [by] John Arrowsmith.
London: J. Murray, 1855.

     1 map : hand col. ; 19 x 30 cm.

     Issued to accompany R. Collinson's report in Journal of
     the Royal Geographical Society 25 (1855), opp.
     p.206.

     Colored to show Collinson's track in the ship Enterprise
     and R. Le M. McClure's track in the ship
     Investigator.

Canadian Arctic—1856   [M135]

Chart Illustrating the Remarks of Mr.
Findlay, on the Probable Course Pursued
by Sir John Franklin's Expedition; and of
Captn. Irminger, on the Arctic Current
around Greenland, [by] A. Findlay.
London: J. Murray, 1856.

     1 map : hand col. ; 31 x 33 cm.

     Issued to accompany A. G. Findlay's report in Journal
     of the Royal Geographical Society 26 (1856),
     opp. p.26.

     Colored to show the probable routes of Franklin's
     ships and the track of the Franklin expedition
     survivors.

Canadian Arctic—1860   [M136]

A Sketch of the Recent Discoveries on the
Northern Coast of North America by
Captain McClintock R.N. in Search of Sir
John Franklin. London: Jas. Wyld, [ca.
1860?].

     1 map: hand col. ; 47 x 34 cm.

     "Published by Jas. Wyld, Geographer to the Queen."

     Detached from an unidentified text; originally folded
     to 19 x 14 cm. and mounted on cloth.

     Apparently derivative of similar maps of the region
     produced by Aaron Arrowsmith for various
     editions of M'Clintock's The Fate of Sir John
     Franklin (London and Boston, various publishers
     and dates).

     Inset: Probable route of the Franklin Expedition [7 x 12
     cm.]

Canadian Arctic—1861   [M137]

Arctic America, Showing the Coasts
Explored in 1859, by Captn. Sir F. L. M.
McClintock and His Officers in Search of
the Lost Ships of Sir John Franklin in
1845, Compiled and Drawn by John
Arrowsmith. London: J. Murray, 1861.

     1 map : hand col. ; 22 x 34 cm.

     Issued to accompany F. L. M'Clintock's report in
     Journal of the Royal Geographical Society 31
     (1861), opp. p. clxxxvi.

     Colored to show coasts explored by M'Clintock,
     Hobson and Young, the track of the ship Fox
     and the probable track of Franklin.

Canadian Arctic—1880   [M138]

[Map of the Arctic Archipelago].
[London?: s.n., ca. 1880].

     1 map ; 34 x 49 cm. on sheet 42 x 56 cm.

     Lithograph, [ca. 1880?].

     Monogram (printed or applied from hand stamp) at
     upper right: EA [?].

On verso in MS. (ink), upper right: Capt. Franklin's 1.
Exped. + Capt. Parry's 2d— of 182 [last digit
obscured].
Does not show expedition routes.

Canadian Arctic—1902   [M139]
Discoveries in the Arctic Sea with
Corrections to 1902. Engraved by J. &
C. W. London: Hydrographic Office of the
Admiralty, 1902.

    1 map ; 94 x 118 cm.
    Sold by J. D. Potter, agent for the Admiralty charts,
       145 Minories.
    "Soundings in fathoms."
    "Small corrections 1–83 IV-05 XII-07."
    Plate no., lower right corner: 21 [remainder torn off]:
       "2118" pencilled on verso.
    At lower left: [1158].
    At upper right: 124.9.
    Manuscript annotation on N.W. coast of Baffin Island:
       Adams own chart. As drawn by Adams.
    G.B. Hyd. Dept. Pl. No.: 2118.

Canadian Arctic—1912   [M140]
Plans in Arctic America. Engraved by
Weller & Addison. London: Admiralty,
1912.

    8 maps ; on sheet 52 x 71 cm.
    Added title: Arctic Sea.
    "Published at the Admiralty, 21st May 1912, under the
       superintendence of Rear Admiral H. E. Purey-Cust
       . . . Hydrographer. Sold by J. D. Potter, agent for
       the Admiralty charts, 145 Minories."
    "New edition 24th July 1912."
    Maps variously attributed to J. E. Bernier, W. E. Parry,
       Edward Belcher, Captn. Hoppner and the ship
       "Arctic."
    Contents: Melville Island: Winter Harbour [36 x 33 cm.]
       — Cockburn I.: Port Bowen [10 x 15 cm.] —
       Grinnell Peninsula: Northumberland Sound [20 x
       15 cm.] — Boothia I.: Elizabeth Harbour [11 x 7
       cm.] — North Somerset I.: Port Leopold [11 x 6
       cm.] — North Somerset I.: Batty Bay [8 x 12 cm.]
       — Boothia I.: Victoria Harbour [8 x 7 cm.] —
       Cockburn I.: Port Neill [8 x 12 cm.].
    The lower right quadrant of the sheet (25 x 31 cm) is
       blank.
    G.B. Hyd. Dept. Pl. No.: 261.
    Handstamped at upper right: 165 30 [and] Increase
       50%.

Canadian Arctic—1920   [M141]
Arctic Sea: Baffin Bay, Sheet 1. London:
Admiralty, 1920.

    1 map ; 62 x 48 cm.
    "1853. With corrections to 1902."
    "J. & C. Walker sculpt."
    "Published at the Admiralty 14th Decr. 1852 under the
       superintendence of Capt. Washington . . .
       Hydrographer. Sold by J. D. Potter, agent for the
       Admiralty charts, 145 Minories."
    "New editions, April 1882. June 1885, May 1892,
       March 1908, 4th Jany. 1911, 1st Nov. 1918;
       Small corrections 1920–783—8–13."
    G.B. Hyd. Dept. Pl. No.: 2177.
    Handstamped "Increase 50%."

Canadian Arctic—1922   [M142]
Ellesmere Island. Ottawa: Northwest
Territories and Yukon Branch. Department
of the Interior, 1924.

    1 map ; 20 x 44 cm.
    "From rough sketch by J. D. Craig—21–8-22."
    "Northwest Territories and Yukon Branch. Department
       of the Interior, Ottawa. 25-3-1924."
    Photostatic reproduction of map in the Hydrographic
       Dept., Admiralty.
    MS. annotations reproduced in photostat: C 9297
       Arctic folio 1 [and] H 8235 [over] 1923.
    Handstamped information reproduced in photostat:
       Hydrographic Departm[ent]. Admiralty. Original
       document. 22 Apr. 1924. [oval, 3 x 5 cm.].

Canadian Arctic—1925   [M143]
Erebus Bay, Surveyed by Commr. W. J. S.
Pullen 1854; J. & C. Walker sculpt.
London: Admiralty, 1925.

    1 map ; 48 x 63 cm.
    Added title: Arctic Sea: Barrow Strait.
    "Published according to Act of Parliament at the
       Hydrographic Office of the Admiralty, Novr.
       27th, 1854. Sold by J. D. Potter, agent for the
       Admiralty charts, 145 Minories."
    "Small corrections—IV-76-1925-(XII-18)."
    Profile of Erebus Bay, lower left (3 x 18 cm.).
    G.B. Hyd. Dept. Pl. No.: 2335.
    At upper right: 362.25.
    Handstamped in title cartouche: Increase 50%.

Canadian Arctic—1931   [M144]
Smith Sound: Kennedy, & Robeson
Channels from Discoveries by the United
States Expeditions under Drs. Kane &
Hayes 1854–61: and in the U.S.S.
"Polaris," under Command of C. F. Hall,
1871–2, as Derived from Charts Published

by the U.S. Hydrographic Office, April
1874. London: Admiralty, 1931.

> 1 map ; 97 x 64 cm.
> Scale 1:1,100,000.
> Included additional 13 lines of text on various
>   authorities used in compilation of map.
> "Published at the Admiralty, 20th April 1875, under
>   the superintendence of Captain F. J. Evans . . .
>   Hydrographer. Sold by J. D. Potter, agent for the
>   sale of the Admiralty charts, 145 Minories."
> "New editions July 78, Augt. 1885, July 1896, Sepr.
>   1904, 22nd Jany. 1915, 10th April 1931. Small
>   corrections."
> Insets: Lady Franklin Sound: Discovery Harbour [13 x
>   18 cm.] — Port Foulke and vicinity [19 x 19 cm.]
>   — Pandora Harbour [5 x 6 cm.] — North Star
>   Bay [8 x 8 cm.].
> Insets variously attributed to R. H. Archer, H. F.
>   Stephenson, the ship Discovery, I. I. Hayes,
>   Charles A. Schott, Allen W. Young, J. F. R. Aylen,
>   and the ship North Star.
> G.B. Hyd. Dept. Pl. No.: 275.
> At upper right: 83.32.
> Handstamped "Increase 50%."

Canadian Arctic—1931　　　**[M145]**
N. Coast of Canada and Arctic Archipelago
Including the North-West Passage with
Corrections to 1926. London: Admiralty,
1931.

> 1 map ; 91 x 117 cm.
> "Published according to Act of Parliament at the
>   Hydrographic Office of the Admiralty Jany. 20th
>   1855. Sold by J. D. Potter, agent for the
>   Admiralty charts, 145 Minories."
> "New editions 8th April 1927."
> "Small corrections 1928—1–14 1929–5-8—11–8
>   1930—1–1—5–8 1931—2–9—4-1."
> G.B. Hyd. Dept. Pl. No.: 2118.

Canadian Arctic—1935　　　**[M146]**
N. Coast of Canada and Arctic Archipelago
Including the North-West Passage with
Corrections to 1926. London:
Hydrographic Office, 1935.

> 1 map ; 94 x 117 cm.
> "Published according to act . . . at the Hydrographic
>   Office . . . Jany. 20th 1855."
> "Sold by J. D. Potter, agent for the Admiralty charts,
>   145 Minories."
> "Engraved 1855."
> "New editions 8th April, 1927."

> "Small corrections 1928—1.4 1929—5.8—11.8
>   1930—1.1—5.8 1931–2.9—4.1 1933—3.15
>   1935—3.11."
> At upper right: 176 36.
> G.B. Hyd. Dept. Pl. No.: 2118.

Canadian Arctic—1938　　　**[M147]**
Davis Strait and Baffin Bay to 75°30'
North Latitude. London: Admiralty, 1938.

> 1 map ; 105 x 64 cm.
> Added title: Arctic Sea.
> "The coast of Greenland from Danish government
>   charts, . . . the remainder from various
>   authorities, including British and American
>   exploring expeditions. . . ."
> "Published at the Admiralty 20th April 1875 under the
>   superintendence of Captain F. J. Evans, R,N.;
>   F.R.S. Hydrographer."
> "New editions July 1887, June 1890, June 1901, 15th
>   May 1925; Large corrections 12th August 1927,
>   5th May 1933, 29th April 1938; Small corrections
>   1938–1812—11.7—12.1—2716—1939—57–
>   5.9—1751—1940—2778." ["1940–2778" in
>   manuscript].
> Inset profiles: View A, Devil's Thumb 124° — View B
>   . . . Kaersorsuak or Sanderson's Hope 22° [and]
>   Dark Head 79°
> G.B. Hyd. Dept. Pl. No.: 235.

Canadian Arctic—1940　　　**[M148]**
The South East Coast of Ellesmere Island
from Surveys by J. W. Wright and R. A.
Hamilton 1938. [London]: Royal
Geographical Society, 1940.

> 1 map ; 42 x 26 cm.
> Scale 1:500,000.
> Detached from *Geographical Journal* 30 (April 1940),
>   opp. p. 329.

Canadian Arctic—1942　　　**[M149]**
Part of Northwest Territories. [Ottawa?]:
Topographical Survey of Canada, 1942.

> 1 map : col. ; 50 x 94 cm.
> Scale 1:2,217,600.
> Added title: Topographical Survey of Canada.
> "W. O. # 116—Nov. 42—I Cdn. Fd. Svy. Coy. R.C.E."
> Typed note (by J. M. Wordie?) on paste-on label (5 x
>   11 cm.) at upper center: Two sheets prepared
>   apparently by Royal Canadian Engineers for
>   Major J. T. Wilson's lecture to the R.G.S. on 14
>   December 1942. Note that the basis of the maps
>   appears to be not of recent date, but that the
>   detail added in some parts shows that there
>   must been a very recent air survey.

Canadian Arctic—1991 [M150]

Areas of Importance in the Lancaster
Sound Planning Region. [Yellowknife,
N.W.T., 1991].

> 1 map : col. ; 80 x 95 cm.
> Added title: Lancaster Sound planning region.
> Color coded to show relative importance of areas for
>   hunting, fishing, and trapping.
> Legend contains parallel text in Inuktitut.
> Issued folded in Lancaster Sound Regional Land Use
>   Planning Commission, The Lancaster Sound
>   regional land use plan (Yellowknife, N.W.T.:
>   Dept. of Renewable Resources, 1991).

ALASKA

Alaska—1868 [M151]

Map of the Yukon or Kwich-Pak River (to
Illustrate Mr. Whymper's Paper),
Constructed and Drawn by J. Arrowsmith.
London: J. Murray, 1868.

> 1 map ; 28 x 45 cm.
> Issued to accompany Frederick Whymper's report in
>   Journal of the Royal Geographical Society 38
>   (1868), opp. p.218.
> Inset: North Pacific Ocean [17 x 26 cm.].

Alaska—1926 [M152]

St. Michael Bay, from a United States
Government Survey, 1900. With
Corrections to 1907; Engraved by Davies
& Company. London: Admiralty, 1926.

> 1 map ; 46 x 44 cm.
> Added title, within neat line: Norton Sound—south
>   shore.
> Added title, above neat line in upper margin: Plans in
>   Alaska.
> "Published at the Admiralty, 10th Aug. 1900, under
>   the superintendence of Rear Admiral W. J. L.
>   Wharton . . . Hydrographer."
> "New edition July 1909; Small corrections IX-11 VI-14
>   1919–1929 1923–9-25 1926—(IV-9)—1606—
>   10–5."
> G.B. Hyd. Dept. Pl. No.: 3143.
> At upper right: 103.31
> Handstamped "Increase 50%."
> Right portion of sheet (46 x 22 cm.) is blank.

EURASIA

Scandinavia—1717 (1726 state) [M153]

A New Map of Denmark and Sweden,
According to ye Newest and Most Exact
Observations, by H. Moll geographer . . .
London: John Bowles, Thomas Bowles,
and Philip Overton, [1726?].

> 1 map : hand col. ; 59 x 100 cm.
> "Printed for H. Moll over against Devereux Court
>   without Temple Bar in the Strand, John Bowles,
>   print and map-seller over-against Stocks Market.
>   Thomas Bowles print & map-seller next to the
>   Chapter house in St. Pauls Church Yard.
>   [erasure?] and by Philip Overton map &
>   printseller near S. Dunstan's Church, Fleetstreet."
> Inset: The North part of Norway, Lapland, and
>   Greenland [23 x19 cm.].
> Includes vignettes and text about Laplanders.
> Detached from Herman Moll, *The World described*
>   (London, 1726).
> Reference: Stevens, World described, catalogue C, no.
>   14, issue (d).

Iceland—1728 [M154]

Het Eyland Ysland in 't Groot.
Amsterdam: Gerard van Keulen, aan de
Nieuwen Brugh, met previlegie, [1728].

> 1 map : hand col. ; 50 x 60 cm.
> On verso in MS. (ink), upper right: 99.
> Possibly detached from Gerard van Keulen, *De
>   Nieuwe Groote Ligtende Zee-Fakkel* (Amsterdam,
>   1728) [cf. Koeman v.4, p. 319 and 395, map
>   226].

Norway—1940 [M155]

Dybdekart i syv blad over de norske
kystfarvann med tilgrensende havstrøk =
Bathymetrical map in seven sheets of the
Norwegian coastal waters and adjoining
seas. Oslo: Norske videnskaps- akademi i
Oslo., 1940.

> 7 maps : col. ; 112 x 81 cm. and smaller
> Scales vary.
> Title from sheet 1.
> Running title, sheets 1–7: Olaf Holtedahl: Dybdekart
>   over de norske kystfarvann med tilgrensende
>   havstrøk.
> "Utarbeidet vesentlig på grunnlag av Norges
>   Sjøkartverks lodde-materiale."

Issued to accompany Olaf Holtedahl, The Submarine
relief off the Norwegian coast (Oslo, 1940).
Reference: OCLC 5444510 (maps dated 1941).

Siberia—1748 [M156]

An Exact Chart of All the Countries
through Which Capt. Behring Travelled
from Tobolski Capital of Siberia to the
Country of Kamtschatka. [London: s.n.,
1705].

1 map ; 17 x 32 cm. on sheet 25 x 41 cm.
Detached from John Harris, *Navigantium atque
itinerantium bibliotheca* (London, 1744–1748),
"Vol. II, Page 1016."
Reference: Mickwitz and Miekkavaara, v.3, p.82.

NORTH ATLANTIC OCEAN

North Atlantic Ocean—1598 [M157]

Scandia, sive regiones septentrionales.
[Venice, 1598].

1 map ; 13 x 18 cm. on sheet 29 x 20 cm.
Detached from Claudius Ptolemaeus, *Geografia cioe
descrittione Vniversale della terra* (Venice, 1598).
p.67 [Phillips 405].
Typeset heading above title: IX. Descrittione della
Scandia, Odé paesi, e dell' isole settentrionali.
Typeset text beneath map and on verso.

North Atlantic Ocean—1646 [M158]

Quest'a carta contiene l'Isolle di Ferro é di
Shutland con la Noruegia Settentrionale, la
longitudine Comincia da l'Isola di Pico
d'Asores di Europa Carta XXXXV. A. F.
Lucini fece. [Florence, 1646].

1 map ; 48 x 73 cm.
Scale ca. 1:2,600,000 at 60° N.
Mercator projection.
From Robert Dudley, Dell' Arcano del Mare (Firenza,
1646–1647), v. 3, bk. 6, no. 49 [Phillips 457].

North Atlantic Ocean—1666 [M159]

De Custen van Noorwegen, Finmarken,
Laplandt, Spitsbergen, Ian Mayen Eylandt,
Yslandt, als mede Hitlandt, en een gedeelte
van Schotlandt. Amsterdam: By Pieter
Goos op 't Water inde Vergulde Zee-
Spiegel, [1666?].

1 map : hand col. ; 45 x 55 cm.
On verso in MS. (ink), upper right: 29.
Possibly detached from Pieter Goos, *De Zee-Atlas, Ofte
Water-Weereld* (Amsterdam, 1666).
References: cf. Koeman v.4, p.197, Goos 1 B, map 29;
Mickwitz and Miekkavaara, v.1, p. 166, atlas no.
80, pl. 30.

North Atlantic Ocean—1671 [M160]

A Generall Chart of the Northerne
Navigation, Discribed by John Seller.
Hydrographer to the Kings Most Excellent
Majesty. Cum privilegio. [London, 1671?].

1 map : hand col. ; 44 x 54 cm.
Detached from an edition of John Seller, *The English
pilot, part I* (London: John Darby et al, 1671–
1791) [cf. National Maritime Mus. Lib. Cat. v.3,
pt.1, p.480, atlas no. 421, pl. 1].
Insets: Part of Nova Zemla [6 x 7 cm.] — The River
Duina in Russia going up to Archangel [11 x 15
cm.] — The Sound [17 x 31 cm.].
Sheet closely trimmed to printed borders; "Genl. chart
of Northern Navigation. 3." in MS. (ink) on verso.
Bookseller's [?] pencilled annotation on verso dates
map 1675.

North Atlantic Ocean—1734 [M161]

Nieuwe gelijk gradige of platte zekaart van
het Noorder deel van Europa.
Vertoonende de geheele Groenlandse en
Moskovise scheepvaard water in elk de
miswysinge van het compas selver moet
verbeeteren = Nouvelle carte marine de la
partie septentrionale de l'Europe
d'emontrant la navigation de Groenland et
Moscovie.—Amsterdam: Gerard van
Keulen, [1734].

1 map ; 60 x 100 cm.
"Nieuwelyks gemaakt en vijgegeven door Gerard van
Keulen. Boek Zeekaard verkooper en graadboog
maker tot Amsterdam an de oost zyde van
Nieuwenbrug en de Gekroonde Lootsman. Met
privilegie. Oversien en gekorrigeert door Ian
Piterse Stuurman na syn eygen ondervindinge
syne nú leermeester in de Konst der Stuurlieden
tot Sardam."

Possibly detached from Gerard van Keulen, *De Nieuwe Groote Ligtende Zee-Fakkel* (Amsterdam, 1734) [cf. Koeman v.4, p.379, map 201 and v.4, p.320, map 201].

North Atlantic Ocean—1758 [M162]

Zusamen gezogene Karte von den Nord-Meeren, zur allgemeinen Historie der Reisen, von M. B. Ingr. de la Marine. 1758. [Leipzig?, 1747?].

> 1 map ; 31 x 43 cm.
> Based on map by J. N. Bellin.
> Probably detached from A. F. Prévost, *Allgemeine Historie der Reisen zu Wasser und Lande* (Leipzig: Arkstee und Merkus, 1747–1774) [cf. Sabin 65406].
> At upper right: No. 1.
> At lower right: T. XVII. C.
> Issued folded to 23 x 15 cm.
> MS. annotation (pencil), upper margin: "From A. C. Aug. '48. August Courtauld to J M W[ordie]."

North Atlantic Ocean—1758 [M163]

Carte reduite des mers du nord pour servir a l'histoire des voyages, par M. B. Ingr. de la Marine 1758. [Paris: J. N. Bellin], 1758.

> 1 map ; 31 x 42 cm.
> Detached from the atlas accompanying J. F. de La Harpe, *Abrege de l'histoire generale des voyages* (Paris [ca. 1780]).
> "Tom. XV" at lower left and "No. 1" at lower right.
> References: Phillips 591 & 5991, no.65.

NORTH PACIFIC OCEAN

North Pacific Ocean—1753 [M164]

Carte des nouvelles decouvertes au nord de la Mer du Sud, tant à l'est de la Sibérie et du Kamtchatka, qu' à l'ouest de la Nouvelle France. Venise: François Santini . . . M. Remondini, [1753 or later].

> 1 map : hand col. ; 45 x 63 cm.
> Scale ca. 1:21,000,000.
> Relief shown pictorially.
> Prime meridians: Ferro, Paris.
> Fifth state of Delisle's map (Tooley FMA, 104).
> "Avertissement" and 2 illustrations of natives of Kamtchatka and Louisiana at top of map.
> "P. II. 44."

North Pacific Ocean—1775 [M165]

The Russian Discoveries, from the Map Published by the Imperial Academy of St. Petersburg. London: Printed by Robert Sayer, Map & Printseller, no. 53 in Fleet Street, 1775.

> 1 map : hand col. ; 44 x 61 cm.
> Shows routes and discoveries of V. Behring, Capt. Tschirikow, their ships St. Peter and St. Paul, and others.
> Detached from an atlas.
> MS. "19" in upper right on verso; verso otherwise blank.

North Pacific Ocean—1776 [M166]

Nuove scoperte du Russi al nord del Mare del Sud si nell'Asia , che nell'America. Venezia: Presso Antonio Zatta, 1776.

> 1 map : hand col. ; 30 x 39 cm.
> Detached from an edition of Zatta's *Atlante novissimo* (Venice, 1779–1784) [cf. Philipps 650 v.1 no.15 and 651 v.4 no.42].
> Shows most of North America and northeast Asia; notes at top discuss recent explorations of the Northwest and Northeast Passages.
> Repaired along center fold and top margin; remnants of guard along top margin.

North Pacific Ocean—1779 [M167]

Carte generale des decouvertes de l'Amiral de Fonte, et autres navigateurs Espagnols, Anglois et Russes pour la recherche du Passage a la Mer du Sud, par M. De L'Isle de l'Academie royale des Sciences &c. [Paris, 1777].

> 1 map : hand col. ; 28 x 35 cm.
> "Publiee a Paris en Septembre 1752."
> At upper right: Suppl. 7e. Carte.
> Inset: Carte dressee sur la lettre de l'Amiral de Fonte par l'ecrivain de la Californie [9 x 10 cm.]
> Apparently a derivative of the map of the same title and imprint date in Delisle's *Nouvelles cartes des decouvertes de l'amiral de Fonte . . .* (Paris, 1753).
> Detached from the atlas supplement to Diderot's *Encyclopèdie* (Paris, 1770–1779) [cf. Phillips 1195; Pedley 454].

North Pacific Ocean—1779 [M168]

Carte des nouvelles découvertes, dressée

par Phil. Buache, Pr. Géogr. du Roi. [Paris, 1777].

> 2 maps ; 14 x 31 cm. and 15 x 28 cm. on sheet 36 x 45 cm.
> Scale ca. 1:35,000,000.
> "Presenteé à l'Acad. des Sciences le 9 Aout 1752 et approuvée dans son assemblée du 6 Septembre suivant."
> On sheet with: Extrait d'une carte Japonoise de l'univers.
> Detached from the atlas supplement to Diderot's *Encyclopèdie* (Paris, 1770–1779) [cf. Phillips 1195; Pedley 452].
> Engraved in lower right: 165.
> Relief shown pictorially.

North Pacific Ocean—1779   [M169]

A Map of the Discoveries Made by Capts. Cook & Clerke in the Years 1778 & 1779 between the Eastern Coast of Asia and the Western Coast of North America, When They Attempted to Navigate the North Sea, also Mr. Hearn's Discoveries to the North Westward of Hudson's Bay. Published by Z. Jackson, for Payne's New System of Universal Geography. [Dublin, 1792–1794].

> 1 map : hand col. ; 16 x 27 cm.
> Detached from John Payne, *Universal geography formed into a new and entire system* (Dublin: Zachariah Jackson, 1792–1794).
> Ms. "1794" in pencil, upper right.

North Pacific Ocean—1788   [M170]

Karte von den N. W. Amerikanischen und N. Oe. Asiatischen Küsten, nach den Untersuchungen des Kapit: Cook in den Jah: 1778 und 1779, entworfen von Heinrich Roberts Lieut.; Neu herausgegeben v. F. A. Schraembl; Gestoch. von I. C. von Lackner. [Vienna], MDCCLXXXVIII [1788].

> 1 map : hand col. ; 40 X 68 cm.
> Scale ca. 1:8,800,000.
> Probably detached from Franz Anton Schraembl, *Allgemeiner grosser Schrämblischer atlas* (Vienna, 1800) [cf. Phillips 694 no. 50].
> Relief shown pictorially.

North Pacific Ocean—1794   [M171]

Chart of the N. W. Coast of America and the N. E. Coast of Asia, Explored in the Years 1778 and 1779, Prepared by Lieutt. Heny. Roberts, under the Immediate Inspection of Capt. Cook; Engraved by W. Palmer. London: Wm. Faden, 24 July 1784.

> 1 map : hand col. ; 40 X 68 cm.
> Scale ca. 1:8,850,000.
> "2d. edition. Published January 1st, 1794."
> Relief shown pictorially.

North Pacific Ocean—1932   [M172]

Yukon River to Point Barrow, Including Bering Strait, Surveyed by F. W. Beechey, R.N., F.R.S., H.M.S. "Blossom," 1826–7. With Additions by Captains Kellett, Collinson, Moore, and Mr. Thos. Hull, Secd. Mast. R.N., 1849–54. Norton Sound from the United States Government Chart. London: Admiralty, 1932.

> 1 map ; 98 x 64 cm.
> Added title: North America—west coast: Alaska.
> "Published at the Admiralty, 17th April 1907 under the superintendence of Rear Admiral A. Mostyn Field . . . Hydrographer. Sold by J. D. Potter, agent for the Admiralty charts, 145 Minories."
> "New editions Jany. 1909, 22nd Aug. 1913, 3rd August 1917, 8th Jan. 1923. Large corrections 1st June 1928, 16th Dec. 1932."
> G.B. Hyd. Dept. Pl. No.: 593.
> At upper right: 355.32.
> Handstamped "Increase 50%."

North Pacific Ocean—1933   [M173]

Bering Strait, from the Most Recent Information, 1884. With Corrections to 1927. London: Admiralty, 1933.

> 1 map ; 98 x 64 cm.
> Added title: Arctic Sea.
> "Published at the Admiralty 21st July 1884, under the superintendence of Captain Sir Frederick J. Evans . . . Hydrographer. Sold by J. D. Potter, agent for the Admiralty charts, 145 Minories."
> "New editions Nov. 1894, Novr. 1906, Jany. 1909, 15th August 1913, 20th July 1917. Large corrections 19th Nov. 1928, 28th April 1933."

G.B. Hyd. Dept. Pl. No.: 654.
At upper right: 123.33.
Handstamped "Increase 50%."

North Pacific Ocean—1933 [M174]
Bering Sea: Eastern Part. Washington,
D.C.: U.S. Coast and Geodetic Survey,
1933.

> 1 map : col. ; 95 x 73 cm.
> Added title: Alaska: west coast.
> "Published at Washington, D.C. Nov. 1928; reissued
> Nov. 1929 by the U.S. Coast and Geodetic
> Survey."
> Additional dates: 28–11/13, 29–11/22, 31–4/30, 32–
> 5/19, 33–2/21.
> Plate no.: 9302.
> Handstamped "Mar 6 1934."

ARCTIC OCEAN AND ISLANDS

Arctic Ocean—1874 [M175]
The Discoveries North of Smith Sound, by
the U.S. Ship Polaris, under the Command
of C. F. Hall, 1871–1873. [Taunton:
Hydrographic Dept., 1939].

> 1 map ; 104 x 60 cm.
> Pencilled note on recto in hand of J. M. Wordie:
> Photostatic copy of chart at Admiralty—courtesy
> of J. W. Wright, June 1939.
> Attributed, in part, to E. K. Kane and I. I. Hayes.
> "Published April 1874 at the Hydrographic Office,
> Washington, D.C. R. H. Wyman, Commo. U.S.N.
> Hydrographer to the Bureau of Navigation."
> Plate no.: 555.
> MS. note reproduced in photostat: Smith Sound—
> Discoveries North of (Duplicate). A 3693 Shelf Tt.
> Handstamped information reproduced in photostat:
> Hydrographic Office. Jan. 18 1875.

Arctic Ocean—1923 [M176]
Arctic Ocean and Greenland Sea, from the
Latest Information in the Hydrographic
Department of the Admiralty, Drawn by
Edward J. Powell under the Direction of
Captn. Hoskyn, R.N. Supert. of Charts;
Engraved by Davies, Bryer & Co. London:
Admiralty, 1923.

1 map ; 85 x 122 cm.
"Published at the Admiralty, 26th Augt. 1872, under
the superidtendence of Rear Admiral G. H.
Richards . . . Hydrographer. Sold by J. D. Potter,
agent for the sale of the Admiralty charts, 145
Minories."
"New editions 1882, Feb. 1886, June 1894, Oct.
1898, May 1899, June 1901, May 1903, April
1905, Sep. 1908, 1st Decr. 1916, 12th Sep.
1919, 9th Feby. 1920, 25th April 1921, 23rd
April 1923; Small corrections 1923—1712."
G.B. Hyd. Dept. Pl. No.: 2282.
At upper right: 249.23.
Handstamped "Increase 50%."

Arctic Ocean—1930 [M177]
Arctic Sea: Melville Sound, Sheet 2. 1859
with Corrections to 1925. London:
Admiralty, 1930.

> 1 map ; 62 x 48 cm.
> "Published at the Admiralty 26th May 1856, under the
> superintendence of Capt. Washington . . .
> Hydrographer. Sold by J. D. Potter, agent for the
> Admiralty charts, 145 Minories."
> "New editions, Oct. 1891, 13th May 1927; Small
> corrections 1928—2–8 1929—5–8 1930—1–1."
> G.B. Hyd. Dept. Pl. No.: 2443.
> Handstamped "Increase 50%."

Arctic Ocean—1932 [M178]
Mackenzie River to Bering Strait, from the
Observations of Beechey, Franklin,
Richardson, Dease & Simpson, Kellet,
Pullen & Hopper, Moore, Collinson,
McClure and Maguire 1856. With
Corrections and Additions to 1927.
London: Admiralty, 1932.

> 1 map ; 61 x 97 cm.
> "Published at the Hydrographic Office of the Admiralty
> Feby. 20th 1856."
> "New editions, Mar. 1882, Dec. 1908. Large
> corrections, 25th May 1928, 30th Sept. 1932;
> Small corrections [none recorded]."
> G.B. Hyd. Dept. Pl. No.: 2435.
> At upper right: 277.32.
> Handstamped "Increase 50%."

Arctic Ocean—1932 [M179]
Arctic coast. Washington, D.C.: U.S. Coast
and Geodetic Survey, 1932.

1 map : col. ; 64 x 109 cm.
Added title: Alaska.
"Published at Washington, D.C. July 1928; reissued
    Sept. 1929 by the U.S. Coast and Geodetic
    Survey."
Additional dates: 28–7/5, 29–9/24, 30–11/13, 32–6/
    4.
Plate no.: 9400.

Arctic Ocean—1954   [M180]

The North Cape to Uyedinyéniya Island
Including the Barents and Kara seas,
Principally from the Russian Government
Charts to 1897. With Additions and
Corrections to 1949. London: Admiralty,
1954.

    1 map ; 65 x 98 cm.
    Added title: Arctic Ocean.
    "Published at the Admiralty, 11th June 1898, under
        the superintendence of Rear Admiral W. J. L.
        Wharton . . . Hydrographer."
    "New editions Mar. 1902, Novr. 1905, 15th May
        1914, 24th Novr. 1916, 21st June 1920, 23rd
        May 1921, 27th March 1925. Large corrections
        18th March 1938, 1st Oct. 1943, 29th Dec.
        1950; Small corrections 1952—1200—12–29
        1953–503—675—677—2694—1954—367–
        369—370—1556—2115—2869."
    G.B. Hyd. Dept. Pl. No.: 2962.
    At upper right: 28.55.
    Handstamped "Cancelled."

Jan Mayen—1662   [M181]

Insvla qve a Ioanne Mayen nomen sortita
est. [Amsterdam: Blaeu, 1662?].

    1 map : hand col. ; 44 x 55 cm.
    Scale ca. 1:126,000.
    Possibly detached from Joan Blaeu, *Atlas major*
        (Amsterdam, 1662).
    Cartouche, lower right, vacant.
    Text in Latin on verso (p. 19–20): Insvlae Ian-Majanae.

Novaya Zemlya—1663   [M182]

Nova Zemla. [Amsterdam, 1663?].

    1 map ; 36 x 48 cm.
    No printing on verso.
    MS. annotations on verso: "Nova Zembla" in ink, lower
        right, "177" [?] in pencil upper right, "Blaeu
        1640" in pencil, upper center.
    First listing in Koeman is in the Blaeu *Atlas Maior* in
        1663, with French text on verso (v.1, p.201,
        map 438).

From collection of J. M. Wordie.
Copy 1 of 2.

Novaya Zemlya—1663   [M183]

Nova Zemla. [Amsterdam, 1663?].

    1 map : hand col. ; 38 x 50 cm.
    Latin heading and text on verso (p. 25–26, signature
        I): Nova Zembla.
    Verso includes hand colored engraving (17 x 22 cm.)
        by Hessel Gerritsz with letterpress title: Figura
        animalis Walrus dicti, & pulli ejus.
    First listing in Koeman is in the Blaeu *Atlas Maior* in
        1663, with French text on verso (v.1, p.201,
        map 438).
    Copy 2 of 2.

Spitsbergen—1662   [M184]

Spisberga. [Amsterdam, 1662].

    1 map ; 37 x 48 cm.
    Detached from Joan Blaeu, *Atlas major* (Amsterdam,
        1662) v.1 [Koeman, v.1, p. 21, map 437].
    Latin text on verso with following title: Spitzberga
        [signature C, p.21, 22].

Spitsbergen—1676   [M185]

Spitzberga. Amstelaedami: apud G. Valk et
P. Schenk, [1676 or later].

    1 map : hand col. ; 40 x 50 cm.
    Detached from an atlas; MS. "36" on verso.
    Probably printed from a revised J. J. v. Waesberge
        plate: according to Koeman, Shenk & Valk
        bought Waesberge's plates in 1676 (v.2, p.162).
        Koeman does not attribute an original
        Spitsbergen map to Shenk & Valk (see v.3,
        p.119–121 and 137–140). Koeman reprints a
        catalog which lists Waesberge maps published in
        Schenk & Valk editions of the Novus Atlas. The
        catalog lists "Spitsberga" as no. 9 (v.3, p.111).

Spitsbergen—1728   [M186]

Nieuwe afteekening van Het Eyland Spits-
Bergen opgegeven door de Commandeurs
Giles en Outger Rep, en in 't Ligt gebragt
en wytgegeven door Gerard van Keulen,
Boek en Zeekaart verkooper aan de
Nieuwen brug met Privilegie voor 15
Jaaren. [Amsterdam]: Gerard van Keulen,
[1728?].

    1 map : hand col. ; 53 x 57 cm.

Detached from an atlas; MS. "134" in upper right and on verso.

First listed in Koeman as appearing in a van Keulen atlas dated 1728 (v.4, p.319, map 227 and p.392, map 227).

Spitsbergen—1764 [M187]

Carte du Spits-Berg suivant les Hollandois. [Paris: s.n., 1764].

> 1 map : hand col. ; 22 x 17 cm.
> Detached from J. N. Bellin, *Le Petite atlas maritime* (Paris, 1764) "Tom. IV No. 22."

Spitsbergen—1899 [M188]

Anchorages on the West Coast of Spitsbergen, from Sketch Plans by Prinz Heinrich von Bourbon and Lieutenant Richard Ritter von Barry in the Austrian Yachts "Fleur de Lys 1 & 2," 1891 & 1892, Published in 1894. Engraved by Edwd. Weller. London: Admiralty, 1899.

> 9 maps ; on sheet 70 x 53 cm.
> "Published at the Admiralty, 8th May 1899, under the superintendence of Rear Admiral W. J. L. Wharton . . . Hydrographer. Sold by J. D. Potter, agent for the Admiralty charts, 145 Minories."
> Contents: Danes I.: Robbe Bay [16 x 14 cm.] — Kings Bay: Blomstrand Harbour [16 x 14 cm.] — Kings Bay: Coal Haven [16 x 10 cm.] — Ice Fiord: Sassen and Temple bays [18 x 25 cm.] — Ice Fiord: Coal Bay [18 x 24 cm.] — Ice Fiord: Green Harbour [27 x 13 cm.] — Temple Bay: Bjona Haven [11 x 12 cm.] — Bell Sound: Middle Hook Haven [16 x 12 cm.] — Bell Sound: Fleur de Lys and Bourbon havens [27 x 24 cm.].
> G.B. Hyd. Dept. Pl. No.: 3020.

Spitsbergen—1910 [M189]

Spitzbergen, bearbeitet von Dr. H. Guttmann. Berlin: Selbstverlag des Herausgebers, N., Chausseeststrasse 27, [ca. 1910?].

> 1 map : col. ; 86 x 58 cm. fold. to 33 x 24 cm. in paper covers.
> Scale 1:1,000,000.
> Added title, from cover: Touristen-Karte von Spitzbergen.
> Imprint from cover.
> Imprint, map recto: Joh. Wilh. Rother Nachf, Berlin C.
> Two columns of text inside front cover.

Shows Salomon A. Andrée's point of departure in 1897 balloon expedition (expedition's remains discovered on White Island in 1930).

Ship routes from Europe in red.

Spitsbergen—1911 [M190]

Magdalena Bay to Red Bay, from Sketch Surveys by Lieuts. Franklin and Beechey, H.M.S. "Trent," 1818. Red Bay from a Survey by Lieut. Guissez of the French Navy, under the Direction of H.S.H. the Prince of Monaco, 1899. London: Admiralty, 1911.

> 1 map ; 74 x 65 cm.
> Added title: Arctic Ocean: Spitsbergen—north coast.
> "Published at the Admiralty, 1st Augt. 1901, under the superintendence of Rear Admiral W. J. L. Wharton . . . Hydrographer. Sold by J. D. Potter, agent for the Admiralty charts, 145 Minories."
> "New edition 28th December 1911; Small corrections [none indicated]."
> Insets (attributed to Lieuts. G. Norselius and E. Arnelius of the Swedish Royal Navy, 1897 and 1900): Danes Gat [26 x 41 cm.] — Fair Haven and approaches [32 x 24 cm.] .
> G.B. Hyd. Dept. Pl. No.: 3203.

Spitsbergen—1911 [M191]

Anchorages on the West and North Coasts of Spitsbergen. Engraved by Davies & Company. London: Admiralty, [1911?].

> 11 maps ; on sheet 63 x 99 cm.
> Maps variously attributed to J. P. Rolleston, George L. Atkinson, Albert the Prince of Monaco, Henry Foster, the Swedish Polar Expedition, and plans by the Swedish and French governments.
> "Published at the Admiralty, 18th May, 1896, under the superintendence of Rear Admiral W. J. L. Wharton . . . Hydrographer. Sold by J. D. Potter, agent for the Admiralty charts, 145 Minories."
> "New editions Aug. 1897, Oct. 1898, April 1900, Aug. 1901, 2nd August 1911; Small corrections XII-16."
> Contents: Bell Sound: Recherche Bay [35 x 41 cm.] — Bear Island: South Haven [20 x 16 cm.] — Cross Bay (Close Cove) [29 x 22 cm.] — Ice Fiord: Skans Bay [28 x 20 cm.] — Ice Fiord: Advent Anche. [15 x 21 cm.] — Bear Island (Cherry I.) [19 x 16 cm.] — Cross Bay: Port Möller [15 x 13 cm.] — Hamburg Bay [7 x 9 cm.] — Beverly Sound [13 x 21 cm.] — Treurenburg Bay [24 x 16 cm.] — Port Signe [8 x 13 cm.] — Cross Bay: Ebeltofts Haven (Cross Road) [11 x 13 cm.].

Right 1/3 of sheet (63 x 29 cm.) is blank.
G.B. Hyd. Dept. Pl. No.: 300.

Spitsbergen—1914   [M192]

Spitsberg (partie nord-ouest), carte dressée
sous la direction du Captitaine Gunnar
Isachsen par l'expédition Norvègienne.
[Paris]: Gravé et imp. par Erhard Fres., 35
bis Rue Denfert Rochereu, [ca. 1914].

1 map : col. ; 143 x 76 cm. on 2 sheets.
Scale 1:200,000.
Added title: Océan Glacial Arctique.
Includes list of expedition members credited with map
compilation: A. Koller, J. Laurantzon, A. Staxrud,
A. Hermansen, J. Petersen-Hansen, K. Haavimb,
N. Ræder, O. Hendriksen, Th. Ween, and T. H.
Barlag.
Eight lines of text list map sources used in compilation,
variously dated 1900–1913.
Insets: [Location map: Svalbard, 20 x 16 cm.] — Mer
de Norvège [19 x 12 cm.].

Spitsbergen—1914   [M193]

Spitsbergen, by Captain Gunnar Isachsen,
R.N.A. [London], 1914.

1 map : col. ; 33 x 30 cm. on sheet 39 x 48 cm.
At upper right: The Geographical Journal 1914.
At lower right: Spitsbergen. Isachsen.
Insets: Bear Island [3 x 4 cm.] — [Location map, 11 x 8
cm.].
Issued to accompany Geographical Journal 45 no.3
(March 1914), opp p. 272; Isachsen's discussion
of the map is on p. 237–242.

Spitsbergen—1918   [M194]

Spitsbergen. [London?]: Ordnance Survey,
1918 Aug.

1 map : col. ; 47 x 41 cm.
Scale 1:1,000,000.
Insets: Bear Island [4 x 5 cm.] — [Location map, 14 x 8
cm.].
On verso in MS. (ink), hand of J. M. Wordie [?]: . . .
R.N. Rudmose Brown
G.S.G.S. plate no.: 2877

Spitsbergen—1919   [M195]

Fra Norge (Tromsø og Varanger) til
Spitsbergen. [Oslo]: Norges Geografiske
Opmaaling, 1919.

1 map : col. ; 133 x 74 cm.
Scale 1:1,000,000.
Added title: Nordishavet.
"Med opmaalingerne fra Staxrud—Hoel-Røvig's
expedtitioner av 1911–18 tilgodegjort."
"Utarbeidet ved Norges Sjøkartverk."
Plate no.: 303.
Handstamps: "Rettet til 1919 Norges Sjøkartvek" [lower
left], "5:19" [lower right].

Spitsbergen—1920   [M196]

Spitsbergen: Map of Klaas Billen Bay &
Temple Bay, Surveyed by John Mathieson
F.R.S.G.S. (Late H.M. Ordnance Survey);
Assisted by George M. Cowan M.C.; and
A. Fleming Campbell. [Edinburgh]: J.
Bartholomew and Son, Ltd., [1920?].

1 map : col. ; 51 x 40 cm.
Scale ca. 1:100,000.
Above title: Scottish Spitsbergen Syndicate.
On verso in MS. (ink), hand of J. M. Wordie [?]: . . .
1919 (1920).

Spitsbergen—1920   [M197]

Spitsbergen: farvand og ankerspladder paa
vest- og nordkysten, optat av Ritmester
Isachsens norske Spitsbergenekspedition
med Marinens D/S "Farm" 1909–1910;
Hydrograferingen er utført av de norske
Sjøofficerer Kaptein A. Hermansen og
Premierløitnant J. C. Petersen-Hansen;
Fotografi efter Tegning av Kaptein Chr. A.
Dahl. Kristiani: Utgivet av Norges
Geografiske Opmaaling, 1920.

9 maps : col. ; on sheet 75 x 91 cm.
Imprint date 1912; 3 handstamps read "Rettet til 1918
[–1920] Norges Sjøkartverk".
Contents: 1. Forland Sundet—Kings Bay—Cross Bay
[64 x 35 cm.] — 2. Blomstrand Hamn [20 x 24
cm.] — 3. Ferrier Hamn [14 x 29 cm.] — 4. Farm
Hamn [20 x 18 cm.] — 5. Vulkan Hamn [11 x 9
cm.] — 6. Green Harbour [20 x 24 cm.] — 7.
Hecla Hamn [11 x 16 cm.] — 8. Norske Hamna
[14 x 14 cm.] — Oversiktskart over Spitsbergen-
sjøkarter [index map, 19 x 18 cm.].
Note in pencil, lower right: Source: Expedition
Isachsen au Spitsbergen, 1909–1910. Resultats
scientifiques, 1916. (Christiana).
Plate no.: 198.
Handstamp, lower right: 7:18.

Spitsbergen—1929 [M198]
Sjøkart yver Bjørnøya upplodingi er gjord
1928, av Rolf Kjær. Oslo: Norges
Geografiske Opmåling, 1929.
> 1 map ; 66 x 57 cm.
> Scale 1:40,000.
> First edition.
> "Reprodusert og prenta i Norges Geografiske
>   Opmåling 1929."
> In upper margin: Det Kongelege Departement for
>   handel sjöfart, industri, håndverk og fiske.
> Plate no.: S 1.

Spitsbergen—1935—Geology [M199]
Geologische Übersichtsskizze von
Spitzbergen, zusammengestellt nach der
Literatur von Hans Frebold, 1935. Berlin:
Gebrüder Borntraeger, 1935.
> 1 map ; 53 x 51 cm.
> Added title, above neat line, upper left: Geologie der
>   Erde. Hans Frebold, Geologie von Spitzbergen
>   usw.
> Above neat line, upper right: Tafel 7.

Spitsbergen—1937 [M200]
Svalbard. Oslo: Norges Svalbard- og
Ishavs-undersøkelser, 1937.
> 1 map ; 53 x 50 cm.
> At lower left: Norges Svalbard- og Ishavs-
>   undersøkelser. Styrar: Adolf Hoel.
> At upper left: Skrifter om Svalbard og Ishavet, Nr. 73.
> Insets: Björnöya [4 x 8 cm.] — [Location map, 19 x 12
>   cm.].

Spitsbergen—1940 [M201]
Nordsvalbard = Northern Svalbard . . . ,
Sjømælingar av Norges Svalbard- og
Ishavs-Undersøkelser 1909–1935. Supplert
med framande sjølmælingar. Oslo: Norges
geografiske oppmåling, 1940.
> 1 map ; 72 x 96 cm.
> Added title: Nordishavet = Arctic Sea.
> At lower left center: Utarbeidt av = Compiled by Rolf
>   Kjær.
> "Prenta Juni 1939; retta til 1st Jan. 1940."
> Handstamp, upper right: Proof 30 Sep. 1942.
> In upper margin: Det Kongelege Departement for
>   handel, sjøfart, industri, håndverk og fiske.

Norges Svalbard- og Ishavs-Undersøkelser, Oslo.
Styrar: Adolf Hoel.
Plate no.: 507.

Spitsbergen—1940 [M202]
Frå Björnöya til Isfjorden, Storfjorden og
Hopen . . . , Sjømælingar av Norges
Svalbard- og Ishavs-undersøkelser 1909–
1936. Supplert med framande sjømælingar.
Oslo: Norges geografiske oppmåling,
1940.
> 1 map ; 72 x 96 cm.
> Added title: Nordishavet: Norge-Svalbard. Nordre blad
>   = Arctic Sea: northern sheet.
> At lower left center: Utarbeidt av = Compiled by Rolf
>   Kjær.
> "Prenta Juni 1939; retta til 1st Jan. 1940."
> Handstamp, upper right: Proof 30 Sep. 1940.
> In upper margin: Det Kongelege Departement for
>   handel, sjøfart, industr, håndverk eg fiske.
> Norges Svalbard- og Ishavs-Undersøkelser, Oslo.
> Styrar: Adolf Hoel.
> Plate no.: 505.

Spitsbergen—1949 [M203]
Svalbard: Central Vestspitsbergen, from
Surveys and Compilation by the
Cambridge Spitsbergen Expedition 1949.
[London]: Royal Geographical Society,
1952.
> 1 map ; 64 x 46 cm.
> Scale 1:125,000.
> Issued to accompany W. B. Harland's report on the
>   Cambridge Spitsbergen Expedition of 1949 in
>   *Geographical Journal* 118 pt. 3 (September
>   1952), opp. p. 330.
> Location map in left margin: Svalbard [7 x 6 cm.].
> Inset map: Index to compilation: scale 1:350,000 [with
>   table of symbols showing contributions of
>   Cambridge Spitsbergen Expeditions (1930, 1938,
>   1949), Oxford Arctic Expedition (1933),
>   Expédition Française au Spitsberg (1946) and
>   Norweigian photo survey (1925)].
> At lower right: Central Vestspitsbergen. Harland.

Spitsbergen—1949—Ice [M204]
Spitsbergen 1:666,666. [Southampton]:
Ordnance Survey, 1949.
> 1 map : col. ; 80 x 75 cm.
> Title above neat line, upper left.

Separate Maps

"Based on a 1:2,000,000 scale Norwegian map dated
    1945, with additional information compiled by
    J. I. B., 1949. Drawn and reproduced by
    Ordnance Survey, 1949."
Colored to show ice caps, glaciers, and ice-free land.
Plate no.: G.S.G.S. (Misc) 358.
Handstamp (oval, 3 x 5 cm.): S.S. control. D.R. 439—3
    Jun 1949. 1st proof. Ordnance Survey south . . .
    [remainder illegible].

SOUTHERN HEMISPHERE

Southern Hemisphere—1740   [M205]

L'hemisphere meridional pour voir plus
distinctement les terres australes. Par
Guillaume De Lisle de l'Academie Rle. des
Sciences. Amsterdam: chez Jean Cóvens et
Corneille Mortier geographes, [1740?].

    1 map : hand col. ; 43 cm. in diam. on sheet 54 x 65
        cm.
    Detached from an edition of Atlas nouveau, contenant
        toutes les parties du monde (Amsterdam: Covens
        et Mortier, [174-?]), no. [3].
    Parallel text in French and Dutch in margins: "Ou se
        voyent les nouvelles decouvertes faites en 1739
        a sud de Cap de Bonne Esperance . . . Dressée
        . . . sur la carte originale de Mr. de Lozier Bouvet
        . . . Extrait du voyage aux terres australes . . ."
    Inset: "Plan et vue des terres du Cap de la Circoncision
        [i.e. Bouvet Island, 8 x 7 cm.] . . ."
    Apparently a later state of a plate first printed without
        marginal text in 1730.
    Plate mark: 497 x 539 mm. plate mark.
    References: Cf. Phillips 595 no.3, 596 no.3; Koeman
        v.2, p.56, C&M 8, no. 3.

Southern Hemisphere—1779   [M206]

Emisfero terrestre meridionale, tagliato su
l'equatore. G. Zuliani inc. G. Pitteri scr.
Venezia: Antonio Zatta, MDCCLXXIX.

    1 map : hand col. ; 32 x 41 cm.
    Scale ca. 1:79,200,000.
    Relief shown pictorially.
    Bookworm damage, left & lower margin.
    Possibly detached from Antonio Zatta, Atlante
        novissimo (Venice, 1779–1785 [1799]) [Phillips
        651].

Southern Hemisphere—1783   [M207]

Southern Hemisphere. Engraved by Willm.
Faden. London: William Faden, 1783 Jan
13.

    1 map : hand col. ; 34 cm. in diam. on sheet 55 x 39
        cm.
    "London. Publish'd according to Act of Parliament
        Jany. 1, 1783 by William Faden, the corner of St.
        Martins Lane Charing Cross."
    Probably detached from an edition of Faden's General
        atlas (cf. Phillips 6047).
    Plate mark 37 x 37 cm.

Southern Hemisphere—1827   [M208]

Der Erde südl: Halbkugel. Augsburg bei
Joh. Walch. Augsburg: Joh. Walch,
[1827?].

    1 map : hand col. ; 18 cm. in diam. on sheet 22 x 26
        cm.
    Detached from an unidentified text; "1827" in pencil
        on verso.
    At upper right corner: 2.

SOUTH AMERICA

South America—1830   [M209]

South America. [Edinburgh]: W. H. Lizars,
[ca. 1830?].

    1 map : hand col. ; 33 x 39 cm.
    "Published by W. H. Lizars."
    Printed plate no. in upper right margin: LXI.
    Probably detached from an edition of the Edinburgh
        geographical and historical atlas (cf. Phillips 761,
        no.60).

South America—1838   [M210]

South America, Sheet V. Patagonia,
Published under the Superintendence of
the Society for the Diffusion of Useful
Knowledge. Engraved by J. & C. Walker.
London: Charles Knight & Co., Ludgate
Street 153, [1838?].

    1 map : hand col. ; 33 x 39 cm.
    Insets: Isle of Georgia [4 x 6 cm.] — The South
        Shetlands and Orkneys [10 x 17 cm.].
    MS. annotation (pencil): "1838."

ISLANDS OF THE SOUTH ATLANTIC

Ascension—1596 [M211]

Vera effigies et delineatio insulæ, Ascenscio nuncupatæ, sitæ altitudine 8 graduum, ad austrum lineæ æquinoctialis = Waerachtighe affbeeldinghe en verthooninghe vant Eylant Asçençion ofte Hemelvaert gelegen op 8 graeden aeñ zuyt zyde vande linea Equinoctial. Baptista à Doetechum sculp. [Amsterdam: Cornelis Claeszoon, 1596?].

> 3 views ; on sheet 31 x 36 cm.
> Detached from an edition of J. H. van Linschoten, *Itinerario, Voyage ofte Schipvaert* (Amsterdam: Cornelis Claeszoon, 1596 or later).
> Engraved binder's instruction, lower right: 142 en 143.
> Reference: Cf. Sabin 41356.

Estados, Islas de los—1933 [M212]

Islas de los Estados. London: Roberts, 1943.

> 1 map ; 45 x 39 cm. on sheet 59 x 49 cm.
> Added title: Carta provisional de la República Argentina.
> Photostatic reproduction of sheet "No. 104" from the 1:500,000 map series Carta provisional de la República Argentina (Buenos Aires: Instituto Geográfico Militar, 1927-).
> "Compilado año 1930. Edición Año 1933."
> Inset: Is. Orcada del Sud [10 x 27 cm.].
> MS. annotation reproduced in photostat: Argentine—Genl.
> Original has handstamp of Royal Geographical Society.
> MS. annotation (pencil) by J. M. Wordie on phototsat: "Orginal at R.G.S. This photographic copy made by Roberts' April 1943."
> Includes attached mimeograph sheet listing sources for compilation (in Spanish).

Falklands—1794 [M213]

Bowles's New One-sheet Draught of Falkland's Islands in the Latitude of 52°,, 0', South, Longitude 60,, 0', west; from London. London: Bowles and Carver, [1794].

> 1 map : hand col. ; 45 x 70 cm.

> "Printed for Bowles and Carver, No. 69 St. Paul's Church Yard. London."
> Printed on verso, at upper right: 37.
> Includes 8 profiles, 3 x 31 cm. or smaller, with collective title: A View of the Sebaldine latterly called Jasons Islands.
> Possibly detached from J. Palairet, et al., *Bowles's universal atlas* (London: Bowles and Carver, [1794–1798]) [cf. Phillips 681, no. 37].

South Georgia—1906 [M214]

Sketch of Cumberland Bay, Sketched by Lieut. A. D. Barff, R.N., H.M.S. "Sappho," Assisted by Captn. Larsen. Engraved by Davies & Company. London: Admiralty, 1906.

> 1 map ; 48 x 35 cm., on sheet 52 x 70 cm.
> "Published at the Admiralty 7th July 1906, under the superintendence of Rear-Admiral A. Mostyn Field . . . Hydrographer; Small corrections II-07 I-12 VII-12 II-13 III-17 IV-18."
> "Sold by J. D. Potter, agent for the sale of the Admiralty charts, 145 Minories."
> Ancillary maps: Southern Ocean: South Georgia [18 x 30 cm.] — Royal Bay [11 x 18 cm.] — Moltke Harbor [11 x 12 cm.] — Cumberland Bay: King Edward Cove [18 x 30 cm.].
> G.B. Hyd. Dept. Pl. No.: 3579.
> Handstamped "Increase 50%."

South Georgia—1927 [M215]

Sketch of Cumberland Bay, by Lieut.-Com. W. G. Benn, R.N., Assisted by Sub-Lieut. E. R. Milner, R.N., H.M.S. "Dartmouth." Engraved by Davies & Company. London: Admiralty, 1927.

> 1 map ; 48 x 35 cm., on sheet 52 x 70 cm.
> "Published at the Admiralty 7th July 1906, under the superintendence of Rear-Admiral A. Mostyn Field . . . Hydrographer. New edition 29th Aug. 1921; Small corrections 1921—1842 11-1—2018—11-26—12-7 1922—1-27—1399—1924—8-28 1926—47—6-17—1515—1927—3-4—860—1342."
> "Sold by J. D. Potter, agent for the sale of the Admiralty charts, 145 Minories."
> Ancillary maps: Southern Ocean: South Georgia [18 x 30 cm.] — Royal Bay [11 x 18 cm.] — Moltke Harbor [11 x 12 cm.] — Cumberland Bay: King Edward Cove [18 x 30 cm.] — Bay of Isles [8 x 13 cm.].
> G.B. Hyd. Dept. Pl. No.: 3579.
> Handstamped at upper right: 269 28, Increase 50%.

South Georgia—1934   [M216]

Harbours and Anchorages in South
Georgia. London: Admiralty, 1934.

    8 maps ; various sizes, on sheet 53 x 71 cm.
    "Published at the Admiralty 12th Sept. 1930, under the
        superintendence of Rear-Admiral H. P. Douglas
        . . . Hydrographer. New edition 8th May 1931;
        Small corrections 1931—8–11—1934 -(XII-7)."
    Contents: Barff Point to Cape George, surveyed by
        Lieut. Commr. J. M. Chaplin, R.N., assisted by
        Midshipman W. P. O'Connor, R.N.R. —
        Stromness Bay: Husvik Harbour — Cumberland
        Bay: Maiviken — Stromness Bay: Stromness
        Harbour — Cumberland Bay: Jason Harbour —
        Elsehul (Else Bay) — Pleasant Cove — Right
        Whale Bay.
    Blank rectangle in lower right (11 x 11 cm.).
    At upper right: 121.45.
    G.B. Hyd. Dept. Pl. No.: 3589.

South Georgia—1938   [M217]

Harbours and Anchorages in South
Georgia, Surveyed by Lieut. Commr. J. M.
Chaplin, R.N., Assisted by Midshipman
W. P. O'Connor, R.N., R.R.S. "Discovery"
Expedition 1926–1930. London:
Admiralty, 1938.

    10 maps ; various sizes, on sheet 104 x 71 cm.
    "Published at the Admiralty 21st Sept. 1931, under the
        superintendence of Vice-Admiral H. P. Douglas
        . . . Hydrographer. New edition 8th May 1931;
        Small corrections 1935—(1–4) 8–5–1937—12–7
        1938—703—1094."
    Contents: Prince Olaf Harbour and approaches —
        Fortuna Bay — Prince Olaf Harbour: North Bay
        — Willis and Bird Islands — Cape Buller to Cape
        Constance — Undine Habour — Larsen Harbour
        — Approaches to Undine Harbour — Blue
        Whale Harbour — Leith Harbour.
    At upper right: 169.43.
    G.B. Hyd. Dept. Pl. No.: 3589.

South Georgia—1938   [M218]

South Georgia. Soundings Mainly from
Surveys by Lieut. Commr. J. M. Chaplin,
R.N., R.R.S. "Discovery" Expeditions,
1925–1930. Topography from Surveys by
the South Georgia Survey Expeditions,
1951–1957, under the Leadership of Mr.
Duncan Carse. London: Admiralty, 1958.

    1 map ; 64 x 98 cm.
    "Published at the Admiralty 23rd May 1958, under the
        superintendence of Rear-Admiral K. St. B. Collins
        . . . Hydrographer. New edition 8th May 1931."
    At upper right: 156.58.
    G.B. Hyd. Dept. Pl. No.: 3597.

South Georgia—1939   [M219]

Harbours and Anchorages in South
Georgia. London: Admiralty, 1939.

    5 maps ; various sizes, on sheet 53 x 71 cm.
    "Published at the Admiralty 7th July 1906, under the
        superintendence of Rear-Admiral A. Mostyn Field
        . . . Hydrographer. New editions 29th Aug.
        1921, 24th May 1929, 15th Aug. 1930; Small
        corrections 1930—1502 1931-4-30—(VII-21)—
        1932—7–9 1934—8–6 1939—1101."
    Contents: Sketch of Cumberland Bay, by Lieut. Comr.
        W. G. Benn assisted by Sub-Lieut. E. R. Miller
        [and] corrections by Lieut. Comr. J. M. Chaplin
        [48 x 36 cm.] — Stromness Bay, by . . . Benn
        [and] . . . Chaplin [18 x 30 cm.] — Royal Bay [11
        x 18 cm.] — Moltke Harbor [11 x 12 cm.] —
        Cumberland Bay: King Edward Cove, by . . .
        Benn [and] . . . Milner [18 x 30 cm.].
    At upper right: 297.45.
    G.B. Hyd. Dept. Pl. No.: 3579.

South Georgia—1957   [M220]

Approaches to South Georgia, from the
Latest Information in the Hydrographic
Department to 1957. London: Admiralty,
1958.

    1 map ; 64 x 97 cm.
    Added title: South Atlantic Ocean.
    "Published at the Admiralty, 23rd May, 1958, under
        the superintendence of Rear Admiral K. St. B.
        Collins . . . Hydrographer."
    G.B. Hyd. Dept. Pl. No.: 3596.

South Georgia—1957   [M221]

Falkland Islands Dependencies. South
Georgia, Surveyed under the Leadership of
Duncan Carse by the South Georgia
Survey Expeditions of 1951–52, 1953–54,
and 1955–56, with Minor Additions from
G. Sutton's Expedition of 1954–55, and
from Admiralty Charts. [London?: s.n.,
1957?].

    1 map ; 122 x 163 cm. on 3 sheets each 64 x 90 cm.

Scale 1:100,000.
"Surveyors: G. Smillie and J. B. Heaney, 1951–52. G.
Smillie, 1953–54. Captain A. G. Bomford R.E.
and S. Paterson, 1955–56."
In lower right margin of each sheet: 500/5/57 S.P.C.,
R.E.

South Orkneys—1943   [M222]
South Orkney Islands. London: Admiralty,
[1943?].

8 maps ; on sheet 71 x 104 cm.
Maps variously attributed to A. L. Nelson and officers
of the ship Discovery II, and Dr. W. S. Bruce and
the Scottish National Antarctic Expedition.
Title proper from largest of maps.
Added title (above title proper): Antarctic Ocean.
"Published at Admiralty, 17th Aug. 1934, under the
superintendence of Captain J. A. Edgell . . .
Hydrographer; Small corrections—1935—3–1—
7–1 1937–1-4—4–2 1938—(II-4)—1943—5–12."
Contents: South Orkney Islands [38 x 83 cm.] —
Sandefjord Bay [15 x 14 cm.] — Uruguay Cove
[9 x 14 cm.] — Queens or Borge Bay [15 x 22
cm.] — Powell Island and Washington Strait [26
x 21 cm.] — Scotia Bay and Mill Cove [26 x 31
cm.] — Ellefsen Harbour [26 x 22 cm.] — Signy
Island [23 x 22 cm.].
G.B. Hyd. Dept. Pl. No.: 1775.
At upper right: 342.45.

South Sandwich Islands—1820   [M223]
South Sandwich Islands, as Charted by
Capt. James Cook, R.N., H.M.S.
"Resolution" in 1775; and by Capt. F. G.
Bellingshausen, I.R.N., S.M.S. "Vostok" &
"Mirnii," in 1820. Compiled by Lieut.-
Commdr. R. T. Gould, R.N. July 1927.
London: Admiralty, 1927.

1 map : col. ; 46 x 32 cm.
"Produced by the Hydrographic Dept. of the
Admiralty, 12th Sept. 1927, under the
superintendence of Rear Admiral H. P. Douglas
. . . Hydrographer. Printed by H. M. Stationery
Office."
Title proper above border in upper margin.
Added title (lower right, within neat line): Mercator
chart of the South Sandwich Islands and the
recently discovered Marquis de Traverse Is. 1820.
Includes "Note" on map sources, 9 lines of text.
MS. note (pencil), upper margin: Not on sale. Given
me by Hydrographer. [initialed] J.M.W[ordie].
G.B. Hyd. Dept. Pl. No.: Misc. 32.
At upper right: 325.27.

South Sandwich Islands—1939   [M224]
South Sandwich Islands, Surveyed by Sub.
Lieut. A. L. Nelson, R.N.R., and the
Officers and Scientific Staff, R.R.S.
"Discovery II," 1930, under the Direction
of Dr. Samuel Kemp, Director of Research.
Commr. W. M. Carey, R.N. in Command.
London: Admiralty, 1939.

1 map ; 98 x 64 cm.
Added title: Southern Ocean.
"Published at the Admiralty, 22nd Novr. 1930, under
the superintendence of Vice Admiral H. P.
Douglas . . . Hydrographer."
"New edition 15th Jan. 1932. Large corrections 14th
Feby. 1936; Small corrections—1939—11-28."
G.B. Hyd. Dept. Pl. No.: 3593.
At upper right: 292.45.
Insets: Candlemas Islands. Nelson Strait [16 x 16 cm.]
— Thule or Morrell Island. Ferguson Bay [12 x 13
cm.].

South Shetlands—1821   [M225]
A Chart of New South Britain Discovered
by Captain Smith in the Brig Williams the
19th of February 1819. Drawn by William
Henry Goddard. [Taunton: Hydrographic
Dept., 1941].

1 map (manuscript facsimile) ; 50 x 77 cm.
Photographic reproduction of manuscript map in the
Hydrographic Department.
MS. annotation reproduced from original: Received
from the Record Office 3rd January 1822.
Insets: On the coast of New South Britain between 62°
and 63° [S.] latitude [17 x 18 cm.]. — George's
Bay [18 x 31 cm.].
Profile: First appearance of the land discovered by the
Williams . . . [5 x 31 cm.].
Handstamped: Hydrographic Department. Copy of
original document.
Typed label (7 x 16 cm.) pasted to lower right margin
of reproduction: Chart accompanying Memorial
from William Smith to the Lords Commissioners
of the Admiralty, December 1821. Endorsement
on back with date 3 January 1822, rewritten on
face of chart after 1913. See *Geographical
Journal* xciv, 316 October 1939. Map F.
Geographical Review xxi. 491 July 1941.
MS. annotation (pencil), to right of label: J. M. Wordie.

South Shetlands—1821   [M226]
Georges Bay. [Taunton: Hydrographic
Dept., 1941].

1 map (manuscript facsimile) ; 39 x 64 cm.
Photographic reproduction of manuscript map in the Hydrographic Department.
Profile insets: Martins Island [4 x 12 cm.] — Penguin Island from the anchorage [5 x 10 cm.] — Cape Melville [5 x 13 cm.].
Handstamped: Hydrographic Department. Copy of original document.
Typed label (6 x 16 cm.) pasted to lower right of reproduction: Bransfield's plan of Georges Bay, South Shetlands. See Geographical Journal xciv, 315 October 1939. Map D. Geographical Review xxi. 491 July 1941.
MS. annotation (pencil), lower left: J. M. Wordie.

South Shetlands—1822   [M227]

A Chart of New or South Shetland, Seen in 1819 by Willm. Smith, Master of the Brig Williams, Surveyed by E. Bransfield, Master R.N. in 1820. J. Walker sculpt. [London]: Published According to Act of Parliament by Capt. Hurd R.N., Hydrographer to the Admiralty, 1822 Nov 30.

1 map ; 42 x 59 cm.
"N.B. This land was known to the old navigators and said to be first discovered by Theodore Gerrards in 1599."
No plate no.
Includes 10 coastal profiles.

South Shetlands—1822   [M228]

Chart of South Shetland, Including Coronation Island, &c., from the Exploration of the Sloop Dove, in the Years 1821 and 1822, by George Powell, Commander of the Same. London: R. H. Laurie, 1822 Nov 1.

1 map ; 59 x 91 cm.
"Published by R. H. Laurie, chartseller to the Admiralty &c. &c. No. 53, Fleet Street, London Novr. 1st 1822."
"Powell's Group [i.e. South Orkney Islands] was discovered on the 6th of December 1821, by the constructer of this chart. . . ."
Profile inset: Appearance of the land, from Desolation Island to Table Island [4 x 33 cm.].
Several repairs on verso.

South Shetlands—1909   [M229]

South Shetlands and Adjoining Islands and Lands Compiled from the Latest Information in the Hydrographic Office. Engraved by Malby & Sons. London: Admiralty, 1909.

1 map ; 65 x 97 cm.
"Published at the Admiralty 1st June 1901, under the superintendence of Rear-Admiral Sir W. J. L. Wharton . . . Hydrographer. New edition July 1909."
"Sold by J. D. Potter, agent for the sale of the Admiralty charts, 145 Minories."
Insets: Deception I., surveyed by Commr. H. Foster . . . 1829 [25 x 18 cm.] — St. George Bay anchorage, surveyed by E. Bransfield . . . 1820 [11 x 12 cm.].
Handstamped in upper right: 209 13.
G.B. Hyd. Dept. Pl. No.: 3205.

South Shetlands—1910   [M230]

The Shetland and South Orkney Islands with the Tracks of the Several Discoverers. J. & C. Walker sculpt. London: Admiralty, 1917.

1 map ; 46 x 65 cm.
"Magnetic variation in 1910 . . ."
"Published at . . . the Hydrographic Office . . . Septr. 7th 1839. Large corrections, 1844; April, 1887, Aug. 1914, Mar. 1901, Sep. 1908; Small corrections X-93 IX-05 VI-09 XI-10 IV-17."
"Sold by R. B. Bate, agent for the Admiralty Charts, 145 Minories."
MS. note (pencil), left margin: "Given me by Adml. Parry to show nomenclature changes, Oct. 1917 [initialed] J.M.W[ordie]."
MS. annotations in pencil, ink, and colored pencil.
G.B. Hyd. Dept. Pl. No.: 1238.
At upper right: 323.14.

South Shetlands—1949   [M231]

Plans in the South Shetland Islands. London: Admiralty, 1949.

8 maps : col. ; on sheet 104 x 71 cm.
Scales vary.
Added title: Preliminary chart.
"Published at the Admiralty, 9th July, 1949, under the superintendence of Rear-Admiral A. G. N. Wyatt . . . Hydrographer; Small corrections 1949— 1309—1897—91–13."
Maps variously attributed to the crews of R.R.S. Discovery and Discovery II, including A. L. Nelson, L. C. Hill, Dr. J. B. Charcot, J. M. Chaplin
Contents: South Shetland Islands. Livingston Island to King George Island [31 x 65 cm.] — Desolation Island [29 x 36 cm.] — Greenwich Island. Yankee

Harbour [21 x 29 cm.] — King George Island.
Admiralty Bay [33 x 20 cm.] — Admiralty Bay.
Visca Anchorage [17 x 14 cm.] — Nelson Island.
Harmony Cove [26 x 28 cm.] — King George
Island. Marian Cove [16 x 21 cm.] — King
George Island. King George Bay [15 x 22 cm.].
G.B. Hyd. Dept. Pl. No.: 1774.
At upper right: 277.49.

South Shetlands—1955   [M232]
Deception Island, Surveyed by Lieut.
Commr. D. N. Penfold, D.S.C., R.N.,
1948–49. London: Admiralty, 1955.
> 1 map : col. ; 65 x 66 cm., on sheet 71 x 104 cm.
> "Natural scale 1/50,000 (lat. 62°57')."
> Added title: South Shetland Islands.
> "Published at the Admiralty 23rd Sept. 1949, under
>   the superintendence of Vice-Admiral Sir Guy
>   Wyatt . . . Hydrographer. New editions 27th
>   Nov. 1953, 30th Sept. 1955."
> Ancillary maps: Deception Island: Whalers Bay and
>   approaches [36 x 46 cm.] — Pendulum Cove [14
>   x 14 cm.].
> Blank rectangle in lower left (29 x 31 cm.).
> Printing proof with paste-on notice: "Note: In addition
>   to any coloured areas shown on this chart,
>   corrections have been made as follows . . ."
> In upper right: 279.55.
> G.B. Hyd. Dept. Pl. No.: 3202.

South Shetlands—1957   [M233]
South Shetland Islands and Bransfield
Strait, Compiled from the Latest
Information in the Hydrographic
Department, 1956, Including Surveys by
R.R.S. "Discovery" and Falkland Islands
Dependencies Survey. London: Admiralty,
1957.
> 1 map : col. ; 64 x 98 cm.
> "Natural scale 1/500,000 (lat. 67°)."
> Added title: Antarctica.
> "Published at the Admiralty 23rd Sept. 1949, under
>   the superintendence of Vice-Admiral Sir Guy
>   Wyatt . . . Hydrographer. New editions 12th
>   Feb. 1954, 15th March 1957."
> Printing proof with paste-on notice: "Note: In addition
>   to any coloured areas shown on this chart,
>   corrections have been made as follows . . ."
> In upper right: 100.57.
> G.B. Hyd. Dept. Pl. No.: 3205.

ISLANDS OF THE SOUTH PACIFIC

Peter I Island—1929   [M234]
Peter I's Öy, ved Nils Larsen, Norvegia-
Ekspedisjonen 1928–29. Olso: Ing. Dahls
Opmåling, 1929.
> 1 map ; 62 x 81 cm.
> Scale 1:50,000.
> Monogram "ER" [?] in lower right.

Various Islands—1941   [M235]
Island and Anchorages in the Southern
Ocean. London: Admiralty, 1941.
> 11 maps ; on sheet 104 x 71 cm.
> Scales vary.
> "Published at the Admiralty, 20th March 1917, under
>   the superintendence of Rear-Admiral J. F. Parry
>   . . . Hydrographer; Small corrections 1919—
>   1936 1921–2-18—10–21 1927—10–1—1930—
>   10–1—11–1 1931—10–1 1932—(IX-23) 1939–3-
>   1—1940—9–17—1941 3–29."
> Maps variously attributed to officers of the following
>   ships: Hinemoa, Lizard, Ringdove, Kekeno, Terror
>   and Aurora. Named officers include D. Mawson,
>   Captn. Fairchild, W. R. Willis, J. B. Grey, J. E.
>   Davis, J. C. Ross, T. Musgrave, J. Edwards, and
>   C. T. Tucker.
> Contents: Macquarie Island [95 x 47 cm.] —
>   Macquarie Island : Hasselborough Bay [17 x 18
>   cm.] — Bounty Islands [15 x 17 cm.]—Antipodes
>   Islands [14 x 17 cm.] — Auckland Is.-Carnley Hbr.
>   : Camp Cove [9 x 10 cm.] — Antipodes Is. :
>   Depôt Anchorage [9 x 10 cm.] — Campbell
>   Island : South or Perserverance Harbour [11 x 21
>   cm.] — Auckland Is. : Hanfield Inlet [7 x 16 cm.]
>   — Auckland Islands [22 x 16 cm.] — Campbell
>   Island [14 x 16 cm.] — Auckland Islands : Port
>   Ross or Sarah's Bosom Harbour [20 x 35 cm.].
> G.B. Hyd. Dept. Pl. No.: 1022.
> At upper right: 102.45.

ISLANDS OF THE INDIAN OCEAN

Kerguélen, Iles de—1788   [M236]
Terre de Kerguelen, appellée par M. Cook,
Isle de la Désolation. Par M. Bonne,
Ingénieur-Hydrographe de la Marine.
Bonne Fil, del?. André sculp. [Paris?: s.n.,
ca. 1788?].

1 map ; 23 x 21 cm. on sheet 32 x 48 cm.
At upper left: Cook, 3e. Voyage.
At upper right: 140.
In MS. (pencil, bookdealer's date?) on verso: 1788.
Insets: Isles découvertes par Mr. Marion du Fresne en
1772; appellées par M. Cook en 1776, Isles du
Prince Edouard [7 x 6 cm.] — Plan du Port
Palliser dans la Terre Kerguelen [12 x 12 cm.] —
Plan du Havre de Noël dans la Terre de
Kerguelen [10 x 12 cm.].
Similar to map in Cook, James. Troisième voyage de
Cook (Paris: Hôtel de Thou, 1785) [cf. Mickwitz
and Miekkavaara, v.3, p. 50, atlas no. 405, map
no. 2].

Kerguélen, Iles de—1949   [M237]

Indian Ocean. Ports and Anchorages in
Iles de Kerguelen from French
Government Charts to 1946. London:
Admiralty, 1949.

19 maps : col. ; various sizes, on 1 sheet 104 x 71 cm.
"Published at the Admiralty 7th June 1946, under the
superintendence of Rear Admiral A. G. N. Wyatt,
Hydrographer. New edition 28th Jan. 1949."
Contents: Port Curieuse — Baie de l'Oiseau — Port
Roland Bonaparte — Port Edmond Perrier —
Port Matha — Baie du Hopeful — Port Fallières
— Port Jules Girard — Baie du Yacht Club —
Port Couvreux — Port d'Hiver — Baie du
Hopeful: Cascade Lozère — Bassin de la Gazelle
— Port Elisabeth — Baie Accessible — Baie du
Morbihan: Port des Iles — Port Jeanne d'Arc —
Anse Betsy — Port Navalo.
Graphic index to above ports on Admiralty chart no.
2398, "Isles de Kerguelen" (1954).
Printing proof with paste on-notice: "Note: In addition
to any coloured areas shown on this chart,
corrections have been made as follows . . ."
In upper right: 38.49.
G.B. Hyd. Dept. Pl. No.: 800.

Kerguélen, Isles de—1954   [M238]

Southern Ocean. Iles de Kerguelen from
the French Government Charts to 1946.
London: Admiralty, [1954].

1 map : col. ; 64 x 98 cm.
"Published at the Admiralty 2nd Nov. 1951, under the
superintendence of Rear-Admiral A. Day . . .
Hydrographer. New edition 26th Feb. 1954."
"With additions and corrections to 1952."
Inset map: Isles de Kerguelen: index to plans on chart
no. 800 ["Ports . . . Iles de Kerguelen" (Admiralty,
1949)].

Inset profiles: View A: lat. 48°39'45" S., long.
69°11'30" E. — View B: lat. 48°56'45" S., long.
70°11'10" E. — View C: lat. 49°47'00" S., long.
68°54'00" E. — View D: lat. 49°29'30" S., long.
70°24'00" E.
Printing proof with paste-on notice: "Note: In addition
to any coloured areas shown on this chart,
corrections have been made as follows . . ."
In upper right: 67.54.
G.B. Hyd. Dept. Pl. No.: 2398.

ANTARCTICA

Antarctica—1630   [M239]

Polus Antarcticus. Henricus Hondius
excudit. [Amsterdam]: Hondius, [ca.
1630].

1 map : hand col. ; 43 cm. in diam.
Scale ca. 1:37,000,000.
Relief shown pictorially.
Prime meridian: [Ferro].
French text, "Description dv Pole Antarctiqve" on
verso.

Antarctica—1650   [M240]

Polus Antarcticus. Ioannes Iansonnius
excudit. [Amsterdam]: Iansonnius, [ca.
1650].

1 map : hand col. ; 43 cm. in diam.
Relief shown pictorially.
Text in Latin on verso: Polus Antarcticus. 103, 104.
Later state of map first published by Hondius [ca.
1630].
Probably detached from Jan Jansson, *Atlantis majoris*
(Amsterdam, 1650) [Koeman ME 164 (11)].

Antarctica—1680   [M241]

[Polus Antarcticus]. [Amsterdam: s.n., ca.
1680].

1 map : hand col. ; 43 cm. in diam.
Dealer's note on verso: Visscher ca. 1680.
Relief shown pictorially.
Prime meridian: [Ferro].
Ms. "64," upper right; verso blank.
Apparently a later state of map published by Hondius
[ca. 1630] and Jansson [ca. 1650], but lacking
title cartouche.

Antarctica—1690 [M242]

Polo australe, ò meridionale, & antartico. [Venice: Coronelli, ca. 1690].

1 map ; 36 cm. in diam. on sheet 66 x 49 cm.

South polar calotte from Coronelli's 3½ foot globe (ca. 1690).

Elaborate cartouche at top includes 15 lines of text on discoveries. Bottom half of diagram includes 112 lines of text between 70–75° S, including the following heading: Del sito, distanza, divisione, e differenti habitatori della terra; no geographic features are shown.

Probably detached from an edition of M. V. Coronelli, *Libro dei globi* (Venice, 1693).

Antarctica—1754 [M243]

Carte des Terres Australes, comprises entre le tropique du Capricorne et le pole Antarcticque, par Phillipe Buache. Delahaye sculps. Paris: [s.n.], 1754.

1 map : hand col. ; 24 cm. in diam. on sheet 44 x 57 cm.

Scale ca. 1:70,000,000 at the Pole.

Beneath title: Ou voyant les nouvelles decouvertes faites in 1739 . . . Partes ordres de Mrs. de la Compagnie des Indes.

"Dressee sur les Memoires et sur la carte original de Mr. de Lozier Bouvet, charge de cette expedition."

"Sous le Privilege de l'Academie Rle. des Sciences le 5 Septembre 1739; Augmentee de diverses vues physiques &c., 1754."

Relief shown pictorially.

Prime meridians: Ferro, Paris.

Inset: Plan et vue des Terres du Cap de la Circoncision.

Includes historical annotations and text: Extrait du voyage aux Terres Australes.

MS. "16" in lower right.

Antarctica—1763 [M244]

Chart of the Antarctic Polar Circle, with the Countries Adjoining, According to the New Hypothesis of M. Buache. From the Memoirs of the Royal Academy at Paris. [Gent. Mag. Jan. 1763]. [London], 1763.

1 map : hand col. ; 19 cm. x 21 cm.

Detached from *Gentleman's Magazine* 33 (1763), opp. p. 32.

Closely trimmed, resulting in loss of "Gent. Mag. Jan. 1763" in upper right.

MS. "23" on verso.

Based on Buache's "Carte des Terres Australes . . ." published in Paris, 1739 and 1754.

References: Klein, G63.1; Tooley Ant., no.63; Jolly, v.1 p.68 (GENT 166).

Copy 1 of 2.

Antarctica—1763 [M245]

Chart of the Antarctic Polar Circle, with the Countries Adjoining, According to the New Hypothesis of M. Buache. From the Memoirs of the Royal Academy at Paris. Gent. Mag. Jan. 1763. [London], 1763.

1 map: hand col. ; 19 x 21 cm.

Detached from *Gentleman's Magazine* 33 (1763), opp. p. 32.

Based on Buache's "Carte des Terres Australes . . ." published in Paris, 1739 and 1754.

References: Klein, G63.1; Tooley Ant., no.63; Jolly, v.1 p.68 (GENT 166).

Copy 2 of 2.

Antarctica—1776 [M246]

A Map of the South Pole, with the Track of his Majesty's Sloop Resolution in Search of a Southern Continent. [T. Bowen sculpt]. [London, 1776].

1 map ; 21 cm. in diam.

Scale ca. 1:65,000,000.

Thomas Bowen's name trimmed from lower right.

Detached from *Gentleman's Magazine* 46 (January 1776), opp. p.16.

Shows tracks from Cook's second voyage, 1773–1774.

References: Jolly, David C. Maps in British periodicals (1990), part 1, p.79, GENT-241; Klein, C.M. Maps in eighteenth-century British magazines, [no.] G76.1

Handstamp on verso: Inner Temple.

Copy 1 of 2.

Antarctica—1776 [M247]

A Map of the South Pole, with the Track of his Majesty's Sloop Resolution in Search of a Southern Continent. [T. Bowen sculpt]. [London, 1776].

1 map ; 21 cm. in diam.

Scale ca. 1:65,000,000.

Detached from *Gentleman's Magazine* 46 (January 1776), opp. p.16.

Shows tracks from Cook's second voyage, 1773–1774.

References: Jolly, David C. Maps in British periodicals (1990), part 1, p.79, GENT-241; Klein, C.M. Maps

in eighteenth-century British magazines, [no.]
G76.1
Handstamp on verso: Inner Temple.
Copy 2 of 2.

Antarctica—1807 [M248]

Countries Surrounding the South Pole.
Neele sculp Strand. London: J. Wilkes,
1807.

> 1 map : hand col. ; 19 cm. in diam.
> "London. Pubd. as the Act directs Octr. 19th 1807, by
> J. Wilkes."

Antarctica—1841 [M249]

Chart of the South Polar Sea. London:
Admiralty, [1841?].

> 1 map ; 61 cm. in diam.
> "Publd. according to Act of Parliament, at the Hydroc.
> Office of the Admiralty, June 1839 and sold by
> R. B. Bate , 21 Poultry."
> Shows various explorer's routes.
> MS. note (pencil) written by J. M. Wordie [?], lower
> margin: "Admiralty-published 1839 (but includes
> Ross' track 1840–41 though not 1841–42 +
> 1842–43)."
> G.B. Hyd. Dept. Pl. No.: 1240.

Antarctica—1842 [M250]

Carta generale dell'Antartica. Benedetto
Marzolla esequi col pennello su pietra, Real
Litografia Militare, Napoli 1842. Naples:
Benedetto Marzolla, 1842.

> 1 map : hand col. ; 34 x 49 cm. on sheet 50 x 65 cm.
> Title from top margin.
> Added title, from center of map: Polo Antartico.
> Detached from an atlas; printed no. "15" on verso.
> Chronological table in upper right: Indicazioni
> de'viaggi intorno al Polo antartico. . . .
> Italian text in bottom margin concluding "Napoli
> Novembre 1842."

Antarctica—1872 [M251]

Southern Regions. New York: G. W. &
C. B. Colton & Co., 1855.

> 1 map : hand col. ; 36 x 34 cm.
> "Entered according to act of Congress . . . by J. H.
> Colton. . . ."
> Detached from a Colton atlas, ca. 1872, map no. 14.
> 3 columns of text on verso with title North America.

Antarctica—1886 [M252]

Süd-Polar-Karte, von A. Petermann. Gest.
v. H. Alt u. Stichart. Gotha: Justus Perthes,
[1886?].

> 1 map : col. ; 34 cm. in diam.
> Scale 1:40,000,000.
> Detached from an edition of Adolf Stieler's *Hand Atlas*
> [cf. Phillips 6238].
> "Umarbeitung 1881. Rev. 1886."
> At upper right: Stieler's Hand-Atlas, no. 11.
> Surrounded by 15 inset maps, various sizes.

Antarctica—1904 [M253]

South Polar Chart. Edinburgh, London:
W. & A. K. Johnston, [after 1904?].

> 1 map : col. ; 43 x 32 cm.
> Detached from an atlas; at lower right: Frontispiece.
> "Engraved, printed and published by W. & A. K.
> Johnston, LImited, Edinburgh & London."
> "Approximate route of Lieutenant Shackleton's
> expedition" in red.
> Includes notes on history of exploration; none dated
> later than 1904.
> MS. annotations (pencil) by J. M. Wordie.

Antarctica—1905 [M254]

Chart of the South Polar Regions, by J. G.
Bartholomew, F.R.S., 1905. [Edinburgh]:
The Edinburgh Geographical Institute,
1905.

> 1 map : col. ; 64 x 64 cm
> 6 inset maps [col. ; 10 x 11 cm.] show history of
> Antarctic exploration from 1760—1903.
> Manuscript annotations in pencil note expedition
> routes in 1909–10, 1928, 1937, and 1947.
> Sectioned, mounted on cloth, and issued folded to 36
> x 29 cm.

Antarctica—1909 [M255]

The Antarctic Regions. London: Stanford's
Geographical Establishment, [1909 or
later].

> 1 map : col. ; 51 x 60 cm.
> "Scale 1:22,429,440. . . ."
> Detached from an edition of Stanford's *London atlas of
> universal geography*.
> "London: Edward Stanford, 12, 13, & 14, Long Acre.
> W.C."
> "London atlas series. 20106."
> Shows routes of exploration through 1909.

Antarctica—1910—Ice [M256]

Ice Chart of the Southern Hemisphere . . . 1874. Originally Prepared for Publication in 1866 by Staff Comr. F. J. Evans, and G. J. McDougall, Master R.N. Engraved by Malby & Sons. London: Admiralty, [1910].

> 1 map : col. ; 61 cm. in diam.
> "Compiled from the voyages of Cook 1772–5, Bellingshausen 1819–21, Weddell 1822–4, Foster 1828–9, Biscoe 1830–2, Balleny 1839, D'Urville 1839, Wilkes 1839, Ross 1841[-]3, Scott 1901–4, and Shackleton 1908–9."
> "Drawn by R. C. Carrington, Hyd. Off: Small corrections X-10."
> "Published at the Admiralty 20th Jany. 1874, under the superintendence of Rear Admiral G. H. Richards . . . Hydrographer. Sold by J. D. Potter, agent for the sale of the Admiralty charts, 145 Minories. New editions October 1874, April 1897, March 1910."
> Show limits of pack-ice and icebergs.
> Includes 3 paragraphs of text.
> G.B. Hyd. Dept. Pl. No.: 1241.
> At upper right: 19.1.

Antarctica—1913 [M257]

The Antarctic Regions. London: Stanford's Geographical Establishment, [1913 or later].

> 1 map : col. ; 51 x 60 cm.
> "Scale 1:22,402,000. . . ."
> Detached from an edition of Stanford's *London atlas of universal geography.*
> "London: Edward Stanford, Ltd., 12, 13, & 14, Long Acre. W.C."
> "London atlas series. 11214."
> Shows routes of exploration through 1913.

Antarctica—1914 [M258]

South Polar Chart, from Various Authorities with Amendments and Additions to 1912. London: Admiralty, 1914.

> 1 map ; 65 x 97 cm.
> "Engraved by Davies & Company."
> "Published at the Admiralty, 1st June, 1901, under the superintendence of Rear Admiral Sir W. J. L. Wharton . . . Hydrographer."
> "Sold by J. D. Potter, agent for the sale of the Admiralty charts, 145 Minories."

> "New editions Octr. 1906, March 1910, 4th Jany. 1911, 9th Octr. 1914."
> Details coastline of Victoria Land and sledge routes taken by Scott (1902–3 and 1911–2), Shackleton (1908–9), and Amundsen (1911–2).
> G.B. Hyd. Dept. Pl. No.: 3177.

Antarctica—1914 [M259]

South Polar Chart, from Various Authorities with Amendments and Additions to 1912. Magnetic Variation Curves for 1912. Engraved by Malby & Sons. London: Admiralty, 1912.

> 1 map ; 64 x 82 cm.
> "Published at the Admiralty, 20th May, 1887, under the superintendence of Captain W. J. L. Wharton . . . Hydrographer."
> "New edition April 1910, 9th Octr. 1914."
> Shows routes of Shackleton, Scott and Amundsen.
> MS. annotations in pencil.
> G.B. Hyd. Dept. Pl. No.: 1240.
> At upper right: 289.14.

Antarctica—1914 [M260]

Antarctic Ocean, Sheet[s] I [through] VIII. London: Admiralty, 1914.

> 2 maps ; on 8 sheets each 70 x 102 cm.
> "Engraved by Malby & Sons."
> "Published at the Admiralty . . . under the superintendence of Rear Admiral Sir W. J. L. Wharton . . . Hydrographer."
> "Sold by J. D. Potter, agent for the sale of the Admiralty charts, 145 Minories."
> Sheets I-VII show adjacent regions between latitudes 60–75°S.
> Sheet VIII (covering 115°W/115°E—67°S/85°S) details Victoria Land coastline and shows sledge routes of Scott (1902–3 and 1911–2), Shackleton (1908–9), and Amundsen (1911–2).
> G.B. Hyd. Dept. Pl. Nos.: 3170, 3171, 3172, 3173, 3174, 3175, 3176, 3206.
> Later issued as: Antarctic Regions, sheet[s] I [through] VIII [1940?–1943?], see M 264 below.

Antarctica—1929 [M261]

Byrd's South Pole Flight, Nov. 29, 1929 3:30 a.m. to 10:07 p.m. Greenwich Mean Time, Constructed by Harold E. Saunders from Navigation Records of Richard E. Byrd, Aerial Photographs by Ashley C.

McKinley and from Surveys by Laurence
M. Gould and Roald Amundsen.
[Baltimore: A. Hoen & Co., 1932].

 1 map : col. ; 32 x 9 cm.
 Scale 1:4,000,000.
 Inset map trimmed from National Geographic Society's
  map "The Antarctic regions" (col. ; 46 x 64 cm.):
  issued in *National Geographic Magazine* 62 (Oct.
  1932), opp. p.484.
 Byrd's route shown in red.
 Mounted on cardboard sheet, 36 x 21 cm.
 Shows names of individual mountains in the Queen
  Maud Range.
 Manuscript inscription (no date): Dear Manny — Here
  is your mountain. It is an historical landmark —
  the western portal of one of the famous glaciers
  of history. With it goes my best wishes. Dick Byrd
  [Emanuel Cohen of Paramount Pictures edited
  the film "With Byrd at the South Pole" (1930); see
  P15 below. "Mt. Cohen" is shown just west of
  Axel Heiberg Glacier].
 Geographic coordinates: E 155°—W 120°/S 78°—S
  90°.
 Oriented with south at top.

Antarctica—1932 [M262]

The Antarctic Regions, Compiled and
Drawn in the Cartographic Section of the
National Geographic Society for the
National Geographic Magazine. Baltimore:
A. Hoen & Co., 1932.

 1 map : col. ; 47 x 55 cm.
 Scale ca. 1:16,000,000.
 "A. Hoen & Co., lithographers, Baltimore, Md."
 Insets variously attributed to H. E. Saunders, A. C.
  McKinley, L. M. Gould, and R. Amundsen.
 Insets: Byrd's South Pole flight, Nov. 29, 1929 . . . [33
  x 9 cm.]. — Antarctic Archipelago [17 x 10 cm.].
  — King Edward VII Land and part of Marie Byrd
  Land [14 x 34 cm.].
 Issued for National Geographic Magazine 62 (Oct.
  1932), opp. p. 484.
 See also inset with inscription by Byrd, M261 above.

Antarctica—1939 [M263]

Antarctica, Produced by the Property &
Survey Branch, Department of the Interior,
Canberra, Australia. Compiled, Drawn and
Lithographed by E. P. Bayliss, F.R.G.S.
Canberra: Property & Survey Branch,
1939.

 1 map : col. ; 124 x 95 cm. on 2 sheets
 Scale 1:7,750,000.
 "L. F. Johnston, government printer, Canberra, A.C.T."
 "For index, authorities consulted, & determinations
  accepted, see accompanying handbook
  [wanting]."
 Insets: Coastal regions of the Australian Antarctic
  Territory [36 x 91 cm] — The Antarctic continent
  in relation to the principal land masses in the
  Southern Hemisphere [25 x 29 cm.].
 Includes notes on history of exploration and shows
  Australian, British and French territorial claims.

Antarctica—1940 [M264]

Antarctic Regions, Sheet[s] VII [and] VIII.
London: Admiralty, [1940?–1943?].

 2 maps ; 70 x 102 cm.
 "Published at the Admiralty . . . under the
  superintendence of Rear Admiral Sir W. J. L.
  Wharton . . . Hydrographer."
 Later issue of: Antarctic Ocean, sheet[s] I [through] VIII
  (1914); see M260 above.
 Sheet VII (covering 60°W/8°E—59°S/75°S) includes
  South Orkneys and Coats Land; sheet VIII
  (covering 115°W/115°E—67°S/85°S) shows coast
  of Victoria Land and sledge routes of Scott
  (1902–3 and 1911–2), Shackleton (1908–9),
  Amundsen (1911–2), and Mawson (1911–14).
 G.B. Hyd. Dept. Pl. Nos.: 3176 [pl. VII], 3206 [pl. VIII].

Antarctica—1942—Ice [M265]

Ice Chart of the Southern Hemisphere,
Prepared in the Naval Meteorological
Branch, 1942. London: Admiralty, 1942.

 4 maps : col. ; 29 x 29 cm. each on sheet 91 x 71 cm.
 "Published by the Hydrographic Dept. of the
  Admiralty, 9th July, 1943, under the
  superintendence of Vice-Admiral Sir John Edgell
  . . . Hydrographer."
 Maps show seasonal limits of pack-ice and icebergs for
  Nov.–Dec., Feb.–Mar., May–June, and Aug.–
  Sept.
 Includes 45 lines of text with heading: Notes on ice
  charts of the southern hemisphere.
 G.B. Hyd. Dept. Pl. No.: 1241.
 At upper right: 71.46 (?).

Antarctica—1943 [M266]

Antarctica. Washington, D.C.:
Hydrographic Office, 1943.

 1 map ; 50 x 78 cm..
 "Latitudinal scale 1:11,250,000."

"Compiled from all available sources to 1943,
    including the results of all American exploration
    from the United States Exploring Expedition,
    1839–1840, to the United States Antarctic
    Service, 1940–1941."
Black and white reproduction of map handstamped
    "Royal Geographical Society Map Room."
"1st edition, March 1943."
"Published at the Hydrographic Office, Washington,
    D.C., March 1943 under the authority of the
    Secretary of the Navy."
MS. annotations reproduced from original: Reduce AB
    to 16.48. — 21 June 1943 Antarctic-General.
Slight MS. annotations on reproduction (col. pencil).
Plate no.: 2562.

Antarctica—1944 [M267]

[Maps of Antarctica, 1944 printing
proofs]. [Edinburgh: John Bartholomew
and Son, 1944].

> 2 maps ; 44 x 57 cm. and 33 x 33 cm. on trimmed
>   sheets
> Smaller of 2 sheets overlaps coverage of regions
>   around Queen Maud Land, but proceeds further
>   north to latitude 35° south.
> Accompanied by 1 p. letter (dated Sept. 7 1944,
>   typed) on John Bartholomew and Son letterhead
>   stationary: Dear Wordie, I am forwarding, as
>   promised, proof of the new Antarctic plate for
>   the World Survey Atlas. The area it is proposed to
>   cover is marked by pencil. The outlying islands of
>   Bouvet and Prince Edward [shown only on
>   smaller proof] will be included in small insets on
>   their respective medians. It is not proposed to
>   proceed further with the printing in the
>   meantime, but we shall be glad to receive any
>   criticisms or corrections that occur to you. Yours
>   sincerely, [signed] John Bartholomew.

Antarctica—1949 [M268]

Falkland Islands & Dependencies.
Compiled and Drawn by Directorate of
Colonial Surveys. [Surbiton]: Directorate
of Colonial Surveys, 1949.

> 1 map : col. ; 75 x 86 cm.
> Scale 1:6,000,000.
> "Published by Directorate of Colonial Surveys D.C.S.
>   10. 1,000/ 3/49 S.P.C.."
> "Photolithographed and printed by G.S.G.S. 1949."
> Shows area from 50° S. to the pole.

Antarctica—1956 [M269]

South Polar Chart Compiled from the
Latest Information in the Hydrographic

Department, 1956. London: Admiralty,
1956.

> 1 map : col. ; 62 x 97 cm.
> "Natural scale 1/11,182,000 (at lat. 90° S)."
> "Published at the Admiralty 22nd April 1949, under
>   the superintendence of Vice-Admiral A. G. N.
>   Wyatt, C.B., Hydrographer. New editions 30th
>   Nov. 1956."
> Printing proof with paste on-notice: "Note: In addition
>   to any coloured areas shown on this chart,
>   corrections have been made as follows . . ."
> Nautical chart also showing territorial claims of various
>   world states.
> In upper right: 341.56.
> G.B. Hyd. Dept. Pl. No.: 1240.

Antarctica—1963 [M270]

Antarctica, Compiled and Drawn in the
Cartographic Division of the National
Geographic Society for the National
Geographic Magazine. Chicago: R. R.
Donnelley and Sons Company, 1963.

> 1 map : col. ; 49 x 64 cm.
> Scale 1:9,820,800.
> Issued with *National Geographic Magazine* 123 no. 2
>   (February 1963).
> "Atlas plate 65."
> Includes extensive historical notes.
> Insets: Subglacial Antarctic [7 x 9 cm.] — Relation of
>   Antarctica to the surrounding continents [17 x 16
>   cm.] — Queen Maud Range [9 x 11 cm.] —
>   McMurdo Sound [8 x 9 cm.].

REGIONS

Bellingshausen Sea—1939 [M271]

Antarctic Regions, between Latitudes 63°S
and 73°S and Longitudes 60°W and
105°W. From All Available Authorities.
Washington, D.C.: Hydrographic Office,
1939.

> 1 map ; 70 x 115 cm.
> Scale ca. 1:4,400,000, or "1° Long. = 1 inch."
> Added title: Pacific Ocean.
> "1st edition, Nov. 1939."
> "Washington, D.C., published Nov. 1939 at the
>   Hydrographic Office, under the authority of the
>   Secretary of the Navy."
> Inset: Peter 1st Land [17 x 13 cm.].
> Plate no.: 5411.

Enderby Land—1955 **[M272]**

The Antarctic, Latitude 52°15′ S. to 71°17′ S., Longitude 27°00′ E. to 90°27′ E. from the Latest Information in the Hydrographic Department to 1954, Including Norwegian Government Surveys. London: Admiralty, 1955.

> 1 map ; 65 x 98 cm.
> Scale 1:2,750,000.
> "Published at the Admiralty, 1st July 1955, under the superintendence of Captain K. St. B. Collins . . . Hydrographer."
> G.B. Hyd. Dept. Pl. No.: 3171.
> At upper right: 180.55.
> Shows Enderby Land and American Highland.

Graham Land—1929 **[M273]**

Discoveries in Graham Land, by Sir Hubert Wilkins. [London]: Geographic Journal, 1929.

> 1 map : col. ; 20 x 18 cm. on sheet 25 x 41 cm.
> In lower right margin: Antarctic regions. Wilkins.
> Detached from *Geographical Journal* 73 (March 1929).

Graham Land—1948 **[M274]**

Anvers Island to Alexander 1. Island, from the Latest Information in the Hydrographic Dept. to 1948. London: Admiralty, 1948.

> 1 map ; 98 x 65 cm.
> Added title: Graham Land.
> "Published at the Admiralty, 12th Novr. 1948, under the superintendence of Vice-Admiral A. G. N. Wyatt . . . Hydrographer; Small corrections 1949—1898—"
> G.B. Hyd. Dept. Pl. No.: 3196.

Graham Land—1950 **[M275]**

Falkland Islands Dependencies, Compiled and Drawn by Directorate of Colonial Surveys in Conjunction with Hydrographic Dept. of the Admiralty. Photolithographed and Printed by G.S.G.S 1948 [–1950]. [Surbiton]: Directorate of Colonial Surveys, 1948.

> 1 map : col. ; on 14 sheets 90 x 63 cm. or smaller
> Scale 1:500,000.

> "Published by Directorate of Overseas Surveys . . . First issue of first edition."
> "Agents for the sale of this map . . . are Edward Stanford, Ltd."
> Coverage complete in 14 sheets.
> "Projection: Lambert Conical Orthomorphic."
> Each sheet includes "Reliability diagram" and graphic "Index to adjoining sheets."
> Contents: Shts. A-L ["I" not used], South Shetlands and Graham Land — sht. [M], South Georgia — sht. [N], South Sandwich Islands — sht. [O], South Orkney Islands.

Graham Land—1952 **[M276]**

Nansen Island to Alexander I. Land, Compiled from the Latest Information in the Hydrographic Department, 1951; Including Surveys by the British Graham Land Survey and the Falkland Islands Dependencies Survey. London: Admiralty, 1952.

> 1 map ; 98 x 65 cm.
> Added title: Antarctica—Graham Land.
> "Published at the Admiralty, 12th Sept., 1952, under the superintendence of Rear-Admiral A. Day . . . Hydrographer."
> G.B. Hyd. Dept. Pl. No.: 3571.

Graham Land—1955 **[M277]**

Falkland Islands and Dependencies 10. Compiled and Drawn by Directorate of Colonial Surveys. [Surbiton]: Directorate of Colonial Surveys, 1955.

> 1 map : col. ; 37 x 36 cm. on sheet 58 x 45 cm.
> "Published by Directorate of Overseas Surveys D.C.S. 960. First edition. 10,000/10/55 S.P.C., R.E."
> "Photolithographed and printed by G.S.G.S. 1955."
> Area bounded by 50°–90°S and 20°–80°W bounded by red border labeled "Falkland Islands Dependancies."
> Possibly issued as a location map for one of the Directorate of Colonial Surveys map series covering the region named. Cf. Public Archives of Canada, *Union list of foreign map series*.

Graham Land—1956 **[M278]**

Plans in Graham Land. London: Admiralty, 1956.

> 10 maps : col. ; various sizes, on sheet 63 x 98 cm.
> Scales vary.
> "Published at the Admiralty 6th Octr. 1950, under the superintendence of Rear-Admiral A. Day . . .

Hydrographer. New editions 25th April, 1952, 23rd March 1956."

Contents: Palmer Archipelago: Melchior Islands — Palmer Archipelago: Schollaert and Neumayer Channels — Graham Land: Hope Bay — Palmer Archipelago: Port Lockroy — Palmer Archipelago: Hackapike Bay — Grandidier Channel: Mutton Cove — Graham Land: Argentine Islands — Marguerite Bay: Neny Island — Doumer Island: South Bay — Graham Land: Debenham Islands.

Printing proof with paste-on notice: "Note: In addition to any coloured areas shown on this chart, corrections have been made as follows . . ."

In upper right: 89.56.

G.B. Hyd. Dept. Pl. No.: 3213.

Graham Land—1957 [M279]

The Antarctic, Latitude 59°27′ S. to 75°00′ S., Longitude 29°00′ W. to 92°27′ W. from the Latest Information in the Hydrographic Department to 1957. London: Admiralty, 1957.

1 map : col. ; 64 x 98 cm.

"Natural scale 1/ 500,000 (lat. 67°)."

"Published at the Admiralty 12th Nov. 1954, under the superintendence of Vice-Admiral Sir Archibald Day . . . Hydrographer. New editions 5th July 1957."

Printing proof with paste-on notice: "Note: In addition to any coloured areas shown on this chart, corrections have been made as follows . . ."

In upper right: 186.57.

G.B. Hyd. Dept. Pl. No.: 3175.

Graham Land—1957 [M280]

Brabant Island to Adelaide Island Compiled from the Latest Information in the Hydrographic Department, 1957, Including Surveys by the British Graham Land Expedition and the Falkland Islands Dependencies Survey, and from foreign Government Sources. London: Admiralty, 1957.

1 map : col. ; 98 x 64 cm.

"Natural scale 1/ 500,000 (lat. 67°)."

Added title: Antarctica: Graham Land.

"Published at the Admiralty 5th Jan. 1951, under the superintendence of Rear-Admiral A. Day . . . Hydrographer. New editions 4th June, 1954, 27th Sept. 1957."

Printing proof with paste-on notice: "Note: In addition to any coloured areas shown on this chart, corrections have been made as follows . . ."

In upper right: 276.57.

G.B. Hyd. Dept. Pl. No.: 3570.

Graham Land—1959 [M281]

Falkland Islands Dependencies. Graham Land. Triangulation and Air Photography. [Tolworth]: Directorate of Overseas Surveys, [1959].

1 map : col. ; 61 x 39 cm.

Scale ca. 1:3,100,000.

"Compiled . . . May 1957. Photographed by D.O.S. and printed by G.S.G.S. 1957. 300/9/59/4198/R."

"D.O.S. (Misc) 233."

Color overprinting shows extent of triangulation and air photography as of September 1959.

Graham Land—1959 [M282]

Falkland Islands Dependencies, Sheet 15. Constructed, Drawn, and Photographed by Directorate of Overseas Surveys 1959 (D.O.S) 710. [Tolworth]: Directorate of Overseas Surveys, 1959.

1 map : col. ; 45 x 62 cm. on sheet 67 x 71 cm.

Scale 1:500,000.

"D.O.S. 710 (Series D401). First edition D.O.S. Published by Directorate of Overseas Surveys 1959."

"Printed for D.O.S. by No. 1 S.P.C.; R.E. 2,200/8/59/4197/R."

"Agents for the sale of this map . . . are Edward Stanford Ltd."

This sheet shows the area 60°W/68°W—70°S/72°S (Palmer Land).

"Projection: Lambert Conical Orthomorphic."

Includes graphic "Index to adjoining sheets"; series complete in 20 sheets.

Graham Land—1960 [M283]

Bismarck Strait with Lemaire Channel, French Passage and Penola Strait, Surveyed by Lieut. C. C. Wynne-Edwards, R.N. and by the Falkland Islands Dependencies Survey 1956–58. With Additions and Corrections to 1960. London: Admiralty, 1960.

1 map ; 64 x 97 cm.
"Natural scale 1/ 100,000 (lat. 65°)."
Added title: Antarctica—Graham Land.
"Published at the Admiralty 12th Aug. 1960, under the
   superintendence of Rear-Admiral E. G. Irving . . .
   Hydrographer."
In upper right: 249.60.
G.B. Hyd. Dept. Pl. No.: 3572.

Graham Land—1960   [M284]

Grandidier Channel, Surveyed by Lieut.
C. J. C. Wynne-Edwards and by the
Falklands Islands Dependencies Survey,
1957–1958. Coastline from Photographs
by Hunting Aerosurveys Ltd., 1956–1957.
London: Admiralty, 1960.

  1 map ; 47 x 64 cm.
  Added title: Antarctica—Graham Land.
  "Published at the Admiralty, 26th Aug. 1960, under
     the superintendence of Rear Admiral E. G. Irving
     . . . Hydrographer."
  G.B. Hyd. Dept. Pl. No.: 3573.

Graham Land—1960   [M285]

Falkland Islands Dependencies. Graham
Land. Hope Bay. [Tolworth]: Directorate
of Overseas Surveys, 1960.

  1 map : col. ; 62 x 58 cm.
  Sheet title: Hope Bay.
  "Published by Directorate of Overseas Surveys D.O.S.
     310. First edition."
  "Printed for D.O.S. by the Ordnance Survey. 2250/3/
     61/1147/OS."
  "Agents for the sale of this map are: Edward Stanford
     Limited. . . ."
  1 sheet from the 1:25,000 series Falkland Islands
     Dependencies (Tolworth: Directorate of Overseas
     Surveys, 1960-).

Graham Land—1960   [M286]

Falkland Islands Dependencies. Graham
Land. Horseshoe Island. [Tolworth]:
Directorate of Overseas Surveys, 1961.

  1 map : col. ; 52 x 62 cm.
  Sheet title: Horseshoe Island.
  "Published by Directorate of Overseas Surveys D.O.S.
     310. First edition 1960. Crown copyright 1961."
  "Printed for D.O.S. by the Ordnance Survey. 2,250/3/
     61/1033/ O.S."
  "Agents for the sale of this map are: Edward Stanford
     Limited. . . ."

1 sheet from the 1:25,000 series Falkland Islands
   Dependencies (Tolworth: Directorate of Overseas
   Surveys, 1960-).

Graham Land—1961   [M287]

Gerlache Strait, C. Wollaston to C. Murray.
From the Latest Information in the
Hydrographic Department 1961. London:
Admiralty, 1961.

  1 map ; 47 x 65 cm.
  "Natural scale 1/200,000 (lat. 64°40')."
  "Including surveys by Commander J. C. Gratton, R.N.,
     and the officers of R.R.S. 'Shackleton' and R.R.S.
     'John Biscoe' 1958–1960."
  Added titles: Antarctica-Graham Land — Palmer
     Archipelago.
  "Published at the Admiralty 7th April 1961, under the
     superintendence of Rear-Admiral E. G. Irving . . .
     Hydrographer."
  In upper right: 121.61.
  G.B. Hyd. Dept. Pl. No.: 3560.

Marie Byrd Land—1939   [M288]

Antarctic Regions, between Latitudes 70°S
and 80°S and Longitudes 130°W and
165°W. From All Available Authorities.
Washington, D.C.: Hydrographic Office,
1939.

  1 map ; 97 x 85 cm..
  Scale ca 1:4,655,000 or "1° Long. = 2.4 cm."
  Added title: Pacific Ocean.
  "1st edition, Sept. 1939."
  "Washington, D.C., published Sept. 1939 at the
     Hydrographic Office, under the authority of the
     Secretary of the Navy."
  Plate no.: 5412.
  Shows Marie Byrd Land and Edward VII Peninsula.

Marie Byrd Land—1960   [M289]

Approaches to Marie Byrd Land from the
Latest Information in the Hydrographic
Department to 1960. London: Admiralty,
1960.

  1 map : col. ; 65 x 98 cm.
  "Natural scale 1/2,750,000 (at lat. 68°00')."
  Added title: The Antarctic.
  "Published at the Admiralty 1st July 1955, under the
     superintendence of Captain K. St. B. Collins . . .
     Hydrographer. New editions 30th Sept. 1960."

Printing proof with paste-on notice: "Note: In addition to any coloured areas shown on this chart, corrections have been made as follows . . ."
In upper right: 365.60.
G.B. Hyd. Dept. Pl. No.: 3174.

"Only the routes taken by Shackleton, Scott, and Amundsen . . . and by the Commonwealth Trans-Antarctic Expedition are shown on this map."
G.B. Hyd. Dept. Pl. No.: 3177.

Ross Sea—1914—Ice [M290]

The Great Ice Barrier & King Edward Land. Cape Crozier to Cape Colbech, S.Y. Terra Nova (Brit. Antarctic. Expedn.. 1910–13.). [London]: Harrison & Sons, [ca. 1914?].

1 map : col. ; 43 x 99 cm.
"Scale 1:1,1000,000."
"Harrison & Sons, Ltd. lith. St. Martins Lane, W.C.2."
Detached from a text; "II" in upper right margin.
Traces face of the Ross Ice Shelf in black; colored to show ice shelf during the 1902 "Discovery" survey and the 1841 "Erebus" survey.
Inset: Junction of barrier with Ross Id. [22 x 24 cm.].
MS. annotation (pencil): Early proof. J.M.W[ordie].

Ross Sea—1957 [M291]

Ross Sea to South Pole from the Latest Information in the Hydrographic Department to 1957. London: Admiralty, 1957.

1 map ; 47 x 64 cm.
Scale 1:4,000,000 at 90° S.
Added title: Antarctica.
"Published at the Admiralty, 29th March 1957, under the superintendence of Rear Admiral K. St. B. Collins . . . Hydrographer."
Shows routes of Shackleton, Scott, and Amundsen.
G.B. Hyd. Dept. Pl. No.: 3177.
At upper right: 98.57.

Ross Sea—1961 [M292]

Ross Sea to South Pole from the Latest Information in the Hydrographic Department to 1961. London: Admiralty, 1961.

1 map ; 47 x 64 cm.
"Natural scale 1/4,000,000 (at lat. 90°)."
Added title: Antarctica.
"Published at the Admiralty 29th March 1957, under the superintendence of Rear Admiral K. St. B. Collins . . . Hydrographer. New editions 28th April 1961."

Ross Sea—1961 [M293]

Ross Sea, Northern Portion. London: Admiralty, 1961.

1 map : col. ; 64 x 98 cm.
"Natural scale 1/2,750,000 (at lat. 68°00')."
Added title: The Antarctic.
"Published at the Admiralty 12th Nov. 1954, under the superintendence of Vice-Admiral Sir Archibald Day . . . Hydrographer. New editions 1st Feb. 1957, 10th March 1961."
Printing proof with paste-on notice: "Note: In addition to any coloured areas shown on this chart, corrections have been made as follows . . ."
In upper right: 73.61.
G.B. Hyd. Dept. Pl. No.: 3173.

Weddell Sea—1956 [M294]

The Antarctic, Latitude 59°27' S. to 75°00', Longitude 33°00' W. to 30°28' E. London: Admiralty, 1956.

1 map: col. ; 65 x 98 cm.
"Natural scale 1/2,750,000 (at lat. 68°)."
"Published at the Admiralty 1st July 1955, under the superintendence of Captn. K. St. B. Collins . . . Hydrographer. New editions. Large corrections 16th Nov. 1956."
Printing proof with paste-on notice: "Note: In addition to any coloured areas shown on this chart, corrections have been made as follows . . ."
In upper right: 321.56.
G.B. Hyd. Dept. Pl. No.: 3170.
Shows Weddell Sea and Queen Maud Land.

Weddell Sea—1960 [M295]

Weddell Sea from the Latest Information in the Hydrographic Department 1960. London: Admiralty, 1960.

1 map : col. ; 47 x 64 cm.
"Natural scale 1/2,750,000 (at lat. 68°)."
Added title: The Antarctic.
"Published at the Admiralty 30th Nov. 1956, under the superintendence of Commodore K. St. B. Collins . . . Hydrographer. New editions 23rd Sept. 1960."

Printing proof with paste-on notice: "Note: In addition to any coloured areas shown on this chart, corrections have been made as follows . . ."
In upper right: 270.60.
G.B. Hyd. Dept. Pl. No.: 3176.

Wilkes Land—1955   **[M296]**
The Antarctic, Latitude 52°15′ S. to 71°17′ S., Longitude 87°00′ E. to 150°27′

E. from the Latest Information in the Hydrographic Department to 1954.
London: Admiralty, 1955.

1 map ; 65 x 98 cm.
Scale 1:2,750,000.
"Published at the Admiralty, 28th Oct. 1955, under the superintendence of Captain K. St. B. Collins . . . Hydrographer."
G.B. Hyd. Dept. Pl. No.: 3172.
At upper right: 304.55.

Paintings, Artifacts, etc.

PAINTINGS

Adam, Richard B [P1]
Admiral Richard E. Byrd in Arctic Costume with His Dog. Signed at lower left "Richard B. Adam Boston July 1928." Signed at lower right: "Richard E. Byrd."

1 art original : pencil and pastels on paper ; 53 x 42 cm.

[Anon., probably William May or George M'Dougall] [P2]
Ships *Pioneer*, *Resolute*, *Assistance*, and *Intrepid* in Winter Quarters (1850–51) in Barrow Strait.

1 art original : pencil and sepia watercolor on paper, heightened with white ; 10 x 15 cm., pasted onto cardboard 37 x 28 cm.
The (erroneous) title "Errobus [sic] & Terror in the Ice" is crudely pencilled on the cardboard mount.
Apparently the original of the chromolithograph in Sherard Osborn's *Stray Leaves from an Arctic Journal* (**531** above), opp. p. 157. Although the lithograph is signed "Lieut. Osborn delt.," in his preface he attributes the "sketches" to William May and George M'Dougall.
This drawing was reproduced as a bookplate [ca. 1992] for G.F. Fitzgerald's polar book collection.

[Anon., probably William May or George M'Dougall] [P3]
Sledge Travelling.

1 art original : pencil and sepia watercolor on paper, heightened with white ; 10 x 15 cm., pasted onto cardboard 37 x 28 cm.
The title "Hauling sledges" is crudely pencilled on the cardboard mount.

Apparently the original of the chromolithograph in Sherard Osborn's *Stray Leaves from an Arctic Journal* (**531** above), opp. p. 240. Although the lithograph is signed "Lieut. Osborn delt.," in his preface he attributes the "sketches" to William May and George M'Dougall.

Blanchard, F. L. [P4]
"The Coming Expedition to the Antarctic, S. S. *Discovery* Lately Launched at Dundee." Signed at lower right "F. L. Blanchard 1901."

1 art original : black and grey watercolor on paper, heightened with white ; 30.5 x 20 cm.
Title from a signed inscription on the back of the drawing.
This drawing was reproduced in the *Illustrated London News*, March 30th, 1901 and in Maggs Bros. Catalog no. 1076, p. 42.

[Browne, William Henry James] [P5]
"H.M.S. *Investigator* in Winter Quarters at Pt. Leopold. Jany. 1849. No. 5."

1 art original : watercolor on paper ; 17.8 x 26.3 cm. in octagonal cardboard mount 26.5 x 35.5 cm.
Title in pencil on verso; "No. 5" in ink.
Made during James C. Ross's 1848–49 expedition in search of John Franklin's party.
Reproduced in Christie's catalog for sale of 10 Nov. 1988, p. 45.

[Browne, William Henry James] [P6]
"A Traveling Party — Tenting for the Night — Regent Inlet. No. 2."

1 art original : watercolor on paper ; 17.6 x 24.9 cm. in octagonal cardboard mount 25.7 x 33.7 cm.
Title in pencil on verso; "No. 2" in ink.
Illegible inscription at bottom center.
Made during James C. Ross's 1848–49 expedition in search of John Franklin's party.

Reproduced in Christie's catalog for sale of 10 Nov. 1988, p. 45.

Hamilton, James (1819–1878) [P7]
Advance and *Rescue* in the Arctic, ca. 1852. Signed at lower left: "J. Hamilton."

> 1 art original : oil on canvas ; 45.5 x 76 cm.
> Presumably inspired by sketches by Elisha Kent Kane, this composition does not appear in Kane's *U.S. Grinnell Expedition in Search of Sir John Franklin* (**372** above).

Hamilton, James (1819–1878) [P8]
Arctic Adventure. Signed at lower right: "J. Hamilton 1856."

> 1 art original : oil on canvas ; 51 x 76 cm.
> Reproduced in Hanzel Galleries catalog for sale of 20–23 October 1991, p. [4].

Hamilton, James (1819–1878) [P9]
Beechey Island, ca. 1852.

> 1 art original : watercolor and brush-and-ink on paper ; 23 x 34 cm.
> Presumably after a sketch by Elisha Kent Kane.
> Provenance: Kane Family.

Hamilton, James (1819–1878) [P10]
Rescue in her Arctic Ice-dock, 1851. Ca. 1852. Signed at lower left: "J. Hamilton."

> 1 art original : oil on canvas ; 35.2 x 30.5 cm.
> Presumably executed after a sketch by Elisha Kent Kane, this scene appears in a wood-engraved vignette at the head of chapter 36 in Kane's *U.S. Grinnell Expedition in Search of Sir John Franklin* (**372** above).
> Provenance: Kane Family.

Hamilton, James (1819–1878) [P11]
Rescue Nipped in Ice, Melville Bay, August 1850. Ca. 1852.

> 1 art original : oil on board, 10.3 x 16.6 cm.
> After a sketch by Elisha Kent Kane, possibly a study for a larger oil. This picture was engraved by John Sartain after Hamilton and published in Kane's *U.S. Grinnell Expedition in Search of Sir John Franklin* (**372** above), facing page 120.
> Provenance: Kane Family.

Kniveton, Frank [P12]
Ward Room on Board the *Terra Nova* during Scott's Last Expedition. Signed at Lower Left "Frank Kniveton 1919."

> 1 art original : oil on canvas ; 45 x 76 cm.
> Painted after a photograph taken during the expedition of 1910–13; the source photograph is reproduced in Victor Campbell's *The Wicked Mate* (**131** above), p. 33.

Welton, Alice (b. 1948) [P13]
Nautilus 90° North. Signed at lower left "Alice Welton."

> 1 art original : watercolor on paper ; 74 x 53 cm.

ARTIFACTS

Byrd, Richard E. [P14]
Pair of Reindeer Skin Mukluks (30 x 21 x 11 cm.), tied together by leather thongs. Cloth label on back of upper: "Manufactured by Lomen Reindeer Corporation, Nome, Alaska."

> Affixed to mukluks is the label of "Jordan Marsh Company 5 Star Cold Fur Storage" with penciled name "Byrd", "Furr Mitts," and the number "69."

Franklin Expedition [P15]
Piece of Cedar Planking from one of the Boats of Sir John Franklin, brought back from King William's Island by Captain Charles Francis Hall 1864–69.

> Fragment of wood (31 x 6 x 4 mm.) encased in lucite block 103 x 152 x 25 mm.
> Descriptive text enclosed in block.
> Accompanying this artifact is the envelope (78 x 137 mm.) in which the fragment was kept until recently. It bears the inscription, in a nineteenth-century hand: 'The piece of wood inside of this Envelope, is a piece of one of the Boats of the lamented Sir John Franklin Arctic Expedition, and was brought to the United States by Captain Hall, from King Williams Island, in the Arctic Ocean, where it was first discovered by Capt McClintock, and afterwards by Captain Hall." The envelope has the printed return address "I. O. O. F. Grand Lodge United States F L T."

Franklin Expedition   **[P16]**
Piece of Stave from a Cask and a Piece of
Metal from a Can Used by the Crews of
Sir John Franklin's Ships, the 370-ton
Erebus and the 340-ton *Terror*, at Beechey
Island during the Winter of 1845–46.

> Fragments of wood (93 x 17 x 7 mm.) and metal (80 x
> 17 mm.) encased in lucite block 100 x 150 x 28
> mm.
> Descriptive text enclosed in block.
> These were found on the island near the graves of
> three crewmen of the expedition, John
> Torrington, 20, John Hartnell, 25, and William
> Braine, 34. The lead-soldered seams in the tin
> cans found at the site caused lead poisoning
> among the crew. These artifacts were picked up
> on the beach by G. F. Fitzgerald on August 7th,
> 1991.

Scott, Robert Falcon   **[P17]**
Naval Officer's Sword. ca. 1901.

> Gilt half-basket with lion's head pommel, the mane
> extending fully down the backstrap. Oval
> cartouche enclosing a foul anchor badge
> surmounted by the Queen's crown. Grip of
> wood covered with white fishskin and bound
> with braided copper wire. Folding flap/lock at
> rear of hilt engraved: "R. F. Scott, R.N."
> Blade (80 cm. long) decorated on both sides with
> etching, signed: J. Gieve & Sons, Portsmouth.
> In black leather scabbard with three engraved brass
> mounts, suspension rings.

FILMS

Ponting, Herbert George   **[P18]**
90 Degrees South: With Scott to the
Antarctic. New York: Milestone Film and
Video, [1992].

> 1 video tape : black and white ; 72 mins.
> Herbert G. Ponting's silent film, restored by the British
> Film Institute's National Film Archive.
> Reference: OCLC 26679322.

Rucker, Joseph   **[P19]**
With Byrd at the South Pole: The Story of

Little America. Photography by Joseph
Rucker and Willard Van Der Veer; Edited
by Emanuel Cohen; Narrative, Floyd
Gibbons; Music by Manny Baer. New
York: Milestone Film and Video, [1992].

> 1 video tape : black and white ; 82 mins.
> Original film made on Byrd's first expedition, 1928–30.
> Reference: OCLC 26204507.

PRINTS AND PHOTOGRAPHS

Anonymous   **[P20]**
The Whale Fishery and Killing the Bears.
[London, 1748].

> 2 engravings ; 16 x 21 cm. each on sheet 41 x 25 cm.
> Detached from John Harris, *Navigantium atque
> itinerantium bibliotheca* (London, between
> 1744–48), "Vol. 2. Pa. 388."
> Title appears between engravings.
> View of whaling fleet at work at top.
> Engraving at bottom includes: The whale from which
> the bone is taken. — The whale louse. — The fin
> fish. — The sea unicorn. — The morse. — A
> harpoon. — A spear.

Cheyne, John Powles   **[P21]**
Views of the Franklin Relics 1850/60.
Descriptive Catalogue of Fourteen
Stereoscopic Slides of the Relics of Sir John
Franklin's Expedition, Brought Home in
the *Fox*, by Captain M'Clintock, in
September, 1859. Photographed by
Lieutenant Cheyne, R.N., at the United
Service Museum, Whitehall, by Permission
of the Council of that Institution, and
Published by Him at His Private Address,
[1860?].

> 13 stereoscopic cards ; 8.4 x 17.5 cm. + photocopy
> of "Descriptive Catalogue" (24 p.), in drop-spine
> box.
> On spine: Stereoscopic slides of the Franklin Relics.
> Incomplete: Slide 1 lacking.

The so-called "Arctic Council" was loose group of "experts" which was formed after the death of Sir John Barrow in 1848 to coordinate the Admiralty's work in the Arctic. At the time of this sitting (1851), Barrow's influence still emanates from his portrait on the wall, flanked by those of Sir John Franklin and his co-commander James Fitzjames, the objects of the search.

"The Arctic Council Discussing a Plan of Search for Sir John Franklin" engraved by James Scott after a painting by Stephen Pearce [**P22**]

Pearce, Stephen (1819–1904)　　[P22]

The Arctic Council Discussing a Plan of Search for Sir John Franklin. [1852?].

> 1 engraving ; 45.6 x 71.6 cm. (plate mark: 58 x 81.9 cm.)
> Engraved by James Scott after Pearce's painting of 1851, now in the National Portrait Gallery.
> Shows Sir George Back, Sir Edward Parry, Capt. Edward Bird, Sir James Clark Ross, Sir Francis Beaufort, Col. John Barrow, Col. Edward Sabine, Capt. W. Hamilton, Sir John Richardson, Capt. M. Beechy, and, on wall behind them, portraits of Sir John Franklin, Capt. James Fitzjames, and Sir John Barrow.
> Faint pencilled signature at lower right: Jas. Scott.
> Small oval blind stamp at lower left: Printsellers Association [C?]BY.
> Pencilled note in lower right corner of sheet: Only 100 copies pub. at 6/6/.
> Reference: Dictionary of National Biography, 2d. Suppl.

Rudge, Chris　　[P23]

Discovery Hut, Hut Point. [Christchurch, N.Z.] : Antarctic Heritage Trust, [ca. 1990].

> 1 poster : col. ; 42 x 60 cm.
> Reproduction of photograph by Chris Rudge.
> Added title: Protecting Antarctica's heritage.
> Interior view of building on the Hut Point peninsula on Ross Island, built by Scott's first expedition in 1902, occupied briefly by Shackleton in 1909, and by Scott again in 1910–13.

Rudge, Chris　　[P24]

Scott's Hut, Cape Evans. [Christchurch, N.Z.] : Antarctic Heritage Trust, [ca. 1990].

> 1 poster : col. ; 42 x 60 cm.
> Reproduction of photograph by Chris Rudge.
> Added title: Protecting Antarctica's heritage.
> Exterior view of building occupied by Scott's 1910–13 expedition.

Rudge, Chris　　[P25]

Shackleton's Hut, Cape Royds. [Christchurch, N.Z.] : Antarctic Heritage Trust, [ca. 1990].

> 1 poster : col. ; 42 x 60 cm.
> Reproduction of photograph by Chris Rudge.

> Added title: Protecting Antarctica's heritage.
> Exterior view of building on Ross Island constructed by Shackleton's expedition in February 1908.

Tittle, Walter Ernest (1883–1966)　　[P26]

Etched Portrait of Richard E. Byrd. Signed "Richard E. Byrd." [192- ?].

> 1 art print : etching ; 16 x 13 cm. on sheet 26 x 21 cm.
> A young Officer Byrd in naval uniform with medals.

PHILATELY AND CURRENCY

American Antarctic Explorers, 1988　　[P27]

Sheet of 50 25-cent Stamps Commemorating American Antarctic Explorers.

> Each block of four includes stamps devoted to Lt. Charles Wilkes, Nathaniel Palmer, Lincoln Ellsworth, and Richard E. Byrd.

American Arctic Explorers, 1986　[P28]

Sheet of 50 22-cent Stamps Commemorating American Arctic Explorers.

> Each block of four includes stamps devoted to Adolphus W. Greely, Elisha Kent Kane, Robert E. Peary and Matthew Henson, and Vilhjalmur Stefansson.

Byrd, Richard E.　　[P29]

Souvenir Envelope with United States Airmail 5 Cent Stamp Tied by "S.S. City of New York Feb 19 A.M. 1930" Duplex Cancellation, Violet Flight Cachet with Small Black Date Stamp "Nov 28 '29" Alongside. Signed "R. E. Byrd."

> Postal cover, 90 x 146 mm.
> About 50 covers were carried on Byrd's pioneering fight, but only a few were signed.

Mawson, Douglas　　[P30]

First Day Cover Commemorating the 50th

Anniversary of the 1911–1914 Australasian Antarctic Expedition, October 18th 1961. With Mawson Commemorative 5d. Stamp Tied to "G.P.O. Adelaide South Aust First Day of Issue 18 Oct 61" Cancellation.

> Postal cover, 92 x 165 mm.
> Cachet, printed in 5 colors, shows a man, sledge, and two dogs.

Mawson, Douglas   **[P31]**

Australia. One Hundred Dollars. 100. [Designed by] H[arry] W[illiamson].

Engraved banknote, 81 x 170 mm., encased in lucite block 95 x 180 x 29 mm.
Australian $100 bill, with portrait of Douglas Mawson wearing a balaclava. Behind Mawson are three geological profiles.
Portrait of astronomer John Tebbutt (1834–1917) on verso.
Engraved signatures of "B[ernie] W[illiam] Fraser, Secretary to the Treasury" and "Johnston [i.e. Robert Alan Johnston], Governor Reserve Bank of Australia."
The bill was first issued on 26 March 1984 and was replaced in 1996.

Index

195

Index

Index

Index

216

Index

Index